Southern Literary Studies
Louis D. Rubin, Jr., Editor

Louisiana Women Writers

EDITED BY

DOROTHY H. BROWN AND BARBARA C. EWELL

Louisiana Women Writers

New Essays

and a

Comprehensive

Bibliography

LOUISIANA STATE UNIVERSITY PRESS   BATON ROUGE AND LONDON

Copyright © 1992 by Louisiana State University Press
All rights reserved
Manufactured in the United States of America
First printing
01 00 99 98 97 96 95 94 93 92   5 4 3 2 1

Designer: Amanda McDonald Key
Typeface: Baskerville
Typesetter: G&S Typesetters, Inc.
Printer and binder: Thomson-Shore, Inc.

Library of Congress Cataloging-in-Publication Data

Louisiana women writers : new essays and a comprehensive bibliography
    / edited by Dorothy H. Brown and Barbara C. Ewell.
        p.   cm.
    Includes index.
    ISBN 0-8071-1743-9
    1. American literature—Louisiana—History and criticism.
    2. American literature—Women authors—History and criticism.
    3. American literature—Women authors—Bibliography.   4. Women and
    literature—Louisiana—Bibliography.   5. American literature—
    Louisiana—Bibliography.   6. Louisiana in literature—Bibliography.
    7. Women and literature—Louisiana.   8. Louisiana in literature.
    I. Brown, Dorothy H., 1926–   .   II. Ewell, Barbara C.
    PS266.L8L68   1992
    810.9′9287′09763—dc20   92-48
                                                              CIP

A version of Clara Juncker's essay "Behind Confederate Lines: Sarah Morgan Dawson" appeared in the *Southern Quarterly*, XXX (Fall, 1991), and is reprinted with the permission of the editor. A version of Ellen Peel's essay "Semiotic Subversion in 'Désirée's Baby'" first appeared in *American Literature*, LXII (1990), and is reprinted with the permission of Duke University Press. A version of Elizabeth Meese's essay "What the Old Ones Know: Ada Jack Carver's Cane River Stories" appeared in a special issue of the *New Orleans Review*, XV (Spring, 1988), and is reprinted with permission.

The paper in this book meets the guidelines for permanence and durability of the Committee on Production Guidelines for Book Longevity of the Council on Library Resources. ∞

To the women writers of Louisiana, in all their infinite variety

Contents

Contents

Illustrations

Photographs of numerous other Louisiana women writers appear in the Bibliography.

Preface

Discovering the women writers of Louisiana has been, for both of us, an unexpectedly rewarding tack in our research. The initial magnet for Barbara was a 1978 project sponsored by the Modern Language Association and the Fund for the Improvement of Post-Secondary Education, "Teaching Women's Literature from a Regional Perspective." Reading Grace King and Ada Jack Carver for the first time nourished the expectation that other writers of their caliber might be hidden in the libraries. For Dorothy, a tireless explorer of fiction, old and new, tracking down all Louisiana women writers became a major preoccupation, leading not only to the Bibliography included here, but to a goodly number of essays and brief biographies as well. Her work is very much at the root of this collection, as it was for the day-and-a-half symposium on Louisiana women writers that we codirected at Loyola University in September, 1986. Organized by the Women's Studies Consortium of Louisiana and funded by a grant from the Louisiana Endowment for the Humanities, the symposium generated an unexpectedly enthusiastic response, resulting in a special issue of the *New Orleans Review,* the publication of other symposium papers and panel transcriptions in *Louisiana Literature,* and the production of an hour-long local television special.[1]

We are pleased to acknowledge all those who contributed to the generation and completion of this collection, a task that has certainly

1. Danella P. Hero, director, and Peggy Scott LaBorde, producer, "A Place of Their Own: Four Nineteenth-Century New Orleans Women Writers," WLAE-TV (New Orleans), 1988. For published essays from the symposium, see Dorothy H. Brown and Barbara C. Ewell, eds., *New Orleans Review: Special Issue on Louisiana Women Writers,* XV (1988); Dorothy H. Brown and Barbara C. Ewell, eds., "Fiction and Louisiana Women Writers," *Louisiana Literature,* V (Fall, 1988), 24–65; Barbara C. Ewell and Dorothy H. Brown, eds., "Drama, Poetry, and Louisiana Women Writers," *Louisiana Literature,* VI (Spring, 1989), 37–80; Jane F. Bonin, "Frances Parkinson Keyes: Mining the Mother Lode," *Louisiana Literature,* V (1988), 71–77; Violet Harrington Bryan, "Evocations of Place and Culture in the Works of Four Contemporary Black Louisiana Writers: Brenda Osbey, Sybil Kein, Elizabeth Brown-Guillory, and Pinkie Gordon Lane," *Louisiana Literature,* IV (1987), 49–65; W. Kenneth Holditch, "Eliza Jane Poitevent, Pearl Rivers, and the Old Lady of Camp Street," *Louisiana Literature,* IV (1987), 27–56; and Ethel C. Simpson, "Ruth McEnery Stuart: The Innocent Grotesque," *Louisiana Literature,* IV (1987), 57–74.

had its sisyphean moments. We are especially grateful to Loyola University and to Dean Julianne Maher for their material assistance, including two timely grants from the Loyola Committee on Grants and Research. For superb and cheerful assistance from the staff of City College, from the library staff of Loyola University, especially Patricia C. Doran, James B. Hobbs, Arthur F. Carpenter, Mark Sutton, Laura Dankner, Diana Madonna, and Sr. Anne M. Ramagos, C.S.J., and the staffs of the Howard-Tilton Memorial Library of Tulane University and the New Orleans Public Library, we are most grateful. We also deeply appreciate the varied but indispensable contributions of Barbara Brown; Joan Fields; Emily Toth; Milly S. Barranger; Elizabeth Brown-Guillory; Thadious Davis; Margaret Dunn; Danella Hero; Gloria Hull; Pinkie Gordon Lane; Susan Larson; Anne Morris; Carol Orr; Pam Parker; Peggy Prenshaw; Edith Roy; Louis D. Rubin, Jr.; Elizabeth Sarkodie-Mensah; Michael Sartisky; Fatima Wickem; Beth Willinger; Andrea Ewell Cox; Jayne Ewell Hagan; Mary Dell Ewell Mixon; Elizabeth Ewell Morgan; Robin Ewell; Robert P. Harrell; Max Harrell Brown; Carolyn Brown; Bruce Brown; and, of course, our husbands, Max Brown and Jerry Speir. We are particularly grateful to the Women's Studies Consortium of Louisiana for inspiring and producing the symposium where it all began. And we feel especially lucky to have had the editorial wisdom and care of Gerry Anders, who has helped us immensely in bringing this work to a shapely end. To all of these individuals—perhaps merely names to you, but supportive, amazing friends to us—we express our gratitude for the virtues of this collection, which they have made possible, and our apologies for its flaws, which are ours alone.

I
Louisiana Women Writers: Essays

Introduction
Re-Viewing the Tradition of Louisiana Women Writers

I NEVITABLY, one aspect of a collection defined by region is a forthrightly chauvinistic desire to show off the literary riches of one's homeplace. We plead guilty. Fortunately for us, Louisiana—singularly romantic even among southern states—has a respectable cache of literary wealth to display. Despite such affluence, few readers actually realize how many writers, male or female, are associated with the state. Not recognizing this literary legacy seems to us a failure of vision, a neglect of the past that distorts our present conceptions of who we are. The most detrimental aspect of this general lapse of consciousness, however, has typically been the systematic exclusion of women (and minorities) from our literary canon. Thus the focus in this collection on writers who are Louisianians (in one way or another) and women (although not often enough nonwhite or lesbian or working-class, pointing up the need for more scholarship on such writers) represents an effort not only to foster a broader appreciation for an overlooked literary tradition of the past, but also to reclaim a diversity that is crucial if we are to redefine our culture flexibly enough to face the challenges of our future together.

The precision of this focus, women writers of a single state—even though it excludes half of the population with one term and relies on arbitrary political boundaries for the other—has another important benefit as well: namely, it highlights thematic and cultural issues that a more inclusive perspective would have diffused. One such issue is the conventionality and deliberate limitation implicit in definitions of gender and place. As Louisianians and as women, the subjects of this volume commonly confront two marginalizing experiences that significantly shape their perspectives and options as writers. The intersection of those experiences provides a provocative context for analysis that allows us to see more clearly the implications of their fictions—and ours.

One aspect of such an analysis is a better appreciation of how these essentially restrictive experiences interact, that is, how being a woman is shaped by Louisiana's peculiar brand of southernness, and how Louisiana—and the South—is constructed by its women. Understanding that interaction could go an important distance toward construing "the female mind of the South," a task that, as Helen Taylor observes, has not yet been adequately undertaken.[1] Certainly, Louisiana women writers represent only a sample of that "mind," and indeed, the authors covered here are only a sample of Louisiana women writers; but the issues raised by their work can help explain an experience that remains subject to a great many myths and far too little understanding.

A natural point of departure is the ambiguity and resonance attached to place, both for women and for the South, as well as for Louisiana women writers. The South, of course, has a notorious "sense of place," one that is reflected by its fictions as well as by its statistics. Rural isolation and a dramatic shared history have contributed much to what Richard Gray calls southerners' "belief in the power of environment, this feeling of attachment to landscape . . . [which is] one of the structuring principles of Southern myth." And as John Shelton Reed's work suggests, this sense of place endures, even late in this century, in southerners' preference for their own states or their identification with local communities and systems of kinship.[2] But place in the South also defines social stratification, particularly for African-Americans, but also for women, who, like blacks, need to "know their place" as the subordinates of white men in an intensely patriarchal culture.

---

1. Helen Taylor, *Gender, Race, and Region in the Writings of Grace King, Ruth McEnery Stuart, and Kate Chopin* (Baton Rouge, 1989), xi. Taylor notes as "pioneering" Anne Goodwyn Jones, *Tomorrow Is Another Day: The Woman Writer in the South, 1859–1936* (Baton Rouge, 1981). Also exceptional in studying southern women is Louise S. Westling, *Sacred Groves and Ravished Gardens: The Fiction of Eudora Welty, Carson McCullers, and Flannery O'Connor* (Athens, Ga., 1985), esp. her chapter on "The Blight of Southern Womanhood," pp. 8–35. See also Kathryn Lee Seidel, *The Southern Belle in the American Novel* (Tampa, 1985).

2. Richard Gray, *Writing the South: Ideas of an American Region* (Cambridge, Mass., 1986), 173. The notion of "sense of place" merits a separate entry in Charles Reagon Wilson and William Ferris, eds., *The Encyclopedia of Southern Culture* (Chapel Hill, 1989), 1137–38. For discussions of the literary sense of place, see Lewis P. Simpson, *The Dispossessed Garden: Pastoral and History in Southern Literature* (Athens, Ga., 1975); and Lucinda Hardwick MacKethan, *The Dream of Arcady: Place and Time in Southern Literature* (Baton Rouge, 1980). John Shelton Reed, "Instant Grits and Plastic Wrapped Crackers: Southern Culture and Regional Development," in Louis D. Rubin, Jr., *American South: Portrait of a Culture* (Baton Rouge, 1980), 35. For a fuller assessment of this phenomenon, see Reed's *Enduring South: Subcultural Persistence in Mass Society* (Lexington, Mass., 1972), esp. chaps. 4–6.

Place for the southern woman (as for the southern African-American) is thus a loaded and doubled term, expressing both a positive, generally productive relation to a physical and cultural reality and an oppressive, limiting experience of social status. Alice Walker, for example, writes movingly of her efforts as a black southerner to reclaim the cultural and geographic territory from which racism has displaced her.[3] But that doubleness of place is precisely what eludes most interpreters of southern women writers. As Helen Taylor observes, many feminist critics, by scrutinizing place as social confinement, have tended to homogenize the specific regional concerns of women writers, subordinating them to formalist and thematic considerations, such as the adoption of certain genres or the modification of female stereotypes, including regionally specific ones—for example, the mammy and the belle. Such emphases, Taylor argues, limit our understanding of how region shapes literary choices. On the other hand, readers without feminist sympathies—sometimes including southern women writers themselves, who often resist any identification with the women's movement—recognize the power of region for a writer such as Eudora Welty or Flannery O'Connor, but fail or refuse to see how that writer's southern sense of place is indelibly marked by her experience as a woman who does "know her place," even if she occasionally refuses to stay in it.[4]

Certainly, place is indispensable for writers. It is, as Welty has eloquently explained, the "raw material of writing," serving as a "lesser angel" of inspiration and giving fiction its life and validity. Place imparts to fiction its necessary illusion of reality. The details and specificities of an environment—its colors and oddities, its "named, identified, concrete" elements—furnish, Welty says, "a plausible abode for [fiction's] world of feeling." But most important, she adds, is the fact that evoking that illusion exposes a point of view—what she calls the "burning-glass" of consciousness—framing and disclosing the world before it.[5] What a writer describes, the details of the landscape she selects in order to make the world of feelings credible, also reveals

3. Alice Walker, "Choosing to Stay at Home: Ten Years After the March on Washington," in *In Search of Our Mothers' Gardens: Womanist Prose* (San Diego, 1983), 158–70.

4. Taylor, *Gender, Race, and Region,* 21–22. See, for example, Welty's comments in interviews, *Conversations with Eudora Welty,* ed. Peggy Whitman Prenshaw (Jackson, Mississippi, 1984), esp. 54, 136, and 250.

5. Eudora Welty, "Place in Fiction," in *The Eye of the Story* (New York, 1978), 121–22, 124–25.

what she sees, what she *can* see. The places of a writer's fiction thus expose both the horizons and the architecture of her vision; they also reveal the adequacy of the fictional furnishings she has selected to accommodate the feelings that are the foundations of her art.

Typically, and as much in their denigration as in their praise, women have been credited with a more precise and searching representation of place than men. William Dean Howells, for example, observed that "the sketches and studies by the women seem faithfuler and more realistic than those of the men, in proportion to their number. Their tendency is more distinctly in that direction, and there is a solidity, an honest observation, in the work of such women . . . which often leaves little to be desired."[6] Howells' approval, of course, reiterates supposed truisms concerning women's eye for detail and their close association with the physical realities of human existence. Generally entrusted with the care and supervision of the places of daily life—the home and its yard, the rooms and furnishings that surround our eating and sleeping and lovemaking and communicating—women are indeed intimates of place, frequently of a single place from which they have neither means nor occasion to wander. That familiarity, enforced or assumed, often—as Howells noted—renders place in women's writing vivid and immediate. But the consciousness or point of view disclosed by those details is distinctive in another way. Whereas men have typically been able to impose individualized perspectives onto their places—their own names, as it were—the shape of places in the writing of women does not always inscribe their personal figures into the design. To the contrary, women's relationship with place, intimate though it be, is usually not one of defining, but of being defined. Their place remains *in* the home, but the homeplace belongs *to* someone else.

For women, then, writing about place has frequently involved a discovery of boundaries and confinement—a recognition of the ways in which their lives and vision are constrained by the familial rules that constitute female experience. As Annette Kolodny suggests, unlike men, who tend to find in places projections of filial dependence or eroticized conquest, women find in their places the borders of their

6. See Elaine Showalter, "Women Writers and the Double Standard," in *Women in Sexist Society: Studies in Power and Powerlessness,* ed. Vivian Gornick and Barbara K. Moran (New York, 1971), 474. See also the pointed comments on feminine confinement and materiality by Mary Ellmann, *Thinking About Women* (New York, 1968), 87–93, 97–101. Quotation from William Dean Howells, *Criticism and Fiction* (New York, 1892), 134.

domestication. Far from imposing their images on the places they inhabit, women more often reiterate the patterns prescribed by patriarchal custom. However, recognizing limits—like those of mortality—can provide the imagination with a special poignance and power. Judith Fryer, for example, explores the fertile encounters with spatial limits that produced the very different fictions of Edith Wharton and Willa Cather.[7] Obviously, the boundaries women encounter—like the artificial constraints of a sonnet or a short story—can tempt, at least from the gifted writer, an evocation of broad significance from the explicit finiteness of her subject: Jane Austen's "miniatures in ivory."

This challenge of boundaries has likewise shaped the literature of Louisiana as part of the South, a place whose cultural and geographical outlines are as vividly marked in the American imagination as the role of gender in the broader human psyche. Like the narrow place defined for women, the South emerged, especially after the Civil War, as a distinctive, separate locus. Northerners and southerners alike found reason to foster the notion of a uniquely traditional culture: its aristocratic values and unshaken loyalties in the wake of military defeat offered a consoling alternative to the harsh realities of late-nineteenth-century America. As Anne Rowe observes, the shifting political climate that encouraged cooperation by conservatives, North and South, gradually transformed northern attitudes toward a former enemy "from one of reform and retribution to that of praise and support" and helped to turn the era of Reconstruction into that of Jim Crow, no less virulently in Louisiana than in the rest of the Deep South. That changing political environment, coupled with the nostalgic "pathos and grandeur of a lost civilization" that the South embodied for the contemporary imagination, beset by the destabilizing forces of postwar industrialization and urbanization, ensured the prosperity of the myth of the South. The national acceptance of this myth, bolstered by the region's long-standing need to justify its peculiar institution of slavery and concomitant racism, resulted in the phenomenon—the virtual industry—of southern literature.[8] Louisiana,

7. Annette Kolodny, *The Land Before Her: Fantasy and Experience of the American Frontiers, 1630–1860* (Chapel Hill, 1984), 12; Judith Fryer, *Felicitous Spaces: The Imaginative Structures of Edith Wharton and Willa Cather* (Chapel Hill, 1986).

8. Anne E. Rowe, *The Enchanted Country: Northern Writers in the South, 1865–1910* (Baton Rouge, 1978), xviii–xix, xix–xx, 138. See also Howard R. Floan, *The South in Northern Eyes, 1831–1861* (Austin, 1958), 184–86; Fred Hobson, Prologue to *Tell About the South: The Southern Rage to Explain* (Baton Rouge, 1983), 3–16; Patrick Gerster and Nicholas Cords, "Northern Origins of Southern Mythology," in their *The New South* (2d

thanks to the popularity of George Washington Cable's exotic stories and novels, enjoyed a particular cachet, which opened opportunities for a number of writers, many of them women. But even long after the war, and well into the following century, the primary impulse of much of the region's imaginative and critical writing remained self-definition. What is the South? What is a southerner? Why is that place so fascinating to us all?

One answer to those questions lies precisely in the limits of the South as a place. As Richard Gray, among others, has noted, the *fact* of the South as a distinct and homogeneous region has increasingly been called into question, but the *idea* of the South as an identifiable structuring principle of culture remains intact.[9] As such, it offers a singularly—and nearly anachronistic—traditional context: a relatively clear set of social expectations by which the self can or must be identified. These social limits are what has made the South valuable both to individual writers and to the nation as a whole, not least by casting the modern struggle for identity in stark and dramatic terms. To know where we are, at least imaginatively, allows us to figure out a little better just where we can—or cannot—go. If our limits are defined for us, if the social map is a given rather than a riddle, then we can see quite immediately what the possibilities are for accommodation or transgression. In the increasingly disoriented, mobile reality of late-nineteenth- and twentieth-century America, such surety was an attractive backdrop for examining identity and "place."

Although, as Michael O'Brien explains, the southern mid-century literary renascence was not historically unique, it was, for itself at least, a singular conjunction of the isolated modern individual against a stable (and idealized) community.[10] At the same time, this revitalized myth of the South was supported by a tenacious ruralism just as most

---

ed.; Urbana, 1989), 43–58, Vol. II of Gerster and Cords, *Myth and Southern History*, 2 vols.; and Barbara J. Fields, "Ideology and Race in American History" in *Region, Race, and Reconstruction: Essays in Honor of C. Vann Woodward*, ed. J. Morgan Kousser and James M. McPherson (New York, 1982), 143–77. The related issue of southern resistance to "northern" influences is explored in Richard N. Current, *Northernizing the South* (Athens, Ga., 1983).

9. Gray, *Writing the South*, xxi. A recent summary of this virtual commonplace appears in *Encyclopedia*, ed. Wilson and Ferris, xv–xvi. See also Michael O'Brien, "A Heterodox Note on the Southern Renaissance," in *Rethinking the South: Essays in Intellectual History* (Baltimore, 1988), 166.

10. O'Brien, "A Heterodox Note," 166.

of America grew urban. This distinctive identity, both within and beyond its borders, thus reinforced the usefulness of the South as an imaginative space. Its remote backwaters and equally remote parlors made the ordinary limits on human behavior—the clogs of prejudice, violence, social stratification—seem somehow less real than they appeared in the complacent and familiar settings of mid-America. Being both part of America and safely separated in its margins, the South offered the nation an exaggerated image of many unacceptable attitudes that Americans disguised from themselves in more familiar environs: a growing consensus condoning racism, a romantic attachment to feudalism and aristocratic status, a nostalgic agrarianism.[11] Sentiments that were inadmissible for a progressive and democratic people, committed to industrialization and urbanization, could be conveniently relegated to a distinct subculture—distinct, at least, from a complacently hegemonic consciousness that was entirely white, mostly male, and predominantly northeastern. Weaknesses could be shunted off as other—"theirs"—while any virtues could be claimed as the dominant culture's own—"ours." In this role as Other, the South, of course, assumes a very feminine part, for women have consistently been assigned this receptive and distancing function in Western culture. Becoming, like woman, "the space," as Alice Jardine writes, "'outside of' the conscious subject,"[12] the South thus became America's most fertile imaginative site, the scene of some of our most significant crises of identity.

Louisiana mirrors the complex role that the South has played in the national consciousness. It, too, defines a space that is both psychic and geographic, a site where the Other—of gender, race, religion, sexuality, ethnicity—is often more clearly demarcated than in the rest of America: a place where social boundaries are frequently equated with precise physical limits: the "white" and "colored" water fountains and schools of segregation, the men-only Carnival clubs and state legislatures, the Negro quarters of towns and small cities, the ladies' entrances of certain shops and clubs. Although Louisiana shares many of these narrowly limited spaces with the rest of the South, it has also given them the distinctive shape of its own anomalous history and

11. Gerster and Cords, "Northern Origins of Southern Mythology," 58; Rowe, *Enchanted Country*, xvii–xx.

12. Alice Jardine, *Gynesis: Configurations of Woman and Modernity* (Ithaca, 1985), 114–15.

culture. Primary among the state's anomalies are the strong French and Catholic strains in its character, manifest in its Napoleonic civil code, its festivals of Mardi Gras and All Saints', its devotion to the culinary arts, and its general tolerance of liquor, languor, and lewdness—within limits. Such peculiarities have redefined in Louisiana—sometimes subtly and sometimes sharply—the cultural and geographic places out of which the South has constructed its prevailing mythologies.

But even within the state, these typically Mediterranean influences are unevenly manifest. Louisiana is divided into two quite dissimilar regions: the mostly Protestant and Anglo-Saxon north and the largely Catholic and French south. Significantly, however, the latter area includes New Orleans, which as Louisiana's largest city tends to project its identity onto the whole state—thus the Louisiana hinterland, in this respect at least, shares the fate of downstate Illinois or upstate New York. Marked as much by its atypicality as by its unmistakable southernness, New Orleans has been an eccentric urban center for the South as a whole as well as for Louisiana. Located at the mouth of North America's greatest river, poised as a border and gateway to the world beyond; with the multiethnic flavor of its French, African, Caribbean, and Spanish influences still pronounced; surrounded by water; at once cosmopolitan and myopically provincial, New Orleans has encouraged conflicting perspectives and definitions. Its divided allegiances were tellingly apparent during the Civil War: never particularly committed to the lost cause, the city fell early in the struggle and escaped many of the worst effects of the South's defining experience. But perhaps more critical to the uniqueness of the city—and thus Louisiana—has been its peculiar treatment of racial difference, the South's most tenacious marker of place. From its earliest period, when the various French colonial proprietors and trading companies responsible for settling the Louisiana territory failed for many years to import sufficient numbers of European women along with male émigrés, the city developed a tacit tolerance for interracial relationships, first with Native Americans and later with Africans from the slave trade. Many of the offspring of such unions remained or became free citizens, constituting a unique social class, *les gens de couleur libre*—free people of color.

Bolstered in the late eighteenth century by free blacks fleeing the insurrections of French Santo Domingo, the *gens de couleur* eventually formed a substantial community in New Orleans, including many individuals of significant wealth and social status. They occupied an anomalous place in southern culture—not quite parallel to the dominant Euro-American classes, as they were throughout the West Indies, but carefully distinguished from slaves. Their acceptance as part of the city's (and the state's) social fabric did not diminish the institutionalized effects of prejudice, but it did work to blur the lines of racial difference: color could not be wholly synonymous with class here, as it often was elsewhere in the South.[13] Even the elaborate classifications of color—mulatto, quadroon, octoroon, griffe, quinteroon, the "black drop" calculated to distant generations—suggest a reluctance to make otherness absolute, certainly among blacks, and perhaps among whites at least a perverse willingness to acknowledge its relativity. Moreover, encouraged by the cultural variety and economic mobility characteristic of a major port, the ambivalences about race in New Orleans likewise extended to the ethnicity of other European and Euro-American newcomers. Social distinctions were typically identified, and often continue to be identified, with places: Yankees in the Garden District; Irish in the Irish Channel; Cajuns in Marrero, Westwego, and elsewhere on the West Bank (of the river); the French (and later Italians) in the Vieux Carré; Creoles occupying the Seventh Ward (downriver) and, later, New Orleans East, which also now includes substantial Vietnamese and Hispanic populations.

Gathered from and diffused onto Louisiana as a whole, these multiple and intersecting identities have complicated the image of both city and state, making them ripe for literary use. New Orleans in particular has been, as Hamilton Basso once wrote, "a symbol of exotic alienness in the national mind," a source of romance that few writers—within or without the state—have cared to resist."[14] Not surpris-

13. For an account of the evolution of Louisiana's distinctive African-American castes, see Thomas Marc Fiehrer, "The African Presence in Colonial Louisiana: An Essay on the Continuity of Caribbean Culture," in *Louisiana's Black Heritage*, ed. Robert R. MacDonald, John R. Kemp, and Edward F. Haas (New Orleans, 1979), esp. 19–25. See also James R. Frisby, Jr., "New Orleans Writers and the Negro: George Washington Cable, Grace King, Ruth McEnery Stuart, Kate Chopin, and Lafcadio Hearn, 1870–1900" (Ph.D. dissertation, Emory University, 1972), 8–23. Frisby's work is cited by Anna Shannon Elfenbein in her study of stereotypes in Louisiana writers, *Women on the Color Line: Evolving Stereotypes and the Writings of George Washington Cable, Grace King, Kate Chopin* (Charlottesville, 1989), 12–19.

14. Hamilton Basso, Introduction to *The World from Jackson Square: A New Orleans Reader*, ed. Etolia S. Basso (New York, 1948), xi. Violet Harrington Bryan's study of the image of New Orleans in literature is forthcoming from the University of Tennessee

ingly, given that dominance and appeal, the literary history of Louisiana virtually overlaps that of its principal city, a fact that is apparent throughout this present work, most notably in the paucity of women writers from the state's northern half represented in the selected essays and in the more inclusive Bibliography.

Writing about Louisiana, then, whether about the rural life of Isle Brevelle or the sophisticated cliques of Uptown New Orleans, and writing as a Louisiana woman both imply writing about life at the margins—at the crossroads of dominant and muted cultures, of role definition and identity, of race and class, of place and places. The peculiar otherness of that experience, imposed onto the more familiar layers of southern myth, gender roles, and color prejudice, is precisely the ingredient that distinguishes the contribution of this group of writers to the fascinating place that Louisiana and its Crescent City occupy in the American psyche.

It has been more than fifty years since anyone has tried to take stock of Louisiana's literary heritage, a serious void that the Bibliography goes a substantial way toward remedying. But even our most rigorous effort at inclusiveness finally demonstrates just how much more work needs to be done. For example, not only the inevitable gaps of data on obscure figures, but the omission even of whole categories—such as that of women writing in French—indicate important scholarship still needed. Both as a research tool and as a challenge to further investigation, the Bibliography is a long-overdue step toward what Adrienne Rich calls the fundamental task of feminist criticism, "re-vision": seeing again what has been written, recognizing what has been lost by unseeing eyes. One dimension of that re-vision is the recovery of many writers whose talents seem undistinguished in isolation, but whose presence among others discloses the essential literary contexts from which writers with greater gifts emerge. As Ellen Moers rightly observed, even Jane Austen could write what she did only because so many others had explored the terrain before her; their failures and partial successes marked the way for her triumphs.[15] Likewise, seeing

---

Press. Two previous works that treat early segments of the city's literary history are Albert Fossier, *New Orleans: The Glamour Period, 1800–1840* (New Orleans, 1957), esp. 238–46; and Robert C. Reinders, *End of an Era: New Orleans, 1850–1860* (New Orleans, 1964). The latter is particularly acerbic on the deleterious "emotional female influences in fiction and poetry," 224.

15. Adrienne Rich, *Lies, Secrets and Silence: Selected Prose, 1966–1978* (New York, 1979), 35; Ellen Moers, *Literary Women: The Great Writers* (New York, 1976), 44.

how many Louisiana women writers there were—and are—makes the achievement of a Chopin or a Grau both less exceptional and more comprehensible. Lesser writers, moreover, can provide valuable cultural data, enriching our understanding of an era, as well as offer glimpses of technique and purpose that their more skillful peers better conceal.

If the Bibliography thus surveys the regions we must traverse, the essays themselves represent a different kind of re-vision, adding evaluation to recovery. Like the Bibliography, they propose another look, often fresh and always perceptive, at the heritage of Louisiana women writers. But their selectiveness also challenges other scholars to pursue the many roads of interpretation that could not all be taken in a single volume. There are, for example, some glaring omissions of writers whose contributions to Louisiana literature are well known: Ruth McEnery Stuart, Anne Rice, Gwen Bristow, Frances Parkinson Keyes, Valerie Martin, and Lillian Hellman, to name only the most obvious. Much more regrettable to us as editors is the paucity of scholarship on Louisiana's African-American women, especially since in the last twenty years that group has produced such a flowering of poets and playwrights, among them Pinkie Gordon Lane, Elizabeth Brown-Guillory, Arthenia Bates Millican, Brenda Marie Osbey, Sybil Kein, Thadious Davis, Gloria Hull, and Mona Lisa Saloy; their work deserves greater critical attention.

Of course, the intent of this volume is not to confirm a canon of Louisiana writers, but to stimulate interest in a rich and vigorous tradition. Obviously, no one collection can encompass the literary variety and wealth that the state has fostered; however, the essays can and do suggest the outlines of that variety. Encouraged only to keep in mind our defining terms, *Louisiana* and *women*, the essayists approach their subjects from a variety of critical positions. Moreover, whereas unfamiliar writers such as Mollie Moore Davis, Berthe Amoss, or Ada Jack Carver invite introductory or biographical comments, their more famous counterparts such as Chopin or Porter permit more specialized approaches. The consequence is a series of essays whose differing perspectives give glimpses of a continuous tradition, punctuated by perceptive insights into the female mind of Louisiana, and thus of the South.

As one might expect, place resonates for these authors; the culture and geography of Louisiana were indeed, for several, crucial to their opportunities as writers. Local colorists, for example—well represented here by Grace King, Kate Chopin, Mollie Moore Davis, and

Alice Dunbar-Nelson—were able to take advantage of the state's popularity as a setting with national audiences in the late 1800s. Even twentieth-century writers such as Ellen Gilchrist, Nancy Lemann, and Shelia Bosworth have successfully capitalized on the state's persistent appeal as setting, although as Randal Woodland points out, not without a distinct awareness of its limitations. The power of Louisiana as an image is directly addressed in the work of Katherine Anne Porter, who spent little time here but whose allusions to the state, as Merrill Skaggs argues, bear important symbolic weight.

The problems of place as social limit are exposed most acutely by the writers of the late nineteenth and early twentieth centuries. Clara Juncker, for example, examines how diarist Sarah Morgan Dawson quietly chafed against the gender roles that wartime Baton Rouge only exacerbated, while Ellen Peel shows how Kate Chopin subtly disclosed the shortcomings of those roles in her tragic portrait of Désirée. But as both essayists suggest, even more unsettling to these writers are the contradictions of race. Linda Coleman addresses the issue most directly in her commentary on the sketches of Grace King, whose sharp realism is consistently distorted by her nostalgic views of blacks. In perhaps the most speculative essay of the collection, Alice Parker ruminates on how Sidonie de la Houssaye, the only representative of Louisiana's important Francophone traditions, usurps the stories of quadroon women to explore territory forbidden to her as a white Victorian woman. Similarly, Elizabeth Meese examines the disruptions in Ada Jack Carver's stories of free people of color in Isle Brevelle, which Carver, like de la Houssaye, appropriates in order to pass over into another culture. In the fiction of Shirley Ann Grau (as in that of Georgia's Margaret Mitchell, whose epic novel Elzbieta Oleksy suggestively compares with Grau's *Keepers of the House*), the conflicts of race are only slightly more submerged than those of gender, although both sharply define the fate of her heroines. Even Berthe Amoss' tales for adolescents, as Sylvia Iskander demonstrates, must confront race and social caste as a consequence of choosing New Orleans as a setting. Conflicts about race and gender are no less apparent in the work of Alice Dunbar-Nelson; however, the lack of a supportive literary community that Dunbar-Nelson experienced in New Orleans as a woman of color—a community that, as Violet Harrington Bryan argues, had it existed, might have enabled her to confront those ambivalences more directly—is made more poignant by the revelation of just such a community's benefits to her older contemporary, Mollie E. Moore

Davis. As Patricia Brady's biographical sketch reveals, Davis could and did rely on the privileges of her race and class to shape her life into graceful southern figures.

That kind of support, shared by most of the white women in this collection, was often essential in creating opportunities to write and publish in a culture that encouraged women to do neither. But reliance on these props frequently obscured the writers' visions of the cramped pedestal of gender that they also occupied. As the essays repeatedly suggest, the failure of King, Chopin, Dawson, Carver, and even Dunbar-Nelson (albeit in a very different way) to extend their tentative analyses of difference to race *and* gender finally restricted their ability to identify the sources of their constraints as women and as writers. Their consequent ambivalence about redefining their places as southern women thus underlines the disturbing opacity of their vision of race.

Such disturbances, however, as Linda Coleman reminds us, can be keys to the patterns that blind and entrap entire cultures. Sharing a native or at least a temporary relation to Louisiana, these writers found in the state a fertile imaginative space from which to examine their specific places in a culture whose limits necessarily mark their work. By exposing some of those markings and by revealing the complexity of these different individuals' struggles to claim their places as Louisiana women writers, the essays, together with the Bibliography, attest to the continuing relevance of their achievement. That we might better recognize the full significance of those places is the hope that binds this collection together.

Sarah Morgan
Dawson in 1899.
Courtesy Special Col-
lections, Hill Memorial
Library, Louisiana State
University Libraries

Behind Confederate Lines: Sarah Morgan Dawson

READERS of Civil War diarists such as Sally Brock Putnam and Julia LeGrand have come to expect a certain narrative morphology from Confederates of the female persuasion: the packing and unpacking of favorite silk dresses, the coming of the Yankees, the nightly flights and shifting places of refuge, the shortage of food and plenitude of chivalry, the (dis)loyal blacks, and the devastating bulletins of loss and death. *A Confederate Girl's Diary* is no exception. Sarah Morgan (Dawson) began her journal in Baton Rouge in 1862 to escape the boredom of a quiet Sunday afternoon, and went on to chronicle a period of American history almost too "massively symbolic in its inexhaustible and sybilline significance."[1] Yet Sarah was not just a dutiful daughter of the Confederacy. Despite the flag of stars and bars she pinned to her bosom to defy the Union soldiers landing at Baton Rouge, she traversed in her diary the boundaries and loyalties that held together the world of southern womanhood. Throughout the turmoils of the Civil War, Sarah retained a fierce pride in her class, her race, and her state, but she oscillated in her writings between respectability and rebellion. The multiple displacements of her journal—from observer to observed, from reader to writer, from masculine to feminine, and from North to South—constitute the gynesis of a writerly Other that defers meaning, truth, and closure. As Alice Jardine explains with Derrida, "Writing is the 'general space' that disrupts all presence and absence and therefore all metaphysical notions of limits (as well as the possibility of transgressing any one of those limits)."[2] Sarah Morgan thus emerges from the pages of her diary as a newly born woman and a budding Louisiana deconstructionist.

The boundaries of Sarah's existence as a "southern lady" are textually represented in the male-authored foreword and introduction to *A Confederate Girl's Diary*. Writing in 1959, James I. Robertson, Jr., emphasizes the leavening effect of the Civil War narratives by women

---

1. Sarah Morgan Dawson, *A Confederate Girl's Diary*, ed. James I. Robertson, Jr. (Bloomington, 1960), hereinafter cited parenthetically by page number in text; Robert Penn Warren, *The Legacy of the Civil War: Meditations on the Centennial* (New York, 1961), 80.

2. Alice Jardine, *Gynesis: Configurations of Women and Modernity* (Ithaca, 1985), 184.

on both sides, whose "observations and experiences give to the war touches of human interest and warmth" (xi). The female diarists with whom the Confederacy was "blessed" thus epitomize the nurturing feminine ideal, also evoked in Robertson's dedication to his wife, "who tolerated neglect and held in check two Rebels as rambunctious as Taylor's Louisianans" (xxv). Robertson presents Sarah to her readers as a younger version of idealized southern femininity, a golden-haired belle of twenty with a "snow-white" complexion and "an hour-glass figure" (xv). Praising Sarah's self-control and balanced judgment, he notes that her dignified conduct "gained her much more male attention than coquettishness would have achieved." Her diary, he concludes, is "feminine, fresh and frank" (xxiii). The original introduction, written by Sarah's son, Warrington Dawson, for the posthumous publication of her Louisiana diary in 1913, predictably stresses the author's maternal virtues—common sense, forgiveness, and martyrdom. A new representative of the family patriarchy, he moreover assumes the voice of authority in praising Sarah's correct word choice and unblotted manuscript pages (xxx). Although both editors assure us that they have merely transcribed the author's original words, they matter-of-factly state that they have omitted passages on "irrelevant topics" (xxiii, xxxi). Sarah's words thus reach her audience through the masculine filters that also strained her life.[3]

Sarah was, in a sense, imprisoned by history. Her story, that of the Civil War, was being written elsewhere—at Manassas, in Washington, and in Richmond. The recurring incidents of feminine war journals—cotton burning, Yankee raids, and all the rest—demonstrate above all the writers' confinement to a male-authored plot. The dawn of Independence Day, 1862, ironically finds Sarah enclosed in the bathhouse while her sister through the weatherboarding tells her of Stonewall Jackson's and McClellan's positions. "This is said to be the sixth battle he [Jackson] has fought in twenty days, and they say he has won them all" (102), records Sarah in her diary, the passive construction and the impersonal "they" testifying to her distance from action and power. "Still no authentic reports of the late battles in Virginia" (223), she complains the following September. In February, 1863, she finally appeals to what she chooses to call "Destiny": "Where do you take us? During these two trying years, I have learned to feel

3. Charles East's new edition of the diary, *The Civil War Diary of Sarah Morgan* (Athens, Ga., 1991), was not available before this essay was completed.

myself a mere puppet in the hands of a Something that takes me here to-day, to-morrow there, always unexpectedly, and generally very unwillingly" (329). An actor rather than an author of history, Sarah is enclosed in a script she cannot control.

In this context, the bathhouse becomes emblematic of the spatial sensibility typical not only of feminine fictions but also of women's history. *A Confederate Girl's Diary* focuses on space, whether exterior, interior, or as Alice Jardine puts it in *Gynesis*, "hidden behind what we used to call Time."[4] Barred from systems of causality, Sarah is fundamentally indifferent to the reasons behind her predicaments, to the linear cause-effect patterns of traditional history. Thus she consistently loses track of time, heroic efforts to the contrary notwithstanding. "I am in danger of forgetting the days of the week, as well as those of the month," she writes a couple of days after the bathhouse incident. "Friday I am sure was the Fourth, because I heard the national salute fired. I must remember that to find my dates by" (107). In September she exclaims, "I had hardly realized spring, when now I find it is autumn" (207). Her sense of space, however, is highly developed, often manifesting itself in images of enclosure and suffocation. In the family mansion: "I am afraid this close confinement will prove too much for me; my long walks are cut off, on account of the soldiers" (87). In Baton Rouge: "Penned in on one little square mile, here we await our fate like sheep in the slaughter-pen" (96). In a boardinghouse in Clinton: "The house really has a suffocating effect on me, there is such a close look about it" (207). About the town of Clinton: "I would hate the dull round of this little place" (207). While Sarah's topographical emphasis usually originates in her feminine (historical) perspective, her spatial imagination occasionally suggests a longing for safety—the security of the womb: "I would dare anything, to be at home again. I know that the Yankees have left us little besides the bare house; but I would be grateful for the mere shelter of the roof" (208).

Sarah's yearning for her white-columned home on Church Street in Baton Rouge indicates her complicity in (re)constructing the walls separating the Morgans and similar prominent families from everybody else. Edmund Wilson notes in "Three Confederate Ladies," a chapter of *Patriotic Gore*, the amazing recurrence of family names in southern war documents: Sarah Morgan in Baton Rouge and Mary

4. Jardine, *Gynesis*, 82. For a discussion of space and femininity, see *ibid.*, esp. 33–34, 88–90.

Chesnut in Richmond share relatives and friends. Their social world, consisting of what Wilson calls "that fraction of the ruling class that is at all public-spirited and well-educated," is thus "extremely limited." Sarah obviously relishes the exclusiveness of her family circle. As the devoted daughter of Judge Thomas Gibbes Morgan, recently deceased when Sarah begins her journal, she carries "an aristocratic sense that has detached itself from planter solidarity."[5]

The "everybody else" expelled from the Morgan universe includes above all the lower classes, blacks, and—to an extent—Yankees. In discussing her milkman, who has commented on the young lady's pride, Sarah declares, "I did not care for what he or any of that class could say; I was surprised to find that they thought at all!" (267). She winces at the sight of "some little clerk in his holiday attire" (137) and particularly dislikes "low white women," too given to gossiping and to intermingling with soldiers, blacks, and "rabble" (397): "'Loud' women, what a contempt I have for you! How I despise your vulgarity!" (79). As for blacks, Sarah praises her servants' loyalty and the pleasant sound of their voices blessing their kind mistress (90), but generally she notices only the absence of her slaves: "What a day I have had! Here mother and I are alone, not a servant on the lot. . . . I actually swept two whole rooms!" (62). The nonidentity assigned to blacks surfaces as well in Sarah's juxtaposition of "cattle, mules and negroes" (337) and in the slaves' textual fragmentation into "black faces" and "shining teeth" (277). Faced with Lincoln's Emancipation Proclamation, Sarah vehemently resists the role reversal feared by members of the ruling class and race: "I would rather have all I own burned, than in the possession of the negroes. Fancy my magenta organdie on a dark beauty! Bah!" (178). The Yankees are, of course, to blame for such threats to well-established southern order. "Yankees can't prosper unless they are pillaging honest people" (337), writes the young Rebel, who "would not forego the title for any other earthly one" (317).

The codes of race and class to which Sarah willingly adhered nonetheless trapped her in the role of southern lady. In her efforts to play the part, she frowns appropriately at a "swearing guerrilla" (47); "reduced" to entering occupied Baton Rouge in a mule wagon, she gives her "whole attention to getting out [of the wagon] respectably" (59).

5. Edmund Wilson, *Patriotic Gore: Studies in the Literature of the American Civil War* (New York, 1962), 278, 269.

Anticipating a Union attack, she notes with feminine vanity, "My chief desire was to wash my face before running, if they were actually shelling us again" (87). At every forced flight, she records in great detail the clothes items lost and saved: "I find myself obliged to leave one of my new muslins I had just finished . . . , the body of my lovely lilac, and my beauteous white mull. But then, I have saved eight half-made linen chemises!" (121–22). Sarah exhibits a good deal of self-irony and humor, however, in relating her struggle to descend from the mule wagon like a queen, and in describing the "disgrace" of herself and her sister Miriam in helping a seemingly wounded Union soldier who, it turns out, is merely drunk. Sarah's subversive irony as well as her consciousness of wearing a mask indicate a distance from the feminine role created for her. "Here I must confess to the most consummate piece of acting," she writes in describing her success in keeping an admirer from embarking upon a whiskey spree (304). Between the signifiers of femininity (lace, downcast eyes, barely audible sighs) and the "self" signified, Sarah (un)consciously inserts a gap of unrepresentable resistance.

The same kind of slippage occurs, predictably, in Sarah's (non)approach to her own sexuality. According to the code, a southern lady was, of course, to remain as pure as Sarah's snow-white complexion, sexual appetites being confined to women of darker hues. Having internalized this prescriptive asexuality, Sarah vows to stab the first soldier who tries to kiss her: "I never dreamed of kissing any man save my father and brothers. And why any one should care to kiss any one else, I fail to understand" (36). When she falls out of her buggy, injuring her lower spine, Sarah worries whether her feet might be exposed, and with ladylike reticence cannot mention to her rescuers an injury so close to her "extremity" (285). In happier moments, Sarah nonetheless demonstrates an unmistakable, if unconscious, attraction to the soldiers swarming around her. After watching a Union detail drill, she notes, "One conceited, red-headed lieutenant smiled at us in the most fascinating way" (68); on being introduced to the "very handsome" Captain Bradford, Sarah compares him to "a moss-covered stone wall, a slumbering volcano, a ———— what you please, so it suggests anything unexpected and dangerous to stumble over" (276). Hidden in the blank is, we may guess, the dangerous sexuality to which Sarah found herself responding. Courted by a Mr. Halsey some months later, Sarah resolves the sexual tension brought about by his visit by staying in her room but sending him a bouquet of flowers with her compliments. The bouquet itself is a writing of contradictions: a bunch of snowdrops tied with three of Sarah's gold-red hairs. With this gesture, Sarah successfully manages (not) to acknowledge her erotic inclinations and thus stays within feminine folds.

Sarah's six-month confinement following her injury may itself have been a bodily articulation of tension, a way of erasing the boundaries between the dutiful and the rebellious daughter.[6] As Elaine Showalter hypothesizes in *The Female Malady*, hysteria, or "the daughter's disease," might be a mode of dissent for women who lack satisfying social, mental, or expressive outlets. Indeed, throughout *A Confederate Girl's Diary*, a subtext of nervous strain runs counter to Sarah's much-advertised calm and reserve. "This suspense is not calculated to soothe one's nerves" (91), she writes when awaiting the arrival of Federal forces in Baton Rouge; she further announces that the shout of "'Picayune Butler's coming, coming' has upset my nervous system" (92). On July 3, 1862, she jots down, "Another day of sickening suspense" (99). After her accident, the connection between mind and body becomes quite explicit: "The uncertainty is really affecting my spine and causing me to grow alarmingly thin . . ." (346). Through her inability to move, Sarah is literalizing feminine passivity, thus speaking with her body what cannot be spoken. Significantly, the mere thought of a change of scene gives her the strength to attempt to walk; an impending enemy attack causes her to *jump* out of bed (332). After her removal to New Orleans, she jubilantly writes, "I am getting well!" (387). Sarah's hysterical illness is, in Dianne Hunter's words, "a discourse of femininity addressed to patriarchal thought." By confining herself to confinement, Sarah signifies in bodily discourse the dissent censored by southern gender systems and, ironically, creates a space of her own.[7]

But the site of challenge, of potentiality, is above all the diary: in the act of writing, Sarah invents a feminine space. Like other women (writers), she struggles against constant interruptions—in her case not only by family members and social visits, but also by cannon fire and enemy assaults. After losing her writing desk (and her home) as she

6. *Cf. ibid.*, 276: "Her slowness of recovery suggests that she had also at last broken down under the continued strain on her nerves."

7. Elaine Showalter, *The Female Malady: Women, Madness, and English Culture, 1830–1980* (New York, 1985), 147; Dianne Hunter quoted *ibid.*, 157. See *ibid.*, 134, for a discussion of hysterics' "desires for privacy and independence." The hysterical attacks of Sarah's sister Miriam and their mother in March, 1864, serve a similar function.

flees the advancing Union troops, Sarah writes using her knees for support in asylums, guest-houses, and aboard the schooner taking her to New Orleans. "I would die without some means of expressing my feelings," she confesses in explaining her efforts to keep her diary intact through losses of practically all other earthly possessions (333). Writing is therapy, a space of privacy undisturbed by the (masculine) systems of power enclosing it. By recording in minute details the destruction of her house—from her mother's shattered armoire to heaps of broken china—Sarah is able to laugh at her losses. Restricted by feminine propriety, she can retreat into the more permissive world of her journal: "How many times it has proved a relief to me where my tongue was forced to remain quiet! . . . [Pens, ink, and paper have] acted as lightning rod to my mental thunder, and have made me happy generally" (76–77).

Through writing, Sarah furthermore attempts to escape her status as text-object, forever surrounded by masculine eyes and performing according to masculine scripts.[8] She is constantly wary (and weary) of the male gaze. "We are certainly watched," she writes about the Union officers passing and repassing her home (99). "I prefer solitude where I can do as I please without being observed," she records about the small town of Clinton, where everybody is "reading" her (207). In recounting her buggy accident, Sarah feels more pain from being "the centre of attraction" (283) than from her injured spine: "I only wanted to get home, away from all those eyes" (284). Although this young lady has internalized her object role to the extent of discussing herself in the third person (109), her writing nonetheless deconstructs the observer/observed dichotomy. In her journal, Sarah becomes a recording Self as well as a recorded Other, a reader as well as the text. Her diary amply illustrates her eye for people and, moreover, suggests the visionary powers with which this seventh child of a seventh child was thought to be endowed (xiii). By presenting herself as a "seer" and observer, Sarah struggles to become the subject of her own existence.

The Confederate girl's efforts to master discourse serve a similar function, much in the style of early black autobiographers' search for literacy. Having received only ten months of formal schooling, Sarah is painfully aware of what she considers her own linguistic shortcom-

---

8. *Cf.* Susan Gubar, "'The Blank Page' and the Issues of Female Creativity," in *Writing and Sexual Difference,* ed. Elizabeth Abel (Chicago, 1982), 73–93.

ings. She repeatedly refers to her diary as "trash" and "stupidity," and further demonstrates anxiety of authorship in describing her reservations about writing for public eyes: "I . . . got in a violent fit of the 'trembles' at the idea of writing to a stranger" (70). Against this background, Sarah's disdain of *ain't* and *her'n* and *his'n* (257) becomes a wish for mastery and control (also) in linguistic terms. She intensely admires Captain Bradford and Colonel Breaux for their conversational and argumentative skills, and takes a similar pride in her own facility with words, as when she catches gentlemen's puns before they are half spoken (305). In search of literacy, Sarah studies "the masters" long hours every day, reading and thinking of reading even as the Yankees are approaching (334). Unconsciously looking for "a different voice," Sarah nonetheless criticizes Boswell ("a vain, conceited prig" [115]) and Johnson ("an old brute of a tyrant" [115]) from what might be a Cixousian feminine border, a no-man's-land of pleasure, dreams, and disruption. Indeed, Sarah announces her desire to read "only what I absolutely love, now" (88) and writes with excitement about a discussion with Colonel Breaux on phrenology and health (248). Sarah's intellectual arousal testifies not least to an intense desire to give birth to her self. Her fantasy is largely fulfilled. At the end of the journal, the Confederate girl of the title proudly declares herself a woman (439).

As Barbara Johnson suggests, the primary autobiographical motivation is the desire to create a being in one's own image, the "desire for resemblance." Yet the expulsion of Otherness necessitated by the dream of resemblance is sabotaged by the "monstrosity" of autobiographical writing: the possibility of giving birth to "a filthy creation," a monster. In Johnson's analysis, the "monstrosity of selfhood" is "intimately embedded within the question of female autobiography" because of the socially prescribed repression of discourses and emotions transgressing "the amiableness of domestic affection." The "woman" of Sarah Morgan's journal is thus not quite the genteel Louisiana lady Sarah wishes (not) to be. What she confronts in her writing is, ultimately, the Other within. In moments of scriptural fervor/fever, she reveals a "monstrosity" related to her difficulty in adapting to a feminine ideal shaped by the masculine, not the feminine, imagination. In the words of Mary Jacobus, "What is repressed necessarily returns, in the language of the unconscious, as an avenging monster."[9]

9. Barbara Johnson, "My Monster/My Self," *Diacritics*, XII (1982), 3, 4, 10; Mary Jacobus, *Reading Woman (Reading): Essays in Feminist Criticism* (New York, 1986), 9.

The face of the Other woman—the *impropre* of Sarah's discourse—shows itself in moments of great emotional intensity. One such moment occurs after an evening spent in the company of educated southern gentlemen: "Why was I denied the education that would enable me to be the equal of such a man as Colonel Breaux and the others? He says the woman's mind is the same as the man's, originally; it is only education that creates the difference. Why was I denied that education? Who is to blame? Have I exerted fully the natural desire To Know that is implanted in all hearts? Have I done myself injustice in my self-taught ignorance, or has injustice been done to me? Where is the fault . . . ?" (249–50). The carefully modulated voice of the southern lady has here given way to an anxious questioning, a syntax ruptured by pain. Other passages, often signaled with "Oh, if I was a man," scream out Sarah's despair at having been made "with a man's heart, and a female form" (139). The monster of *A Confederate Girl's Diary* is caged in a feminine (textual) body but has a feminist face.

Although Sarah's questioning of boundaries was confined largely to the private space of her journal, her writing entered into a dialogue with other sexual/textual practices that allowed for similar dislocations. In and outside her diary, Sarah merged her voice with those of other women, establishing the sort of feminine community linked across masculine borders that Carroll Smith-Rosenberg first identified.[10] Not only did she fill her textual space with women—most notably her mother and sisters—she also consistently emphasized the contribution of her sex to the war effort: "Honestly, I believe the women of the South are as brave as the men who are fighting" (137). Her feminine loyalties extended beyond enemy lines, to "the many mothers, wives, and sisters who wait as anxiously, pray as fervently in their faraway homes for their dear ones, as we do here" (80).

Female bonding surfaces as well in moments of fun and jollity. As Nathalie Davis demonstrates in "Women on Top," an essay in *Society and Culture in Early Modern France*, the privileged time of carnival and festivity allowed for female disobedience to traditional hierarchical power structures.[11] Although Davis limits her discussion to preindustrial Europe, the frolic of Sarah and her sisters during the Louisiana

10. Carroll Smith-Rosenberg, "The Female World of Love and Ritual: Relations Between Women in Nineteenth-Century America," *Signs*, I (1975), 1–29.

11. Nathalie Davis, "Women on Top," in Davis, *Society and Culture in Early Modern France* (Stanford, 1975), 124–51.

sugar-cane harvest echoes the "unruly" women of Davis' account. Entering the dark of the sugarhouse, described as if it were a sensuous underworld, Sarah and her female companions discard all dignity and abandon themselves to disorderly merriment: "Anna flew around like a balloon, Miriam fairly danced around with fun and frolic, while I laughed" (274). In the sugar purgery, the young women cleanse themselves of genteel restrictions as they chase their gentlemen friends from corner to corner. In the process, they establish a symbolic, if temporary, inversion of gender roles.

Interestingly enough, Sarah's opposite move—toward calm and control—functions as a similar usurpation of phallic territory. Throughout *A Confederate Girl's Diary,* Sarah identifies with her father, both psychologically and politically. Against her mother's weakness, she posits a self-imposed coolness reminiscent of the balanced, dignified Judge Morgan. Moreover, she contrasts the quiet, gentlemanly speech of Union soldiers with the abusive violence of female secessionists (72–73). "To cry, faint, scream or go off in hysterics," she argues, will only land one in prison (394–95). Although Sarah in this passage has in mind the Custom House jail, the implication is nonetheless that to avoid feminine incarceration, one must assume phallic powers. Against this background, her first meeting with Union officers in Baton Rouge takes on new significance: the Confederate flag pinned on her bosom signals sexual and political difference, but the pistol hidden in her skirt covertly denies the difference, making her in several ways one of "them." "A pistol in my pocket fills up the gap," she writes in describing what she might do if attacked. "I am capable, too" (24). Sarah presents herself, in other words, as a phallic woman. And, as Jane Gallop reminds us, "For a woman as woman to assume power is to introduce a crack in the representation of power." [12]

Sarah's fantasies of cross-dressing signal a similar desire to efface gender boundaries. In describing the "Home Guard" of Louisiana men, Sarah expresses her longing "to give them my hoops, corsets, and pretty blue organdie in exchange for their boots and breeches!" (138). Although she makes this statement to ridicule "cowards," it also suggests Sarah's own wish to get her hands on the paraphernalia of masculinity. In another, extended passage, she again indulges in dreams of putting on men's clothes (and roles): "If I was a man—oh, wouldn't I be in Richmond with the boys! . . . What is the use of all

12. Jane Gallop, *The Daughter's Seduction: Feminism and Psychoanalysis* (Ithaca, 1982), 120.

these worthless women, in war times? If they attack, I shall don the breeches, and join the assailants, and fight. . . . How do breeches and coats feel, I wonder?" (119–20).

The entry progresses to describe Sarah's unsuccessful attempt to try on a suit belonging to her brother Jimmy. "If I only had a pair of breeches," she writes, awaiting a Federal attack, "my happiness would be complete" (140). This (proposed) blurring of gender distinctions amidst the chaos of war implies that women need not be confined to a uni-form, to what Sandra M. Gilbert in "Costumes of the Mind" calls "a single form or self."[13] "If some few Southern women were in the ranks," Sarah speculates, "they could set the men an example they would not blush to follow. Pshaw! there are *no* women here! We are *all* men!" (25).

Sarah's costume fantasy is, again following Gilbert, an attempt "to name not what is fixed but what is fluid in herself." The elastic ego boundaries of the "woman-as-process" born on the pages of Sarah's diary resist closure and integration, as the writing "subject" dissolves into other characters and emerges as kaleidoscopic selves. Sarah dives into the minds and hearts of Anna and Miriam, projecting her own emotions onto her sister and companion and, in turn, finding their feelings and actions mirrored in her own. This extension of "self" is evident also in the various Sarahs writing the journal. Not only does the mature Sarah Morgan Dawson add footnotes and postscripts to the diary of her youth, but the young woman of the Civil War constantly displaces selves, strategies, solutions. As Judith K. Gardiner notes in "On Female Identity and Writing by Women," the "model of the integrated individual was predominantly male, and women writers show that this model of characterization is inappropriate to their experience."[14] Much like the "knowing" mirror squinting at Sarah "from a thousand broken angles" when she returns to her destroyed home, the signifying "subject" reflected in *A Confederate Girl's Diary* reaches the reader from numerous directions. And considering that Sarah wrote primarily for her own I's, the mirroring process becomes as open-ended as the diary itself.

The merging of Self and Other is a source of both energy and fear

13. Sandra M. Gilbert, "Costumes of the Mind: Transvestism as Metaphor in Modern Literature," in *Writing and Sexual Difference*, ed. Abel, 177–91.

14. *Ibid.*, 215; Judith Kegan Gardiner, "On Female Identity and Writing by Women," in *Writing as Sexual Difference*, ed. Abel, 185. On "woman-as-process," see Jardine, *Gynesis*, 40–49; or Julia Kristeva, "Woman Can Never Be Defined," in *New French Feminisms*, eds. Elaine Marks and Isabelle de Courtivron (New York, 1981), 137–66.

in Sarah's writing. The deconstruction of difference leads, on the one hand, to a dissolution of North/South hatreds, as in Sarah's increasing compassion for Union soldiers and her identification with northern mothers and sisters (136, 79). Writing from a feminine position situated in the Imaginary realm of the unconscious, Sarah challenges traditional representations of meaning and ideology. In a recurring nightmare, for example, a soldier leads Sarah to a hill overlooking a scene of battle: "I could see the Garrison, and the American flag flying over it. I looked, and saw we were standing in blood up to our knees, while here and there ghastly white bones shone above the red surface" (83). In writing her unconscious, Sarah floods masculine symbolic systems with bodily fluid(s), thus exposing the nonmeaning within. As Sarah states in 1865, "I don't know what tempts me to do it [write] except perversity; for I have nothing to say" (405). The "nothing" of Sarah's discourse of desire represents precisely the meaninglessness surrounding her.

On the other hand, the stirrings of unconscious drives cause Sarah to exorcise Otherness in its most recognizable shapes and forms: "vulgar" women, the lower classes, blacks (see, for example, pp. 396–97). In distancing herself from the Other(s), Sarah hoped, of course, to eliminate alien(ating) parts of herself. Even Sarah's sympathy for the enemy soldiers might originate in a desire for Sameness: what the Confederate writer tries to establish across political borders is perhaps the resemblance between enemies of similar zeal, class, and race. In describing a group of Union officers, Sarah thus writes with approval: "Fine, noble-looking men they were, showing refinement and gentlemanly bearing in every motion. One cannot help but admire such foes!" (29).

Sarah's (de)construction of boundaries thus establishes her diary as an electric field in which concepts such as Woman, Truth, and War are endlessly vibrating. Sarah tries to separate "truth" from "lies" but ultimately has to erase the distinction. Wondering about news from Vicksburg and Port Hudson, she reflects: "If it is true, it is all for the best, and if it is *not* true, it is better still. Whichever it is, it is for some wise purpose; so it does not matter" (395). She emphasizes that she does not record "events" or "reliable information" (143) and scorns people who can "only take in one idea at a time" (225). Predictably, Sarah thus expresses the deferral and plurality characteristic of her medium—writing. And by reversing and traversing traditional hierarchies of order and belief, Sarah constructs herself as a deconstructionist.

In the end, however, Sarah's questioning of limits was silenced by male gatekeepers. At the close of the journal, Sarah, Miriam, and their mother are forced by physical, mental, and financial necessities to seek admittance to the occupied city of New Orleans and the house of the eldest Morgan brother. In a scene resonating with symbolic significance, the crippled, mute, and almost unconscious Sarah takes the Oath of Allegiance, administered by Union soldiers. In a Kristevan reading of the situation, she enters a system of signification that in women's writing "is seen from a foreign land . . . from the point of view of an asymbolic, spastic body."[15] In this (linguistic) realm, she is increasingly reduced to silence. The representative of masculine author-ity, generically and appropriately called "Brother," forbids her to write letters and notes. Even Sarah's diary entries become short and scarce.

Nonetheless, Sarah ends her journal on an important note of ambiguity. Despite her enclosure in masculine (sign) systems, Sarah enjoys in New Orleans a certain independence: she regains her health and enjoys considerably more freedom of movement than the imprisoned Confederate officers who invite her to visit the Custom House jail. As Sarah comments, "Position of affairs rather reversed since we last met!" (404). To an extent, at least, the women of the Confederacy emerged from the war as "triumphant survivors"—the heirs of a system that had for so long disinherited them.[16]

The silence of the last pages of *A Confederate Girl's Diary*—and beyond—originates ultimately in what Alice Jardine calls "an inability of words to give form to the world—a crisis in the function of the *techne.*" At the opening of her journal, Sarah writes, "There is no word in the English language that can express the state in which we are, and have been, these last days" (16). Three years later, after the deaths of two brothers within a week, Sarah no longer searches for words to describe her pain. Instead, the pistol fired at Lincoln concludes her (printed) diary and, indeed, sets the Confederate girl of the title free. The shot marks Sarah's entry into modernity—the collapse of "master discourses," the chaos and fragmentation of Western existence.[17] Sarah's dislocations of traditional conceptional habits—Woman, Meaning,

---

15. Kristeva, "Woman Can Never Be Defined," in *New French Feminisms*, eds. Marks and Courtivron, 166.

16. Gilbert, "Costumes of the Mind," in *Writing and Sexual Difference*, ed. Abel, 211.

17. Jardine, *Gynesis*, 100. Concerning Sarah's pain and increasing reticence, *cf.* Florence Nightingale's demand for the right to pain as an antidote to the (mental) inactivity of women's lives, discussed in Showalter, *Female Malady*, 65.

Region, and others—thus place her in the intellectual company of today's theoretical haut monde—a fashionable circle that would undoubtedly have pleased both Sarah the Louisiana lady and Sarah the feminist deconstructionist.

Portrait of Grace King
as a young woman.
Courtesy the Historic New
Orleans Collection, Mu-
seum/Research Center, Acc.
No. 1974.25.27.214

Grace King, *right,* and
her sister in the
parlor.
Courtesy the Historic New
Orleans Collection, Mu-
seum/Research Center, Acc.
No. 1974.25.25.6

View of Grace King's
former New Orleans
home, 1749
Coliseum.
Photo by K. W. "Jake"
Jacobs

At Odds

Race and Gender in Grace King's Short Fiction

> White women don't work on racism to do a favor for someone else, solely
> to benefit Third World women. You have to comprehend how racism
> distorts and lessens your own lives as white women—that racism affects
> your chances for survival, too, and that it is very definitely your issue.
> Until you understand this, no fundamental change will come about.
>
> —Barbara Smith

W HEN the complex links between sexism and racism are
understood as a compounding of material and spiritual
difference and deprivation, the late-nineteenth-century short stories
of Grace King appear in an at once more sympathetic and more critical light. A Louisiana native, King was a significant figure in her own
day both locally and nationally, but until very recently, her work has
been unfortunately ignored, even amidst the contemporary feminist
revival of regional women writers.[1] No doubt at least one reason for
her marginalization has been King's white-apologist position on race.
To acknowledge the importance of Grace King's fiction, however, is
not to condone its racism. What is valuable is an understanding of the
limitations that interlocking racism and sexism imposed on King and
her representation of Louisiana women.

King is often quoted as having said: "I am not a romanticist, I am a
realist '*à la mode de la Nouvelle-Orleans*'. I have never written a line that
was not realistic, but our life, our circumstances, the heroism of the
men and women that surrounded my early horizon—all that was romantic. I had a mind very sensitive to romantic impressions, but critical as to their expression."[2] These social and literary definitions have

---

1. Two important studies have appeared since the completion of this essay: Helen
Taylor, *Gender, Race, and Region in the Writings of Grace King, Ruth McEnery Stuart, and
Kate Chopin* (Baton Rouge, 1989); Anna Shannon Elfenbein, *Women on the Color Line:
Evolving Stereotypes and the Writings of George Washington Cable, Grace King, Kate Chopin*
(Charlottesville, 1989). Taylor's investigation of King and her peers offers valuable re-
gional and literary contexts, as well as thoughtful analysis of the intersection of race
and class in King's short fiction and novels. Elfenbein examines the types and traditions
embodied in King's work.

2. Grace King, quoted in Fred Lewis Pattee, *A History of American Literature Since
1870* (New York, 1915), 362.

passed through the same distorting, conservative lens that blinds King to the parallels between sexism and racism that appear in her stories. In her fiction she seeks and accomplishes realism of circumstance but persists in a romantic ideology. Anne Goodwyn Jones believes that after the Civil War, southern women were often "conservative as an ideal" but "radical in feeling," able to articulate a "critique, implicit or direct, of racial and sexual oppression, of the hierarchical caste and class structures that pervade cultural institutions, and of the evasive idealism that pushes reality aside."[3] The step from implicit to overt or direct critique, however, required an acknowledgment of a structural cultural problem and its responsibility for harmful racial and gender differences. King, instead of making that acknowledgment, believed that each woman, whether black or white, was responsible for an individual reconciliation to existing racist and sexist loss and displacement, and that only through such personal reaction and public responsibility was the cultural harmony she envisioned possible. Although social problems, as King perceived them, were closely and often painfully brought forward in her stories, cultural causes and conflicting points of view remained unexamined. Radical collective reconstruction encompassing the goals and values of both races and both genders was far from her imagining.

Grace King had felt a desire to write as early as age ten, but it was not until invited by the northern literary establishment to counteract the negative and popular postwar image of the South created by George Washington Cable that she actually composed her first story, turning to her native Louisiana for her material and to her mother's oral tradition of storytelling for a model.[4] The foundation of her fiction is a faith in female experience and values. Following her conservative Presbyterian ideology, King believed that when open to female nurturance and when strengthened and guided by their own experiences and memories, women could reconcile themselves to their personal, political, and social displacement, overcoming pride, self-delusion, ignorance, and inexperience.[5]

3. Anne Goodwyn Jones, *Tomorrow Is Another Day: The Woman Writer in the South, 1859–1936* (Baton Rouge, 1981), 45. See also Helen Taylor, "The Case of Grace King," *Southern Review,* n.s., XVIII (1982), 686–87, and Paula Giddings, *When and Where I Enter: The Impact of Black Women on Race and Sex in America* (New York, 1984), 42–43.

4. Grace King, *Memories of a Southern Woman of Letters* (New York, 1932), 48. King discusses her mother's storytelling in several sections of *Memories:* 18, 21, 63, 183.

5. King occasionally does offer male characters in similar displaced circumstances but rarely allows them reconciliation, instead offering them as examples of failed virtue,

King located her stories in the public and private experience of New Orleans women during and after the Civil War. Her desire to tell a lively yet realistic story and her belief in a need for a unifying regional reconciliation took her across race and class divisions: her characters lead us behind the locked gates of the Catholic girls' school, into the sitting rooms of Uptown ladies, out on the streets with quadroon vendors, and into the memories of former slaves and their former mistresses. The boredom and disappointment of the married woman who only a year before had been the belle of the ball, the alienation created between a mother and child by the child's mixed race in a segregated society—when taken together, these race- and gender-defined dramas promise to modern readers a complex subjective view of the female world in New Orleans before the turn of the century. Like Mary Wilkins Freeman and Sarah Orne Jewett, her northeastern counterparts, Grace King reacted to the gap created in her postwar society by turning the culture inside out: women's private virtues and values became public solutions.

Men—and a Protestant God—created King's world, but to women fell the responsibility of seeing that the patriarchally defined life was lived fully and properly. By acting according to their God-granted instincts as mothers and family members, and guided by established southern values of loyalty, women could reconcile their own and others' lives to the fallen world in which they found themselves. The women who people King's fictional world were displaced by war from their homes, their families, and their perceived class birthrights. But her fiction is neither a lament nor a search for the causes of this alienation; it is instead a prescription for reconciliation. Failure centers upon individual moral weakness, which perpetuates and worsens the original, inevitable circumstance in which the person finds herself. Typically in King's stories, the perspective of age and experience occasions a reevaluation of the real nature of a loss, revealing that faded friendships, not diminished social status or relinquished material objects, were the central tragedies. In the closing scene of "A Delicate Affair," for example, an ill-tempered and proud old woman is reunited with her childhood best friend, now dying and poor; the jealousy and disloyalty that severed their friendship fade in the face of death, leaving only memories and loving "murmuring." As in the clos-

---

e.g., the old general's pride in "Drama of Three," Beau's masking and deception in "Bayou L'Ombre," and Paul's lack of loyalty in "Making Progress." See David Kirby's discussion of "the fallibility of men" in his *Grace King* (Boston, 1980), 16.

ing scenes of Toni Morrison's *Sula,* one is left in King's story with a clear sense of the place of friendship in women's survival: "If Mr. Horace had not slipped away, he might have noticed the curious absence of monsieur's name, and of his own name, in the murmuring that followed. It would have given him some more ideas on the subject of woman."[6]

For other King heroines the separation is not physical but purely psychological. Survival sometimes sends a woman on a journey away from herself—and pride, jealousy, and self-denial replace the "natural" feminine instincts of love and nurturing. Madame Aurore in "On the Plantation," for example, has put aside romantic love in favor of religious fanaticism and service to her brother. Implying a criticism of this masked life, King contrasts Aurore's narrow existence with the growth and fulfillment being experienced by her peer and old friend, Eugénie, who after years as a widowed mistress of a girls' school is planning to remarry and to adopt a young orphaned student. Eugénie's opening up, however, enables Aurore to do so as well: "It was worth so much difference, so many differences,—the reconciliation; the crossing over from such a separation in their natures to meet again as they had started in life, heart open to heart, tongue garrulous to tongue, all revealed, understood, nothing concealed,—absolutely nothing. For there was a generous rivalry in loyal self-surrender and confession."[7]

As so often in King, these women find the answers in a return to the original bonds of female friendship and the values learned there, able finally to articulate their feelings and needs in ways that pride, vanity, and artifice had disallowed. This return is not, however, an escape into immaturity or irresponsibility; nor does it represent an overt critique, like Morrison's, of the cultural forces that create the initial divisions, teach the false pride, condone the masking, or benefit from the alienations of self and between women. Although the women do reunite, although they do regain their self-nourishing memories and revise their goals, their newfound wisdom is placed in service of King's conservatively defined feminine roles—their reward is found in their self-sacrifice to the fathers whose egos and fortunes were lost in the war, to the orphaned children, and to their own newly formed families. Not all stories, of course, have what King would term

6. Toni Morrison, *Sula* (New York, 1973), the "1965" chapter; Grace King, *Balcony Stories* (1893; rpr. Ridgewood, N.J., 1968), 219, hereinafter cited parenthetically by page number in the text.

7. Grace King, *Monsieur Motte* (1888; rpr. Freeport, N.Y., 1969), 177, hereinafter cited parenthetically by page number in the text.

happy endings: memory sometimes fails to be reconciled with reality; individuals fail to make the necessary self-sacrifice; or ignorance and innocence stand in the way of success. These are individual failures, assigned by King to a woman's inability to act her feminine role in service of others—regardless of circumstance.

This pattern of individual loss and displacement being offset by active self-knowledge and self-sacrifice is found in stories both with predominantly white and with predominantly black protagonists. The opportunities for reconciliation, however, the accuracy of the causes for what King judges as wrong action, suffer from King's complicity in the southern woman's role as apologist and from her stated goal of debating for northern readers George Washington Cable's view of the South. As Anne Goodwyn Jones points out: "Where the northern woman could (in Gerda Lerner's variation on Simone de Beauvoir) 'see man as "the other,"' the identification of the southern woman with the southern white man in mutual grief over the destruction and loss of the war and in mutual fears during Reconstruction might well retard that perception. The Yankees often became her 'other.'"[8] One might expand that "other" to include all black men and women. Although King's own perceptions and realist's sensibility create scenes and characters that threaten to disrupt her ideologically conservative surface, the fabric remains finally and always racist, and the resulting image of Louisiana's black women is frustratingly limited and distorted.

Only two of King's short stories, in her three full collections—*Monsieur Motte* (1888), *Tales of a Time and Place* (1893), and *Balcony Stories* (1893)—deal primarily with black characters; both appear in *Balcony Stories,* the collection containing her briefest sketches. "A Crippled Hope" is the story of a former slave, "little Mammy," whose life's work, during and after slavery, has been to nurse others, first the slaves at the auction block where she was kept by slave traders, and later the white women who hire her to nurse themselves and their families. The story is told in the spirit of the entire collection—as a story-within-a-story told to give "balm to some woe." Little Mammy's loyalty is the healing message. But other messages, far less positive and more provocative than King may have intended, are offered. This is a story built on stereotypes.[9] Little Mammy's goodness is defined

8. Jones, *Tomorrow Is Another Day,* 25.

9. For a wealth of information on the lives of black women before and after the war, see Giddings, *When and Where I Enter,* and Eugene D. Genovese, "Life in the Big House," in *A Heritage of Her Own,* ed. Nancy F. Cott and Elizabeth H. Pleck (New York, 1979), 290–97. For a specific discussion of the lives of Louisiana's black women, see

largely in contrast to the negatively portrayed blacks around her. Her handicap, a deformed leg, is the result not of a cruel slave master but of a thoughtless and unloving mother, and Mammy's anger at her situation focuses not on the slave trader who mistreats her but on the mother who dropped her: "All the animosity of which little Mammy was capable centered upon this unknown but never-to-be-forgotten mother of hers; out of this hatred had grown her love—that is, her destiny, a woman's love being her destiny. Little Mammy's love was for children" (*BS*, 106).

Gender seems to transcend race; little Mammy has "a woman's love" and "destiny," a destiny of self-sacrifice shared by all successful women in King's fiction. Out of adversity, and alone, she has created a meaningful role in life, puzzling out a crude artificial limb for herself (thus enabling herself literally to stand on two feet), and exercising the maternal instinct both to survive and to serve others. Her difficult fate is termed universally female: "God keeps so little of the truth from us women" (116). But the racial apologist has the last word, for little Mammy's strength ironically enslaves her: "Out of her own intelligence she had forged her chains" (116).

Whereas King's white characters are expected to sacrifice their lives for their families, little Mammy's role in King's hierarchy of care is to serve white women. Her own needs or desires for a family appear only ambiguously and tentatively, as absences and gaps—as what is not remembered. While she was still a slave, the narrator suggests, "she could hear of the outside world daily from the passing chattels—of the plantations, farms, families; the green fields, Sunday woods, running streams; the camp-meetings, corn-shuckings, cotton-pickings, sugar-grindings; the baptisms, marriages, funerals, prayer-meetings; the holidays and holy days. Remember that, whether for liberty or whether for love, passion effloresces in the human being—no matter when, where, or how—with every spring's return. Remember that she was, even in middle age, young and vigorous. But no; do not remember anything. There is no need to heighten the coloring" (117).

Amidst this highly romanticized and distorted picture of the slave's world, King recognizes universal female needs and desires, then stops herself as if she has gone too far with a character who must remain

Doris Dorcas Carter, "Refusing to Relinquish the Struggle: The Social Role of the Black Woman in Louisiana History," in *Louisiana's Black Heritage*, ed. Robert R. MacDonald, John R. Kemp, and Edward F. Haas (New Orleans, 1979), 163–89.

apart because of "coloring." In the next paragraph, King more fully inscribes little Mammy's wants. Rather than allow little Mammy her own black community/family, King projects little Mammy's affections into the circle of the white extended family: "It would be tedious to relate, although it was not tedious to hear her relate it, the desperations and hopes of her life then. Hardly a day passed that she did not see, looking for purchases . . . some master whom she could have loved, some mistress whom she could have adored. Always her favorite mistresses were there—tall, delicate matrons, who came themselves, with great fatigue, to select kindly-faced women for nurses; languid-looking ladies with smooth hair standing out in wide *bandeaux* from their heads, and lace shawls" (117–18).

King's ideal of an extended family with a white nuclear core supported by loyal black servants was typical among antebellum women. The reason, according to Paula Giddings, was that southern white women "found themselves enmeshed in an interracial web in which wives, children, and slaves were all expected to obey the patriarchal head of the household, as historian Anne Firor Scott observed. The compliance of White women became inextricably linked to that of the slaves. . . . As it was often asserted by slavery apologists, any change in the role of women *or* Blacks would contribute to the downfall not only of slavery, but of the family and society as well." [10] Perhaps this situation necessitated King's broad racial generalizations presenting black families as fragmented not only by the cruelty of the slave traders (whom King does, without doubt, condemn), but also by their own irresponsible natures. For example, as a group black women are "careless" mothers. The implication is that they are properly able to act out their maternal instincts only when caring for the children of others. Little Mammy, the exceptional black, finds her own final place in "freedom" as a servant to the white "families" she was denied before the war: she was "the only alleviation God left them after Sheridan passed through" (123). Again, little Mammy's reward for her self-sacrifice is not a family of her own or even service within her own black community, but a place at the bedside of the ailing white community— a place that historical records suggest was seldom actually accepted by black women after the war. [11]

10. Giddings, *When and Where I Enter*, 42–43.
11. Herbert G. Gutman, *The Black Family in Slavery and Freedom, 1750–1925* (New York, 1976), 443.

The roles of memory and time in little Mammy's life also emphasize King's failure to account adequately for essential differences in what she appears to see as the common virtues of women. Like the other orphans in King's stories, white and black, little Mammy lacks a familial collective memory, a possession King sees as an essential feminine tool for self-definition; lacking a mother and even a consistent extended family, little Mammy knows her past only through what she is told. Unlike the white orphans, she never finds a way to fill this gap in her life—unless, perhaps, by her own story/memory, which she tells over and over in the service of her white mistresses to ease their fears and uncertainties.

All time is for little Mammy relative and inductively defined: "She had no way of measuring time except by her thoughts and feelings. But in her own way and time . . ." (111). This experience of time is in fact quite typically feminine.[12] Although they may experience time differently than men—cyclically, in its dailiness—the *use* of women's time is most often defined for them by men. For little Mammy, a victim of both race and gender, time is defined first by white men, the slave traders, and later by white women, her "mistresses."

The extent of the limitations imposed on black characters in King's fiction is evidenced in the contrast between "A Crippled Hope" and the story that immediately follows, "One of Us." The latter, too, is a typical King story of feminine self-sacrifice. A middle-aged white opera singer seeks meaning in life through looking after the welfare of others, in this case orphaned children of the war. But the psychic center of this second story, which focuses solely on white characters, is the failure of romance—the relationship this woman might have had, the story hers might have been. "Evidently, when rôles do not exist in life for certain characters, God has to create them," the narrator muses, adding, "But the rôle I craved to create for my friend was far different—some good, honest bourgeois interior, where lips are coarse and cheeks are ruddy, and where life is composed of real scenes, set to the real music of life, the homely successes and failures, and loves and hates . . . where romance and poetry abound *au naturel*" (*BS,* 138).

Although the opera singer is not allowed the fulfillment of her do-

12. See Elaine Showalter, "Women's Time, Women's Space: Writing the History of Feminist Criticism," *Tulsa Studies in Women's Literature,* III (Fall, 1984), 29–43; Julia Kristeva, "Women's Time," trans. Alice Jardine and Harry Blake, in *Feminist Theory: A Critique of Ideology,* ed. Nannerl O. Keohane, Michelle Z. Rosaldo, and Barbara C. Gelpi (Chicago, 1982), 31–53.

mestic romance, and her role as caretaker becomes necessary and admirable because of the effects of the war, the possibilities of that role have at least existed for her. No such romance is even imagined for little Mammy—her romance is with the plantation life she is never allowed, and her substitute role is to nurse the white victims of a war that destroyed her "lover."

Despite her realist's intentions—but perhaps predictably, given her apologist's agenda—King's images of black family life appear severely limited when set against the realities historians and sociologists have uncovered in the last twenty years. One recurring element of this scholarship is the integrity, not the disintegration, of the black family both during and after slavery. The available statistics and records show that when able, slaves entered into long-term legal or common law marriages, and that "slave marriages were universally respected in the slave community unless a couple were separated either voluntarily, by 'divorce,' or involuntarily by sale." Paula Giddings observes that after the war, "among the first and perhaps most important decisions that freedmen and women made was the re-establishment of family ties."[13] This is not to say that these relationships, defined and limited as they were by slavery and its aftermath, were without problems. Between black men and women were not only the tensions of their freedom to define their sexual lives apart from white men (an issue only very indirectly touched upon by King), but also the tensions created by the caste hierarchy within the slave community. Giddings argues, for example, that in preferring the position of house servant to that of field worker, black women confirmed the social inferiority of such work when measured by the myths of idle southern white womanhood. Unlike the early historian E. Franklin Frazier, however, Giddings considers the power achieved by female house servants to have been essentially gender-limited: "Slave women maintained their authority over the domestic domain—as women have traditionally done—while Black men had no authority over the traditional male spheres of influence."[14] Whether black women did in fact have this domestic authority, power struggles and differences no doubt complicated black family life, posing some of the same problems historically created by gender differences.

13. Nancy Woloch, *Women and the American Experience* (New York, 1984), 178. Giddings, *When and Where I Enter,* 57. See also Gutman's discussion of the federal census figures in *Black Family,* 444.

14. Giddings, *When and Where I Enter,* 62, 58.

King's portrayal of the slaves' relationship to a master or mistress may be confirmed in its external features by the current scholarship on black history, but the spirit of that relationship is very differently interpreted today, undermining completely the myth of the happy, servile black. Eugene Genovese believes that "in the reciprocal dependency of slavery, especially in the Big House, the slaves needed masters and mistresses they could depend on; they did not need masters and mistresses to love them. But the whites needed their servants' love and trust." This and other critical interpretations construct a very different picture than King does of the power relationships operating behind the scenes of the extremely complicated black and white social structure. The woman behind the Mammy mask, for example, was a "worldly-wise, enormously resourceful" person. And Herbert G. Gutman's statistical study, which is used by many current researchers, suggests that the lessons learned by these women were not automatically put to use for white families after the war, but were more often employed in reestablishing and founding the women's own families.[15]

Despite its perhaps accurate presentation of King's white narrator's perceptions, then, the attempt to portray to northern readers the shiftless mother of "A Crippled Hope" as a realistic norm is undermined by the historical facts. In reality, little Mammy might well have founded her own family, not merely fulfilled the needs of the war's displaced and broken white families. Yet the fractured or nonexistent black family remains the standard in King's short fiction, affirming her complicity in the postwar patriarchal wisdom that the "superior white race, with its roots deep in the experiences of law and government, had the obligation of teaching the inferior Negro race, with its history of 'four thousand years of barbarism,' the precious knowledge of citizenship. The weaker race had corresponding obligations: implicit obedience, deference, loyalty, and hard work."[16]

Discomforting for King, however, was her belief that not male law and government, but rather female instinct, experience, and values were the roots of wisdom and the means of reconciliation. Because of this gender focus, King's fiction often finds women bonding despite racial differences; in place of racial paternalism she inserts a racial

15. Genovese, "Life in the Big House," 291; Gutman, *Black Family,* 443.

16. Guion Griffis Johnson, "Southern Paternalism Toward Negroes After Emancipation," in *The Black Man in America Since Reconstruction,* ed. David Reimers (New York, 1970), 38.

maternalism. "Bayou L'Ombre," for example, from *Tales of a Time and Place*, is a direct, elaborate, and extended comparison of white and black female experience. Set on a Louisiana plantation at the end of the war, and taken very probably from King's own wartime experiences, the story encompasses all variety of responses to the changes the war created in the plantation structure, although most generally it is yet another story of white women's loss and displacement. The three young white female characters have been taken to the plantation after the Federal occupation of New Orleans and are thus, for King, deprived of the youth that would have belonged to them as wealthy white Louisiana belles. Serious as this loss is, the critical losses of the plot are not material or even physical; they are instead losses of a patriarchally defined "family" and of a corresponding faith in southern patriarchal values. The girls' reconciliation comes through their own real and immediate experiences of war, which replace the dangerously romantic illusions they brought with them. Acting on their newfound knowledge and out of maternal instinct and ingrained family loyalty, they mature into the women King believes are essential to reconstruction.

One of the central redefinitions that must take place in order for these young women to adjust to their changed world concerns their extended family, including their relationships to their slaves, both house and field. From their white women's perspective, there are good slaves and bad, loved and feared. The good, Uncle John and Peggy, the loyal house servants, are the stereotypes of apologist literature: they are wise in exercising their loyalty and in their defense of their mistresses—even wily in becoming tricksters not for their own sakes but for their white "family's," against the "enemy." Uncle John has been left in charge, but rather than allow him the real, if veiled, power that history tells us many house servants exercised, King comically undermines his efforts, even symbolically leaving him impotent as his gun stands empty.[17] The important action is left to the women, black and white. For Peggy, the black woman, however, power comes through her gender and is placed again in service of her white family, against the interests of those of her own color. Peggy, like little Mammy, is a maternal figure who exercises traditional female wit to aid the girls in their plot to free what they perceive to be Confederate soldiers. For her, war is like a fight between husbands and wives, a

17. See Genovese, "Life in the Big House," 292.

temporary engagement with little radical consequence: "She worked, inspired by all the wife-lore of past ages, the infiltrated wisdom that descends to women in the course of a world of empirical connubiality, that traditionary compendium to their lives by which they still hope to make companionship with men harmonious and the earth a pleasant abiding-place."[18] Specific racial issues are erased in favor of "universal" gender conflicts. As in "A Crippled Hope," the common bonds of female values and instincts are valued only as they serve the white family and cause.

King's exploration of the antebellum relationship between mistress and slave is unique to "Bayou L'Ombre," and it yields some of her most interesting and complicated scenes. Point of view, for example, shifts revealingly in the section of the story in which she dramatizes the female field-slaves' responses to freedom—no white characters are present. The scene opens after Lolotte, the youngest white child, has responded to the news that Federal soldiers are approaching the plantation; she fears that they will "kill us all" (*TTP*, 20). The shift to the slave quarters dramatizes King's belief that the locus of change, the real threat to her young white characters, is with the black women whose actions will undermine completely and most intimately the whites' perceptions of family and place. The emotionally vivid and tense scene opens with a wealth of romantic racial stereotypes as happy black women wash clothes in an idyllic setting, their work not having vanished as had their white counterparts':

> Under the wide-spreading, moss-hung branches, upon the broad flat slope, a grand general washing of the clothes of the small community was in busy progress by the women, a proper feminine consecration of this purely feminine day. The daily irksome routine was broken, the men were all away, the sun was bright and warm, the air soft and sweet. . . . a return, indeed, for one brief moment to the wild, sweet ways of nature, to the festal days of ancestral golden age (a short retrogression for them), when the body still had claims, and the mind concessions, and the heart owed no allegiance, and when god and satyr eyes still might be caught peeping and glistening from leafy covert on feminine midsummer gambols. (21)

The scene is broken by the news of the approaching soldiers, and the white narrator's voice enters to question the black women's reactions; her tone continues in its paternalistic condescension but simultane-

18. Grace King, "Bayou L'Ombre," in *Tales of a Time and Place* (New York, 1893), 42, hereinafter cited parenthetically by page number in the text.

ously suggests uncertainty and ambiguity. Have their "rude minds" comprehended the changes already taking place on the plantation? Has a mother's instinct already told them of their infants' "superiority over others born and nourished before them"? But, perhaps sensing disloyal sympathy in these questions, the apologist narrator quickly slights her racial Others, condemning their part, or lack of one, in the war—"the water-shed of their destiny" being formed "without their knowledge as without their assistance" (24).[19] Next she shifts again to acknowledge uncomfortably the limitations of a maternalistic point of view, of subsuming race under gender: "Was this careless, happy, indolent existence genuine, or only a fool's motley to disguise a tragedy of suffering? What to them was the difference between themselves and their mistresses? their condition? or their skin, that opaque black skin which hid so well the secrets of life, which could feel but not own the blush of shame, the pallor of weakness" (25).

The scene that follows answers these questions, implying both knowledge and desire on the part of these black women. The white narrator is caught up in the drama of the women slowly and passionately articulating their desired freedom. King's identification with them, however, is limited, as is apparent in the contrast between this scene and the one it foreshadows in tone and content, a scene in which the white mistresses discover King's matriarchal alternative to patriarchal values. King sees common problems, not solutions, in these paralleled quests for freedom. From her point of view, whereas the white mistresses are culturally and intellectually prepared for their newfound freedom, the black women are not. Although the initial scene is taut with exuberance, although the goal and needs may be just, these women are not yet equipped to handle the freedom they seek. Ignorance leads to failure. The black women violate the patriarchally defined bond of family as well as King's code of self-sacrifice, creating divisiveness and chaos. Almost immediately they begin to fight with one another over what should be done; one woman drops her child (again, the bad mother) to rush to freedom, and many run without thought of husbands or families. Only one woman remains, the African "primitive" Black Maria, who in the violent action that

19. King's judgment is undermined by historical facts. Black enlistment, both North and South, was significant. See Charles Vincent, "Black Louisianians During the Civil War and Reconstruction: Aspects of Their Struggles and Achievements," in *Louisiana's Black Heritage*, ed. Macdonald *et al.*, 85–87.

closes the scene keeps her daughter-in-law from running with the others.

This scene strongly contrasts with the largely cerebral one that follows, in which the white mistresses, betrayed by their white male cousin, act in orderly and sensible ways to discover for themselves that change is necessary and desirable. Significantly, the narrator moves from external description to interior monologue, her identification with the characters perhaps now easier and clearer: "Thank God that Nature was impartial, and could not be drilled into partisanship! If humanity were like Nature! If—if there had been no war! She paused, shocked at her first doubt; of the great Circumstance of her life it was like saying, 'If there had been no God!'" (50).

Before the young white women can reach a cultural reconciliation, however, they must face a far more immediate and intimate disruption of their world view: "This was not a superficial conflict to sweep the earth with cannons and mow it with sabres; this was an earthquake which had rent it asunder, exposing the quivering organs of hidden life. . . . The anger of outraged affection, betrayed confidence, abandoned trust, traitorous denial, raged within them" (37). The girls vacillate between anger, hurt, and fear, envisioning their "pastoral existence together" (38) as a thing never to be regained, perhaps even a farce from the start.

That the girls' memories and experiences are in question puts at risk what is for King a woman's grounding center. These young white women have suffered from a false and romantic image of war because their experiences of it have been remote and vicarious. Their beliefs about the nature of their relationship to the black women, however, grow out of their immediate experience. King here has an opportunity to examine more closely the intimate harm done by institutionalized slavery. It is left untaken. Instead, perhaps to reinforce her own harsh final judgment of the other black characters or to offer the white characters justification for their past behavior toward their slaves, King mediates the crisis by placing the loyal Black Maria before the young mistresses' disillusioned gaze. Loyalty being a just ideal, King now vacillates between a racist's inability to join independently achieved virtue to blackness and a woman's acknowledgment of gender as a common bond: "Black Maria! They might have known it! They looked at her. No! She was not! She was not negro, like the others. Who was she? What was she? Where did she come from, with her white features and white nature under her ebon skin? What was the mystery that enveloped her? . . . Why was she, alone of all the negroes, still an alien, a foreigner, an exile among them?" (39–40). Value in color is resisted. Only because Maria is unlike the others, perhaps even supernatural, can the young whites acknowledge strength in this woman who has walked "as if she were free through slavery" and now assumed "slavery . . . when others hailed freedom, to be loyal in the midst of treason" (40).

Maria, more "African" and thus closer to her primitive intuitions, acts from an instinct of loyalty that transcends circumstance. Yet in the end the strongest impressions concerning Maria are not of her strength or her bond with the white characters, but of her behavior as a judgment on the failure of the other black women. For King, differences between relative freedoms should not and do not excuse disloyalty, and thus for the errant slaves there is narrative punishment and ironic mocking. Although the war's end coincides with the end of the story, and these women will in fact be freed, their expected immediate freedom turns out to have been only part of an ill-conceived plot on the girls' cousin Beau's part.

King's narratively achieved just desserts could not and were not meant to gloss over the real and unavoidable losses of power and past security that the South faced after the war. King knew those losses only too well—they had encouraged her to turn to fiction in the first place—and for her, the foundation of a healing reconstruction rested in the bravery and loyalty, the womanly love and nurturing exhibited by the young women in "Bayou L'Ombre." Yet she remained equally certain that those characters' white skins gave them insights and responsibilities unavailable to black women. The most that she could allow blacks was their ignorance: "uneducated, barbarous, excited; they could not help it; they could not be expected to resist all at once the momentum of centuries of ancestral ferocity" (48). On the other hand, she denied even this backhanded kind of forgiveness to the white men, northern or southern, who created and perpetuated divisions.

In a number of her stories, Grace King turned to postwar interracial relationships. New Orleans after the Civil War was the world she knew best, a world different from most others in its racial history and circumstance.[20] For example, members of the distinct and long-standing

20. See John W. Blassingame, *Black New Orleans, 1860–1880* (Chicago, 1973).

community of free people of color in New Orleans had known relative freedom, been educated, and held professional and other responsible positions in the larger community. This base served the former slaves well, for the majority of the previously free blacks understood the common bond of race and the consequences of divisiveness and therefore worked toward the mutual good in the reforms they sought. But in experience and culture, and even in religion, the two black groups were different. Problems arose, especially as people long used to relative freedom began to lose some of their previous rights and to see their social lot cast in with people with whom they had less in common than with the white community that was now rejecting them. One consequence was that exact degree of color took on increased meaning and value.[21]

Grace King examines the crisis of color and identity in two parallel stories, "The Little Convent Girl" (another of the *Balcony Stories*) and "Madrilène" (in *Tales of a Time and Place*). Both are complicated and unusually symbolic stories tracing the long-term consequences of interracial relationships—displaced children. In the first, a young girl has been sent by her white father to be raised in a northern convent. As the story begins she is in mourning for the death of her father and is dressed in black, a symbolic foreshadowing of the story's concluding racial twist. Placed on board a riverboat to travel to New Orleans to meet the mother she's never known—"on account of some disagreement between the parents" (148)—the sheltered and excessively passive young girl is exposed for the first time in her life to the human energy and passion that the convent sisters had worked hard to bridle in their charges. Her brief shipboard forays into her small reserves of inquisitiveness and action little prepare the young woman for the surprise awaiting her on the docks in New Orleans: a mother who is black. Unable to adjust to this truth, displaced from her past and her accustomed self-image, she dies at the close of the story. The simple message, of course, might be the "tragedy" of miscegenation, but the story is complicated by King's symbolic, detached handling, replacing her more usual narrative manipulations and pronouncements.[22] The

21. For an extended discussion of the complicated political and social relationships within the postwar black community, see David C. Rankin, "The Politics of Caste: Free Colored Leadership in New Orleans During the Civil War," in *Louisiana's Black Heritage*, ed. Macdonald, *et al.*, 107–46.

22. For a useful psychological reading of the story, see Jones, *Tomorrow Is Another Day*, 121–26. See also Clara Juncker, "The Mother's Balcony: Grace King's Discourse of Femininity," *New Orleans Review*, XV (1988), 39–46.

girl's apparently accidental death can easily be read as a suicide. Unable to find worldly reconciliation with a mother whose cultural realities are far removed from her own, denied that mother or any real mothering (part of King's critique of Catholic practice), the girl surrenders herself to the river, beneath which, the riverboat's pilot has told her, is "that great mother-stream" (155). Although King here acknowledges that racial divisions create social and personal crises, she leaves causes uncritiqued and solutions symbolic. Real social reconciliation seems beyond her imagining.

The second of King's stories on the general theme of race and identity begins from a less commonly considered perspective. Madrilène, a white girl who intentionally has been led to misbelieve that she is a person of color, lives her life hoping for death, her only perceived means of achieving the white skin and status she so badly desires:

> When she was a little child, half naked, all dirty from the streets, she had begged to be left in the cemetery, "with the dead, with the good dead, with the white dead;" and as she said then, she as childishly said now: "Maybe I might die, and you might slip me into one of these tombs here—who would know? And then on resurrection-day . . . on resurrection-day I would rise with the others. We resurrect white, do we not, Monsieur Sacerdote? I would be found out otherwise. All white—white limbs, white faces, white wings, white clothes. Not yellow—not black corpses rising with their white bands." She closed her eyes and shuddered. "Oh, the fearful sight! And if I arose with the white, would they turn me out, do you think?" (*TTP*, 138)

This scene, like many in Morrison's novel *The Bluest Eye,* maps the distorted geography of self-hatred created by internalized racism.[23]

The tragedy's focus moves from the distortion of an individual soul to the social consequences of intraracial bitterness and conflict, a familiar King theme that displaces concern for the roots of racial structures in favor of a critique of chaotic and uncivilized black community life. First, in another instance of cross-racial loyalty and intraracial hostility, a black mother kills Madrilène because the woman's son has frightened some white children and Madrilène has punished him: "She slapped him vigorously. 'Dare! dare!' she said, 'dare frighten white children again!'" (128). Next we discover that Madrilène's initial betrayer—the one who convinced her she was not white—was the quadroon mistress who had adopted Madrilène as a child, a woman who treats her servants "as, let us hope, few mistresses treated their slaves" (154). In fact, in King's eyes the entire neighborhood is morally

23. Toni Morrison, *The Bluest Eye* (New York, 1970).

corrupt and thus unable to offer Madrilène a model for family: "Very few of what are called regular parents live about a cemetery. Ties and relationships assume a voluntary and transient character in that careless neighborhood" (136).

Out of desperation, in the absence of a nourishing family, Madrilène grovels doglike for whatever attention and information she can gather from an aging and disheveled cemetery attendant. White-skinned and male, he is her God, regardless of his being an outcast among his own race. Without family, without faith, and without community, Madrilène lacks what are to King the essentially feminine means of survival. As in "The Little Convent Girl," King seems unable to conjecture a positive social or individual solution for a woman who by circumstance or birth cannot fit squarely within one racial community or another. Instinctive loyalty to her white race brings Madrilène only alienation, disdain, and finally death. The little education she has received from Monsieur Sacerdote, her sometimes benevolent god, brings her only confusion—her mind is chaotic and her language dysfunctional: "It was only thought, and in words not her own. Her own words, from the common store of language about her, could not have expressed her thoughts; or perhaps the thoughts as well as the words were foreign to her; perhaps the thoughts were transplanted with the words from the books read aloud to Monsieur Sacerdote in surreptitious hours, in that stolen acquirement which neither Madame Laïs nor her family suspected. Reading! They would as soon have provided her with a looking-glass" (144).

Madrilène's confusion makes her vulnerable to the weaknesses of pride and self-concern, which King believes are fatal. King adds to these personal failures the circumstantial problems of masking, a false social situation, and a denial of natural relationships. Madrilène has no one to whom or for whom to be loyal. The tools of reconciliation, memory and language, are undermined. There is little hope for anything but a tragic end. Her only and final escape is into nothingness, to "sightlessness, dumbness, deafness, to nullity" (178)—a bitterly ironic achievement of the lack of color she so desperately sought.

In the final twist, Zizi Mouton, the Voodoo woman who forces Madame Laïs to reveal Madrilène's birthright, makes clear that she has had the power to do so all along and has finally forced the truth not for Madrilène's sake but in revenge against Madame Laïs. Here is final proof of the failure of values within the black community, and in the end, despite her whiteness, Madrilène must share in the black community's fate, a judgment King foreshadowed in the opening lines of the story in her description of the cemetery frequented by Madrilène: "Those [houses] which by necessity did face it had the aspect of houses accustomed to look at worse things in life than death—houses that had not enjoyed the sad privilege of falling from a higher estate or disappointing hopeful prospects, but which had been preordained from the beginning to degradation and ostracism" (119).

In this story and in "The Little Convent Girl," King locates what seems to have been for her one of the most terrifying and unanswerable consequences of postwar black-white relationships, an innocent child caught in the web of muddied and chaotic social structures. That King blamed miscegenation, not racism, as the prime cause of the difficulty is evident when one contrasts the resolutions of these two stories with that of her first story, "Monsieur Motte."

The works collected in *Balcony Stories* and *Tales of a Time and Place* were written at a time when King's stories seemed to flow by necessity from her pen, as if she had "to get relief from them." It was in writing "Monsieur Motte," however, that she felt and articulated her most didactic purpose: to defend her region and to clarify the "truth" of its racial circumstances and relationships. Although the story's resolution does justify southern faith in the integrity and primacy of family, albeit a newly constituted and temporary one, the racial premise and conclusion are neither optimistic nor satisfying.[24]

Three women inhabit this story. The first, Marie, a young orphan of the war, has grown up and been educated in the school of the second, Madame Lareveillère, a widow; the third is Marcélite, the quadroon servant of Marie's dead parents and now hairdresser to the school. Marcélite is also—unknown to Madame or Marie—the young girl's benefactor. The early scenes in the story create what is apparently an accurate picture of the energy and intimacy between many young white girls and their black servants. For King this relationship, mirroring as it does the maternal bond, is appealing and just, so long as it is kept within acceptable social limits of mistress and servant. With the revelation of a very different relationship between Marie and Marcélite, one in which Marcélite has assumed not only the motherly role of emotional parent, but also the normally white and male role of financial parent, peace becomes chaos. But King's familiar tools of

---

24. King, *Memories*, 99. Again, for a thoughtful and extensive analysis of this story, see Jones, *Tomorrow Is Another Day*, 99–117.

reconciliation are then employed. Marie, who in memory and fact has been displaced from her family, is loyal to Marcélite and is rewarded with a new family—not with Marcélite, but with Madame and her counselor and soon-to-be husband, Monsieur Goupilleau.

Madame, too, has suffered loss, but hers carries with it adult responsibilities—her vanity and pride have kept her from reestablishing a family. In choosing now to care for Marie and to act on her feelings for Goupilleau, she finds fulfillment and a future. This newly constituted nuclear family, however, so mirrors the antebellum family in structure that it offers Marcélite only token reward for her loyalty and her resourcefulness. Although Goupilleau seems to elevate Marcélite to the status of heroine when he reflects, "'They say, Eugénie, that the days of heroism are past, and they laugh at our romance!'" (MM, 103), Marcélite loses her place as provider, her function as mother, and even her prewar role as confidante. In fact, even though Marie would follow Marcélite out of a sense of responsibility, there is no opportunity in New Orleans society for a such a relationship. King articulates this harsh reality through Marcélite's grim self-deprecation: "'Go with me! Go to my home! A white young lady like you go live with a nigger like me!'" (100). Such self-effacement—after already having suffered through hours of self-destructive turmoil over her failure to have planned for the day Marie would graduate and when the truth of their relationship must be revealed! All of Marcélite's earlier pride and self-respect disappears, implying an understanding on King's part of the loss of personal integrity caused by racial structures. Again, though, despite her accurate description of the effects, King remains limited in her search for causes. The narrative implies that the war and the chaotic family structures it created are the problems. The solution is to reconstruct as closely as possible antebellum circumstances, within which individuals can again find meaning and identity.

Marcélite's descent structures the story. Early on, King sketches a realistic scene of working-class racial tension between Marcélite and Jeanne, the immigrant housekeeper at the school:

> The white woman did not lack judgment. She was maintaining her own in a quarrel begun years ago; a quarrel involving complex questions of the privileges of order and the distinctions of race; a quarrel in which hostilities were continued, year by year, with no interruptions of courtesy or mitigation by truce. This occasion was one of the perquisites of Jeanne's position of *femme de ménage,*—slight compensation enough when compared to the indignities put upon her as a white woman, and the humiliations as a

sensitive one by *"cette négresse Marcélite."* But the duration of triumph must be carefully measured. Marcélite's ultimatum, if carried out [by calling Madame to settle the dispute], would quickly reverse their relative positions by a bonus to Marcélite in the shape of a reprimand to Jeanne. (17–18)

Thus this small battle is won by Marcélite, who calls upon her native wit to manipulate Jeanne to a commonsense conclusion. But even though wit can prevail at this level of struggle, it is Marcélite's ignorance and her failure to plan that causally lead in the end to the crisis with Marie. Marcélite's only resources are instinct and "untamed African blood," and even these have been muddied by "a civilization which had tampered with her brain, had enervated her will, and had duped her with false assurances of her own capability" (51). To King, Marcélite is out of her element, unnaturally placed in a position of responsibility, as were many blacks after the war, and the results are harmful to all involved. Marcélite cannot offer Marie a permanent model for reconciliation.

The mixed victory and tragedy of the original resolution of "Monsieur Motte" was later made even more complex by the transitional ending King added when she used the story as the opening chapter of a novel of the same name. In this extension, white women's losses are the focus, especially Marie's loss of identity: "But for the future,— looking for it there was no future" (104). Although the family Bible that Marcélite has given her provides Marie with a name and a social place, it fails to offer a physical place, her land, to confirm her position. She remains at the school with Madame, but that is no longer appropriate; she has graduated and should move on. Perhaps most fatally, like the young white mistresses in "Bayou L'Ombre," she has lost faith in her memory and perceptions of reality.

In this new ending Marcélite, too, is left unreconciled, out of place because of both her race and gender: "As Marcélite, there was nothing to accomplish except the part of a faithful servant. As Monsieur Motte, what could she not do?" (106). From this point in the novel, however, Marcélite becomes a shadowy, unhappy figure, and the plots focus primarily on Marie's and Madame's lives. Marcélite does finally return, without narrative development or explanation, in this closing scene to the novel: "It was not Madame Goupilleau, but Marcélite, who walked behind the bride that night to the altar, for so Marie Modeste had commanded. It was not to Madame Goupilleau, but to Marcélite, that the bride turned for her first blessing after the ceremony" (326).

The new nuclear family contains "Marie Modeste, her husband, her children, and Marcélite" (327). Although King again allows Marcélite the feelings of a mother, they are granted within this disturbingly reconstructed family, strongly reminiscent of the black-mother/white-child bond of the antebellum South, a conclusion reinforced by the fact that Marie has regained her family's estate and their new home will be the one from which Marcélite first carried the orphaned Marie. For King, Marcélite can regain her lost identity within this new context, giving up her independent position as hairdresser. The story ends like a fairy tale: "They all live well, happily, prosperously together; for in giving hearts, God assigned destinies" (327).

King saw storytelling as a feminine activity, and her stories as feminine forms, organic and nondidactic. These beliefs necessitated a connection between Grace King the writer and Grace King the woman. The conflicts of that position are revealed in King's remembrances of her mother, wherein she delights in her mother's spontaneity and ingenuity as a storyteller but reminds us that when it came to judgments, her mother always relied on her father "and seemed to have a horror of forming her own." And of this paternal judgment she recalls a "cold, stern repression of feeling as a measure of good breeding."[25] She faced, then, conflicting goals and strictures—a desire for realism yet a deeply planted distrust of expressing her own feelings or trusting her own evaluations. War and the loss of close family members had taught her much about social circumstance, class, and race that her fiction could reveal only in indirect, perhaps even unintended, ways. Among these areas so difficult for her to approach directly was the complicated intersection of race and gender. The southern apologist, eager to speak to and with a northern audience, needed to soften the evils of slavery by offering in its place the possibilities for change inherent in the positive values of that much-flawed system. The woman easily found such values in her own experience and was able to fictionalize them comfortably out of her own and a collective female memory. The white woman sought a common bond with her black sister, sometimes at the expense of her own identification with southern white men—but never with an unbiased eye to the very real material and social differences between white and black female experience, and always to the detriment of the black woman. Virginia Woolf's familiar call for the "incandescent mind" might seem to be appropriate here.[26]

25. King, *Memories*, 67, 30, 31.
26. Virginia Woolf, *A Room of One's Own* (New York, 1929), 58.

Perhaps if King had been less racially self-conscious, less inclined to rewrite rather than to reflect, we would have a more consistent vision of the postwar South from a white woman's perspective. But perhaps too we ought to be happy at least for the occasional emotional obstacles and impediments that create welcome disruptions in the surface of King's homogeneous ideal. If even more of her questions and doubts had surfaced, she might have discovered not only her own part in the repressive racial structure of postwar New Orleans, but also the intersection between racism and sexism in patriarchal southern ideology where her own spiritual deprivation met the material and spiritual deprivation of her black sisters.

Kate Chopin.
Stone and Kimball Papers,
the Newberry Library,
Chicago

**Kate Chopin's New
Orleans residence
at 1413 Louisiana.**
Photo by K. W. "Jake"
Jacobs

Semiotic Subversion in "Désirée's Baby"

AT first "Désirée's Baby," published in 1893 by Kate Chopin, seems no more than a poignant little story with a clever twist at the end.[1] Yet that does not fully explain why the tale is widely anthologized, why it haunts readers with the feeling that the more it is observed, the more facets it will show. In "Désirée's Baby" Chopin, best known as the author of *The Awakening*, has created a small gem, whose complexity has not yet been fully appreciated. As I explore that complexity, my broader goal is a theoretical one: I plan to show not only that a semiotic and a political approach can be combined, but also that they *must* be combined in order to do justice to this story and to others like it, stories that lie at the nexus of concerns of sex, race, and class.

A semiotic approach to the work reveals that despite its brevity, it offers a rich account of the disruption of meaning, and that the character largely responsible for the disruption is Désirée Aubigny, who might on a first reading seem unprepossessing. She is a catalyst, however, for the subversion of meaning. When the semiotic approach is supplemented by a political one, it can be seen that Désirée casts doubt on the meaning of race, sex, and class in antebellum Louisiana.[2] In this drama of misinterpretations, she undermines smugness about the ability to read signs, such as skin color, as clear evidence about how to categorize people.

The disruption culminates when Désirée, whom everyone considers white, has a baby boy who looks partly black. When she is rejected by her husband, Armand, she takes the infant, disappears into the bayou, and does not return. Armand later finds out that he himself is black, on his mother's side. Désirée, although unintentionally, has dev-

1. Kate Chopin, "Désirée's Baby," in Per Seyersted, ed., *The Complete Works of Kate Chopin* (2 vols.; Baton Rouge, 1969), I, 240–45, hereinafter cited parenthetically by page number in the text. I would like to thank Robert Arner, William Bush, Gillian C. Gill, Margaret Homans, and Gila Safran-Naveh for their comments on this paper.

2. I am using *semiotic* to refer to the study of signs in the broad sense, to the study of systems by which we create signification, decipher meaning, and gain knowledge. I am also using *political* broadly to refer to societal power relations, not just electoral politics.

astated him by means of these two surprises, one concerning her supposed race and one concerning his own.

Combining semiotic and political approaches, my analysis consists
of four steps: I trace how the surprises to Armand disrupt signification; question whether they are actually as subversive as they first appear; shift the focus more definitively to Désirée to show how the story
associates her with certain enigmatic, subversive absences; and finally,
discuss how the story criticizes, yet sympathetically accounts for, the
limitations of Désirée's subversiveness.

The story takes place in a Creole community ruled by institutions
based on apparently clear dualities: master over slave, white over
black, and man over woman. Complacently deciphering the unruffled
surface of this symbolic system, the characters feel confident that they
know who belongs in which category and what signifies membership
in each category. Moreover, as Emily Toth has observed, in the story
the three dualities parallel one another, as do critiques of their hierarchical structures.[3]

Within this system of race, sex, and class, the most complacent representative is Armand Aubigny, Désirée's husband. Confident that he
is a white, a male, and a master, he feels in control of the system. In
order to understand how his wife challenges signification, we must
take a closer look at the surprises that Armand encounters.

The tale begins with a flashback to Désirée's childhood and courtship. She was a foundling adopted by childless Madame and Monsieur
Valmondé. Like a queen and king in a fairy tale, they are delighted by
her mysterious arrival and name her Désirée, the "wished-for one,"
the "desired one." She, like a fairy-tale princess, "grew to be beautiful
and gentle, affectionate and sincere,—the idol of Valmondé" (240).
When she grew up, she was noticed by Armand, the dashing owner of
a nearby plantation. He fell in love immediately and married her. She
"loved him desperately. When he frowned she trembled, but loved
him. When he smiled, she asked no greater blessing of God" (242).
They were not to live happily ever after.

Soon after the story proper opens, Armand meets with the first

3. Emily Toth, "Kate Chopin and Literary Convention: 'Désirée's Baby,'" *Southern
Studies*, XX (1981), 203. See also Robert D. Arner, "Kate Chopin," *Louisiana Studies*,
XXV (1975), 47. By comparing race, sex, and class, I do not mean to imply that the
three give rise to identical problems.

surprise. He, other people, and finally Désirée see something unusual in her infant son's appearance. She asks her husband what it means, and he replies, "'It means . . . that the child is not white; it means that you are not white'" (243). Désirée writes Madame Valmondé a letter pleading that her adoptive mother deny Armand's accusation. The older woman cannot do so but writes: "'Come home to Valmondé; back to your mother who loves you. Come with your child'" (243). When Armand tells his wife he wants her to go, she takes the child and disappears forever into the reeds and willows along the bayou.

Thus, Armand's first surprise comes when he interprets his baby's appearance to mean that the child and its mother are not white. What seemed white now seems black. Désirée, with the child she has brought Armand, has apparently uncovered a weakness in her husband's ability to decipher the symbols around him.

Ironically, Désirée's power comes from the fact that she seems malleable and adaptable. She has no known origin. Into an established, ostensibly secure system she comes as a wild card—apparently a child without a past. As a wild card, the girl appears blank to those around her, or at most appears to possess nonthreatening traits such as submissiveness. Désirée seems to invite projection: Madame Valmondé wants a child, Armand wants a wife, and both deceive themselves into believing they can safely project their desires onto Désirée, the undifferentiated blank screen. Actually, however, her blankness should be read as a warning about the fragility of representation.

One aspect of Désirée's blankness is her pre-oedipal namelessness.[4] As a foundling, she has lost her original last name and has received one that is hers only by adoption. Even foundlings usually receive a first name of their own, but in a sense Désirée also lacks that, for her first name merely reflects others' "desires." In addition, namelessness has a particularly female cast in this society, since women, including Désirée, lose their last name at marriage. Namelessness connotes not

4. In this way, as in many others, Désirée closely resembles what the psychoanalyst and literary theorist Julia Kristeva calls "the semiotic" (*le sémiotique*). She uses the term in an idiosyncratic way to refer to the instinctual, pre-oedipal stage when an infant has close ties to the mother and signifies through gesture, rhythm, intonation, and mobile, prereferential heterogeneity. Even after the oedipal phase represses *le sémiotique*, the latter strives to return. See Julia Kristeva, "From One Identity to an Other," in *Desire in Language: A Semiotic Approach to Literature and Art*, ed. Leon S. Roudiez, trans. Thomas Gora, Alice Jardine, and Leon S. Roudiez (New York, 1980), 124–27; and the first section of her *La Révolution du langage poétique* (Paris, 1974), 17–100.

only femaleness but also blackness in antebellum Louisiana, where white masters can deprive black slaves of their names. Although Désirée's namelessness literally results only from her status as a foundling and a married woman, her lack of a name could serve figuratively as a warning to Armand that she might be black.

But he sees only what he desires. Before the wedding he "was reminded that she was nameless. What did it matter about a name when he could give her one of the oldest and proudest in Louisiana?" (240). On this virgin page Armand believes he can write his name, the name he inherited from his father or, more broadly, the patriarchal Name of the Father. In addition, as a father, Armand wants to pass on that name to his son. Before he turns against his wife and baby, she exclaims: "'Oh, Armand is the proudest father in the parish, I believe, *chiefly because it is a boy, to bear his name;* though he says not,—that he would have loved a girl as well. But I know it isn't true. I know he says that to please me'" (242; emphasis added).

The approaching downfall of Armand's wife, and hence of his plans for his name, is foreshadowed by the relationship between Désirée's blankness and another name, that of the slave La Blanche. The mulatta's name refers to the whiteness of her skin, but *blanche* can also mean "pure" or "blank," recalling Désirée's blankness. La Blanche is Désirée's double in several ways. Neither has a "proper" name, only a descriptive one. During the scene in which Armand rejects his wife, he explicitly points out the physical resemblance between the women:

> "Look at my hand; whiter than yours, Armand," [Désirée] laughed hysterically.
> "As white as La Blanche's," he returned cruelly. (243)

The story also links the two women through their children, for the mistress first notices her son's race when she compares him to one of LaBlanche's quadroon sons. And perhaps Armand is the father of La Blanche's son, as Chopin's southern readers would have recognized.[5] The two women—and even their sons—may have parallel ties to Armand because of the possible sexual connection between slave and master. So much doubling hints that the slave's racial mix has foreshadowed that of the mistress.

Because La Blanche's name refers to her in the visual but not the

---

5. Cynthia Griffin Wolff, "Kate Chopin and the Fiction of Limits: 'Désirée's Baby,'" *Southern Literary Journal*, X (1978), 128.

racial sense, her appearance illustrates the contradiction of a racial system that is based on color but does not consider visual evidence conclusive. In this discourse a person who looks white but has a "drop" of black "blood" is labeled black. As Joel Williamson has pointed out, the "one-drop rule" would seem definitive but in fact leads to the problem of "invisible blackness." [6]

Miscegenation, which lies at the heart of the contradiction, marks the point at which sexual politics most clearly intersects with racial politics. Theoretically, either parent in an interracial union could belong to either race. Nonetheless, "by far the greatest incidence of miscegenation took place between white men and black female slaves." [7] Even when the white man did not technically rape the black woman, their relationship tended to result from, or at least to be characterized by, an imbalance of power in terms of race, sex, and sometimes class. Ironically, descendants of such a union, if their color was ambiguous, embodied a challenge to the very power differential that gave birth to them.

"Désirée's Baby" calls attention to the paradoxes that result from miscegenation and the one-drop rule. La Blanche and Désirée look white but are considered black, whereas "dark, handsome" Armand (242)—whose hand looks darker than theirs—is considered white. Since the established system of meaning allots power to Armand as a white, a male, and a master, it would not be in his interest to acknowledge the absurdity of "invisible blackness," as seen in La Blanche—a white-looking woman who is "really" black and a slave. Désirée's entry into the symbolic system forces him to confront the contradiction he ignored in La Blanche. Désirée is also a white-looking woman, but one whom his name has placed in his *own* class. A form of poetic justice ensures that the same one-drop rule that enables him to keep

6. Joel Williamson, *New People: Miscegenation and Mulattoes in the United States* (New York, 1980), 98. Although Louisiana made legal distinctions on the basis of relative racial composition (quadroon, octoroon, and so forth), the plot of "Désirée's Baby" hinges on the strict application of the one-drop rule. To avoid confusion, I generally follow the terminology of the society portrayed in the story, using the one-drop rule in deciding how to refer to a character's race and referring to "mulattoes" only when the context demands it.

7. James Kinney, *Amalgamation: Race, Sex, and Rhetoric in the Nineteenth-Century American Novel* (Westport, Conn., 1985), 19. See also Winthrop D. Jordan, *White over Black: American Attitudes Toward the Negro, 1550–1812* (Chapel Hill, 1968), 138, and Judith R. Berzon, *Neither White nor Black: The Mulatto Character in American Fiction* (New York, 1978), 9.

La Blanche as a slave causes him to lose Désirée as a wife. After the first surprise, Armand sees Désirée's blankness as blackness, not *blanche*-ness.

It is crucial to note that Désirée is disruptive not because she *produces* flaws in the signifying system, but because she *reveals* flaws that were already there. In a sense, she acts as a mirror, revealing absurdities that were always already there in the institutions, but repressed. Her blankness has reflective power. In another sense, Désirée's potential as a mirror is one of her attractions for Armand, for he wants her to bear a child that will replicate him. But he desires only a flattering reflection: hence his happiness at having a boy and his fury at the baby's blackness. Armand blames and smashes the mirror that has produced a black reflection. An outsider observing Armand's generally harsh treatment of slaves might, however, see his baby's darkness as another instance of poetic justice, the return of the oppressed.

Similarly, if the baby's darkness comes from his mother, whom Armand dominates, then the child's appearance represents the return of another oppressed group, women. To reproduce the father exactly, the child would have to inherit none of his mother's traits. In a metaphorical sense the first surprise means that Armand learns that his son is not all male but half female. The infant is an Aubigny but has inherited some of Désirée's namelessness as well, for we never learn his first name (nor that of his double, La Blanche's child). More generally, paternal power, the name of the father, seems to have failed to compensate for the mother's blackness or blankness.

To blame someone for the baby's troubling appearance, Armand has followed the exhortation "Cherchez la femme." In particular, he is looking for a black mother to blame. He is right to trace semiotic disruption to Désirée, but the trouble is more complex than he at first realizes.

The first surprise stemmed from a misinterpretation, a rash response to Désirée's question about her son's appearance: "'What does it mean?'" (243). The end of the story brings the second surprise—black genes came to the baby from Armand, through his own mother. Early on, readers have learned that old Monsieur Aubigny married a Frenchwoman in France and stayed there until his wife died, at which point he brought eight-year-old Armand to Louisiana. Only at the very end of the story, after Désirée and her baby have disappeared and her husband is burning their belongings, does he come across a letter from his mother to his father: "'I thank the good God for having so arranged our lives that our dear Armand will never know that his mother, who adores him, belongs to the race that is cursed with the brand of slavery'" (245). As Joseph Conrad suggested, the "heart of darkness" lies within the self: the letter unveils Armand's "dark, handsome face" to himself.

At this point, several shifts occur. One takes place between wife and husband. For Armand, his wife was originally a screen onto which he could project what he desired. When he found a black mark on the screen, he rejected it. Now he has learned that the mark was a reproduction of his own blackness. The mark, which he considers a taint, moves from her to him.

Another shift takes place between sons and fathers. As Robert Arner implies, Armand at first rejects his baby for being the child of a white man and a black woman but then finds that the description fits himself.[8] Like blackness, the half-female nature attributed to the baby has also moved to Armand, who discovers his own black mother. Certain changes also affect female characters. An intergenerational shift occurs between women as well as men, for the role of black mother has gone from Armand's wife to his mother. A similar shift occurs in his encounter with the letter itself: before reading it, he attributes it—like the taint of blackness—to Désirée, but he then discovers Madame Aubigny at the origin of both. He has sent his wife away and burned her letters, yet the letter of the black mother remains.

Thus two surprises have profoundly disturbed Armand. As in the Hegelian dialectic of master and slave, these two surprises have shaken the structure of white over black, male over female, and master over slave. Armand, the figure who seemed to belong to the dominant race, sex, and class, is shown to be heir to blackness and femaleness and to belong to the group "cursed with the brand of slavery." The repressed has returned and drained meaning from the established system of signification.

Great as these surprises in "Désirée's Baby" may be, they are less subversive than they at first appear. The fact that they shake Armand's concept of meaning and punish his arrogance does not mean that they actually change the inequality of power between the sexes, between the races, or between the classes, even on his plantation. Armand

8. Robert D. Arner, "Pride and Prejudice: Kate Chopin's 'Désirée's Baby,'" *Mississippi Quarterly*, XXV (1972), 133.

might be less sure of his ability to tell black from white, but he probably will not free his slaves. Moreover, although the story invites readers, through the traumas experienced by Armand, to pity the suffering caused by inequalities of power, it does not impel them to wonder how those inequalities could change. In other words, the surprises are more disruptive in a semiotic than in a political sense; they endanger the system of *signification* more than the system of *domination*.

What strikes today's readers as conservative is not odd, given the ideologies of the particular historical period in which Chopin set the story and the period in which she wrote it—or the magazine in which it first appeared, *Vogue*, whose readers (of both sexes) tended to be rich, white New Yorkers. Although Chopin was writing after the Civil War, she set the story in the slaveholding South and, like many other whites of her historical moment, was not herself free of prejudice against blacks and slaves. Still, if some of Chopin's attitudes seem conservative by today's standards, she was not as racist as many of her contemporaries. According to Barbara C. Ewell, even in "Désirée's Baby" Chopin showed "at best, equivocal feelings about race." Chopin gradually came to write less stereotypically of African-Americans and to have "more success, and perhaps more sympathy, with characters of mixed blood."[9] She held relatively progressive ideas about women, but her feminism, like that of many nineteenth-century thinkers, was hobbled by notions of female purity and martyrdom, these being particularly evident in "Désirée's Baby."

The text directs sympathy less toward black characters than toward characters on the margin between black and white. The story urges us to consider it a pity that Désirée and Armand, brought up as white, must undergo the trauma of receiving the news that they are black. But we are hardly urged to pity the much larger number of people who have lived as enslaved blacks since birth. The implication is that being black deserves no particular sympathy unless a person was once considered white. The broader effects of race and its relation to slavery remain unexamined.

The problem arises in part because Chopin is using the Tragic Mulatto convention, which appears repeatedly in American literature.[10]

9. Barbara C. Ewell, *Kate Chopin* (New York, 1986), 67, 68.

10. For more information on the Tragic Mulatto, see Berzon, *Neither Black nor White*, 99–116; Sterling A. Brown, "The Negro Character as Seen by White Authors," *Journal of Negro Education*, II (1933), 192–96; Barbara Christian, *Black Feminist Criticism: Perspectives on Black Women Writers* (New York, 1985), 3–4 and *passim;* Toth, "Kate Cho-

It is often easy for white readers to identify with the Tragic Mulatto, because she or he typically is raised as white and only later discovers the trace of blackness. Yet the discourse of "tragedy" introduces problems, partly because it implies resignation to the inevitable. The tragic outcome may be attributed to the miscegenation that created the mulatto in the first place, to society's unfair treatment of a mulatto condescendingly portrayed as being "as good as" a white, or to the mulatto's "black" vices. In the final analysis, all three possibilities play on readers' racism. The very idea of a Tragic Mulatto suggests that mulattoes may be more tragic, more deserving of pity, than people of purely black ancestry (in one limited sense this may even be true: mulattoes deserve pity because, unlike blacks, they may be rejected by both races).

Moreover, pity almost by definition is inadequate as a political response and can even have a conservative effect. The limitations of pity are best observed by looking at the traces of sexism that, like traces of racism, appear as a residue in the text. The parallel between racism and sexism here is complicated because the story's insufficient concern for blacks and slaves corresponds to its excessive concern for women. Of course, excessive concern can be debilitating for women by enclosing them in a construct where they are defined solely as victims.

The tale most strongly urges readers to show such concern for women in the scene where Désirée walks away, apparently to her death. The effect is enhanced by the sympathetic way in which the entire story has represented her. She is good: "beautiful and gentle, affectionate and sincere." She is appealing: "'Armand,' she called to him, in a voice which must have stabbed him, if he was human" (243). She is vulnerable: "Désirée had not changed the thin white garment nor the slippers which she wore. Her hair was uncovered and the sun's rays brought a golden gleam from its brown meshes. . . . She walked across a deserted field, where the stubble bruised her tender feet, so delicately shod, and tore her thin gown to shreds" (244). This doelike character joins a long line of women who, by dying at the end of a story or a novel, call forth readers' tears. In particular, Tragic Mulattoes tend to be mulattas.

Any scrutiny of such endings raises the discomfiting possibility that

---

pin and Literary Convention," 201–208; and Jules Zanger, "The 'Tragic Octoroon' in Pre–Civil War Fiction," *American Quarterly*, XVIII (1966), 63–70.

they rely on feminine vulnerability in order to move readers. A strong, rebellious, surviving heroine might not provide such a tidily tragic closure. I am not suggesting that Désirée's pain should be presented less sympathetically; rather, I am questioning the implication that a less vulnerable woman would deserve less concern. Such an attitude endorses female weakness. Even on the dubious assumption that Désirée freely chooses to go to the bayou, that choice fits all too well into the literary tradition of heroines allowed to demonstrate strength only in self-sacrifice.

The connection of pity with race, class, and sex is noteworthy in a scene that includes the double of Désirée's baby, La Blanche's quadroon son. When Désirée gestures the quadroon boy away, a telling detail is mentioned: he wears no shoes whatsoever, but his bare feet are described merely as coming in contact with a polished floor (243), which would feel soothing on a hot day. He probably wears no shoes outdoors either, but it is only "delicately"—if inappropriately—shod Désirée who is shown walking painfully through the field, only she who is presented as suffering from the lack of sturdy shoes. Here the stress on feminine vulnerability combines with the acceptance of black slavery, as if it were a pity for a person such as Désirée to suffer: a member of the weak sex, someone who at least used to belong to groups that do not deserve such treatment—the race with "a golden gleam" in their hair and the class with the right to "tender feet."

For these reasons, even though the meanings of race, sex, and class are threatened by Armand's surprises, those two events do not seriously disturb the system of power relations. The story invites sympathy for Désirée partly on the sexist grounds that feminine women are weak and on the racist grounds that white members of the master class do not deserve to be treated like black slaves. The traces of sexism and racism as factors in the story's appeal may account for the fact that this is the single Chopin story that remained in the literary canon for the half-century during which she was forgotten. It also conformed to what Poe and others valued: the (apparent) death of a beautiful young woman.

Some of the problems that I have described can be mitigated if one thinks carefully about the text—or rather, about what is missing from the text. Shifting the focus more definitively to Désirée discloses certain enigmatic, disruptive absences.

Almost everyone who has written on the story has mentioned, favorably or unfavorably, the concluding revelation about Armand's mother. This final twist recalls the surprise endings of Guy de Maupassant, who strongly influenced Chopin. Even while evoking sympathy for Désirée, the twist essentially turns backward to tradition and male power: first, the very presence of a plot twist may reflect Chopin's inheritance from Maupassant, a literary forefather; second, the focus of narrative point of view in the ending is Armand, upholder of conservative values; and third, the female character earns sympathy largely through a sentimental convention—through powerless, victimized innocence. In fact, my discussion itself has so far concentrated on surprises undergone by Armand, a figure of male conservatism. I agree with Cynthia Griffin Wolff that we should cease analyzing the surprise ending, favorably or unfavorably, and look elsewhere.[11]

Instead of focusing on the male-centered ending, we should turn to Désirée, who is absent from it. Although submissive, the young woman does have some power. Her boldest action is disappearance, but she does act. Although she neither desires nor anticipates the havoc she wreaks, she does catalyze the entire plot.[12]

Through Armand, we have already started to see how the meanings of race, class, and sex are crumbling. Désirée offers two greater challenges to meaning because (1) she may not be wholly white and (2) she may not die in the bayou. These are enigmas, in the sense Barthes used in S/Z.[13] They remain inconspicuously unsolved, both for readers and, apparently, for the other characters. The enigmas are silent, formless absences that cannot be found in any specific location.

To begin with, Désirée may be black—and thus a black mother—after all. If she is black, that mitigates some of the racism I discussed earlier; instead of being a white character who deserves sympathy for unjust treatment, including the accusation of being black, she is a black character whose unjust treatment, minus the accusation, *still* on its own account deserves sympathy. Because of her name and her catalytic role, Désirée in any case represents desire, one of the major forces that drive people to cross the boundaries between sexes,

---

11. Wolff, "Kate Chopin and the Fiction of Limits," 125–26. For further discussion of Maupassant's influence, see Per Seyersted, *Kate Chopin: A Critical Biography* (Oslo, 1969), 73.

12. *Cf.* Arner, "Pride and Prejudice," 137.

13. Roland Barthes, *S/Z*, trans. Richard Miller (New York, 1974), 209–10. Among other critics who have written on the work, I have not found any who mentions these two points.

classes, and races: perhaps interracial desire has also given birth to her. If a French person may be black, as Madame Aubigny was, then who is clearly white? Although Armand's blackness surprises him, his race is at least knowable. His wife's possible blackness and, even more important, the *impossibility of knowing* her race reveal the fragility of meaning more than Armand's knowable race does.

This racial ambiguity also has a broader implication. Just as it is possible to distinguish between dark and light skin, so it is possible to distinguish between a written word and the page on which it is written. But the *significance* of the color or word is not so easily discerned, for skin color does not necessarily make a person's race obvious, and writing does not necessarily convey unambiguous information. The racial ambiguity in the story metaphorically threatens the certainty of knowledge based on writing. Indeed, some of the characters' own writings fail to provide desired knowledge: for example, Désirée's letter to Madame Valmondé asks for, rather than asserts, proof of racial purity, and the older woman's response fails to answer the agonized plea for knowledge. (It is particularly appropriate that the information lacking in these letters concerns Désirée's race.) The *presence* of a traditional, *male*-oriented twist *located* at the end of the story veils a troubling, *female*-oriented *absence*—of knowledge based on skin color or on writing—that has *no particular location*.

Désirée is troubling in another way as well. The tale says, "She disappeared among the reeds and willows that grew thick along the banks of the deep, sluggish bayou; and she did not come back again" (244), but it never actually says she dies. Just as it is possible that she is partly black, so it is possible that she (with the baby) is alive. If so, that survival mitigates some of the sexism I discussed earlier. Désirée deserves sympathy even if she does not pay for it with her life. In addition, if she does not kill herself, she is saying in effect that life is worth living even if she is black and has lost Armand's love. Indeed, by escaping, she has freed herself from those who once projected their desires on her.

Even if she does kill herself and her child in the bayou, it is significant that the deaths are absent from the text. If Désirée has any black ancestors, she represents the subordinated race, class, and sex, or—if Désirée is wholly white—she and her son in combination represent the subordinated groups. By omitting explicit mention of the characters' deaths, the work allows some hope for the future, however slight, for the subordinated race, class, and sex the characters represent.

Like the impossibility of knowing Désirée's race, the impossibility of knowing her death offers a challenge to complacency about knowledge. In addition, Désirée's chance of survival connotes freedom from traditional meaning. She came as a child without a past; her total disappearance from her old life means that, if alive, she has again completely freed herself from her past, from tradition. Thus her possible survival metaphorically represents an escape from the established system of meaning.

As the two unsolved enigmas suggest, the challenge to meaning tends to operate negatively, through non-sense—as does Désirée herself. She sometimes cries out unconsciously and involuntarily, or remains completely silent. These traits appear in the scene where she notices her baby is black:

> "Ah!" It was a cry that she could not help; which she was not conscious of having uttered. . . .
> She tried to speak to the little quadroon boy; but no sound would come, at first. When he heard his name uttered, he looked up, and his mistress was pointing to the door. (242–43)

Désirée at first seemed no threat to the signifying structure she had entered, but the very inarticulateness of this blank card reveals that the system of signification sometimes breaks down.

Désirée's enigmas—the possibility that she is black and the possibility that she and her baby are alive—to some extent counteract the racism and sexism that would exist if the story clearly stated that she was white and dead. It is important that the enigmas are not just difficult but decipherable puzzles that, when solved, would clearly state that Désirée was black and alive. Instead, the enigmas have the elusive indeterminacy typical of Désirée.

Armand first thinks his wife is white, but he decides he has misinterpreted her. He thinks his wife is black and solely responsible for their son's blackness, but again Armand finds he has misinterpreted. Although unsettling, both incidents leave intact the hope that knowledge can correct misinterpretations. Yet the absences associated with Désirée erode some of that semiotic hope. Because the readers—and probably the characters—never know whether she is partly black or whether she survives the bayou, the story throws into question, at least in some cases, the very possibility of knowledge.

It would be satisfying to end on that note, but I must add that Désirée still disrupts the practice of domination less than she disrupts semiotic practice. Although sympathetic to her, Chopin also presents a critique indicating that the young woman, as a product of her society, has internalized so many of its values that she can never fully attack it. The author subtly indicates that in spite of the disruptiveness of Désirée's enigmas, her subversiveness remains limited, for three main reasons.

To begin with, Désirée is excessively dependent on the unconscious. Those who consider her weak and controllable, an invitingly blank screen, eventually learn of her power. But a problem remains: Désirée is herself "unconscious," in the sense that she is unaware. She is, for example, the last to realize that her child is not white, and it never occurs to her that her baby's blackness comes from her husband. On another level, she often seems unaware of herself, driven by her own unconscious. Her actions after discovering the baby's race seem trancelike, as if in a dream—or a nightmare. And, as we have seen, she sometimes speaks or cries out involuntarily. On still another level, Désirée's lack of political consciousness could also be seen as a kind of unconsciousness. None of this detracts from her raw power, but uncontrollable power can be as dangerous to those who wield it as to others.

The second restriction on Désirée's subversiveness comes from a certain negative quality in her. Through her silence (and inarticulateness), through the story's silence about her enigmas, and through her final absence, she disrupts her society's signifying system by revealing its contradictions and meaninglessness. She does destroy complacency about knowledge. Yet all this is not enough. Destruction often must precede creation but cannot in itself suffice. Désirée creates nothing but a baby, whom she certainly takes away, and perhaps kills.

Even Désirée's destructiveness is limited, for she possesses another negative trait: she is "essentially passive." [14] She is discovered by Monsieur Valmondé, she is discovered by Armand, she is filled with joy or fear by her husband's volatile moods, and, while lying on a couch and recovering slowly from childbirth, she is visited by Madame Valmondé. It must be acknowledged that she writes to Armand during their engagement, but she sends only "innocent little scribblings" (244) that, as his later rejection shows, fail to win his permanent loyalty. Désirée is immersed in her husband's value system and never stands up to him, not even to interpret the meaning of his dark skin or the baby's, much less to criticize his racism, his sexism, or his treatment of slaves. When she finally acts, she pleads ineffectually with her husband, writes ineffectually to her mother, and then takes the most

14. Ewell, *Kate Chopin,* 71.

passive action possible—she disappears. Like the suicide of Edna Pontellier in *The Awakening,* Désirée's disappearance is hardly a triumph.

The third weakness lies in Désirée's lack of a sense of political solidarity. She acts only individually or as part of a nuclear family, never as part of a broader group. She fails to acknowledge ties with anyone outside the family who belongs to her sex or to her newly attributed race and class. Her similarity to La Blanche, for instance, fills her with horror.

In fact, in Désirée's final efforts to win back Armand she is seeking someone she thinks is her diametric opposite—a white male, assured of his place as master. The only exception to Désirée's final solitude is her baby. But even he cannot represent any kind of positive political bonding. In the first place, if she indeed commits suicide, she probably murders him as well; and even if they both live, she probably fails to see him as linked to her in shared oppression. Nothing indicates that she loves him as anything more than a son.

Désirée's individualism resembles that of other characters.[15] For instance, the general condition of blacks and slaves never really comes into question. Madame Valmondé, like Désirée, regrets that one individual, Armand, treats his slaves cruelly, but not that he or other people own slaves in the first place. Instead of recognizing the institutional nature of exploitation based on race, class, and sex, Désirée and others seem to feel that problems stem from the lack of certain personal qualities, such as pity or sympathy. "Young Aubigny's rule was a strict one, . . . and under it his negroes had forgotten how to be gay, as they had been during the old master's easy-going and indulgent lifetime" (241). Indulgence rather than emancipation is presented as the alternative to Armand's harshness. In a similar vein, individualizing love is shown as the "antidote to the poison of Armand's racial abstraction."[16] His love for his wife and baby causes him to treat the slaves well for a while. This makes Désirée happy, but she does not question whether one man's moods should have such power over other people.

Chopin sympathetically but critically shows that her characters de-

15. Wolff makes a similar point and comments that because of the story's personal and interior approach, "the dilemma of 'color' must ultimately be construed emblematically, with the ironic and unstated fact that human situations can *never* be as clear as 'black and white.'" "Kate Chopin and the Fiction of Limits," 127–28. I agree on the emblematic meaning but believe that race (like sex and class) has a literal function as well.

16. Arner, "Kate Chopin," 52.

fine problems in terms of the lack of individualistic qualities such as love and mercy, not in terms of the subordination of one group by another. I do not mean to say that individual virtues totally lack value, only that they may not suffice to solve certain problems. As we have seen, because the story does not explicitly say Désirée and her baby die, it may spark hope for subordinate groups; nothing, however, develops that hope beyond sentimentality. In short, although some characters feel pity for slaves, blacks, and women, the assumption that they are inferior goes unquestioned. In this ideology, superiors should have a sense of noblesse oblige, but they remain superior. Concerning sex, race, and class, Désirée upsets systems of meaning but—by failing to connect the personal with the political—stops short of attacking hierarchical power structures. Disruption of meaning could lead to, and may be necessary for, political disruption, but Désirée does not take the political step.

Instead of attacking the meaningfulness of racial difference as a criterion for human rights, Désirée takes a more limited step: she reveals that racial difference is more difficult to detect than is commonly supposed. In this view, suffering can result if people classify each other too hastily or if, having finished the sorting process, people treat their inferiors cruelly. Armand, for example, labels himself too hastily as white and labels Désirée too hastily (perhaps) as black; then, having classified her as inferior, he goes on to treat her cruelly. The two concepts are linked, for superiors should be restrained from behaving cruelly by the ever-present possibility of misclassification—Armand is black and Désirée may be white. But the system of racial difference, with its built-in hierarchy, persists. In this system, superiority is still meaningful; the only difficulty lies in detecting it. It is no wonder that those viewed as inferior do not unite with one another.

Chopin presents these three reasons—unconsciousness, negativeness, and lack of solidarity—to help explain why Désirée does reveal her society's lack of knowledge but fails to change its ideological values, much less its actual power hierarchies. The force of just one of these three influences can be seen by comparison of "Désirée's Baby" with *Pudd'nhead Wilson,* which Mark Twain published the next year. Unlike Désirée, Roxana is conscious and takes positive action, but both characters lack unity with a group. Thus Roxana, who suffers from only one of the three disadvantages, still cannot manage to bring about notable subversion. Indeed, Désirée poses so little threat to the dominant power structures that she holds a relatively privileged position for most of her life. Yet subversiveness need not be bound so tightly to traits, such as unconsciousness, that make it self-limiting. It is characteristic that this tale, representing Désirée's values, uses darkness to symbolize evil and light to symbolize innocence.[17]

Désirée's semiotic subversiveness should be taken seriously. Her disruption of meaning may even be necessary—but Chopin skillfully suggests it is not sufficient.

17. Mark Twain, *Pudd'nhead Wilson and Those Extraordinary Twins* (1894; rpr. New York, 1980). Wolff, "Kate Chopin and the Fiction of Limits," explores the symbolism without commenting on its racism, 129, but the problem is recognized by Ewell, *Kate Chopin*, 71, and by Arner, "Kate Chopin," 54–55.

Sidonie de la Houssaye.
Courtesy J. John Perret

Evangeline's Darker Daughters
Crossing Racial Boundaries in Postwar Louisiana

"Why must man's vocation be always to distinguish himself from the animals?"

—Jean Baudrillard

"Everybody knew what she was called, but nobody anywhere knew her name. Disremembered and unaccounted for, she cannot be lost because no one is looking for her, and even if they were, how can they call her if they don't know her name? Although she has claim, she is not claimed."

—Toni Morrison, *Beloved*

THE heroine of Longfellow's 1847 poem, Evangeline, was immediately adopted into the complex Creole/Acadian culture of south Louisiana, which had longed for such a myth of origin.[1] She is emblematic of the double diaspora that sent her forebears first to colonize Acadia (Nova Scotia) and then to flee southward when the British expelled them. She likewise symbolizes the values assigned to white females in the Francophone cultures of the New World.

In comparison, Evangeline's darker sisters and cousins, through even more profound dislocations, experienced continuous exclusions from their geographical and cultural roots: there was no new home in the New World for African-American women. Miscegenation further complicated issues of identity. In New Orleans, city of brotherly sin, with the attendant rituals and mysteries, a mythos arose in the early nineteenth century concerning the mixed-blood women who had come to represent female beauty, sensuality, and sexuality in their unmediated (most dangerous) form.

1. A lovely statue of Longfellow's romantic heroine, the tragic victim of political/ religious persecution and an ill-fated love, resides permanently in the state park that bears her name. There are many ironies in the fact that an elite planter/mercantile Creole culture should see itself reflected in the words of a New England poet and that it should identify with a representative of the Acadian culture generally relegated to an inferior socioeconomic status. Of course, love and tragedy ennoble, and never was a culture more mythopoetically inclined than that of south Louisiana. In terms of symbolic resonances, it is curious to juxtapose the figure of Evangeline with that of the Voodoo priestess Marie Laveau.

Alice Parker

Although the presence in white Creole society of these exotic women is authenticated by primary documents and historical accounts, I will be arguing that the "quadroon" and "octoroon" (like the "mulatta") were in effect cultural products, created to serve white male interests in the pre–Civil War period. The fact of their mixed blood bears witness to the appropriation of generations of African-American women. By the time we meet them in the text that I will be examining, these women—whose "otherness" is calculated down to a thirty-second of African "blood" but whose appearance might be "whiter" than most Euro-Americans—had submitted to over a century of male appetites, both proprietary and sexual. The least we can reasonably suppose is that black and mixed-blood women were more often in a position of chosen than of choosing, or were manipulated into a choice that was far from free.

How then do we read *Les Quarteronnes* [quadroons] *de la Nouvelle-Orléans,* a work written by an upper-class Creole lady and set in the early part of the nineteenth century, in which the victims are held responsible for the crimes perpetrated on them?[2] Sidonie de la Houssaye, the author, allegedly borrowed a whole trunkful of "original" materials from the period left by her grandmother, and even her grandmother's voice, in order to ensure the fidelity of her account. And yet I am left with an uncomfortable sense that one of us, de la Houssaye or I, does not know how to read. Or rather, if it is true that speech and desire are synchronic, then the stories de la Houssaye tells are not the same as the stories I interpret. My point is not merely that acts of reading and writing are culturally determined, but that we read with a good deal more than our "minds," and further, that texts both provide a sort of generic map for interpretation and perform according to patterns that scientists are now labeling chaotic (which, given our present models and reality structures, may appear uncanny). De la Houssaye's reader has an immediate sense of having strayed into alien spaces, of trespassing in a land of unrecognizable flora/fauna, speech, and customs. While we are trying to get our bearings, authorial choices complicate the interpretive process further by encouraging our complicity with an elite French Creole culture, whose private reserve we are only to view as voyeurs, donning the (white) male gaze

2. Sidonie de la Houssaye [Louise Raymond], *Les Quarteronnes de la Nouvelle-Orléans* (2 vols.; Bonnet Carré, La., 1894–95). Hereinafter referred to in the text by volume and page number.

that has appropriated representation of the female body since at least the Renaissance.

De la Houssaye appears to be nervous about boundaries that define social identity and therefore prescribe a fixed location, assign her a place of subjectivity. Thus, while adventuring into a psychosexual territory literally unthinkable for a "lady" of her class and time, she would like us to believe that she has both feet planted firmly on terra cognita. In the name of her grandmother, de la Houssaye means to claim the territory staked out by the ideologies of phallocentrism and early capitalism (known, interestingly, as "free" enterprise), and through her portraits of the mixed-blood "queens" of New Orleans society at the turn into the nineteenth century, to help us pass to the other side, to (tres)pass the limits with impunity. In order to protect her name and her reputation on this dangerous excursion, she will use the cover of Victorian morality as she (paradoxically) exploits the codes and disguises necessary to double back or "pass" into a "dark continent" of primal desire. It is likely that in addressing the "other," who is at once white male and mixed-blood female, de la Houssaye literally did not know what she was saying.[3] Thus her purpose is manifestly to conceal her desire, the desire of the "other" Victorian, who, culturally speaking, as a woman has no libido. The writer here stands in a place of erasure; she must "steal the father's tongue" as well as his name/symbols/disapproval ("no") in order to constitute herself as literary subject/agent.

In this essay I propose to come to terms with the discourses that constitute race, gender, and class in the text of *Les Quarteronnes*. What interests me in the narrative is a series of re-presentations of the complex phenomenon of passing. Prototypically, the term *passing* refers to crossing racial boundaries. In addition, de la Houssaye's work plays (havoc) with class boundaries, sexual transgressions, and gender identity. The "author" is also un-certain, signing with a pseudonym, "Louise Raymond," and using her grandmother to legitimize her sources and her voice. The modalities of passing are inscribed in *Les Quarteronnes* in terms of the codes (speech, dress, manner, taste, milieu, ethics, religion, sexuality) that determine subjectivity. These codes, or

---

3. Jacques Lacan in *Séminaire, Livre XX: Encore* (Paris, 1975) writes that the woman can only be written with the *the* barred (68); that "she" is the "other of the other" (75); that she neither exists nor can signify anything (69); that she can only exist as mother (90) and has no unconscious (91); that "women are excluded from the nature of things which is the nature of words," and thus "they do not know what they say" (68).

systems of signs, can be manipulated or exchanged for analogous symbolic structures. This is a process that Josue Harari calls "transcoding." Moving from one language to another "demonstrates the reciprocal power that each . . . possesses to provoke and modify the discourse of the other."[4] The transcoding involved in passing likewise has the power to interrogate and undermine the categories that given codes establish and maintain. For example, the passing involved in moving from one race to another destabilizes the codes that determine racial identity.

In staging lengthy encounters with the "other" woman/race/culture in both public and private domains, de la Houssaye brings to "light" facts that more than one family would have desired to keep secret (I, 1). Nowhere is this illicit information more evident than at the liminal point figured in the text by the quadroon ball; here the reader has an observation station from which to contemplate where and how the races meet and exchanges occur. At the ball, reason meets fantasy, reality encounters the imaginary. The word *meet* is of course tricky, because what we are really dealing with are rituals of desire. A central concern of this essay will be to analyze the erotic economy figured by the term *quadroon,* particularly the surplus of sexual energy that threatens the orderly, bourgeois social interaction of Creole culture. The ball is dangerous, like a dark wood into which a hero adventures at his peril; however, the separation from the known does not hold promise of cultural renewal; rather, the boundaries are fortified to protect the integrity of the divisions between the gentleman and the brute, the angel and the demon. Once he crosses that line, as does the hero of the first story, Charles Rennes, he enters the shifting terrain of the anomalous: all of the sociometric markers disappear. Charles is "astonished, subjugated" upon perceiving his new Circe, and instantly becomes her slave, forgetting his family, his name, the land to which he will no longer be heir, the entire bourgeois scene with its attendant values (I, 8). Passing through the portals into the space of the Other, where behavior is orchestrated in response to alien codes, threatens to disrupt not only the social identity of the individual, but also the discourse that produces identity as such (I, 9). The nightmare of the colonizer—that the victim will turn bloodthirsty—begins to take form.[5]

---

4. Josue V. Harari, *Scenarios of the Imaginary: Theorizing the French Enlightenment* (Ithaca, 1987), 34.

5. See Frantz Fanon, *The Wretched of the Earth* (New York, 1968), 61–62.

Like the young Des Grieux in *Manon Lescaut,* Charles has never before looked at or thought about women. Now a "cyclone of passion" delivers him to an eighteen-year-old enchantress whose "disorderly life" characterizes the "women of her race" (I, 9). No one is rich enough to keep this "vilest, most debauched, cruelest of Satan's creatures" (I, 10), already credited with the "shame and desolation of some of the most honorable families." We are told that "like the chameleon she can take on any color, appear to have every virtue, she who is vice incarnate" (I, 11). In an important sense these texts are *reading* lessons or "textbook" cases: on the one hand, upper-class white men are functional illiterates in the psychosexual domain represented by the quadroons. Creole women, as we shall see, represent a "sex which is not one"—a lacuna in the linguistic sign system on which the sexual economy is based; written in invisible ink, they can neither read nor be read.

There is a constant interplay in *Les Quarteronnes* between the persona of the author, who is obliged to uphold proper Creole standards of behavior and to maintain a position of solidarity with the men of her class, and the voices of the quadroons, which carry the weight of the stories. Doubtless de la Houssaye did not intend some forms of passing we glimpse through gaps in the narrative. In fact, her narrative strategies disrupt discursive systems that distinguish white from black, male from female, proper from improper, as the boundaries that protect such binary pairs are continually transgressed. The process of "othering" that separates the *we* from the *they,* the known from the unknown (strangers), has to be undermined for the text to exist at all. In coming to terms with the quadroons—and in making sense of the legacy of her grandmother—de la Houssaye has to enter the scene. Passing in this case is a process by which the writer constructs identities that transport her out of cultural positions that were severely restrictive in the late Victorian period. At the same time, as a colonizer, she writes both from and in the place of the Other.

In attempting to "make relive for a moment . . . a race which today, thanks to education and especially to religion no longer exists," three years of research were insufficient, de la Houssaye admits, to generate a text that could only be produced by dissolving generational markers and giving back the word (*rendre la parole*) to her grandmother (Introduction). In letting the grandmother "tell what she knows," Houssaye installs a scene of desire for the (m)other in which the "originary" or libidinal traces "relive." Although literature com-

monly challenges its own assumptions and laws, the disjunctures here
are shocking. An exemplary small-town schoolmistress relates the unthinkable: scandalous tales of sex, seduction, greed, violence, and incest. The text conceals an unmistakably uneasy relationship to the
codes of her culture. Was Lillian Smith correct in thinking women are
"disloyal to civilization"?[6] In any case, one can read a barely repressed
desire in *Les Quarteronnes* to explore an other (exotic) sensibility, sexuality, sensual élan. The moralistic disclaimers, which might have convinced earlier readers, no longer insulate the text from manifestations
of libidinal energies. All of the forbidden territories are transgressed:
the "author" passes as male, independent of work and family, young,
rich, exotic, beautiful, seductive, and above all, powerful. In the narrative, the existence of mixed-blood women, the quadroon and octoroon, is proof of how boundaries *can* be subverted.

Taking off and landing are both dangerous and exhilarating; the
"author" is at greatest risk in terms of credibility and legitimacy at the
inception and conclusion of the fictional work. It is also at these initial
and final moments of stress that a scene of desire may be most trans-
parent. De la Houssaye recounts the cry of joy (*jouissance*) that escaped her upon discovery of her grandmother's papers, the "origin" of
"these stories [that] had all the charm of the incredible attached to fairy
tales of the Arabian Nights" (I, 1). Above all, referents for the anec-
dotes had to be kept hidden, which is what constituted their appeal
for contemporary newspapers, which both staged the exploits and
hypocritically protected the interests of the (white) families involved.
Victorian society particularly enjoyed the space in which the private
was re-presented as public. As a threshold where the two came together, the quadroon ball held special attraction for society writers of
the time; the ball figured the "abyss" between the two worlds (public/
private; moral/erotic; white/black). Like de la Houssaye, her "grandmother" resides at some remove from the marvelously evil city where
the action occurs. She listens "avidly" to the accounts her husband
reads to her of the quadroons, "their supernatural beauty, their
luxury or rather their extravagance and the follies that were done for
them" (I, 1). The illicit spaces figured by the "queens of the period"
paradoxically "forced" white women "to remain in the shadows, entirely neglected by those who owed them help, love and protection"

6. Lillian Smith, *The Winner Names the Age: A Collection of Writings by Lillian Smith*,
ed. Michelle Cliff (New York, 1978), 191.

(I, 2). Men from the best classes attended the intimate dinners and balls of the quadroons, "and if it wasn't an honor it was certainly a pleasure (jouissance)" (I, 2). Merging with her source, the writer admits that she too reads the papers "more than she should," seeking out particularly stories of the "splendid parties" given by the quadroons, descriptions of their "fabulous outfits, jewelry, and carriages," so much more interesting than politics or wars (I, 24).

Further on we will look at how the pleasure represented by the quadroons is produced, whose interests it serves, and what forms it takes. Of course, what de la Houssaye had intended (to mask her pleasure, which has all of the hallmarks of an erotics of reading and writing) was a study in immorality and perversion, for which the Others (quadroons) were to assume the entire burden of responsibility. As in Freud's scenario (hysteria and the oedipal drama), the sins of the fathers were to be visited on the children. In fact, as worthy daughters of Eve, the quadroons have no fathers at all—this trace is entirely covered, with the exception of an occasional Cuban, who does not count in Creole culture (I, 25). The text reveals no clue at all as to how the "dark" women came to have "mixed" blood, or indeed how the category of "blood" came to define race. The male counterpart of the female quadroon is conspicuously absent from the novel; it is not difficult to understand de la Houssaye's purposes in removing the father, lover, and/or brother figures from the quadroon's life, which the author will divert into a quite different trajectory.

The most notable lapse in historic memory as the text records it is the institution of slavery, which provided the impetus for categories of racial distinction in the United States. Knowing that de la Houssaye lived through the Civil War, we might be all the more surprised had not recent work in historiography alerted us to the fictional processes at work in historical narrative. Here white men are the victims of the quadroons, who figure as miracles of spontaneous generation, typically beyond kinship denominations, although occasionally connected to an aunt or sister. Both the author and the reader know, however, that some of the "best blood" of New Orleans ran in their veins. Like the heroine of Gayl Jones's *Corregidora*, they are also childless, heedless of the injunction to "make generations" in order to pass down patrilineal messages ("The important thing is making generations. They can burn the papers but they can't burn conscious. . . . And that's what makes the evidence. And that's what makes the verdict."). Typically situated in an educational and ethical vacuum (a no-place, or atopia), de la Houssaye's quadroons are continually compared to beasts, in obvious reference to a division of the animal kingdom into higher and lower species. As Gayatri Spivak reminds us, the gaze directed toward the subaltern is always down.[7]

In her provocative "Mama's Baby, Papa's Maybe: An American Grammar Book," Hortense Spillers suggests that we have not yet begun to interrogate the categories of race and gender as they relate to African-American women. She notes that captive women on this continent were outside categories that regulate gender in their alienation from native and European kinship systems and in their removal from domesticity, and were outside the sociolects that authorize human interaction because of their status as chattel.[8] In de la Houssaye's work the dark women and their paler sisters have, in fact, odd rapports with "gender": on the one hand a surplus, or overdetermination, of the category, and on the other a rather unconvincing imitation of it.

The problem is that "femininity" as a trope in the nineteenth century excluded material functions (maternity, nurturance, education of children, socioeconomic management of domestic resources, and so on) and problematized the ontological status of women, who were assigned only a phantom presence. If, as Spillers argues, the institution of slavery did not in fact permit African-American women to constitute themselves in *terms* of gender, the rarified environment of Victorian domesticity produced a paradoxically similar effect in elaborating for the "wife" and "mother" a transcendence of the material world, separating the woman from her body, her sexual impulses, and her desire. The only "real" women were the Others, the darker sisters, who were suddenly in the position of filling the void where gender used to be. De la Houssaye inflects this gender overdetermination/ underdetermination problematic in *Les Quarteronnes,* following the dominant discourses of her society, yet she subverts these discourses at the same time. The pleasure her grandmother finds in reading is of course the pleasure de la Houssaye takes in writing, giving the text an (erotic) energy that helps us negotiate in the land of difference where, like her quadroons, de la Houssaye's narrative signs change their color and their message like "chameleons" (I, 26).

7. Gayl Jones, *Corregidora* (New York, 1975), 22; Gayatri Chakravorty Spivak, *In Other Worlds: Essays in Cultural Politics* (New York, 1987), 264.

8. Hortense J. Spillers, "Mama's Baby, Papa's Maybe: An American Grammar Book," *Diacritics,* XVII (1987), 66–76. This is a complex argument from which it is impossible to extract a single passage without falsifying the perspective.

In fact, the systematization of categories derived from societal norms breaks down from the beginning; in the spaces between black and white, between female and male, between moral and illicit, interesting discoveries occur. The distortions that take place when boundaries are blurred are crucial to an understanding of how identity is constructed. Further, border disputes—over parentage, for example, or over what percentage of "black blood" it takes to be classified "black" even though one appears "white"—help us recognize how "objective" and even "scientific" categories are contaminated by ideological assumptions that constitute the rationale for oppression. What interests are served by the construction of the quadroon, a creature in de la Houssaye's work who is deprived of family and name (patronym), who is at once alluring and sterile, but could be one of our own (sisters)? It is in the borderlands that the worst dangers lurk; de la Houssaye has given us a whole Pandora's box—her grandmother's trunk—of libidinal figures and tropes. Even though the frame is negative, when we interpret the signs we find, as with the dreams Freud helps us unravel, a genuine treasure trove of messages to be deciphered. The text encodes nothing so much as ambiguity and ambivalence—the novelist's discomfort in the face of choices she is obliged to make for the sake of plot, characterization, and so on. Thus the beautiful Octavia dresses with an unexpected decency, and in spite of the perception that quadroons "had no heart and gave themselves to the highest bidder," Octavia adores Alfred—while her idol invests in her exactly as he might a rare painting or a fancy racehorse (I, 25–26). Later we learn that it was, ironically, Alfred's innate nobility that prevented him from loving such a "vile, wretched creature" (I, 26). Eventually, when he must dispose of her in order to contract a "proper" marriage, she is recast as a she-devil and witch who must be sent back to Satan (I, 30, 32). The quadroon whose taste and appearance were so distinguished "one would never suspect she had a drop of black blood in her veins" now exemplifies "the taste of her race" (I, 25, 33).

Mary V. Dearborn observes that the quadroon provides a space in which "limits are tested," boundaries are fluid—a "locus of protest." It is a fictional space of ambivalence and the uncanny. For de la Houssaye's compatriot Grace King, the threat to boundaries in the mulatta represents a place of tragic discovery, and ultimately a death of the self: in King's "The Little Convent Girl," when the heroine discovers her mother is black, she drowns herself. In desperation she affirms the homogeneity of a "unitary" self by eliminating the Other. King suggests that the child, who is never found, may have disappeared through a "hole in the floor of the upper river" to the "underground river, to that vast, hidden, dark Mississippi that flows beneath the one we see."[9] Is this an inscription of the (un)conscious where boundaries do not obtain?

Although (white) men could freely embrace darker women, black and white women, according to ideologies of gender, sexuality, and family, were immured in roles that kept women fragmented and separate. A visitor to New Orleans in 1836 was perplexed:

> I have often heard of the beauty of quadroons. I found them pretty. They are a virtuous and amiable looking people, and have the appearance of being virtuous: but they are generally prostitutes and kept mistresses. Young men and single men of wealth have each a quadroon for his exclusive use. They are furnished with a Chamber and a sitting room and servants, and the comforts and elegancies of life. It generally costs from $1,500 to $2,000 a year to keep a quadroon. I am informed that the quadroon is faithful to a Proverb in these attachments. Married men in this City are frequently in the habit of keeping quadroons.[10]

Although the quadroons appear virtuous and amiable (but only "pretty"), they fulfill functions that are in conflict with these attributes. For whose pleasure and profit are they mistresses? Is it for Creole husbands and fathers, whose honorable status is unaffected by keeping dark women in bondage?

We know that a woman "of honor" is an anomaly, that the woman's "honor" derives only from the man for whom she preserves her chastity. For Sidonie de la Houssaye, confronting the inner spaces where the "Other" could be concealed, rationalizing the scandal, turning sexuality into a comprehensible discourse (of the Other) was an ethical necessity and an obsession. Who were these latter-day sirens who bewitched the scions of so many important families, threatening to disrupt the very markers of Creole society? Writing/unwriting/rewriting de la Houssaye got more than she bargained for. In attempting to map the "ecstatic," the passion that "astonishes" and "subjugates" (I, 8–9), she found herself in a dangerous space, where the Other (daughter,

9. Mary V. Dearborn, *Pocahontas's Daughters: Gender and Ethnicity in American Culture* (New York, 1986), 139, 141–42; Grace King, "The Little Convent Girl," in *Balcony Stories* (Boston, 1893), cited *ibid.,* 145.

10. Herbert A. Keller, ed., "The Diary of James D. Davidson," *Journal of Southern History,* I (1935), 348, cited in Catherine Clinton, *The Plantation Mistress* (New York, 1982), 212.

sister?) lurked in primal splendor. Once the voyage was launched, there was no controlling the vessel, much less the seas into which it had descended. Ideological pressures only made the currents unfathomable, and the little rudder of Victorian morality was a sadly inadequate guide.

Paradoxically, *Les Quarteronnes* teaches us how to read the ideologies concealed in the discourse of decolonization generated after the Civil War. De la Houssaye herself suffered the downward mobility that afflicted many Creole families, and likewise succumbed to a romantic revision of the past, even more evident in an Evangelinesque tale of the exodus from Acadia entitled *Pouponne et Balthazar,* a story of star-crossed lovers fleeing to the maternal French arms of Louisiana. In *Les Quarteronnes,* de la Houssaye both reproduces and subverts the inherited story: the Other may have neither legal nor political power but is still threatening (like the repressed, which can return in unforeseeable ways) as siren and witch. Outside the pale of mainstream society, the quadroons are free agents for the perpetration of evil (according to a system that links "black" with magic, of which implied qualifiers are also "female" and "blood"). Ayi Kwei Armah, in *Two Thousand Seasons* (1979), and other African writers have begun the work of recoding such a system by insisting on qualifying the "destroyers"—slave-dealers and colonizers—as *white,* and complicitous Africans as "zombies."[11]

De la Houssaye's quadroons operate through a series of symbolic castrations of the men they lure into their clutches. Since they are bewitched, the white men are not responsive to the codes of their people: diverted from their legitimate families into sexual commerce with the darker women, they will, it is inferred, waste their seed and their money, the sublimated representative of the phallus. Sexual initiative rests with the quadroon female in this scenario. Such an uncanny commerce, like a contract with the Devil, is irreversible and can only be canceled by total ruin. Like dangerous tropical plants, the quadroons figure a space in which sons and husbands can be entrapped in noxious blooms and devoured (*vagina dentata?*). Removed from the exchange system of alliances among the propertied classes, these men represent the dashed hopes of the white patriarchy. They lose their value-generating potential. The wives, children, and aged

11. Sidonie de la Houssaye, *Pouponne et Balthazar* (New Orleans, 1888); Ayi Kwei Armah, *Two Thousand Seasons* (Chicago, 1979).

parents they abandon along the way become in turn valueless commodities, severed now from the (male) sources of production.

Opening her text to the language of desire by displacements that permitted her to write of and through the Other, de la Houssaye could interrogate the system of surplus value on which a racist, mercantile Creole society depended. Dahlia—the exception that proves the rule—has undergone a *rite de passage:* educated in a convent in Baltimore (most Louisiana convents would not accept black women), and acknowledged by her father (II, 39), she is cultivated, pious, and can "pass" as a proper lady. The other quadroons typically bear the names of no man's family, and re-present "gender" in a pure, unalloyed form. They are products of a cultural moment in which the repressed magma of the psyche has erupted in bizarre (uninscribable, uncontrollable) manifestations. They are characterized by their negativity in an economy of excess, using their unholy power (Voodoo) as Satanic consorts. As Creole men are drawn into the Magic Circle, privilege is exchanged for pleasure; "honest" money (extracted from the work of slaves and peons) is now tainted as it returns to the lower echelons of society whence it came.

Once we recognize the complexity of the category "gender," two analytical movements converge: on the one hand, gender is entirely coded, can only be articulated through a given cultural language; on the other, gender is determined by a binary logic of which "male" and "female" is the prototypical pair, according to a discourse of Western metaphysics that privileges the same/presence, and which we are learning to deconstruct. In other words, the cultural language that writes gender does not speak "naturally." Thus when de la Houssaye proclaims that this "race" has now "disappeared" as a result of "education" and "religion," the principal tools of acculturation (and in this case, of the destruction/assimilation of the Other), she is expressing a scene of her desire and her fear of/for history and a mythical past, and paradoxically, for liberation and for writing. Because the Other is *essentially* uninscribable.

De la Houssaye's project is to gain access to a language of desire whose grammar and syntax are illicit by transposing libidinal energies, relocating sexual codes in stories of a marginal Other. With the mediating discourses of white culture eliminated, the quadroons are produced in the text through an exclusion of all signifiers that do not have a material relationship to the referent, so that primacy is given to a language of the body. The originary topos is the jungle, although the current reality of Voodoo practices made antecedents superfluous. In a childish state of arrested psychosocial development, the quadroons re-present the negative of every attribute of Victorian womanhood: pampered, spoiled, immodest, spontaneous or even wild, they expect immediate gratification of senses that respond to only the strongest stimuli—bright colors, rich fabrics, glittering jewels, fragrant blooms and perfumes, the stuff of which dreams (the unconscious) are made. Paradoxically, in the midst of their "natural" materialism (like children, they have no sense of the "value" of money) and hedonism, mixed-blood women are credited with an artistic sensibility that inspires an exquisite sense of taste, choice, and arrangement. One might say that sexual and esthetic grids are superimposed, or that these economies intersect. De la Houssaye notes that Creole women copied the quadroons at a distance, but with little success. They did not have "it" (sex, sensual élan?).

The signs that situate mixed-blood women in *Les Quarteronnes* derive from the ethnic mix of New Orleans Creole society, whose less refined elements are ascribed to Latin American sources. The quadroons are further identified with pagan foremothers—for example, Circe, Cleopatra, Helen, and Medea—and with figures such as ondines (water spirits), sirens, and bacchantes. Like Octavia, initiated by her mother into the occult science of poisons and potions, they may have diabolical power. For Dr. Verdier, her ex-lover's uncle, Octavia's secret knowledge is more fearful than war, which conditioned him to death (I, 33). Associated also with dangerous animals, naming procedures in effect *mark* the quadroon with what Spillers calls "overdetermined nominative properties." They virtually stick to the body of the darker woman, like the epithets African-American women continue to attract: "Embedded in bizarre axiological ground, they demonstrate a sort of telegraphic coding; they are markers so loaded with mythical prepossession that there is no easy way for the agents buried beneath them to come clean." In de la Houssaye's work the mythological roots are purposefully exposed, although in Spillers' terms they do not "come clean" because, like mythological symbols or psychic-releasing mechanisms, they evoke an immediate, nonrational response.[12]

The attribution to "blood" of culturally produced behaviors as well as an "unnatural" beauty of body and speech is a probable cause of the quadroons' "uncanny" seductiveness. In this sense "blood" figures

12. Spillers, "Mama's Baby," 65.

a constellation of meanings overburdening the subject of discourse, here the quadroons. The purer attraction (a real oxymoron) of their paler sisters cannot compare; although de la Houssaye moves into metalanguage each time a comparison is inevitable, in order to avoid bringing black and white into material contact (on the level of the signifier), one cannot help thinking of Maxine Hong Kingston's use of the word *ghosts* to qualify everyone except Chinese and Japanese, and of, more recently, Toni Morrison's skinless creatures in *Beloved*.[13] In fact, the quadroons and octoroons are as perfectly at home in their bodies as the Creole women are estranged from theirs, a typology that persists in the discourse of the female body as it continues to be written. Interestingly, Creole children are sent away to colder climates to be educated (where their sensual/sexual development may be slowed or arrested?), the girls to convents in Canada and the boys to schools in Germany.

De la Houssaye's text stages a continuous decoding-recoding process that problematizes narrative and cultural schema. Messages constructed by the text do not "make sense," since the excess (of beauty, sexuality, power, color, blood) with which figures of the Other are burdened is necessarily unstable. The boundaries are impossible to police: signs accumulate to reinforce a fragmentation of women's lives along classist and racist lines; white women are all "angels in the house." Alfred D.'s young wife, Angèle (!), who succeeds Octavia the quadroon, seems oblivious of her body and the storm of revenge brewing about her. Yet the fact that Creole women, as dutiful wives, risk their lives to bear numerous children, belies their innocence. Similarly, the bestiality of their husbands undermines the romance of Creole marriage. In fact, de la Houssaye positions white women beyond the narrative frame—like Madame Pierre Saulve, immured in The Magnolias, the Saulves' city residence, who inspires tenderness but not passion (II, 9, 21, 85). The gender arrangements of "everyday life" bring to crisis literary figures and tropes that traditionally code gender, the one continuously interrogating the other. Thus Creole wives, like Hermine Saulve (II, 72ff.), are capable of calling into play unsuspected personal resources to provide for themselves and their children when their husbands defect for one reason or another.

De la Houssaye herself was married at thirteen, had six children—

13. Maxine Hong Kingston, *The Woman Warrior: Memoirs of a Girlhood Among Ghosts* (New York, 1975), *passim;* Toni Morrison, *Beloved* (New York, 1987), *passim.*

four sons and a daughter survived—then lost her husband when she was forty-three. Her daughter died when de la Houssaye was fifty-four, leaving her with eight grandchildren to raise. She was in her mid-sixties before she could devote herself to writing full-time, having responsibility also for a school she opened after the Civil War to support herself and her family. With the survival tactics women learned from the war, she persevered and functioned as a unique source of instruction and intellectual stimulation for the children of Franklin, Louisiana, for several decades. She was also a major, unacknowledged informant for the Louisiana stories of George Washington Cable.[14] So again one wonders from what sources emanate this text, what kinds of desire are being inscribed.

De la Houssaye's ambivalent relationship to the prescriptive codes that determined gender echoes the (self-)image of a Creole woman published by the New Orleans literary society Athénée Louisianais the first year the writing competition was opened to women (1879). The winning essay notes that Creole women are distinguished by their sweet disposition, which does not fail under the most dire circumstances, including the deaths of loved ones and loss of fortune. Christian virtues sustain them even when the men become fanatic, egotistical patriots, expressing the chauvinism of "my country before all else," or as in the postwar period, worship the golden calf. The writer rejects, like many women before and after, the heroism of the battlefield in favor of peace, harmony, and the brotherhood of nations. A similar effort to analyze how ideology operates through discourse is evident in the Civil War journal of Julia LeGrand, who wrote from the Federally occupied city of New Orleans in 1862: "I long to be rid of the evil and suffering which spring from the passions of men! Claptrap sentiments and political humbugs! I almost hate the word 'Flag' even!"—recognizing specifically the ways in which gender inf(l)ects historical accounts.[15]

The postcolonial (post-Emancipation) spaces in de la Houssaye's narrative are at once the dark and the light, a divided, doubled, Janus-

14. Biographical information on Sidonie de la Houssaye comes from Velma Savoie, "The Life and Writings of Mme. Sidonie de la Houssaye" (M.A. thesis, Louisiana State University, 1936).

15. Madame Armand Cousin, "La Femme Louisianaise avant, pendant, et après notre dernière guerre," *Procédés de l'Athénée Louisianais* (1879), 331; Julia LeGrand, *The Journal of Julia LeGrand: New Orleans, 1862–1863,* ed. Kate Mason Rowland and Mrs. Morris L. Croxall (Richmond, Va., 1911), 44–45.

like vision of the female that faces both directions but cannot see, much less read, the Other. Borrowing Gayatri Spivak's description of a recent Indian work, we could call it a "sinister vision of the failure of social cement in a decolonized space where questions of genital pleasure or social affect are framed" (framed on the Other?). As in the narrative Spivak analyzes, the body is here a "place of knowing in the text"; however, "knowledge is not identity but irreducible difference," so that "what is known is always in *excess* of knowledge." The ability to read or know in de la Houssaye's work is invested exclusively in the male gaze in its position of exteriority with regard to the divided female (black and white) body, the "place of knowing." But since there is no "outside the text," what we have here is Lacan's "barred subject" that "yearns to find itself again," the lost object that represents desire; the "lost object is the support of the subject." [16] If, according to Lacanian psychoanalysis, all subjects are barred (castrated), the woman writer experiences her loss of self, of identity, more acutely than the man because of her position as object rather than agent in discourse. The fact that a woman *is* writing dislodges homosocial arrangements in which men communicate with men, and brings to crisis epistemological issues (who knows what/whom, and how). The "disadvantaged" text Spivak analyzes encourages us to ask why the locus of knowing is in the body, to interrogate the relationship between sexuality and "truth."

In de la Houssaye's text knowledge, like pleasure, is endlessly deferred. The clues in her grandmother's trunk set us on a trail that leads in circles: the content of the unconscious is by definition buried. *Les Quarteronnes* generates knowledge by writing on the body of the Other. The novel re-presents desire, excess, and loss. The lost or suppressed text tells us, the readers, that the quadroon as an African-American woman has been diverted from her material/historical function as wife, mother, sister for black men and women, the "real" community from which she has been extracted or abstracted. The knowledge produced by our reading is a paltry imitation of what we know, which is of course the accumulated experience we bring to the process, our interaction with the text.

16. Spivak, *In Other Worlds*, 264, 261, 254 (emphasis added); Jacques Lacan, "Of Structure as an Inmixing of an Otherness Prerequisite to Any Subject Whatever" (transcription of a 1966 address), in *The Languages of Criticism and the Sciences of Man*, ed. Richard Macksey and E. Donato (Baltimore, 1970), 194, 189.

As Spillers says of the "captive body," the economic, the figural, and "the real" merge as we read de la Houssaye's text, which "brings into focus a gathering of social realities as well as a metaphor for *value* so thoroughly interwoven in their literal and figurative emphases that distinctions between them are virtually useless." Sexual value is precisely of the kind that can be endlessly reappropriated. So that although the scene of captivity appears to be restaged in de la Houssaye's work, no reader can fail to understand that political power remains in the domain of the privileged white classes. In the locution "free" women of color, as Spillers notes for the term "liberated": "No one need pretend that the quotation marks do not *matter.*" [17] Although de la Houssaye tries to hold the quadroons *accountable* for the excesses (capital expenditures) committed in their *name,* the late-twentieth-century reader knows who really profits, and that the flaws are systemic. So although we are literally *led* to believe that the quadroons will do anything for money, we know that in this luxury economy the women have the status of prized possessions. The real entrepreneur is not Octavia, but her lover's uncle, who triples the fortune his nephew then sows about like "wild oats."

When I began this project I thought that the trace that had to be obscured for the story (of the quadroons) to be told was a tale of miscegenation, of the rape of the powerless by the powerful. I now think that gender is a central element in the drama, and that the division by "blood" into identities that qualify as black and white is modeled on an originary binary pair, male and female. In handling the dangerous materials drawn from the book of the "unconscious," de la Houssaye opens up space between Self and Other, between parent and child. In one of the stories, for example, the prodigal is the father, summoned home by his young son. In a further mythical reversal it is the son who, like Oedipus, sacrifices himself so that order can be restored (I, 81–82). According to this economy, the phantom (bodyless) wives and children have only sickness and death as means by which to recall the husband or father, but the likelihood is that only a commodity drained of its value or value-generating potential will return. What Spillers calls "originating metaphor[s] of captivity and mutilation," which return in "endless disguise," direct the destinies of the tyrants as well as the victims. [18]

17. Spillers, "Mama's Baby," 68.
18. *Ibid.*

"Expenditure for a sign": the exchange of surplus value (money, sexuality) takes a tragic turn in a story from *Les Quarteronnes* in which a child is sacrificed in another value substitution of the child for the father. Here the incest motif that is covered over in dramatizations of patrilinear succession and miscegenation is foregrounded. When Alfred D. abandons his mistress to assume family "responsibilities" by settling down in a "normal" way, by marrying the sixteen-year-old cousin whom he can entrust with the incubation of "his" child, fulfilling his uncle's dream of merging family interests, Octavia the quadroon designs an act of vengeance unmatched in the annals of lex talionis. Octavia kidnaps Alfred's daughter and raises the child as her own, training her in the arts of seduction. Eventually, as the reader anticipates with horror, Octavia lures the girl's brother, a sensual young man spoiled by his grieving parents and grandfather, into an incestuous commerce with his sister. In the final act of the drama Octavia apprises Alfred of the girl's "origin" so that the father (a lawyer "standing before" the law) can witness brother and sister in each other's arms and destroy all concerned, including himself. The effective linking of the quadroon with the cruel, implacable fate that animated Greek tragedy was doubtless conscious. But the behavior of the hero is less than exemplary; the messages leave a modern reader nonplussed. In whose name and to what end could such a story come to be written? The last person who could furnish answers to such questions is the author herself.

Is de la Houssaye writing "in the name of" white women, who as silent participants in Victorian culture seem to have no language, and to exist only as objects of speculation (as Irigaray uses the term in *Speculum of the Other Woman*)?[19] Certainly she could not "mean" to indict the men of "honor" who commit adultery, forge checks, literally or figuratively kill their wives and children, waste their fortunes (the worst of all possible sins). Are the wives responsible? If Hermine Saulve's husband, Pierre, behaves like a brute, is it *her* fault (I, 86)? Beyond the mea culpas, she learns to function on her own as embattled women always do, a subtext the author does not own (I, 3).

The story we miss most is the material history of persons of African-American descent in the nineteenth century. Instead, de la Houssaye tells us of Jeannette—or "Adoreah," as she is known—and her blonde sister, educated by their young mistress, who separates from

19. Luce Irigaray, *Speculum de l'autre femme* (Paris, 1974).

them and their mother (her nanny) only when she marries a rich Canadian, at which point she frees them and gives their mother a substantial sum of money. But the latter keeps the money and puts the children into domestic service, from which they do not escape until Jeannette-Adoreah is sixteen (I, 10). By the time she is eighteen she is consummately perverse (I, 11). The metonymic slide on de la Houssaye's part as she moves from race/blood to disorder/seduction reinforces the separations encoded in nineteenth-century systems of perception that the text tries to bring into new balance. In a sense it is a brave attempt to eliminate conflict (between the races, and especially between different classes of women) as Freud describes the process in *Beyond the Pleasure Principle*.[20] A modern reader must engage in a different balancing act, knowing the "facts" of black women's history, both as slaves and as freed persons of color. I can only read such a text with lucidity and the courage to admit complicity with what Spillers calls "The Great Long National Shame."

From slave narratives and other documents Paula Giddings uncovers the stories of black women in a constant struggle to protect themselves and their daughters from white male sexual aggression. The Otherness of racial imprint would color the discourse about bodies in the nineteenth century, a discourse relating science and sexuality, the development of capitalism and bourgeois order. If, as Michel Foucault alleges, the discourse on sexuality is sustained by a regime of power/knowledge/pleasure, the important issues are "the fact that we speak of it; who speaks of it; . . . the institutions that incite us to speak of it, that package and diffuse what is said; in sum the global 'discursive fact,' the 'putting into discourse' of sex." In no way would I argue that Sidonie de la Houssaye escapes a Victorian discursive economy, nor could I remove her from the subject position she is assigned as a Creole woman in small-town southern Louisiana. But she does illustrate Foucault's contention that the repression hypothesis with regard to sexuality is ill-founded; what we see instead is a compulsion to speak of "it," to put it into discourse.[21] It is in this regard that we could call the text truly "performative."

What the text performs are all the excesses, from exposure to ec-

20. Sigmund Freud, *Beyond the Pleasure Principle*, trans. and ed. James Strachey (New York, 1961). See esp. Freud's conclusion, pp. 56–58.

21. Paula Giddings, *When and Where I Enter: The Impact of Black Women on Race and Sex in America* (New York, 1984), 42–46; Michel Foucault, *Histoire de la sexualité: La Volonté de savoir* (Paris, 1976), 12, 18–20 (my translation).

stasy, that threaten bourgeois society. In undermining hypocritical codes of conduct with their multiple standards (male and female, black and white: *cf.* Sojourner Truth's "Ain't I a woman?"), the text performs duplicitously by saying one thing and doing another. In her compulsion to expose the scandal, de la Houssaye opens her text to the fruit of the tree of knowledge that Victorian culture forbade. By writing (on) the body of the Other, by telling the "secret," she can move in a space that her gender and class prohibited, but which as a writer she has the power to explore with relative freedom. The real chameleon is thus the writer herself. With Pierre Saulve, she can lift the charming little quadroon in her arms, experience a "frenetic desire" to possess her, "to suffocate her with caresses" (II, 23). In the "place" of Violetta, in turn, she can misbehave, be impudent, petulant, sensual. Like a druidess of ancient times, she can be a conjurer (I, 29). She can live in a palace surrounded by incomparable foods, flowers, furnishings, and servants. She can dress in rich jewels and Parisian silks, wear ermine wraps or sensual dressing gowns, spend all her time shopping, dancing, flirting, exposing her incomparable beauty at the opera and in town. With impunity she can, as "author," both name the quadroons and *call them out of their name.*[22]

Legitimacy is played off against illegitimacy; the Creole wife and children could die from inadequate provisions or actual abuse (II, 68–70) on the part of a husband who is encouraged, in the system of exchange, to choose the superfluous over the necessary, his sexuality being coded as an excess that must be expended regardless of the means. According to this system of putting sexuality into discourse, the man bears no responsibility for his choices, since they are not free. It is assumed that if he changes from a "gentleman, a good father, a tender spouse" into "a vile debauched wretch," it is due to forces beyond his control, namely the quadroon (II, 68). It does not occur to Hermine, nor presumably to de la Houssaye herself, that Pierre's "injustice and cruelty" are endemic to the patriarchal, bourgeois system in which they are located, of which he is an agent and producer, but which likewise produces him. When Saulve abandons his family, how-

22. In using the expression, to "call a person out of his/her name," traditional among blacks, at least in the South, as an extremely derogatory form of address, I am thinking particularly of the way Sherley Anne Williams employs it in *Dessa Rose* (New York, 1986) as a way of figuring a relationship between a black woman and a white woman, in which the names have to be evacuated before a real relationship can be joined.

ever, a new economy of subsistence ("use" value) is instituted in the household, from which all surplus is banished, even the children's schooling (II, 73). But although the combined initiative of Hermine and the children is self-sustaining for a while, the only son falls ill, and the family risks loss of the patronym with his death. The two systems then confront each other in the persons of Pierre's eldest daughter, Marie, and his mistress, Violetta. In the name of her desperate brother, Marie initiates an odyssey across town to seek her father. There she witnesses firsthand the transformation of men "from the choicest circles of society" who are no longer men at all, drunk, obscene, brutalized by debauchery. Faced with the women assembled at Violetta's dinner/orgy, whom she at once sees and refuses to countenance, Marie's final defense is a categorical exclusion: they "could not belong to the same sex as she" (II, 77).

The unaccustomed sight of such a child, pale and deprived of speech, literally struck dumb, so that she resembles "a statue of innocence and despair," temporarily restores a sort of order, brings the company to its senses, creates a new emotional charge, and magnetizes the wayward father, who follows his daughter home to his dying son. An extraordinary aspect of the scene is the willingness of the author, in violation of Victorian codes of class and gender, to thrust young Marie into contact with the Other woman, who in the text becomes her shadow/double. Marie is a sign of the "proper" young lady, in the sense of appropriate and appropriated. Although she recovers her father, Marie loses her fiancé to the same quadroon mistress and decides, finally, to take refuge in religion and become a nun. Interestingly, Violetta herself in her later years, "like all the old quadroons who had been famous wenches in their younger days, became devout" (II, 129). The work closes on the double image of the "angel and the demon" that had fragmented Victorian women into the Lady and the Other, the light and the dark.

The text of *Les Quarteronnes* inscribes complex relationships between the body and bourgeois ideology. The female body, which is exclusively dark (the white body is conspicuous by its absence, like the lady's *name*, which must never be exposed to public view), is improper, although it may be appropriated by any (entre)preneur with enough money. In the Creole world marriage is a property alliance: the woman is an object of exchange, her body an incubator, a vessel, for the patrimon(e)y and for reproducing a (man's) name. Women "of color," whose dresses, "cut down" to reveal shoulders and breasts, cling to bodies as perfect as the forms of the Venus de Medici, have exclusive rights to the body in (of) the text. With hair that cascades down to her waist, embellished only with flowers or brooches, unimpeded by the bonnets worn by proper ladies (I, 8), the quadroon is a sign looking for a signifier as the "lady" is a signifier looking for a material referent. Within the textual domain of the quadroon, the private is made public, the secret scandal revealed. Pleasure of the body (jouissance) is coded as negative, sex and death associated in a literal way when a lover leaps to his death to protect his mistress, a child dies to redeem his father, and most horrifying of all, a double murder consummates the incestuous coupling of a brother and a sister.

We would be foolish to trust that the whole of any story could be told, naïve to believe we could find the origin of any narrative. Still, to permit ourselves to be titillated by the sexual exploits of the "other" Victorians, our great-grandfathers, material or fictional, is to admit complicity with the racist, classist, and sexist heritage of our country and its high, medium, and low culture. In *Beloved,* Toni Morrison speaks movingly about the record of violence enacted on the body of the African-American woman and her children. Morrison's conclusion recalls to the reader the fate of the title character, a phantom, who had to be ritually resurrected for the story of bondage and survival to be written: "Everybody knew what she was called, but nobody knew her name. Disremembered and unaccounted for, she cannot be lost because no one is looking for her, and even if they were, how can they call her if they don't know her name? Although she has claim, she is not claimed."[23] Writers like Morrison, Gayl Jones, and Sherley Anne Williams are at least constructing the narrative space in which to (re)member and (re)insert the unclaimed souls into culture.

"Covered over" in de la Houssaye's work, or figured as an absence (negative space) in the text, are the mind and spirit of the quadroon and her people. Similarly, one notes a discursive refusal of signs or signifiers that would code the body of the white woman. The dialectical opposition of body and mind that are (re)produced in the text as quadroon and Creole would persist into the twentieth century and indeed into present readings of dark and light, self and other, sensual and spiritual, and all binary pairs that keep concepts of dominance and exchange firmly in place. Reading such a text brings us face to face with our own classism, sexism, and racism, so that we cannot help but wonder . . . what if Evangeline had been black?

23. Morrison, *Beloved,* 274.

Narrative procedures in de la Houssaye's work call the quadroons out of their names by insisting on the figural investment of the term *quadroon*. Calling them "quadroons" makes them anomalies in terms of sociometrical reference, leaving them suspended in a limbo of presocial space where there is no possibility of them signifying in their own name. It denies them nominative or subject status, thus reenacting a discourse of appropriation in which they are inserted as commodities in a closed economy of sexual exchange. What is missing is a sense of human value, as Bessie Head describes it in the African village of Serowe: although the place is neither exceptional nor prosperous, "there is a sense of wovenness, a wholeness in life here; a feeling of how strange and beautiful people can be—just living."[24] After all, we only expect writers to pursue their work with lucidity and courage. Perhaps Sidonie de la Houssaye did as well as she could, but as readers we must be prepared to demand more of our own analysis, to search for the missing traces and names, to refuse to take her "at her word." Sometimes it helps just to interrogate a founding metaphor: the trunks in our attics may not all contain treasures. As ugly a blight on our collective history as it is, African-American women writers have begun rewriting the narrative(s) of slavery and its aftermath in an attempt to look at it with "different" lenses, to reinvent the memories if necessary, to deconstruct the ideologies that have kept the names from being known, to exorcise our fears and write our desire(s), to initiate new reading and writing practices, to call us all back.

24. Bessie Head, *Serowe: Village of the Rain Wind* (London, 1981), x. This study of a large Botswanan town where Head lived in exile from South Africa for ten years is a paradigmatic view of a traditional African community.

Mollie Moore Davis.
Courtesy the Historic
New Orleans Collection,
Museum/Research Center,
Acc. No. 85.65.L

During the last years
of her life, this typi-
cal French Quarter
building at 505 Royal
was Mollie Moore
Davis' home.
Photo by K. W. "Jake"
Jacobs

Mollie Moore Davis
A Literary Life

MOLLIE E. MOORE DAVIS was nationally known at the turn of the century for her novels, short stories, and poetry. A popular author who wrote for mass-market magazines, she used southern settings and themes to considerable advantage, garnering good reviews during her lifetime. Although much of her work is still enjoyable reading, her literary reputation has not survived the eclipse of the romantic style. In New Orleans, at any rate, of more importance than her work was her life—as much a conscious creation as any novel. For thirty years, her influence on the cultural and intellectual life of the city was immense.

Mollie Moore came from that class of Americans who defined themselves as "quality folks."[1] Community leaders in small-town and rural America, quality folks saw themselves—and were seen by others—as respectable, responsible, and somehow superior. Although not wealthy, they viewed themselves as civilized and supported the institutions of civilization: they were the mainstays of the local schools, churches, and projects for community or cultural uplift.

Mary Evelina Moore, the second of nine children, was born in 1844 to just such a family in Talladega, Alabama. Her father had come from Massachusetts to the newly opened Creek frontier to make his fortune. He completed medical training and married in Alabama, but he was never very successful. In 1855 the Moores loaded furniture, household goods, and children into a wagon and set out on the long journey west. In central Texas, their destination, they rented a small piece of land, scratching out a living by farming and hunting, while the doctor also practiced medicine. A hand-to-mouth existence was the pattern of their lives for years to come.[2]

---

1. Mollie Moore Godbold, Mollie Moore Davis' niece, namesake, and a writer on family history, titled her reminiscences about the Moore family "Quality Folks." Mollie Moore Godbold to Evelyn Jahncke, March 29, 1954, in Jahncke Papers, Historic New Orleans Collection (hereinafter cited as HNOC).

2. All the information on Davis' early life in this essay is taken from Clyde W. Wilkinson, "The Broadening Stream: The Life and Literary Career of Mollie E. Moore Davis" (Ph.D. dissertation, University of Illinois, 1947), 1–109.

Young Mary clearly stood out in the family as unusually intelligent and talented. Her opportunities, though, were limited by poverty. Her mother, not particularly well-educated herself, taught the children all she could. Their official schooling was sporadic, frequently interrupted by an absence of nearby schools or a lack of money to pay fees, by the family's frequent moves, and in Mary's case, by her mother's need for help with the house and her brothers.

In 1860 the sixteen-year-old girl became second assistant at a private school in the east Texas town of Tyler, teaching the smaller children. The same year, Dr. Moore noted that the Tyler *Reporter*, one of two local newspapers, had printed a "poem by Mollie (that is Mary)."

This public change of name was no mere happenstance. Young Mary Evelina had begun the transformation of herself into Mollie Evelyn Moore, poetess (as she declared herself in the 1860 census)—and very much a personage. She signed her work Mollie E. Moore, and when she married she continued to use that name for a few years. She then published as M. E. M. Davis and Mrs. Mollie E. Moore Davis, and signed her letters Mollie Moore Davis.

Names were obviously significant to her. In the semiautobiographical *Jaconetta: Her Loves*, set in exactly this pre–Civil War period, the narrator, also called Mary, rejects her commonplace name—"Those around me addressed me by the more homely name [Mary] bestowed upon me"—to assume a name of her own choice.[3] The author had done the same, and the change was final. Never again was she known as Mary.

Mollie E. Moore's poetic output was spurred by the approaching Civil War, the beauties of nature, and family sorrows; the local paper began to refer to her as "the song bird of Texas." The patriotism provoked by the war gave Mollie her chance both to achieve a wider audience and to further her education. Patriotic poetry was at a premium in southern newspapers, and by 1861, when she was seventeen, her poems began to be reprinted in other Texas papers, including the Houston *Telegraph*, owned and edited by E. H. Cushing. Cushing, an avid reader with wide-ranging literary interests, saw something special in the as-yet-undeveloped work of the young country girl. He and his wife invited her to make a visit of several months with them in Houston.

Mollie arrived at the Cushings' home in 1862 and began an educa-

3. Mollie Moore Davis, *Jaconetta: Her Loves* (Boston, 1901), 1.

tion both in books and in life-style. The metropolis of Houston, with some 10,000 residents, offered an array of entertainment—theaters, libraries, newspapers, concerts, and lectures. This was living, and after her restricted opportunities, Mollie was ready to live and to learn. Houston and the Cushings themselves became her finishing school and her college, exposing her to wealth, gracious living, and the most intellectual company the city had to offer. The Cushings, like her later acquaintances, did not grasp just how impoverished her youth had been.

For the next five years Mollie alternated living with the Cushings and living at home. She wrote prolifically—mostly poetry, which was published by Texas newspapers. Cushing made plans for the publication of the first collected volume of her poetry; Cushing and Cave of Houston would bring the book out, although it would be printed in New York.

The publication of *Minding the Gap and Other Poems* in 1867 and the reprinting of the volume, along with additional poems, two years later, established Mollie's place in Texas letters; a few critics outside the state reviewed the book, and Professor James Wood Davidson of Columbia University praised her work in his *Living Writers of the South*. She was also profiled in Mary Tardy's *Living Female Writers of the South*.[4]

Mollie's personal situation stood in stark contrast with her professional success. Her mother died in 1867, and for the next seven years—throughout her twenties—Mollie cared for the Moore family. Her father was hard-pressed financially, and her writing became the source of much-needed income. Through Cushing's influence she became a weekly contributor to the Galveston *News*, which paid her a regular small salary. She was devoted to her family, but the difference between the domestic drudgery at home and the freedom she had enjoyed with the Cushings was painful. Visits to her friends in Houston and an active social life in Galveston were bright spots, but her family responsibilities greatly constrained her life.

"Counsel," one of her most famous poems, was written at this time. Reflecting her feeling that friendship was almost holy, the poem advised: "Therefore, lest sudden death should come between, / Or time, or distance, clasp with pressure true / The palm of him who goeth forth," and concluded, "Lest with thee henceforth, night and day, /

---

4. James Wood Davidson, *Living Writers of the South* (New York, 1869); Mary T. Tardy, *Living Female Writers of the South* (Philadelphia, 1872).

Regret should walk." Mollie herself took this advice to heart: she was known for her delicate attentions to her friends—complimentary notes about a reading or a piece of writing, personal poems written to celebrate special events in their lives, support for their activities, and frequent visits. "Counsel" appeared in the Galveston *News* in 1870; it was frequently reprinted well into the twentieth century.[5]

In 1872 Cushing and Cave published another edition of her poems, including many from the first edition, but newer work as well. The dedication of the second part to a knight with all "the grace and pride of Chivalry" signaled her romance with the man she would marry in 1874, Thomas E. Davis. Major Davis, a former Confederate officer, had set up a very successful tobacco business in Galveston; he was a well-to-do and popular member of the society Mollie adorned. During their courtship and the first year of marriage, she published very little.

Once again, though, hard times struck: Major Davis' business failed in the financial panic of 1875. Not only did he have to find a way to make a living—at forty—but, honorably, he also insisted on paying all his debts, a pledge that burdened the Davises financially for some years. He turned to newspaper work in Houston, using the Cushing connection to find a job. By 1877 he was editor of the Houston *Telegram*. Mollie also began writing regularly for a living again, first for the Galveston *News* and then for the Houston *Telegram*.

In 1879 the Davises made the move that defined their lives: Major Davis accepted a position as an associate editor of the New Orleans *Times,* and by August they had moved to the Crescent City. They rented rooms downtown on Carondelet Street, in an area honey-combed with boardinghouses. Newspaper salaries were not high, and the couple still may have been burdened with debt. Besides money worries, Mollie Davis suffered severe emotional shocks in 1879: both her father and E. H. Cushing, virtually her second father, died that year; she suffered a miscarriage; and she showed symptoms of the family lung ailment, apparently tuberculosis, that had afflicted her mother and three of her brothers.[6]

What sort of city had the Davises chosen for their new start? The antebellum New Orleans of unlimited economic opportunity—one of

5. Mollie Moore Davis, "Counsel," in *Selected Poems by Mollie E. Moore Davis* (New Orleans, 1927).

6. New Orleans City Directory (hereinafter cited as NOCD), 1880; "List of Letters," New Orleans *Times,* August 3, 1879, p. 9; "List of Autographed Books," 2, in Jahncke Papers; Wilkinson, "Broadening Stream," 110–13.

the richest cities in the country, an entrepôt of international trade and an important theatrical and artistic center—had disappeared with the war. New Orleans in 1879 was poor: the mouth of the river was silted over, few ships docked in the port, business was lackadaisical. The city was dirty and poorly lit, few streets outside the downtown area were paved, and the water supply was unsafe. Disease infested the place. Not only endemic illnesses such as typhoid, smallpox, malaria, and diphtheria, but also recurrent epidemics—a devastating attack of yellow fever had killed four thousand the previous summer—gave New Orleans a frightful reputation.[7]

From such unpromising materials, Mollie Moore Davis molded the life she wanted. To an extent the Cushings were her models, but she lacked their comfortable fortune. Rather than money, her tools were imagination, intelligence, charm, and talent. She was able to live modestly—and as the Gilded Age grew more flamboyant, to make such a life seem a virtue.

A downtown boardinghouse lacked flair: she needed a setting with a certain cachet. A new acquaintance, George Washington Cable, influenced her search for the proper milieu. Cable had dropped full-time reporting some years before for the more lucrative profession of bookkeeping, but had continued to write articles for the local papers. Soon after their arrival, the Davises met Cable through mutual friends in the newspaper business. In 1879 he was enjoying—and suffering from—the first flush of celebrity: *Old Creole Days* had come out in May of that year and had become an immediate success. On August 13, he autographed a copy, "To Mrs. Davis (Mollie E. Moore) . . . with the prayer to heaven she may live to look back upon these present times and call them with something of affection, Old Creole Days." Appealing to Davis' strong imagination and romantic streak, Cable's tales sent her house hunting in the oldest part of the city, the Vieux Carré, or French Quarter.[8]

For Anglo-Americans, moving to the Quarter was extremely odd. In 1879 that part of the city was, not to put too fine a point on it, a decaying slum. Since the glory days of the 1830s, there had been a long slide downward. There were still pockets of gentility, individual

---

7. Joy J. Jackson, *New Orleans in the Gilded Age: Politics and Urban Progress, 1880–1896* (Baton Rouge, 1969), 4, 21; John P. Dyer, *Tulane: The Biography of a University, 1834–1965* (New York, 1966), 146–48.

8. Louis D. Rubin, Jr., *George W. Cable: The Life and Times of a Southern Heretic* (New York, 1969), 34–37, 73; "List of Autographed Books," 2, in Jahncke Papers.

houses or blocks where appearance was maintained and respectability reigned. Some of the old Creole families still remained, too stubborn or entrenched to abandon their fine homes to the encroaching deterioration of the neighborhood, or simply too poor to be able to do so. The panics of 1837 and 1857, the Civil War, and postwar depression had impoverished many of the former gentry. Those of the grand old families who could afford it had generally deserted the Quarter for the Esplanade ridge or, occasionally, Uptown.

Undaunted, Mollie Moore Davis sallied forth downtown, searching Royal Street for a suitable home. Through a veil of myth, she saw and wrote of the Quarter, which in her mind became the setting for a (mythical) Creole aristocracy. But the shrewdness of the Texan who had had to make do all her life also came into play. On the moderate salary earned by a newspaperman and the bits she was then paid for her writing, the Davises could not afford an impressive establishment in the newer parts of town. In the Quarter, Davis found some of the cheapest rentals in New Orleans. Turning unpleasant reality inside out, Davis could drape any deficiencies in their living arrangements in the rosy gauze of romance—and by extraordinary force of character, convince others to accept her view.

She persevered, moving in 1880 to an apartment in the third block of Royal Street, and to another in the same block the following year, when Major Davis joined the *Picayune* as a reporter. In 1882 Mollie Davis finally found what she had been looking for in the fourth block of Royal, three buildings down from Conti. Here the Davises would live for over twenty years. Both sides of the block were lined with small shops—boots and shoes, hairpieces, fancy goods, furniture; there were also a plumber, a cutler, and a bank.[9]

The Davises' new home, 84 Royal Street (later 406, when streets were renumbered in 1894), was a typical Vieux Carré three-story brick townhouse with a wrought-iron balcony on the second story supported by an iron colonnade. The shop downstairs was rented to a piano tuner. Entered through a heavy, dull-red door to the left of the shop, the narrow carriageway "whose walls [were] wrought in fantastic arabesque by the mould and the peeling plaster" emerged into a small, brick-paved courtyard with a cistern and other necessary offices. Against a wall rested "an enormous high-shouldered, mildewed earthen jar, like those wherein the Forty Thieves did hide themselves."

9. *D. H. Holmes Fancy Goods . . . 1883 by J. Popper* (map), Richard Koch photographs of Royal and Conti streets, *ca.* 1903, Curatorial Collection, HNOC; NOCD 1881–1885.

In Davis' eyes "this old court" was clothed in the mystery and romance of the past:

> In this old court what feet have strayed
> ....
> The powdered dame in gold brocade
> The courtly beau, the saucy jade
> ....
> Their ghosts the silences pervade
> In this old court.

Davis embellished the courtyard consciously in keeping with her ideas—with lush green plants in clay pots and with Don Estaban, a large red macaw whose cage hung in one of the surrounding arches.[10]

A curving flight of steps at the end of the passageway led up to a hall, which opened into graceful, high-ceilinged rooms with tall windows facing onto a plant-filled balcony overlooking Royal Street. Gauzy drapes and louvered shutters could shut out the street, but Davis often threw them open to enjoy the stream of exotic people below—the "calla tout chaud" girl, the praline woman, "colored nuns, 'nigger' musicians, Indian women with gombo filé." A special pleasure was watching from her balcony "all the processions at Carnival time"; Momus, Proteus, and Comus all paraded on Royal Street.[11]

During their first five years in New Orleans, Major Davis strove to establish his credentials as a newspaperman, and Mollie Davis revamped her writing career while also busily making friends, creating her French Quarter environment, and battling ill health. Each summer she fled the humid, oppressive heat of New Orleans, usually making the trek by train and wagon to the dry hills of west Texas. There she had her own room in her brother Tom's house. His children were forbidden to disturb her while she wrote, but she also spent time with the family walking, riding, and engaging in other exercise. While en-

10. Vieux Carré Survey, squares 39–40 (406 Royal St.), HNOC; NOCD 1883–1904; "Keren-happuch and I," New Orleans *Picayune*, November 30, 1884, p. 11; "In This Old Court," *Art and Letters*, I (August, 1887), 122; Mollie Moore Godbold, "Letters from Pearl Davis Jahncke, and Other Material Regarding M. E. M. Davis, Compiled for Mary Evelyn Jahncke in 1956," in Jahncke Papers, 19; Mollie Moore Davis, "An Old House in Royal Street," in Jahncke Papers.

11. Vieux Carré Survey, squares 39–40 (406 Royal St.), HNOC; Godbold, "Letters," in Jahncke Papers, 19; Mollie Moore Davis to Ella Farman Pratt, March 4, [1888], Dr. Horace A. Horton Papers, Rare Books and Manuscripts, Howard-Tilton Memorial Library, Tulane University (hereinafter cited as TU); Interview with Charles L. Mackie, October 29, 1988.

joying this sort of recuperation, she also gathered raw material, which she refined in her literary work.[12]

From 1872 until 1879, her writing had been spotty—frequently interrupted for long stretches and marked by inferior work. Force of circumstances now pushed her into a new phase. During the nineteen years she had been publishing, Davis' natural idiom had been poetry, and her market had been primarily newspapers—notorious for the low fees paid their writers. Like most southern women writers, Davis needed the money she earned: writing was no ladylike avocation, but her business, and she began to work hard at it. Earlier, she had written occasional short stories; now, because prose paid better than poetry, she pursued the craft in earnest and began to find her voice in stories for children. She analyzed her own talent for this audience: "I have been very much associated with children all my life. I 'get on' wonderfully with them."[13]

In 1879, shortly before moving to New Orleans, Davis had broken into the lucrative and expanding children's-magazine market. She placed a story that year with *Wide Awake,* a recently founded illustrated magazine for children published by Daniel Lothrop in Boston. She was a steady contributor to the periodical until it ceased publication in 1893.[14] In these new stories she exploited popular forms: black dialect, which Joel Chandler Harris had recently popularized; Creole settings, for which George Washington Cable had paved the way; and frontier life, based on her Texas background. The latter stories, depicting her most immediate experiences, are the most clearly realized. Her use of black dialect, an immensely popular genre at the time, is heavy-handed and hard going for a modern reader; her more sparing representation of Texas accents is much more effective. The picturesque backgrounds to the Creole stories are well sketched, but the characters are overly romanticized.

Prose became Davis' usual form of literary expression, but she continued to write poetry for special occasions and for her friends. In the nineteenth century, poetry was considered basic to civilized life. The literate were expected to write poetry: lovers wrote poems to each other's charms, friends wrote poems in each other's autograph books.

12. Godbold, "Letters," in Jahncke Papers, 4–16.
13. Wilkinson, "Broadening Stream," 129; Davis to Pratt, March 4, [1888], in Horton Papers.
14. Wilkinson, "Broadening Stream," 109; Frank Luther Mott, *A History of American Magazines* (5 vols.; Cambridge, Mass., 1936–68), III, 508–509.

Given this cultural centrality, a poem was almost always commissioned for important public ceremonies; it would be read during the event and published in the program and in newspaper accounts. Following the lead of the poet Mary Ashley Townsend, Davis was frequently called on to write such occasional verse: for the dedication of the San Jacinto Monument in Houston; for Woman's Day at the North, South, and Central American Exposition; for the commemoration of the settlement of Louisiana; for celebrations at the Round Table Club and Tulane University; and for a reunion of University of Virginia alumni.[15]

Davis also wrote pieces now and then for the *Picayune,* a major cultural force in New Orleans. Eliza Jane Nicholson, the first southern woman to publish a major newspaper, had breathed new life into a humdrum provincial journal. In the 1880s, under Nicholson's guidance, the *Picayune* introduced a society column (a boon to the social historian), led reform movements against the lottery and for public education, and published many writers who later became famous. The paper also brought together many of the city's most creative and talented people. Because of Major Davis' position, the couple became friendly with the Nicholsons and with the other writers associated with the paper.[16]

The *Picayune* was one of the movers in the economic and cultural revitalization of New Orleans in the mid-1880s, as the city started to stir from its long postwar torpor. Businessmen and community leaders dreamed of a return to prewar golden days. Street paving and electrification were visible symbols of the city's awakening.[17] Hand in hand with commercial development went an intellectual flowering. Antebellum New Orleans culture had favored music and the theater, supporting both touring and resident theatrical and opera companies. Not surprisingly, the city continued to be a regular stop on the traveling circuit for major stars and for more mundane touring companies; in the 1880s literature and the arts flourished as well. Certainly writers and fine artists had worked in New Orleans before the Civil War, but since the late 1870s a self-conscious community of writers and artists, friends and acquaintances, had grown up—meeting so-

15. Wilkinson, "Broadening Stream," 113–63 *passim;* Scrapbooks, in Jahncke Papers.

16. *Dictionary of American Biography*, XIII, 499; Lamar Whitlow Bridges, "A Study of the New Orleans *Daily Picayune* Under Publisher Eliza Jane Poitevent Nicholson, 1876–1896" (Ph.D. dissertation, Southern Illinois University, 1974).

17. Dyer, *Tulane,* 148.

cially, forming clubs and organizations, criticizing and nurturing one another's work.[18] Their ranks would be swelled by new artists attracted to the city by the developments of the eighties.

Besides the *Picayune,* two other institutions were especially vital to the city's cultural growth in the 1880s: the World's Fair of 1884–1885 (officially styled the World's Industrial and Cotton Centennial Exposition), and Tulane University, along with its coordinate women's college, Newcomb.

The World's Fair was supposed to spur the sluggish New Orleans economy, but it became a financial, logistical, and organizational nightmare. (As a *Picayune* reporter, Major Davis covered the exposition for its five-month run. Because of the quality of his articles, he was promoted to a position on the editorial staff, which led to his eventual appointment as editor in chief of the paper.)[19] Culturally, however, the fair, particularly the Women's Department, was a great success. Disorganization and financial embarrassments delayed the opening of the department, but the selection of the redoubtable Julia Ward Howe as director solved those problems. Howe made friends in the city, including Mollie Moore Davis, and began raising money through benefit entertainments. The displays, which finally opened in the middle of January, 1885, were of mixed value. The best of them was the Creole Exhibit: Howe persuaded members of the old white Creole families to lend memorabilia, portraits, furniture, and all manner of things. (For most white New Orleanians in the post–Civil War period, *Creole* was a narrowly defined, elite designation reserved for white descendants of original French and Spanish colonists; Creoles of color were not invited to participate.) The exhibit was much commented on; it validated Mollie Davis' fascination with Creole society and the French Quarter.[20]

Howe also hired the New England artists William and Ellsworth Woodward and brought them down to teach arts and crafts to New Orleans women. After the fair ended, the Woodward brothers stayed in the city and were instrumental in forming the outstanding Newcomb Art School. Although they lived Uptown, both—especially

18. Jackson, *Gilded Age,* 123; Robert C. Reinders, *End of an Era: New Orleans, 1850–1860* (New Orleans, 1964), chap. 10; Judith Bonner, "*Art and Letters:* An Illustrated Periodical of the Nineteenth Century," *Southern Quarterly,* XXVII (January, 1989), 60.

19. D. Clive Hardy, *The World's Industrial and Cotton Centennial Exposition* (New Orleans, 1978), 8, 20; Bridges, "Study of the New Orleans *Daily Picayune,*" 291–92.

20. Hardy, *World's Industrial and Cotton Centennial Exposition,* 14–15.

William—were staunch defenders of the architectural merit of the French Quarter and were early preservationists.[21]

More important than the World's Fair to the cultural life of New Orleans was Tulane University. The University of Louisiana, located in New Orleans, had been known primarily for its medical school; in the 1880s, with new funds and a new president, and reorganized and renamed, Tulane University became the intellectual center of the city. The opening exercises were held in October, 1884; over five hundred students were enrolled. In 1887 the university was joined by a woman's Newcomb College.[22] The early faculty, including Alcée Fortier, John Rose Ficklen, Jennie Caldwell Nixon, and the Woodward brothers, were seen as social assets; they became part of Davis' circle and moved freely in local society.

Now in her forties, Davis continued educating herself. She organized a weekly French class, which met at her home. More daringly, she founded the second women's club in New Orleans. Although the club movement was in full bloom in the North, women's clubs were suspect in the South; they represented a radical departure from the notion that a woman's proper place was in the home. The first two clubs in New Orleans were started by writers, already accustomed to nontraditional roles. The first, the Woman's Club, was founded by Elizabeth Bisland in 1884, and the second, the Geographics, by Davis in the same year. In the days before the *National Geographic* and television, the world was a mysterious and glamorous place; armchair travel was a passion of the educated. The Geographics seriously studied the countries of the world; one country at a time was selected, and each member presented a paper on some aspect of it—religion, art, literature, topography—until the club had thoroughly covered that nation. Davis was elected president for life by her fellow members.[23]

Wealth and antebellum family background were the usual, but not indispensable, qualifications for entry into New Orleans society. The Davises were talented, intelligent, literate, and well mannered; their circle of friends grew ever wider as they became the guests of the wealthy and the well connected. Their own entertaining became more frequent, although never more elaborate. In 1885 Davis established Friday as her formal day to receive callers. At simple afternoon receptions she welcomed friends from Tulane, from her clubs, from the

---

21. *Encyclopaedia of New Orleans Artists, 1718–1918* (New Orleans, 1987), 420–24.
22. Dyer, *Tulane*, chap. 4.
23. Lillian Brewster Sauer, *Women's Clubs of New Orleans* (New Orleans, 1930), 6–7.

Picayune, and, increasingly, from both Uptown and downtown society. Writers congregated in her drawing room—Elizabeth Bisland, Martha Field (who wrote as Catherine Cole), Lafcadio Hearn, Eliza Jane Nicholson, Mary Ashley Townsend (the poet Xariffa), Ruth McEnery Stuart, May W. Mount, Grace King, George Washington Cable, and Kate Chopin (during a visit to the city from St. Louis). The artists came too—William and Ellsworth Woodward, Brors Anders Wikstrom, Mary Given Sheerer—and their paintings graced her walls. Then there were Creole and Anglo members of "society." In scrapbooks, Davis carefully kept clippings of newspaper stories about her entertainments. She had a genius for social life—and she loved it.[24]

In October, 1884, she placed her first short story (for adult readers) with a nationally circulated magazine. Founded less than a year earlier, the *Current* was one of the most important ventures of Chicago literary circles. It mixed public-affairs commentary with fiction and poetry; its contributors included some of the most brilliant writers in the nation.[25]

Although a national reputation was her aim, Davis also felt a responsibility to the local intelligentsia. She worked with her friend Mary Ashley Townsend on the distinguished *Art and Letters,* a journal with illustrations by the Woodwards and Wikstrom. Her only published contributions were two poems, but she was sympathetic to the undertaking, which proved unfortunately short-lived.[26]

Davis became steadily more successful in the 1880s and 1890s. She was published by the leading magazines of the country. She continued to write stories regularly for *Wide Awake,* as well as for *Harper's Young People, Youth's Companion,* and other magazines for children. In 1888 and 1889 she began to publish poems and stories in *Harper's* and other well-known magazines, appearing in the prestigious *Atlantic Monthly* in 1893. Her best stories continued to be those with a Texas frontier theme, although those with a romantic New Orleans background were probably more popular.[27]

In the 1880s she also began to reimagine her own past, using sup-

24. New Orleans *Picayune,* December 6, 1885, p. 5; M. E. M. Davis, *Keren-Happuch and I* (New Orleans, 1907), 9–22; Scrapbooks, in Jahncke Papers.

25. Wilkinson, "Broadening Stream," 116; Mott, *History of American Magazines,* III, 54.

26. Bonner, *"Art and Letters,"* 66; Davis to Pratt, March 4, [1888], in Horton Papers; Mollie E. Moore Davis, "The Poet's Wife," *Art and Letters,* I (February, 1887), 21; Davis, "In This Old Court."

27. Wilkinson, "Broadening Stream," 129–38.

posedly autobiographical sketches as a vehicle to popularize her fantasies for public consumption. She began in 1884 in the *Picayune* with "Keren-happuch and I," a series of pieces on her adventures in house hunting and living in New Orleans. Although describing the city and its inhabitants factually, she heavily modified the "I" character and established a fanciful tone toward her own life that was at odds with its sharp-edged realities. In the opening piece, "We Come to Town," she wrote: "One day I was sitting on the steps of a plantation-house, very idle and, in truth, horribly *ennuyée*. . . . All at once I sat up inspired . . . 'Keren-happuch . . . Let us go to New Orleans.'"[28] This is the first mention of the mythical family plantation home, which Davis gave the elegant name La Rose Blanche; the remaking of her life had begun.

Davis embroidered on the theme of a prosperous past in a series of sketches published in *Wide Awake,* beginning in December, 1886. In her story "In War Times at La Rose Blanche," the first-person narrator, an eight-year-old girl, relates loosely connected incidents of life on a plantation during the Civil War. The family is well-to-do, the house is large, and the father has an impressive library of the classics—both a financial and an intellectual status symbol. Devoted slaves serve the happy group; there is even a personal body servant for each child. Most people assumed that the series was a generally accurate account of Davis' girlhood; even her close friends believed that she had come from a privileged plantation background rather than the hardscrabble childhood of fact.[29]

The series was extremely popular; readers responded to its romantic representation of plantation life and its humane view of innocent boys fighting on both sides in the Civil War. The public response caused the publisher of *Wide Awake,* Daniel Lothrop, to bring out the collected series in 1888—Davis' first published book of prose. It was received very favorably.[30]

"In War Times at La Rose Blanche" also created a false impression of Davis' age. The narrator is eight years old—eight years younger than Davis was at the time in question. The difference probably was not intended to deceive, but was merely a fictional device to appeal to her youthful audience. However, when 1852 (rather than the correct

28. New Orleans *Picayune,* November 30, 1884–March 29, 1885.

29. Wilkinson, "Broadening Stream," 123; Ruth Ramay, "Mollie E. Moore Davis," *Current Topics,* II (November, 1891), 3–5.

30. Wilkinson, "Broadening Stream," 123.

1844) began to appear in print as her birth date, she did not correct it, and 1852 still appears in major reference works. Even her husband was confused about her birth date: he knew that she had not been born in 1852, but he had 1845 placed on her tombstone—and got the month and day wrong to boot.[31]

The misunderstandings about Davis' background and age may have been begun accidentally, but there is no doubt that she deliberately cemented the false impressions in the public's mind with the publication of *Jaconetta: Her Loves* in 1901. Long after she might have provided the facts, she returned to the form of the autobiographical sketch—emphasizing again a youthful narrator on a plantation.

Whatever the desires that led her to an involved reinventing of her past, Davis had long wanted a child. She had yearned over her brother Tom's baby—the "sweet little darling that I would like to keep in my arms all the time." She had suffered at least one miscarriage, and at forty-two was unlikely to bear a child. In 1886 she and the major adopted Fannie Pearl Moore, the four-year-old daughter of her brother Hartwell, who was experiencing family difficulties. In the nineteenth century, adoptions among family members were common; there was neither stigma nor secrecy involved in them. Davis had been a responsible and loving sister to all her brothers. Hartwell could feel sure that his young daughter would have a happy and secure upbringing.

Davis renamed the little girl Mary Pearl, but the child was always called Pearl. A plump cherub with masses of blonde curls and large round eyes, Pearl was as pretty as an illustration on a chocolate box and the darling of her parents' hearts. Davis doted on "the dear funny little Girl, whose sunniness . . . pervade[s] the Old House, bringing the joy of April into every nook and cranny of it." Indeed, so devoted was Davis that she frequently styled herself "Mother of Pearl" in correspondence; friends, such as the children's author Gelett Burgess, also began to use the name affectionately.[32]

While devoting herself to young Pearl and to her writing in the late 1880s, Davis still suffered periods of illness. Apparently she was

31. *Ibid.*, 125–26; Perpetual Care, Bill 3616, Contract Book 9, Metairie Cemetery.

32. Godbold, "Letters," in Jahncke Papers, 5; Interview with Mrs. C. Dawson Moore, Jr., October 20, 1988; Newspaper clipping in scrapbook, in Jahncke Papers; Davis, *Keren-Happuch*, 9; Mollie Moore Godbold to Evelyn Jancke, August 16, 1956, in Jahncke Papers; Mollie Moore Davis to Adèle Townsend Stanton, [March 1, 1892], Townsend-Stanton Family Papers, TU: "List of Autographed Books," in Jahncke Papers, 1.

free of lung trouble by this time, but she continued to complain of ill health to her friends and to suffer periods of exhaustion. She continued to leave New Orleans in the summer, now with Pearl in tow. They spent time in Beaver Meadow, Alabama; in Mexico—where Pearl contracted a serious case of typhoid; and in west Texas with the Moores.[33]

Socially, Davis' place was secure; the *Times-Democrat* declared that "she is one of the most widely known women in society, and . . . scarcely any public gathering of note is complete without her presence." Her Friday reception days had evolved into what she considered a salon: the notion was so compelling to her that she placed a clipping entitled "The Salon in America" in her scrapbook; she probably wrote the piece. The article, in effect, describes Davis' style of entertaining: conversation was the order of the day; dancing, refreshment rooms filled with food, and formal programs would have interfered with the salon's purpose. "A salon is a woman's work. . . . It is a place of resort for men and women of brains and wit, where fashion is subservient to mind, and where the twaddlers cease to twaddle."[34]

The Friday receptions that made Davis' reputation in New Orleans social tradition were the "Fridays in February." In 1890 she began hosting special entertainments on the Fridays of Lent; in 1891 she formally settled on the Fridays in February, a feature of the Carnival season for the next decade and more. Refreshments were simple: black coffee, sherry, and small cakes. No hired waiters or butlers served the guests; rather, Davis prevailed on the young debutantes of her acquaintance to serve—and they considered it an honor. Davis received guests at one end of the drawing room, assisted by several of her close friends. Pearl and her small friends were always included; they enjoyed mingling with the guests and following the young ladies around.

No invitations were sent: simply, the right people knew that they would be welcome. The "worthwhile New Orleans folk" and "all the well-known strangers" assembled at the house on Royal Street on those Friday afternoons from three until six. A few came by carriage or cab, but most probably walked or arrived on the mule-drawn (after 1896, electric) streetcars of the Clio line, which ran up Royal Street.

33. Wilkinson, "Broadening Stream," 130; Mollie Moore Davis to Adèle Townsend Stanton, *passim*, Townsend-Stanton Family Papers; Mollie Moore Davis to William Beer, *passim*, William Beer Papers, TU.

34. Newspaper clippings in Scrapbook, in Jahncke Papers.

By the mid-1890s, Davis' guest list had been considerably enlarged by out-of-town visitors come to enjoy the "must-do's" of Carnival—her Fridays were one of them. Like other society matrons, Davis welcomed the admirals and officers of visiting fleets (both American and foreign), generals and bishops, explorers and archaeologists, poets and historians. Unlike some hostesses, she was particularly fond of actors, inviting theatrical troupes such as those of Madame Helene Modjeska, Otis Skinner, and Joseph Jefferson. Other celebrities—Eugene Field, Frances Willard, Horace Fletcher, Thomas Nelson Page, Charles Dudley Warner, Joaquin Miller, Josiah Royce, Booth Tarkington—lent further glamour to her salon.[35]

In 1895, Davis entered the third phase of her career. At fifty-one, an age when many writers are repeating the works of their youth, she published her first novel, *Under the Man-Fig*. Houghton Mifflin of Boston, which published all her subsequent novels, printed 1,650 copies, all of which sold. Although not a best seller by any means, the book earned favorable reviews and provided a respectable start for her new literary endeavor.[36] (Today *Under the Man-Fig*, like Davis' later novels, reads almost as if it consisted of two mismatched works precariously joined together. The plot is romantic and unrealistic, and the main characters are wooden dolls whose dialogue is nobly highfalutin; but the array of colorful secondary characters, the Texas setting, and the country life-style give the book vitality.)

Throughout the late 1890s Davis concentrated on longer works. In 1897 Harper's published a collected edition of her stories. Containing some of her best, the volume garnered excellent reviews. The same year she published a history of Texas for children. Although her output of short stories had slowed as she concentrated on novels and other book-length manuscripts, the stories she produced were well received. In 1899 she broke into the premier wide-circulation magazine for fiction writers, the *Saturday Evening Post*. During the next few years she wrote mainly for the *Post*, which consistently featured stories by major writers; she also occasionally placed stories in *Smart Set* and the *Atlantic Monthly*.[37]

Davis also published three novels in this general period: *The Wire Cutters* (1899; 2,500 copies); *The Queen's Garden* (1900; 2,500 copies);

35. Godbold, "Letters," in Jahncke Papers, 20–22; "Cynthia St. Charles' Letter," New Orleans *Item*, February 15, 1914, Sec. 2, p. 2; Louis C. Hennick and E. Harper Charlton, *The Streetcars of New Orleans* (Gretna, La., 1975), 78–80; Davis, *Keren-Happuch*, 9–22.

36. Wilkinson, "Broadening Stream," 140–41.

37. *Ibid.*, 144–46, 152–57; Mott, *History of American Magazines*, IV, 671–86.

and *The Little Chevalier* (1903; 3,000 copies), as well as the fictionalized memoir *Jaconetta: Her Loves* (1901; 2,500 copies). The plots continued to be very romantic, and Creole and plantation life were highly idealized. Of these works, *The Wire Cutters* is the strongest—largely because of its authentic presentation of Texas frontier life, Davis' forte as a writer. The story line involves two secret adoptions, cases of mistaken identity, highly unrealistic ideas about heredity, and a hero of godlike magnanimity. But the novel comes to life when the Texans come on stage. The vivid characterization of their frontier eccentricities is almost Dickensian in flavor. The postmaster, an important supporting character, is modeled on Davis' brother Tom. The descriptions of the postmaster's family, friends, house, neighbors, politics, and general way of life are taken directly from an 1881 journal or letter (the first and last pages are missing) that Davis wrote while visiting Tom's family in west Texas.[38]

Davis' adult life had been periodically interrupted by bouts of illness. At the beginning of 1903, she was so ill that she canceled her Fridays in February (the *Picayune* announced that she and Pearl would be at home in a very private way to their special friends). Davis at first believed this to be merely another spell, but it was the first sign of cancer. The Fridays in February were never resumed.[39]

Davis rallied from the first attack. She had a wedding to plan: Pearl was engaged to be married to Paul F. Jahncke in October. To compound the difficulties of planning a society wedding, the Davises lost their home. City officials decided to tear down the 400 blocks of Royal (where the Davises lived) and of Chartres, backing on Exchange Alley; in that square block they planned to construct a large building to house the Supreme Court of Louisiana and other government agencies.[40]

Davis had assumed that the family would be able to remain in their home until after the wedding, but instead the "demolition man" insisted that they vacate as soon as their lease expired—probably sometime in the summer of 1903. Determined to stay in the Quarter, Davis lamented that "there are so few desirable houses in this street." Through the good offices of her landlady of twenty years, Mary Zaeringer, she found the best substitute possible for her cherished home. In the next block of Royal, Mrs. Zaeringer owned another handsome,

38. Wilkinson, "Broadening Stream," 147–51, 159–63; Godbold, "Letters," in Jahncke Papers, 4–16.

39. New Orleans *Picayune*, February 1, 1903, Sec. 3, p. 2.

40. Wedding invitation, in Jahncke Papers; Vieux Carré Survey, squares 39–40, HNOC.

albeit smaller, three-story townhouse; she and her youngest sons lived upstairs. To accommodate their famous tenant, the Zaeringers moved to another of their properties, just outside the Quarter.[41]

The Davises moved into their new house at 505 Royal and began refurbishing it. While superintending preparations for the wedding, Davis suffered another attack, but the ceremony and festivities went successfully. The strain of moving, sprucing up the new house, and staging a grand wedding had been great for a woman as ill as Davis. She was exhausted: "I have been laid up, like a log in an eddy, ever since Pearl's wedding."[42] But again she rallied. This was to be the pattern of her cancer: illness and activity alternated, but the spells of illness grew longer, the intervals of activity shorter. During periods of remission, she still hoped to recover and tried the doctors' experimental treatments.

As the disease progressed, her life was pared down to the essentials. She had no energy for entertaining, visiting, or attending her beloved opera and concerts. She seldom left the house during the last five years, confined to the sofa by often agonizing pain. But she continued to see her close friends and family and to write, publishing a few poems and stories.

In 1906 she had a story called "The Forerunner" in the *Atlantic Monthly*. The narrator is visited by the Messenger of Death. He does not tell her exactly when her death will be, simply that it is coming. She accepts the inevitability of the message and promises to "keep my hand to the plow as long as God grants me the blessing of life."[43] Clearly Davis suspected that her illness was terminal, but like the narrator, she kept her "hand to the plow" until almost the end. She was hard at work on her final novel to be published. *The Price of Silence* (1907; 4,000 copies) was her most successful work.[44] Like earlier stories, it turns on the question of adoption and heredity, but introduces a theme of miscegenation and implied interracial romance.

Even during the last few months of her life, Davis continued to write, taking a daily hypodermic of morphine "to ward off pain past

41. Vieux Carré Survey, squares 39–40, square 62 (505 Royal St.), HNOC; *Letters of M. E. M. Davis to Kate Minor of Southdown Plantation* (Tokyo, 1955), 6–7; Mollie Moore Davis to William Beer, n.d., in William Beer Papers; NOCD 1903–1904.

42. NOCD 1903–1904; Davis to Beer, n.d., William Beer Papers; *Letters of M. E. M. Davis*, 8, 12.

43. "The Forerunner" in *In Memoriam: Mary Evelyn Moore Davis, Entered into Rest New Year's Day, 1909* (New Orleans, 1909), 13–14.

44. Wilkinson, "Broadening Stream," 163.

bearing." She published her last book, *The Moons of Balbanca* (1908; 2,000 copies), a series of children's stories dedicated "To the dearest of little people—Paul, Mary Evelyn, and Edward," her grandchildren. That year she also made a will, making her husband universal legatee and leaving personal keepsakes to family members and to friends. She apologized to a friend for the "tiny-bit" check she sent for a good cause: "I am sure you must realize how it is with us, now that my own pen is perforce idle, and illness presents so many claims."[45]

During her last year she finished at least one, possibly two, works dealing with the themes of mixed blood and interracial romance that she had touched on in *The Price of Silence*. Her early works about blacks had been standard formula pieces of the era, written in an exaggerated dialect; they presented black characters stereotypically as childish layabouts or slavishly devoted servants. Now she was ready to attempt a somewhat more serious—although still stereotyped— portrayal. In an early review of Grace King's work, Davis had admired her treatment of "the passionate, savage life, boiling under the lazy child-like good-humor" of blacks, and this was the aspect she decided to consider.[46]

The manuscript was finished but unpublished when she died. Her husband and daughter conferred with Jennie Nixon, a longtime friend who taught English at Newcomb, about this manuscript; reportedly, they then destroyed it.[47] It seems more likely, however, either that the manuscript was not destroyed or that a second copy existed, for this work was probably the novella *The Ships of Desire*, published posthumously by Davis' granddaughter, Evelyn Jahncke. The protagonist, Yvonne du Quesnay, is a New Orleans mulatta who loves and enslaves a young white planter through their passion, and whose love turns to hatred when he leaves her to marry a white woman. Though Yvonne is portrayed as tainted by low passions because of her race, her situation is presented somewhat sympathetically. Of accomplishing this work, Davis wrote, "It has been something of a comfort to me to realize that the mental and spiritual *can* so dominate the physical, [in] spite of agony. The story is not a pleasant one, but I think it about the best work I have ever done."[48]

In the final months of her life, Davis wrote to a friend, "If it were

45. *Ibid.,* 166, 177; *Letters of M. E. M. Davis,* 16, 19.

46. *Louisiana Authors: Proceedings of a Round Table Held at the Louisiana State Chautauqua on July 19, 1893* (Monroe, La., 1893), 7–9.

47. Wilkinson, "Broadening Stream," 163.

48. *Letters of M. E. M. Davis,* 23–24.

117

not cowardly ... I would beg you *to pray for my passing,* I suffer so much." Finally, on January 1, 1909, in the early hours of the morning death released her from her frightful pain. Her body, draped in a white satin mantle tied with broad white satin ribbons, was placed on a bier completely covered with masses of white roses and lilies. The romantic image would have pleased her: she looked like "the Lady of Shalott floating down the river in her floral barge."[49]

49. *Ibid.,* 23; *In Memoriam;* Grace King, Introduction to Mollie E. Moore Davis, *Selected Poems* (New Orleans, 1927), 16; Grace King, *Memories of a Southern Woman of Letters* (New York, 1932), 334; New Orleans *Picayune,* January 2, 1909, p. 4.

Alice Dunbar-Nelson.
Courtesy the Amistad Research Center, Tulane
University

Race and Gender in the Early Works of
Alice Dunbar-Nelson

N UNS and praline women, Creole belles and beaux, musicians and rejected lovers, fishermen and Mardi Gras Indians, all the characters of the New Orleans environment, speaking in distinctive voices using their diverse dialects—Alice Dunbar-Nelson mined the same vein as George Washington Cable, but as Vernon Loggins wrote, "Mrs. Nelson found types in New Orleans which her master [Cable] had neglected, and she treated them in sketches which are frail and at the same time redolent of a delicate sympathy."[1] In this assessment, the use of the word *master* in reference to Cable says much about the black male critical establishment's evaluation of Dunbar-Nelson, a black woman writer—most notably the presumption that she was subordinate to the prominent male white writer. The primary differences between Dunbar-Nelson and Cable were that she dealt mainly with Creoles of color, whom she cleverly disguised for her reading audience as Creoles of *any* color, her basic assumption being that racial distinctions meant little in terms of essential Creole attitudes; and that the protagonists of most of her early stories were women—indeed, in several of the sketches she explicitly dramatized contemporary issues of women's rights.

In her 1916 article "People of Color in Louisiana, Part I," Dunbar-Nelson discussed the difficulty of defining the term *Creole:*

> The native white Louisianian will tell you that a Creole is a white man, whose ancestors contain some French or Spanish blood in their veins. But he will be disputed by others. . . . It appears that to a Caucasian, a Creole is a native of the lower parishes of Louisiana, in whose veins some traces of Spanish, West Indian or French blood runs. The Caucasian will shudder with horror at the idea of including a person of color in the definition, and the person of color will retort with his definition that a Creole is a native of Louisiana, in whose blood runs mixed strains of everything un-American, with the African strain slightly apparent.[2]

1. Vernon Loggins, *The Negro Author: His Development in America to 1900* (Port Washington, N.Y., 1964), 318.
2. Alice Dunbar-Nelson, "People of Color in Louisiana, Part I" (1916), rpr. in *An Alice Dunbar-Nelson Reader*, ed. R. Ora Williams (Washington, D.C., 1978), 143–44.

Dunbar-Nelson's fascination with Louisiana's Creoles of color is apparent in her history and in many of her stories. Yet whether she herself could be classified as a Creole is not readily apparent. According to the family history she wrote in a letter to her first husband, Paul Laurence Dunbar, her mother (Patricia Wright) was born a slave in Opelousas, Louisiana, and as Gloria Hull points out, the racial identity of her father (Joseph Moore), generally acknowledged to have been a seaman, was questionable. Hull discusses Dunbar-Nelson's probable ancestry in her article "Shaping Contradictions," but refers only briefly to the New Orleans experience.[3] After researching Dunbar-Nelson's early life in New Orleans and her relationships with colleagues at Straight University, I have found that many of her early works reflect her experiences as a participant in the activities and social life of the city's Creoles of color. In the racially segregated and patriarchal New Orleans community, she was more vocal on matters of women's rights than on racial matters in her fiction. Later, in Delaware, where she became involved in both the black women's club movement and the Harlem Renaissance, her fiction and poetry became more explicit on the subject of race but, surprisingly, less expressive about gender.

Born in New Orleans in 1875, Alice Ruth Moore lived at 56½ Palmyra Street in Uptown New Orleans; she was an Episcopalian in her childhood, until being sent upstairs to sit in the separate Negro church gallery upset her so terribly that she gave up the church: "Many things will be forgiven by me in this world. But the circumstances which destroyed my faith in Rich and Trapnell [pastors of St. Andrew's Episcopal Church, New Orleans] and turned me from the Episcopalian Church will never be effaced from my mind."[4]

Alice Ruth Moore attended Straight University (now Dillard University), founded by the American Missionary Association in 1869 to educate blacks, but open to all regardless of race, creed, or color. As a Straight College graduate, she was among an impressive group of future black elite including, for example, Louis A. Martinet, who founded the New Orleans *Crusader* newspaper and who, as attorney for the Comité des Citoyens, struggled in the *Plessy* v. *Ferguson* court case for the rights of blacks freely to ride the city's streetcars.[5] Moore

---

3. Gloria T. Hull, ed., *Give Us Each Day: The Diary of Alice Dunbar-Nelson* (New York, 1984), 297; Gloria T. Hull, "Shaping Contradictions: Alice Dunbar-Nelson and the Black Creole Experience," *New Orleans Review*, XV (Spring, 1988), 34–37.

4. Hull, ed., *Give Us Each Day*, 122–23.

5. *Catalogue of Straight University, 1891–92* (New Orleans, 1892), includes the names of faculty and students and the curriculum; Louis A. Martinet, M.D., was a

was an active community member at a very young age as an elementary schoolteacher, journalist, and participant in the city's social and literary circles, especially in her work with the Delta Sigma Theta sorority.

At twenty, she published her first book, *Violets and Other Tales* (1895). Her early poetry caught the attention of Paul Laurence Dunbar, already a prominent black poet although only two years her senior. He noticed her picture and a poem, probably in the *Boston Monthly Review*, and fell in love, courting her through letters; the first reply from Alice was mailed from Palmyra Street, May 7, 1895. In Dunbar's early correspondence he asks her to send him a photo: "Please let me have your photo as soon as possible and don't consider me selfish for saying that I would rather not send you mine" (June 25, 1895).[6]

Much has been written about the color difference between Paul and Alice as one of her mother's major objections to the ensuing marriage, but it is not clear from the correspondence that this was the primary issue. Mrs. Moore wrote to Paul on November 3, 1897, from West Medford, Massachusetts: "You have surprised me quite a lot as I thought you & my daughter were friends,—nothing more. I scarcely know what to say to you about this important matter. You are a perfect stranger to us, I do not know anything of you. . . . My daughter is young & for her to take such a serious step and perhaps regret it & be unhappy the remainder of life would be dreadful." Thus Mrs. Moore's reluctance may have arisen partly out of simple protectiveness and lack of knowledge about this suitor who, although a public figure, was known to her mainly through his correspondence with her daughter. Still his color, the dialect poetry that he was known for, his willingness to be a part of the minstrel tradition (as displayed in his musical *Clorindy*, a collaboration with Will Cook)—these did not endear him to Alice's self-made, society-oriented, properly Victorian, southern family. On the other side, Mrs. Dunbar, who acknowledged having been born a slave and having earned her living as a laundrywoman before Paul made money with his poetry and could set her up in a

---

graduate of Straight University's Law Department, 1876; in 1892 Alice Ruth Moore was a member of the Middle Class of the Preparatory Division of the College Department.

6. All letters mentioned in the text are from Sara S. Fuller, ed., *The Paul Laurence Dunbar Papers* (Microfilm; Columbus, Ohio, 1972). Letters are hereinafter cited in the text by date only. See also Virginia Cunningham, *Paul Laurence Dunbar and His Song* (New York, 1969), 172.

nice home in Washington, D.C., was not too happy with the marriage either. As Paul wrote to Alice on October 29, 1897: "Is my mother pleased at the marriage? Well, dear, to tell the truth, she doesn't hanker after it, but she is reconciled and is prepared to love you. Before I left home she had begun to enter pretty heartily into my enthusiasm." In spite of the hesitancy of both mothers, Paul and Alice felt themselves ready financially and emotionally to marry; they were wed on March 6, 1898.

Throughout the letters to Paul and in her early poems, short stories, and essays written primarily in New Orleans, Alice Ruth Moore appears as an ambitious, upwardly mobile, romantic young woman, light-complexioned and of mixed ancestry, who adopted the life-styles and values of the New Orleans Creoles of color. Like Grace King, she was brought up in the Creole tradition, but in her literature and general perspective she was an outsider looking in.

Violets and Other Tales was published by the *Boston Monthly Review* in 1895, three years before Moore married Dunbar. The vignettes and poems (twelve poems, seventeen tales and sketches) were largely descriptions of the social practices of New Orleans Creole culture and the role of women, especially the conflict between career and family, a topic that engaged most women writers at the turn of the century. Her second collection, *The Goodness of Saint Rocque* (1899), was published after her marriage by Dodd, Mead, and Co., Paul Laurence Dunbar's major publisher.[7] In this volume, composed of fourteen stories (two of them, "Little Miss Sophie" and "Titee," reprinted from the first volume), the work is more fully developed. The settings, dialects, and customs of New Orleans are presented in greater detail. Although *Saint Rocque* has none of the sketches that foreground feminist issues, as in "The Woman," "A Story of Vengeance," and "At Eventide," and that accordingly help to characterize *Violets*, both volumes, which contain Dunbar-Nelson's most memorable fiction, bear the seeds of the feminist and racial concerns she would confront more overtly in her later fiction, poetry, and nonfiction when she had left New Orleans, separated from Paul Laurence Dunbar (1902), and become a significant part of the black women's club era and the Harlem Renaissance from her adopted home in Wilmington, Delaware.

7. Alice Dunbar-Nelson, *Violets and Other Tales* (1895) and *The Goodness of St. Rocque and Other Stories* (1899) are reprinted in Gloria T. Hull, ed., *The Works of Alice Dunbar-Nelson* (3 vols.; New York, 1988). All references to these collections are to this edition, which will be cited parenthetically by volume and page number in the text.

Paul Laurence Dunbar considered Moore's early stories comparable to those of George Washington Cable and Grace King. In a February 16, 1896, letter to Moore he wrote: "Your determination to contest Cable for his laurels is a commendable one. Why shouldn't you tell those pretty creole stories as well as he? You have the force, the fire and the artistic touch that is so delicate & so strong."

"Those pretty creole stories" were sometimes very violent, but they were the romantic ("beautiful" and "tragic") tales that Americans loved to read during post-Reconstruction, told delicately with a "woman's touch." To make her stories marketable and reflective of her perceptions of life and the role of art, Dunbar-Nelson camouflaged the issue of race, even though matters of race and gender are easily apparent to the late-twentieth-century reader. Her protagonists are for the most part women who act silently and secretly, in the end accepting their isolation from the community in which they live. They reflect the dilemma of young Alice Ruth Moore herself, who did not have, perhaps could not have, a voice in New Orleans literature that clearly identified her as a southern black woman. In the stories where she mentions race at all, it is only indirectly, in description—"dusky-eyed" and "small brown hands" (Sister Josepha), "wizened yellow woman" and "dat light girl" (Claralie)—or by place names, particularly of streets and neighborhoods, such as Rampart Street or "the lower Districts" in "A Carnival Jangle." When she raises issues of women's rights in these early stories and poems, as in the frequently anthologized "I Sit and Sew," her criticism focuses on the plight of all women, with no mention of the particular problems of the black woman. And her stand on women's issues in these first volumes is always ambivalent.

In the 1890s the story "Little Miss Sophie" would have been read as a typical tale of "tragic heroism," centering as it does on a young woman whose lover has rejected her but who still loves and works to save him in his distress. To readers of that day, the story must have seemed another version of Cable's *Madame Delphine* (1881) or "'Tite Poulette," but Dunbar-Nelson makes the white youth irresponsible while she allows the quadroon mistress to retain her innocence.

The narrator of Dunbar-Nelson's story, who speaks from the perspective of a neighbor looking in on Miss Sophie's life, is reminiscent of Cable's style of narration, especially in "'Sieur George" or "Jean ah-Poquelin" of *Old Creole Days* (1879). Miss Sophie is praying in church when a wedding party arrives; she stays to enjoy the ceremony and finds that her lover of five years ago is about to be married. After the wedding, she overhears a conversation about the young man's unfortunate circumstances: his business has failed, and he is unable to inherit his uncle's wealth because he does not have the family ring necessary for identification.

> "Well, you're all chumps. Why doesn't he get the ring from the owner?"
> "Easily said—but—It seems that Neale had some little Creole love-affair some years ago and gave this ring to *his dusky-eyed fiancée.* But you know how Neale is with his love-affairs, went off and forgot the girl in a month." (I, 147; emphasis added)

Having received the ring from Neale, Sophie had pawned it to be able to attend to her father before his death. Now she resolves to raise enough money to recover the ring from the pawn shop in order to return it to her former lover and save him from financial disaster. She carries increasingly bigger black bundles of clothes to sew, and skimps on fuel and food until she becomes a mere waif. Her work has always been "her only hope of life," but now the ring becomes even more the meaning of her life—so much so that when she finally recovers it (on Christmas day), she dies with it "clasped between her fingers on her bosom" (I, 141, 154).

To any reader knowledgeable about New Orleans culture, the words *dusky-eyed* would signify that Sophie was a quadroon (a racial designation: one-fourth black; but unlike Cable, Dunbar-Nelson does not explicitly use the term). The status of free antebellum quadroon women was, predictably, ambiguous.[8] Many did not wish to marry free men of color, and certainly not men who were any darker than they. The result was the *plaçage* arrangement, which became conventional in antebellum New Orleans society, whereby a white man had a liaison with a woman of color, set her up in an apartment or house, and provided for the children of their union, while also legally marrying a white woman and having a "legitimate" family. "Little Miss Sophie" suggests such a situation, but in this case, the young man has long since broken off the liaison; it is suggested that he has had several such affairs before his marriage.

Dunbar-Nelson's ambivalence toward race is reflected in the theme as well as the images of the story—for example, in her use of the color white, which is always associated with the good, pure, and innocent,

8. For a more detailed discussion of the New Orleans *gens de couleur,* see John W. Blassingame, *Black New Orleans: 1860–1880* (Chicago, 1973), and Rodolphe Desdunes, *Our People and Our History,* trans. Sister Dorothea Olga McCants (*Nos Hommes and Notre Histoire* [Montreal, 1911]; rpr. Baton Rouge, 1973).

whereas black is associated with guilt. In the church, Miss Sophie is comforted by "the beneficent smile of the white-robed Madonna" (I, 140); she herself is "a slight, black-robed figure" leaning her head against the Virgin's altar (I, 142). When she hears of Neale's loss of his business, she cannot bear to think of the sorrow of "the white-gowned bride" (I, 148). In death, Miss Sophie lies with the ring clasped between her fingers, on "a bosom white and cold, under a cold, happy face" (I, 154).

Like Cable and King, Dunbar-Nelson tended to stereotype her Creole characters in clipped, aphoristic statements about their attitudes and traditions. For example, Miss Sophie could never have demeaned herself by telling Neale where the ring was and letting him find the means to buy it back from the pawnshop. "That good, straight-backed, stiff-necked Creole blood would have risen in all its strength and choked her. No; as a present had the quaint Roman circlet been placed upon her finger,—as a present should it be returned" (I, 148).

"The Goodness of Saint Rocque," the title story of Dunbar-Nelson's second volume, is replete with such aphorisms. Although ostensibly about two young Creole women (Creoles of color: "dark-eyed" Manuela, and Claralie, "blonde and petite") who fight both with Voodoo charms and with novenas to St. Rocque to win the attentions of Theophilé, the desired young man, the story is also a sketch of Creole customs and a detailed picture of the New Orleans landscape. The protagonists, as in "Little Miss Sophie," are women; the male character is an object to be won.

Manuela has considered Theophilé her "own especial property"; then she and a group of her Creole friends spend a day at "Milneburg-on-the-Lake" (the same resort on Lake Pontchartrain that Mark Twain memorialized in *Life on the Mississippi* (1883) as "the West End, a collection of hotels of the usual light summer-resort pattern, with broad verandas all around, and the waves of the wide and blue Lake Pontchartrain lapping the thresholds. Thousands of people come by rail and carriage to West End and to Spanish Fort every evening, and dine, listen to the bands, take strolls in the open air under the electric lights, go sailing on the lake, and entertain themselves in various and sundry other ways.").[9] There, Theophilé dances every waltz and quadrille with Claralie, while Manuela can only try to keep up appearances by dancing with many of her other suitors.

The next day finds Manuela walking down Marais Street to the

9. Samuel Clemens, *Life on the Mississippi* (1893; rpr. New York, 1968), 382–83.

house of a Voodoo woman. "The little walk of broken bits of brick was reddened carefully, and the one little step was scrupulously yellow-washed, which denoted that the occupants were cleanly as well as religious" (I, 7). The Voodoo woman, a "little, wizened yellow woman" with "long grimy talons"—not glamorous like Cable's Palmyre, but just as icy and mysterious—gives Manuela a charm to wear and advises her to make a novena to St. Rocque at the cemetery of St. Rocque (the cemetery is as important here as it is in Grace King's "Madrilène").[10] The Voodoo's charm and Manuela's novena begin to work against Claralie's novena, and both women await the outcome, neither revealing her feelings, as destiny is played out—"For your Creole girls are proud, and would die rather than let the world see their sorrows" (I, 13). Nevertheless, the wizened one is correct; her charm finally does win out, and at the birthday party of Theophilé's sister, Theophilé (never knowing the cause of his renewed affection for Manuela) places Manuela at the table next to his mother: "When a Creole young man places a girl at his mother's right hand at his own table, there is but one conclusion to be deduced therefrom" (I, 15–16). Dunbar-Nelson's second volume thus opens with a story very much in the Cable tradition—humorous, aphoristic, with detailed observations of Creole customs that would have been an instruction even to Frowenfeld of Cable's *Grandissimes* (1880).

Another story in the same volume gives slightly more explicit consideration to racial and gender problems in the New Orleans of the nineteenth century. "Sister Josepha" is the tale of a young novice who had come to the convent as an orphan fifteen years earlier—just one of the many "scraps of French and American civilization thrown together to develop a seemingly inconsistent miniature world" (I, 157–58). At the time of the narration, she is eighteen, having become a novice at sixteen shortly after she had refused a willing couple's offer to adopt her and had "fled like a frightened fawn into the yard." She refused because of the man's obvious admiration of her physical charms: "She was fifteen, and almost fully ripened into a glorious tropical beauty of the type that matures early. . . . It was doubtless intuition of the quick, vivacious sort which belonged to her blood that served her" (I, 158–59). The sensual imagery used to describe the attractive young woman is unusually direct for Dunbar-Nelson; it is

10. *Cf.* Grace King, "Madrilène; or, The Festival of the Dead," in *Tales of a Time and Place* (New York, 1893), 119–78.

more in line with Kate Chopin's descriptions of Edna Pontellier, as when Edna reminds Doctor Mandelet of "some beautiful, sleek animal waking up in the sun."[11]

The ceremonies held at St. Louis Cathedral in Josepha's eighteenth year—the beautiful colors and lights, but also the intrusion of the outside world and especially the brown eyes of a young serviceman, who looks at Josepha with pity—make the young novice wonder again at her decision to stay in the convent, "this home of self-repression and retrospection" (I, 168). She decides to run away into the great city, perhaps to find the brown eyes again, but then, overhearing three older nuns whispering, she realizes that she is without identity, having "no name" and "no friends," only "her beauty" (I, 170). Finally, realizing that she does not know *who* she is or *what* she is (black or white), she goes back into the convent and "vanishe[s] behind the heavy door" (I, 172). (Refuge in the convent when in doubt of one's identity or the evils that await one is a resolution of many Creole tales, for example, Cable's "'Sieur George," Dunbar-Nelson's "Odalie," or historically, the life of Henriette Delille, who not only fled into the convent because of her reluctance to go the way of the rest of her relatives—Creoles of color—and attend the quadroon balls, be selected by a white man, and spend the rest of her life as his faithful mistress, but actually went much further and established an order for women of color, the Sisters of the Holy Family.)[12]

In *Violets*, four sketches are specifically directed toward the dialogue prominent in most major periodicals at the turn of the century on the role of women in the home and in the world of work. As early as 1863, when one would think that the attention of the public would have been focused on the Civil War, Augusta Jane Evans had published *Macaria*. She dedicated it to the Army of the Confederacy; yet many who condemned her political affinities heartily supported her insistence that the proper role of wives was to be devoted homemakers. The New Orleans *Tribune*, a black newspaper, published an excerpt from the book in its religious column under the title "'Married Belles'—What a Woman Says." According to Evans: "Women who so far forget their duties to their homes and husbands, and the respect

11. Per Seyersted, ed., *The Complete Works of Kate Chopin* (2 vols.; Baton Rouge, 1969), II, 952.

12. For a detailed history of Henriette Delille and the founding of the Sisters of the Holy Family, see Sister Audrey Marie Detiege, *Henriette Delille, Free Woman of Color; Foundress of the Sisters of the Holy Family* (New Orleans, 1976).

due to public opinion, as to habitually seek for happiness in the mad whirl of so-called fashionable life, ignoring household obligations, should be driven from well-bred, refined circles, and hide their degradation at the firesides they have disgraced." [13]

On through the late nineteenth century many editors, black and white, seemed intent on publicizing the opinions of women who supported the conventional idea that a woman's place was in the home, even in view of changing trends in women's employment, a declining number of marriages, and increases in the divorce rate. In June, 1894, for example, in the same issue of *Lippincott's* that included Paul Laurence Dunbar's novel *The Uncalled,* Eleanor Whiting argued in the article "Woman's Work and Wages" that "women bettered themselves financially, legally, and socially by becoming indirect wage-earners through marriage rather than direct wage-earners in the world' of business." The work of women, she argued, would result in lower wages for men, would be detrimental to the children, and would take away the home's "greatest source of well-being"—the mother. [14] In her first published volume, the young Alice Ruth Moore joined in the debate with "A Story of Vengeance," "At Eventide," "The Woman," and to a lesser extent, "Violets."

In "A Story of Vengeance," Dunbar-Nelson uses the style of oral narrative, as Grace King did in *Balcony Stories* (1893). The story begins: "Yes, Eleanor, I have grown grayer. I am younger than you, you know, but then, what have you to age you? A kind husband, lovely children, while I—I am nothing but a lonely woman" (I, 198). The narrator's decision to enter the literary world and achieve fame instead of marriage and family had resulted from her lover's apparent rejection and her vengeful decision not to forgive him when he returned. Nevertheless, after her initial act of vengeance, she hesitates and wants to show him mercy because of her womanly tendency to put irrationality and passion above reason: "Strive as I did, I could not repress it [a deluge of pity]; a woman's love is too mighty to be put down with little reasonings" (I, 104); but her former lover resists her belated change of heart, and she is left alone.

In "At Eventide," a similar choice must be made between career

13. Augusta Jane Evans, *Macaria; or, Altars of Sacrifice* (1863; rpr. New York, 1887); "'Married Belles' — What a Woman Says," New Orleans *Tribune,* March 29, 1865.

14. Eleanor Whiting, "Woman's Work and Wages," *Lippincott's Magazine,* May 22, 1898, p. 676.

and family. This time the woman decides to become a singer, to submit to ambition, even though doing so will destroy her chances for a home, for her lover believes: "My wife must be mine, and mine alone. I want not a woman whom the world claims, and shouts her name abroad. My wife and my home must be inviolate" (I, 162). She becomes the great singer of her dreams, but her fame passes, and she asks her beloved to take her back. In a stern voice he again tells her that he does not want a "soiled lily," a "gaudy sun-flower"; what he desires is a "modest, shrinking violet"—and besides, he has married another (I, 165).

In both "A Story of Vengeance" and "At Eventide," the woman who follows her ambition and career is hurt in the end because she has forgone the charms of family life. In the sketch "The Woman," the topic of "whether woman's chances for matrimony are increased or decreased when she becomes man's equal as a wage earner" is handled as a debate going on in a club. The narrator, the secretary of the club, puts forth her thoughts: to her the question more logically is, *"Why should well-salaried women marry?"* (I, 21, 22; Dunbar-Nelson's emphasis). After explaining all the reasons why she should not marry—she may go where she pleases ("provided it be in a moral atmosphere"), her earnings are her own, she gains men's respect—the secretary weakens and points out that irrational falling in love and deciding to marry are natural in women nonetheless.

"Violets," the title story of the volume, is more romantic than the other three tales. The author employs the same kind of time lapse she used in "Vengeance" and "At Eventide." A young woman who sends her lover a lock of hair and flowers does not mail the letter that explains the meaning of the package, but keeps it and constantly rereads it, remembering the past. One Easter she is buried, covered with violets and other flowers. The lover, now married, runs across the lock of hair and violets and asks his wife if she ever gave them to him. She proudly says no, and tells him to throw them into the fire. He does, but as they begin to burn he remembers and grieves, for a moment at least. The burning of the violets is a requiem to the dead love. In this tale, inspired by Byron (whom Dunbar-Nelson mentions here and in "A Story of Vengeance"), marriage again falls far short of its romanticized ideal. Dunbar-Nelson's attitude toward marriage as revealed in several of her early stories is often as negative as that of Grace King or Kate Chopin; for her characters, too, marriage often entails the loss of one's dreams. On the other hand, Dunbar-Nelson could not divorce herself from the conventional idea that women have an often-irrational impulse to marry.

The Goodness of Saint Rocque was dedicated to "My best Comrade, My Husband," as could be expected of a loving wife of the 1890s; however, when Dunbar-Nelson separated from Dunbar in 1902 and moved with her family to Wilmington, Delaware, other dimensions of her personality took precedence. She became politically and socially active not only as a prominent member of the black women's club movement, but also as a teacher, lecturer, and journalist; simultaneously, her writing became more overtly race-conscious, although not so clearly gender-conscious.

Having secretly married a young teacher and colleague at Howard High School (where she taught for eighteen years) in 1910—four years after Paul Dunbar's death—Dunbar-Nelson later divorced him and subsequently married the journalist Robert Nelson in 1916. During her years in Wilmington, until her death in 1935, she was actively involved in the Federation of Colored Women's Clubs, the League of Colored Republican Women, and the Delta Sigma Theta sorority. At various times from 1915 to 1931, she campaigned for women's suffrage; worked with other women to found the Industrial School for Colored Girls in Marshalltown, Delaware; headed the Anti-Lynching Crusaders in Delaware; and was executive secretary for the American Friends Inter-Racial Peace Committee. She was a member of the delegation of prominent black citizens who presented racial concerns to President Harding at the White House in 1929. That delegation argued in behalf of sixty-one Negro soldiers who had been sentenced to life imprisonment because of their participation in the Houston riot of 1917; nineteen had been executed by hanging. Dunbar-Nelson's diary for 1930 reveals that she also became emotionally and legally involved in devising a way of getting pardon for a young man named Russ, who had been sentenced to death for raping a white woman. When Dunbar-Nelson and the others sympathetic to the cause lost the fight, she reflected: "The end of Theodore Russ. . . . Life snuffed out at the end of a noose. . . . How I wish all those who sent him to his fate could swing alongside of him."[15]

15. Hull, ed., *Give Us Each Day*, 376. The biographical information is primarily from this book. In addition, see *Notable American Women, 1607–1950: A Biographical Dictionary* (3 vols.; Cambridge, Mass., 1971), II, 614–15. For a detailed discussion of the black women's club movement, see Paula Giddings, *When and Where I Enter: The Impact of Black Women on Race and Sex in America* (New York, 1984), particularly her description of the

Dunbar-Nelson and her third husband coedited a progressive black newspaper, the *Advocate,* from 1920 to 1922; Robert Nelson also edited the Elks' newspaper, the Washington *Eagle,* from 1925 to 1930. In the 1920s and 1930s Dunbar-Nelson was a friend and critic of several of the leading figures of the Harlem Renaissance, including Jessie Fauset, Alain Locke, and Georgia Douglas Johnson.

Although Dunbar-Nelson's first two collections of stories—the only volumes of her work published in her lifetime—dealt implicitly with racial concerns, only in her later, uncollected tales does she address those troubling issues as directly as she had the conflicts of women in *Violets* and *The Goodness of St. Rocque.* The apparent shift in her willingness to employ racial themes in her literary works roughly coincided with the changes in her personal life, particularly her move to Wilmington and her consequent activity as a journalist, literary critic, clubwoman, and diarist. The difference is evident in several of these later stories. As Gloria Hull indicates, in "The Pearl in the Oyster" and "The Stones of the Village," Dunbar-Nelson deals with the themes of race and "passing" much more explicitly than in her earlier collections of New Orleans stories.[16] The difficulty of getting stories on such themes published is no doubt a major reason she did not pursue them more aggressively. As Hull has noted, "When she proposed enlarging . . . 'The Stones of the Village,' into a novel, Bliss Perry of the *Atlantic Monthly* discouraged her in 1900 by saying that the present American public disliked 'color-line' fiction."[17]

A similarly realistic treatment of race published in the early twentieth century was "Hope Deferred." The short story, which deals with a young black man's difficulty in finding a job as civil engineer and his subsequent decision to become a strikebreaker during a strike of waiters in the city, is thematically comparable to the earlier "Mr. Baptiste" (*The Goodness of Saint Rocque*), about an old Creole man who is killed during a longshoreman's strike in New Orleans.

---

search for identity by three writers of this period — Jessie Fauset, Nella Larsen, and Zora Neale Hurston, 189–93.

16. See Hull, "Shaping Contradictions." "The Pearl in the Oyster," *Southern Workman* (1900), "Hope Deferred" (*The Crisis,* 1914), and "The Stones of the Village" (formerly unpublished) are reprinted or printed for the first time in Hull, ed., *Works of Alice Dunbar-Nelson,* III, 51–64; 178–88; 3–33.

17. Gloria T. Hull, *Color, Sex, and Poetry: Three Women Writers of the Harlem Renaissance* (Bloomington, 1987), 19.

As in most of Dunbar-Nelson's early stories, there is no certainty that Mr. Baptiste is a man of color. "He was small: most Creole men are small when they are old. . . . Mr. Baptiste was, furthermore, very much wrinkled and lame. Like the Son of Man, he had nowhere to lay his head, save when some kindly family made room for him in a garret or a barn" (I, 111–12). To sustain himself, Mr. Baptiste has developed an unusual occupation: he hangs around the levee and picks up fruit from the steamships before the shippers discard it, then trades the fruit to his many customers for nice home-cooked meals. Besides being a survivor, Mr. Baptiste is a lover of the old traditions; the arrival of immigrants with their newfangled ways threatens to destroy his way of life. When the Irish longshoremen who handle the shipments of cotton go on strike with no concern about harm to the fruit industry, the black longshoremen continue working. The reader's first awareness that Mr. Baptiste is probably a Creole of color comes in the narrator's observations that in the confrontation between the black and the Irish longshoremen, Mr. Baptiste sides with the blacks:

> "Bravo!" cheered Mr. Baptiste.
> "Will yez look at that damned fruit-eatin' Frinchman," howled McMahon, "Cheerin' the niggers, are you?" and he let fly a brickbat in the direction of the bread-stall. (I, 122)

Mr. Baptiste is killed instantly. After the body has lain unclaimed in the morgue for days, he is buried unnamed in potter's field.

The emphasis in "Mr. Baptiste" is on the old man's attempt to hold onto tradition and to reestablish his identity by tenuously connecting himself with the black community in the face of the intrusion of the immigrants, whose "negative treatment" was "certainly in keeping with common attitudes in New Orleans at the turn of the century."[18] Grace King's references to "dagos" in "Madrilène" and other stories, like Cable's pondering of the question of immigration in *Doctor Sevier* (1882), reflect the increasing American fear of immigration as the twentieth century approached.

As in "Mr. Baptiste," a labor strike leads to the tragic demise of a black man's dreams in the later story "Hope Deferred." The local color of the earlier story—expressed in the descriptions and dialogue of the characters and the clearly evoked presence of the French Market,

---

18. Roger Whitlow, "Alice Dunbar-Nelson: New Orleans Writer," in *Regionalism and the Female Imagination*, ed. Emily Toth (New York, 1985), 122.

the wharves, the levee, the Mississippi River, the rhythmic song of the stevedores heaving cotton bales, and the steady sounds of the compression machines—is missing in "Hope Deferred." There is not the same attention to details of setting and landscape. The locale could be any urban center in one of the border states of the South. The most insistent description of environment centers on the August heat, which makes the young man's disheartening search for employment along the main street even more burdensome.

The theme of immigration is also significant in this story, as it was in "Mr. Baptiste": the restaurant owner who gives the young man a job after his waiters walk out on strike is a foreigner (the narrator cannot with certainty identify his nationality). But the overriding theme is not confrontation between cultures or between tradition and change (with both conflicts entailing a search for identity); the theme in "Hope Deferred" is obviously racism and injustice. The young man, Edwards, is clearly a black, as is his submissive wife. The strikers hate him for being a "scab," but the missile they throw into the restaurant, upsetting the dishes that Edwards is holding and causing him to spill soup on an influential white customer's suit, is only the context of the action; the important incident is not the white man's reprimand, but Edwards' violent retaliation for his abusiveness as well as his rejection of Edwards' earlier efforts to secure a position as an engineer. In Ralph Ellison's *Invisible Man* (1958), the black surgeon, ridden out of town on a rail for daring to practice his chosen profession, ends up in a mental asylum with shell-shocked veterans; in Dunbar-Nelson's story, the hapless civil engineer ends up in a prison workhouse, he and his wife having to wait much longer for the realization of their dreams.

Much of Dunbar-Nelson's poetry also became more overtly race-conscious over time. The contrast is evident in two very different poems about flowers, a subject of which Dunbar-Nelson was especially fond. In "Violets," published in 1917, the speaker's new lover recalls wild violets she once had: "I had not thought of violets of late, / The wild, shy kind that springs beneath your feet / In wistful April days." Having forgotten wild nature and the naïve love of beauty for its own sake, she had begun to think only of violets in artificial settings—florists' shops and party corsages—"And garish lights, and mincing little fops / And cabarets and songs, and deadening wine." Her lover has made her think again of "sweet real things"—"wild violets shy," and her "soul's forgotten gleam" (II, 81–82). Although written after Dunbar-Nelson left New Orleans, this simple love poem reflects the themes and language of her earlier fiction and poetry.

"April Is on the Way," for which she won an honorable mention in the *Opportunity* contest of 1927, does something very different: it is about lynching, a subject she would once have thought unsuitable for poetry. The speaker is a young man running from a lynch mob. The constant refrain is "April is on the way"; that is, spring has returned and there is hope of the Resurrection and an end to his pain and suffering. But in his feverish imagination, the speaker asks: "(Dear God, was that a stark figure outstretched in the bare branches / Etched brown against the amethyst sky?)" His observation of a little boy lightly rolling a hoop down the road contrasts with his awareness of his own bloody feet "clutched" by the earth's "fecund fingers." All about him nature warns but also gives hope of renewal. In "Violets," the speaker is reminded of "the perfect loveliness that God has made" in wild nature; the speaker of "April Is on the Way" remembers "the infinite miracle of unfolding life in the brown February fields," but simultaneously he hears the hounds baying. In "April Is on the Way," Dunbar-Nelson seems at least to recognize the futility of trying to escape from the "real," which is both beautiful and terrible (II, 89–91).

According to Elizabeth A. Meese, "Although the appropriated woman speaks without a voice of her own, the very act of writing, of speech, signals her defiance and requires that she transgress or (un)cross the double-cross of difference as constituted by phallocentrism."[19] As a published black woman writer and freethinker in nineteenth-century New Orleans, Alice Dunbar-Nelson was certainly a rarity. Her colleagues as writers were probably the male journalists who had written for the newspapers published originally by free men of color—*L'Union,* founded in 1862, which later became the *Tribune de la Nouvelle-Orléans* and continued in existence to 1869, followed by the *Louisianian* (1870–1881) and the New Orleans *Crusader* (1890–1897). Rodolphe L. Desdunes was her peer; Louis A. Martinet, lawyer, politician, and journalist, was her elder. It is very unlikely that she would have known the white women writers Grace King, Mollie E. Moore Davis, and Ruth McEnery Stuart, or the journalists Eliza Jane Poitevent Nicholson (Pearl Rivers), editor and publisher of the *Picayune,* and

19. Elizabeth A. Meese, *Crossing the Double-Cross: The Practice of Feminist Criticism* (Chapel Hill, 1986), 12.

Elizabeth Gilmer (Dorothy Dix). The women of color of New Orleans were popularly viewed as George Washington Cable's pretty but tragic quadroons and octoroons, the landladies of neat, well-run boarding-houses, nurses, prostitutes, or Voodoo women. The *African* women were seen as the praline, flower, and cala vendors, who sold their words of wisdom with their wares.

Black women artists were invisible, and often silent, since for the most part they were not recognized or published, and their distinctive voices remained unheard. Thus, although Alice Dunbar-Nelson, like other black writers, frequently drew on oral discourses in the black community for her fiction, she shaped her tales of Creole life for a largely white reading audience. And though she explored contemporary feminist concerns in several of her earlier stories, the predominantly male black intellectual society of New Orleans was unresponsive.

After Dunbar-Nelson departed the closed patriarchal culture of New Orleans and entered the northern black women's club movement and the Harlem Renaissance, her literature did become more overtly race-conscious, but she remained silent or ambivalent on the question of gender. As a literary critic, she reviewed many of the significant new works by black writers such as Langston Hughes, Georgia Douglas Johnson, and James Weldon Johnson. She knew the major writers and leaders of black organizations personally, although she never felt totally at ease with the clubwomen or the political leaders.[20] She read widely, being pleasantly astounded by the freedom of thought and expression in such works as D. H. Lawrence's *Lady Chatterley's Lover*. But as Hull has pointed out, the Harlem Renaissance did not encourage black women writers: "The overall definition of the Harlem Renaissance automatically excludes or devalues the contribution of the women writers. The prevailing concept of the period is that it was a time of racial assertion and poetic freedom. As the discussion of their themes and methods revealed, the majority of the women wrote aracial or quietly racial works in traditional forms. Hence, they are never taken to represent the era. Their poetry is usually described as 'personal,' and this adjective, as applied, becomes a synonym for female/feminine, and thus connotes a devaluation or dismissal of the work."[21]

20. See Hull, *Give Us Each Day* and *Color, Sex, and Poetry, passim.*
21. Gloria T. Hull, "Afro-American Women Poets: A Bio-Critical Survey," in *Shakespeare's Sisters: Feminist Essays on Women Poets*, ed. Sandra M. Gilbert and Susan Gubar (Bloomington, 1979), 174.

In the male-dominated Harlem Renaissance, Dunbar-Nelson became reticent about feminist issues, choosing instead to emphasize race. In submerging the Woman Question in her literature under the Negro Question, she followed the lead of most black clubwomen, who were dedicated to both defending the civil rights of blacks and upholding the reputation of black women, who had from slavery been associated with the image of sexual promiscuity. As Deborah E. McDowell puts it: "Even in [Nella] Larsen's day, the Freudian 1920s, the Jazz Age of sexual abandon and 'free love'—when female sexuality, in general, was acknowledged and commercialized in the advertising, beauty, and fashion industries—black women's novels preserve their reticence about sexuality. . . . Jessie Fauset and Nella Larsen could only hint at the idea of black women as sexual subjects behind the safe and protective covers of traditional narrative subjects and conventions."[22] Even in the tales—such as "Hope Deferred" or "The Stones of the Village"—that treat the problems of race more explicitly than the earlier collections, Dunbar-Nelson omits the voice of gender (the protagonists in these race-conscious tales are most often male) and dedicates herself to the problem of racial identity.

Nevertheless, except for a few poems and stories, these volumes—*Violets and Other Tales* and *The Goodness of Saint Rocque*—remain Dunbar-Nelson's most valuable creative expressions. The inhibited, disguised voice of these works draws the story of the black New Orleans woman of the late nineteenth century into the history of New Orleans literature, and—as Hélène Cixous says of women's writing—the discovery of Dunbar-Nelson's work creates a new history: "Personal history blends together with the history of all women, as well as national and world history."[23]

22. Deborah E. McDowell, ed., *"Quicksand" and "Passing," by Nella Larsen* (New Brunswick, N.J., 1987), xiii.
23. Hélène Cixous, "The Laugh of the Medusa," *Signs,* I (1976), 882.

Ada Jack Carver.
Courtesy the Historic New
Orleans Collection, Mu-
seum/Research Center, Acc.
No. 1981.330.30

What the Old Ones Know
Ada Jack Carver's Cane River Stories

I N the 1920s, Ada Jack Carver (1890–1972) won some of the country's most prestigious literary awards: the O. Henry Memorial Award (several times), *Harper's* Prize, and others. Furthermore, she published stories in such reputable magazines as *Harper's* and the *Century,* and her work frequently displayed her preoccupation with substantial themes. Carver's fiction, set in Louisiana's Cane River country, explores the spaces between such conflicting forces as culture (Creole, black, mulatto, and the locally important category known as "redbone"), generations (grandmothers and grandchildren), and values (tradition and materialism). Many of the pieces in *The Collected Works of Ada Jack Carver* [1] demonstrate how "fiction" composes a field within which powerful human struggles of identity and meaning are explored and elaborated, and they often do so with an immediacy displayed by only the best southern writers.

Carver was born and raised in Natchitoches, in an upper-middle-class family with solid religious (Baptist), professional (judges, attorneys, and legislators), and political associations (her grandfather had been a Confederate colonel). She attended Louisiana's Normal School (the state teachers' college) and Judson College, and in 1918 married John B. Snell, who was on the faculty of the Normal School. A son was born a year later, and in 1920 the small family moved to Minden. The first son died accidentally (he fell into a tub of scalding water) only two days before Carver gave birth to a second child in 1921. It is curious to note the commonly held belief that Carver's eventual literary silence was occasioned by the guilt and grief surrounding her son's death. This view may, for some, be a comforting one (in that it affirms "proper" gender roles, rather like the "necessity" of Edna's death at the end of *The Awakening*), but Carver's personal chronology and publishing history offer no support for it. In his dissertation, "Ada Jack Carver: A Critical Biography," Oliver Jackson Ford, in fact, suggests that the opposite may have been true: "The child's accidental death

---

1. Mary Dell Fletcher, ed., *The Collected Works of Ada Jack Carver* (Natchitoches, La., 1980); hereinafter cited parenthetically by page number in the text.

came as a severe blow to the mother, and the tragedy for several years came near taking the joy out of existence. Although she had always written to some extent, she began to devote more time to her stories in an attempt to decrease her sorrow."[2] Indeed, a review of her literary output demonstrates that Carver's greatest productivity followed her son's death.

Literary silence, as Tillie Olsen has demonstrated in her book *Silences*, presents a complex, multivarious terrain. Olsen explains in brief: "Literary history and the present are dark with silences: some the silences for years by our acknowledged great; some silences hidden; some the ceasing to publish after one work appears; some the never coming to book form at all."[3] Ada Jack Carver's writing life offers just such a complex mystery, the solution to which we may never discover, although an examination of her work might reasonably permit us to narrow the field of possibilities.

Carver began writing in 1908. The stories of this early period— "The Ring"; "The Story of Angele Glynn"; "A Pink Inheritance"; "The Joyous Coast"—are conventional pieces that focus on trite concerns of the white middle and upper classes of the day: a husband's Civil War regiment's reunion, female ghosts, and party dresses. Carver's characters, moved by "the irresistible rhythm of Dixie," are both victims and—as such—victimizers according to white southern culture's historic biases of race, sex, and class (23). The stories are tidy; everything is accounted for as human and narrative problems are predictably resolved. Published from 1915 to 1917, they were written when Carver was in her mid-to-late twenties and show signs of her youth and lack of experience as a writer. It is, of course, possible that their conventionality simply displayed Carver's shrewd assessment of what was required to enter the literary scene of the moment, and her resolve to do so.

Of more enduring interest are Carver's stories from the late 1920s, the first of which, the widely republished "Redbone," appeared in 1925—four years after her son's death. These works are set in the agrarian, traditional culture of Cane River (the Isle Brevelle area), which Carver preferred to the more predictable and confining small-town culture of Minden. In 1925 she wrote to her friend Caroline

2. Oliver Jackson Ford III, "Ada Jack Carver: A Critical Biography" (Ph.D. dissertation, University of Connecticut, 1975), 109.
3. Tillie Olsen, *Silences* (New York, 1978), 6.

Dormon, a noted Louisiana botanist: "I have been rather busy since you left. First, of course, there is church. I don't go every night, but as often as I can. I would much rather ride in the moonlight, and worship in my own way. But I rarely ever—really—do just what I want to do!" In addition, she frequently felt burdened by social and familial obligations; Carver continues: "Yesterday—just as I sat down at my desk—a car of people from Shreveport came to spend the day with me! I raved inwardly and tore my hair—but after I became resigned to the inevitable, I really enjoyed them. One of them was my own sister, Judith, of course. But even sisters can interfere with 'the muse', can't they? We had a lovely time, however."[4]

The conflicting demands on her exacted a psychic and artistic price. For example, in a 1925 letter to Cammie Henry, an arts patron and personal supporter, Carver wrote: "I have been so busy since my return [to Minden from Melrose Plantation]—and have been with my friends a lot. There are some darling people here and they are good to me. But they know only half of me! Or rather they don't know the real me at all,—and my *self*—my soul—sort of gets lost up here some times. It's really very difficult for me to write in my present environment and I'm longing to start my house in the woods."[5] In a letter of the same year she wrote Carrie Dormon an even more explicit assessment of the tensions in her life: "I can do nothing here. I will be a nervous wreck in a few years if people don't let me carve out my life to suit myself."[6]

Melrose Plantation provided Carver with an interruption or break in the oppressive social and domestic expectations for white middle- and upper-class women. Located on Isle Brevelle, an area largely owned and developed until the twentieth century by free people of color and their descendants, Melrose Plantation had fallen to white ownership as early as 1847, and had come down eventually to Cammie Henry, who ran the place as an artists' colony, which Carver frequented. The environs afforded Carver both an escape and subject matter for her stories, in which Isle Brevelle served as the locus of racial, cultural, and geographical differences. As Ford notes, Carver experienced a "desperate sense of polarity and limited options" with

4. Ada Jack Carver to Caroline Dormon, July 1, 1925, in Melrose Collection, Cammie G. Henry Research Center, Eugene P. Watson Library, Northwestern State Library, Natchitoches, Louisiana; hereinafter cited as Melrose Collection.

5. Quoted by Ford, "Ada Jack Carver," 70.

6. Ada Jack Carver to Caroline Dormon, July 8, 1925, in Melrose Collection.

respect to "the roles open to her. Either she wrote seriously or lapsed into the social whirl, for no other alternatives were apparent to her."[7] She clearly associated serious writing with Melrose and Cammie Henry, and the social merry-go-round with Minden and society.

The interest Isle Brevelle offered to the southerner—respecter of categorical boundaries, quantifier of blood, enumerator of genealogy—rested in ambiguity, in transgressions of the conventional. Its inhabitants were African, French, Spanish, Indian, and Anglo-Scotch-Irish: the psychic landscape of ethnicity was as curious as the rich, mysterious topography of the swamps, rivers, and bayous. Ford observes, "By writing about 'Redbones,' mulattoes, and Blacks, Ada Jack could avoid any allegations regarding her own propriety, for such characters would be considered curious, amusing, and exotic by the more privileged whites."[8] Similar speculation has been offered concerning other white southern women writers, such as Julia Peterkin (the South Carolinian who won a Pulitzer Prize for *Scarlet Sister Mary* in 1928): namely, that they acquired a certain freedom, not unlike other freedoms white women of their class have claimed through the agency of black women, by writing outside their own race and class. What this freedom is, how it functions artistically, and what its limits are, present some of the most interesting questions concerning white American women writers in the early twentieth century.

These questions cannot be answered easily, if at all. The best we can do in many cases is to sketch the barest outline of struggle, tension, and rupture. In the late nineteenth and early twentieth centuries, women writers wanted everything. They wanted artistic freedom and at the same time husbands and families, which in certain classes meant social prominence with its attendant pressures and obligations. Writers such as Mary Wilkins Freeman made equivocal and denunciatory comments when pressed to elaborate on how sexual politics were figured in their stories.[9]

In her Cane River stories, Carver explores an uncharted territory in some ways similar to the terrain she herself entered as a woman trying to write professionally, to take her work as an artist as seriously

7. Ford, "Ada Jack Carver," 126.

8. *Ibid.*, 120.

9. See chap. 2, "Signs of Undecidability: Reconsidering the Stories of Mary Wilkins Freeman," in my *Crossing the Double-Cross: The Practice of Feminist Criticism* (Chapel Hill, 1988), 19–38, for a discussion of how Freeman recants with respect to the sexual politics of her story "The Revolt of Mother."

as her socially sanctioned role as wife and mother (young society matron). What appears to fascinate Carver the most is *un certain on ne sait quoi*, a "something unaccounted for" in the quantification of blood and specification of racial and cultural origins: an excess of some kind that manages to escape inherited stereotypes and that provides the driving force for discursive production. The what-is-left-over (excess) and perhaps even the what-cannot-be-said (the unspeakable) provide the fulcrum for her most successful stories; as something unspecifiable, resisting or eluding representation, the something unaccounted for warrants more and more writing. The notion first appears in "Redbone," a prize-winning story published in *Harper's* in 1925. This story of the redbone planter Baptiste Grabbo is set in the Côte Joyeuse area, and opens with the following description: "And here among the whites and blacks there dwell in ecstatic squalor a people whom, in the intricate social system of the South, strangers find it difficult to place. For although they may be bartered with, jested with, enjoyed, despised, made friends and enemies of—yet in the eyes of those born to the subtle distinction they are forever beyond the pale" (62).

Because these people do not represent "pure" categories, they defy those making "the subtle distinction"; they are themselves subtle, somehow obscure and difficult for the white writer to "figure" (out). Carver runs up against the form that is "beyond the pale" and resorts to stereotypes, the means by which she has learned to represent the identity of the Other: "They are a mixture of Spanish, French, and Indian, and God only knows what besides; and along the Côte Joyeuse, a region given to phrase and to fable, they are dubbed 'redbones' because of their dusky skins so oddly, transparently tinted. They are shiftless and slovenly, childlike and treacherous; and yet from somewhere, like a benediction, they have been touched with something precious" (62). In a double gesture, Carver (as)signs the redbones to a stereotypically subservient place (and they are bad servants at that) and tries to redeem them by making them mysterious at the same time, although neither gesture succeeds in presenting them as human.

The story relates Baptiste's celebration of his son's birth in terms dictated by a "creed" that Carver describes as "past understanding," built on "things vaguely heard and remembered; things felt and but dimly divined; superstitions drilled into him by the wrinkled old crones of his race. His religion is compounded of Catholic altars where candles burn through the thick dim smoke from the swinging incense bowls; of pinewoods tremulous like a sounding organ; of forest fires and thunders and winds; of fetishes against the powers of darkness; of a moon that comes up red from the swamp; of a wilful river that doles out life and death" (65). Thus, the ways of nature, the rituals of Catholicism, and black and Indian culture assume similarly exotic properties in a story about the unspecifiable difference of Otherness.

The reader watches the exoticism of the "something unaccounted for" being played out, providing a way of understanding Baptiste's choice of carved tombstones as a birth present to his wife Clorinda. The inappropriate gift becomes ironically appropriate when Baptiste murders and buries Olaf, the hired man whom he discovers in an adulterous relationship with Clorinda. Even this event is not fully accounted for, as the stereotypes of racial identity exhaust their capacity to specify:

> The Indian in Baptiste performed the deed with neatness and despatch, so that Olaf for an instant knew only a face before him—high cheek bones, thin straight lips, and comic eyes that were sad. The Spanish in Baptiste dug the grave and the French tossed a rose upon it.
>
> But the something unaccounted for that made him what he was sent him dragging back to the house, his face the color of leaves. (79)

The "something unaccounted for" is the mark of Baptiste's humanity, the excess beyond the stereotype of identity as ethnicity. The tombstone guards the fiction's concluding revelation—the mysterious bones discovered many years later, after the death of Baptiste, as the gravediggers prepare to bury Clorinda next to her husband.

Through the "something unaccounted for," Carver explores with increasing complexity the mysteries of identity as a singular, "pure" construct. Her approach is exemplified in "Treeshy," which was published in *Harper's* in 1926, won an O. Henry Memorial Award and was selected for O'Brien's *Best Stories* that year. The story begins with a mysterious young painter from Gascony who is called Prometheus, his real name forgotten. The young man is befriended by the narrator's grandfather, who offers him a bed for the night. He disappears just as mysteriously as he appeared, leaving an unruffled bed and a note of gratitude, claiming to have given the town a gift. The first part of the story ends with the double mystery of the identity of the young man ("Perhaps . . . he was just one of those fauns or a god or something out of mythology") and the gift ("What [had] the young man left for the town?") (86–87).

The rest of the story concerns another pair of mysteries centered on the character Treeshy, a light-fingered seamstress who never uses the things she takes (silk stockings, for example, although she has a wooden leg). The painter's gift slowly becomes apparent through the progression of items Treeshy steals. She is both familiar (she sews for everyone) and mysterious, again figured in ethnic terms as an excess: "There was actually something sort of Dutch about old Treeshy. . . . But then there was about her something Irish too, and something Spanish and French. . . . of every land and clime and yet of none. She was engagingly and disconcertingly herself" (89). In spite of her peculiar behavior, Treeshy possesses "great poise and tremendous *savoir-faire*," as well as "a puzzling surety"—"as if she knew things beyond the common ken" (89). Of course, she has a secret knowledge and motive that none of the others recognizes. In her capacity as savant one night near Christmas, she explains to the outcasts in her abandoned refuge of a house: "They's *this* that I know regardin' the Virgin. . . . she knowed things she couldn't talk on. It says: 'and them things she hid in her heart'" (91). Only when Treeshy is dying are the mysteries of her own heart revealed: she stole to support her illegitimate daughter, now a famous young violinist—the artist's gift to the town, and the secret Treeshy kept hidden.

Age in Carver's stories serves as a vehicle for wisdom and values. It is most evident in two of her best stories, "The Old One" and "The Raspberry Dress," both published in 1926. "The Old One" concerns Nicolette, her grandson Balthazar, and his new wife Rose—free mulattoes of French descent living on Isle Brevelle. Rose is an outsider, French but "not a native of Isle Brevelle . . . not even a Catholic—a common girl, with no raising," from a town in northern Louisiana (120). The story revolves around the issues of dominance, space in the house, and ownership of possessions, focusing on Nicolette's old bed, where she and her children were born, where her husband died and she too will die. At first the bed—a "tacky old thing"—embarrasses Rose; then she learns of its value to white antique-hunters from Natchitoches (120). Despite Nicolette's refusal to sell it, Rose promises it to the visitors, hoping to purchase a car with the proceeds. Similar in some respects to Alice Walker's "Everyday Use," the story turns on the transformation of traditional culture, with its emphasis on use value, to the urban economy of surplus value.[10]

The contest of wills between Rose and Nicolette creates the textual

---

10. Alice Walker, "Everyday Use," in *In Love and Trouble: Stories of Black Women* (New York, 1973), 47–59.

body. Rose pretends to be pregnant; as a countertrick Nicolette feigns illness and takes to her bed, thus preventing Rose from selling it. Each perceives the other's dissimulation. In a final ironic turn, Granny dies in her bed, but the bed is sold to Poleon, the store-owner, to pay for her funeral. Carver thereby affirms the values of traditional culture and indicts the economy of the urban middle class (the white treasure-hunters), as well as the youthful outsiders like Rose.

Like its individual inhabitants, the community of Isle Brevelle cannot prevent change. Cars and Technicolor movies bring different images. As Balthazar explains to Rose, "A old un, they is made different" (129). Earlier generations of French mulattoes, according to Carver's narrator, "had guarded the blood in their veins. Ignored by the whites, ignoring and scorning the blacks, they had kept themselves to themselves" (148). One unquestioned point is obvious, however: certain essential transgressions of racial lines had taken place at one time or another, and the notion of "purity" installs itself, this time, in the place of the "impure."

"The Raspberry Dress," one of O'Brien's *Best* for 1927, tells another story of intergenerational relationships between a grandmother, Eugénie Laston, and her favorite granddaughter, Aline. Eugénie, nearly sixty, has worn black mourning clothes, which she despises, for almost twenty years. She hoards her money in the hope of fulfilling her dream: to recapture the joys of her youthful days in New Orleans, represented in the memory of being painted in a red, pigeon-throated silk dress. Now she lives on in a two-story steamboat house. Her daughters spend most of their time making gray, look-alike dresses for their ten growing girls. Eugénie, however, sees herself in the young Aline, who, rebellious and lovestruck, wants a dress of another color.

Having received a letter from an old New Orleans friend, Eugénie plans her trip: a reunion with the artist and old times. In her black widow's clothes, she goes into town and purchases a raspberry silk dress and a red fan. As her departure draws near, Eugénie perceives Aline's unhappiness. A young boy whom she loves is captivated by a town girl with a pink ruffled dress. Rather than attempting to repeat her own youthful experience, Eugénie gives Aline the raspberry dress, recapturing her past through her granddaughter, who "was her very image, herself grown young again" (146). Because of the relationship between grandmother and granddaughter, and their characterization as pleasure-seeking women, "The Raspberry Dress" exceeds in both interest and significance Carver's earlier stories in which clothing served as a symbolic center.

Without question, Carver took her various roles seriously. In her letters she worries about the performance of her duties as a wife, wanting her husband to perceive her as having common sense (which he never did). In a letter (1925) to Carrie Dormon she comments parenthetically: "In justice to my husband, I must tell you a compliment he gave me last night. He said he would not have a hair on my head changed, or a kink in my brain either. So evidently he must be satisfied with his witch-wife."[11] Carver sought as well to fulfill her responsibilities as a mother, worrying about her duties to her son. To Cammie Henry she wrote in 1925: "I am thrilled and quite appalled at all the things in life I want to do. And now every day I must devote a certain definite time to my little son, to his mental and spiritual needs. I'm afraid I take my mothering rather seriously—but it is a solemn thing to have a child, isn't it?"[12]

Carver was also plagued in her later years with bad health— debilitating attacks of asthma, headaches, "nerves." In an undated letter to Cammie Henry, she wrote, "But for your beautiful, serene understanding, (and that of John, my mother, and Lyle [Saxon]—and perhaps a few others) I should have despaired long 'ere this, and either blown out my brains or settled down as one of the 'popular young matrons' of Minden, going happily to clubs and playing bridge! etc."[13] The *on ne sait quoi* of identity characterized as well Carver's struggle as a southern woman with the conflicting demands of life and art, family and personal desire. Woolf's analysis in *A Room of One's Own* produced strong resonances in Carver, who presented, again in a letter (1931) to Cammie Henry, a summary of the woman writer's all too familiar circumstances: "I have just finished *A Room of One's Own*. You remember I told you I would order it! How I wish I had written it. I could have, I think—Oh, for that five hundred pounds a year, and that room of one's own. And Oh that one's mind could be truly 'incandescent' and free of hatred and grievances, bitterness, anger—so that one could write calmly."[14]

Carver's identification with Woolf did not stop there. In an address

11. Carver to Dormon, July 1, 1925, in Melrose Collection.
12. Ada Jack Carver to Cammie Henry, April 5, 1925, in Melrose Collection.
13. Ada Jack Carver to Cammie Henry, n.d., in Melrose Collection.
14. Quoted by Ford, "Ada Jack Carver," 125.

to the Minden Book Club, she reiterated some of the same sentiments. Having praised Elizabeth Madox Roberts' novel *The Great Meadow*, Carver lamented Roberts' failure to make the shift to realism and naturalism, epitomized in the work of Sinclair Lewis: "One might wish that Miss Roberts . . . would leave her mountains for a while, and give us a book of Main Street; or a novel having for hero Babbitt, that pathetic, misunderstood creature immortalized by the venomous Sinclair Lewis, a writer, who, it would seem, can see only one trait in any man and only one aspect of our national life." Citing the passage in *A Room*, "that charming and learned essay," in which Woolf discusses the writer's need to rid him- or herself of anger and bitterness, Carver suggests that an inability to do just that might be Lewis' limitation: "He has a grudge, an antipathy; he desires to protest, to preach, to proclaim an injury, to pay off a score." [15] It is possible to read in this juxtaposition of characters—Roberts, Woolf, and Lewis—a cause of Carver's silence: she failed to make the shift in style and subject matter that she knew the literary moment required for continued success. Such a view is reinforced by a letter to Cammie Henry in 1928: "I'm still planning to do something 'modern,' however—something about the new generation—I've been studying them for a year or two—because so far they've never been interpreted right. Not that I might do it any better!—but any way, it will be a relief some day to turn to the present-day after living so much in an atmosphere that is dead and foul." [16] The major turn from local color and regionalism was, however, one that Carver and many other women writers in her tradition never made, and constitutes a literary moment worth serious investigation.

Carver's stories are simply and carefully crafted, but because of limitations in engaging the complex issues of race and class relationships, they play in a small register. It is curious to consider, as all of her critics do, why she wrote so little after her remarkable success of the 1920s. Following that decade she wrote and produced *The Clock Strikes Tomorrow*, a children's play, in 1935, and a story, "For Suellen with Love," in 1949. It is possible to take this last story as the "modern" one Carver promised Cammie Henry. The resemblance in voice and strategy to works by Eudora Welty is striking:

15. "Mrs. Snell Addresses Book Club on the Subject 'Adrift Among Books' Wednesday," Minden (La.) *Herald*, February 19, 1931.
16. Ford, "Ada Jack Carver," 117–18.

"Suellen," someone would say, a grownup probably, "tell what happened to your Uncle Clint."

And that would start Suellen off. Why, her Uncle Clint was in jail, Suellen said. He had killed three men and a child in cold blood, a small innocent new-born babe; and naturally they had locked him up. And now his children were running about the streets half-clad. . . . And in two or three weeks, Suellen said, her cousins were coming to live with her, a whole tribe of cousins like an orphan asylum; for her father planned to adopt them, and had already written her Uncle Clint in jail, and the cousins would share her room. (*CW*, 188)

Welty's prose, however, moves musically with the rhythms of southern speech and is rich with humor. The following passage from "Why I Live at the P.O.," collected in *A Curtain of Green and Other Stories*, published in 1941, years before Carver's "modern" piece, points up Carver's limitations when she tried to make the shift:

I says, "Papa-Daddy, you know I wouldn't any more want you to cut off your beard than the man in the moon. It was the farthest thing from my mind! Stella-Rondo sat there and made that up while she was eating breast of chicken." [17]

Pearls, fabrication, family interactions, appear in both of these first person narratives, but the similarities stop at a superficial level.

Although Carver's silence remains a mystery, there are a number of reasonable ways of accounting for it: (1) she exhausted her limited range of familiarity with the people who were the primary subjects of her best fiction; (2) Isle Brevelle changed gradually but markedly, requiring stories that Carver was not able to tell; (3) her regenerative and productive trips to Melrose Plantation, where she could live in the company of artists, were too infrequent an antidote to the domestic and social claims of Minden (she wrote to Carrie Dormon in 1925, "If I could get to Briarwood and Melrose oftener my periods of pure inspiration wouldn't be so few and far between!"); [18] and/or (4) her increasing respect for these Other people narrowed the gap between them and herself, accentuating the differences she already felt between herself and other Minden matrons, thus demanding silence to ensure relative equanimity.

It is probably the case that each of these scenarios holds a little truth and accounts for some of the pressure Carver felt at the end of her

17. Eudora Welty, *Collected Stories of Eudora Welty* (New York, 1980), 47.
18. Ada Jack Carver to Caroline Dormon, August 6, 1925, in Melrose Collection.

career. Until more of her unpublished material becomes available and other parts of the immense story that constitutes our literary history are refigured to answer certain questions about women writers, the mystery of Ada Jack Carver's silence, like the *on ne sait quoi* that she explores in her fiction, must remain a limit text of our intellectual and sociocultural paradigms.

Katherine Anne
Porter.
Courtesy Special Collections, University of
Maryland at College Park
Libraries; Paul Porter

The Louisianas of
Katherine Anne Porter's Mind

SETTINGS in Katherine Anne Porter's stories are not always precise or explicit. In spite of twentieth-century pronouncements about the imperative need for specificity in fiction, her stories occur frequently in no-place or any-place. When her location is rural, we usually infer Texas; and when it is a small town, we sometimes assume it is southern. Often, however, Porter leaves her geographical locales deliberately vague, especially in those stories that are primarily psychological sketches or character studies about a place in the mind.

Louisiana, in Katherine Anne Porter's fiction, is also a place in the mind. Although an actual state carries the name, the Louisiana of Katherine Anne Porter's imagination is formed more of the ingredients used in nineteenth-century local-color stories than of raw earth. The most vivid Louisiana locale in those stories is the city of New Orleans as George Washington Cable popularized it. As I have noted elsewhere, "Cable's New Orleans . . . is a city of many faces. It is often the scene of great wickedness; Cable speaks of the 'loose New Orleans morals of over fifty years ago.' . . . But wicked or not, and including scenes of Creole decay as it does, Cable's city exerts a unique fascination."[1] Louisiana, of course, was settled by the French; in particular areas it still retains vestigial signs of a French culture, and that was even more the case in Cable's time. Cable devoted most of his literary attention to the two distinct groups among Louisianians of French extraction, the Creoles and the Acadians. Although definitions of *Creole* abound, Creoles in general trace their origins at least partly to France's upper classes; the Acadians are descendants, by way of Nova Scotia, of French peasants. It is the exotic, aristocratic but decaying, moral-law-breaking life imputed to the Creole, however, that most arrested the attention of American readers, and of Katherine Anne Porter.

In "Magic," for example—perhaps Porter's most ephemeral exercise in reproducing literary stereotypes—a Creole mulatto maid brushes

---

1. Merrill Maguire Skaggs, *The Folk of Southern Fiction* (Athens, Ga., 1972), 171.

her employer's hair and tells "hair-raising" stories of Basin Street brothel life and its brutalization of the "girls" who are its stock-in-trade. New Orleans has, since the mid-nineteenth century, represented in American literature the alluringly and titillatingly lascivious, the Catholic place where all Protestant sexual taboos are shockingly violated.[2]

After being featured as the docking place in those keelboat and "ringtail roarer" tales published as newspaper fillers before the Civil War, New Orleans was also, at the end of the nineteenth century, the literary location of drunken or violent release, of gambling dens and racetrack depravity. It is where all ignorant travelers, whether arriving by way of the Mississippi or the Gulf, were lured to lose their hard-earned money. After Cable's treatment in *Old Creole Days* (1879) and *The Grandissimes* (1880), New Orleans was also seen as the literary capital of Louisiana's plantation life, which in turn was assumed to be based on callous brutalization of blacks. In short, New Orleans has always been portrayed in American literature as the continent's most colorful and hazardous city, the tourist mecca for all who wished to witness the delightfully wicked or taste the extraordinary decoctions of the Other.

To understand superficially Katherine Anne Porter's depiction of Louisiana, all one need know is that she relies on these traditional literary views and southern stereotypes. For example, Louisiana is briefly mentioned in "The Journey" as a place of memorable sweetness and scarring loss. *The Old Order*'s grandmother stops there on her way to Texas, buys a house, plants an orchard, buries a husband, and takes a loss on her investment in a sugar-refining business. After she settles on a more productive farm in Texas, her two sons try to run away back to Louisiana so that they can eat sugar cane. The growth of the sugar-refining industry is a central episode in Cable's history, *The Creoles of Louisiana* (1885); but more sinister elements of the Cable version of Louisiana life are picked up later, in "The Witness," where Uncle Jimbilly describes black slave torture in rice fields and swamps.

The point, I think, is that the luridly appealing Louisiana that Porter experienced in her reading was far more real to her than any aspect or element of the Louisiana she discovered when visiting or

2. For a thorough and detailed description of the Louisiana Creole stereotype, with its many ramifications, see the chapter "The Creole," *ibid.*, 154–88. "Magic" and the other Porter stories quoted in this essay appear in Katherine Anne Porter, *The Collected Stories of Katherine Anne Porter* (New York, 1965), hereinafter cited parenthetically by page number in the text; "Magic" can be found on pp. 39–41.

living there. The fictional Louisiana that the previous century had prepared for her was also more practically important to her work. Louisiana and New Orleans are intensely felt and imagined places in *her* mind. Not surprisingly, then, that setting shimmers like Poe's City in the Sea when Porter creates two of her strongest psychological masterpieces: New Orleans itself is the symbolically appropriate location for key events in Parts 1 and 2 of "Old Mortality," and perhaps even more significantly, the microcosmic farmhouse location of "Holiday" is said to be "not far from the Louisiana line" (408). This essay will explore these two centrally important fictions, primarily asking what they reveal of the life of Porter's mind.

"Old Mortality," one of the brilliant trio of short novels (or long stories) in *Pale Horse, Pale Rider,* is one of Porter's densest and most inexhaustible fictions. After reading Joan Givner's biography of Porter, as well as the *Conversations* Givner edited, we know now that Porter's preparation for "Old Mortality" started with her invention of an aristocratic family and a conventionally proper childhood, from which she then appeared to be rebelling as she wrote her ostensibly autobiographical stories about Miranda's growing up.[3] Porter's inventions unpack like onion rings. By the time each reader reaches what she takes to be a core, she has no guarantee that she is seeing accurately through her stinging eyes.

The three parts of "Old Mortality," for example, invite—and support—many very different interpretations of its structure. The parts can be seen to represent Miranda's childhood, adolescence, and adulthood; or the past, present, and future as each impinges on and alters Miranda's life; or three ways in which a remote and seemingly peripheral or ignorable relative—in this case, Gabriel—can affect the world view of a little girl; or the intrusions of three mysterious female strangers—Amy, Miss Honey, and Cousin Eva—each of whom teaches Miranda a different truth; or it can be interpreted as a "the more things change, the more they stay the same" story, in three phases. All of these readings—and several more besides—seem to be to be supportable by the text of "Old Mortality." But when we focus on what *Louisiana* represents in "Old Mortality," we can interpret the three parts of the piece as three answers to the question, What does it mean to be a southern woman?

One of the things being a southern woman means, in "Old Mor-

---

3. Joan Givner, *Katherine Anne Porter: A Life* (New York, 1982); Joan Givner, *Katherine Anne Porter: Conversations* (Jackson, Miss., 1987).

tality," is being incarcerated. As Miranda looks on or listens to family stories, she registers facts that suggest her Aunt Amy was imprisoned in stifling conventions and expectations, which confined her and hastened her death, as much as her corset stays—giving her at last an eighteen-inch waist—confined and destroyed her body. Amy demands the heroine's right to affect her own novel, but remains to the end entrapped by its insidious fictions. In Part 2, Maria and Miranda are "immured" in their convent school, and escape its discipline momentarily only to discover the far more terrible entrapment that Miss Honey, living "outside," represents and gracelessly endures. In Part 3, eighteen-year-old, married Miranda encounters Cousin Eva, the suffragette who has been repeatedly jailed for her political activities. Eva seems bound up in her own need for negative attention, and she repeatedly suggests a negative model to avoid—until Miranda realizes that they think alike. The story ends, then, suggesting the possibility that Miranda is entrapped in her own family's ways of seeing, reacting, and avoiding or distorting truth.

The story begins, with deliberately confusing ambiguity, by describing Amy: "She was a spirited-looking young woman, with dark curly hair cropped and parted on the side, a short oval face with straight eyebrows, and a large curved mouth." We are seven lines into the story before we realize that the "she" in question is merely the figure in a photograph, a dead woman. She seems alive; and that is the point to remember about long-dead but still actively mourned Amy. It is also the key fact the story presents us; for we are in a world in which we cannot absolutely know what is fact and what is fiction, what is lively truth and what is dead legend—or, as Miranda's family expresses it, what is fact and what is poetry. Amy belongs to the world of poetry and legend. That characterization is our first reason to question whether she existed, at least as her family describes her. To what degree is Amy a family fiction? And to what extent, in this family, does created myth replace verifiable reality?

Porter deftly but repeatedly reminds us that in this family (which was once supposed to have been closely modeled on her own), nobody's word can be trusted, not even for the simplest declaration. For example, the photograph of Amy is said to be deficient because it does not show her hair and smile (174); yet the story's first sentence establishes that it shows both. Miranda's father, Harry, claims that no fat women were in the family, but Miranda knows of two fat aunts. Harry also tells his daughters to "go away, you're disgusting," if they fail to observe the conventions requiring girls to be clean and neat; yet he himself is still remembered for breaking much more strongly held conventions, about honor, when he shot at an undefended beau of Amy's. Gabriel, Amy's husband, produces a poem commemorating Amy that contains no factually accurate statements, nor any details that actually relate to Amy. The family approves because it understands that poems do not need to be "true." Their love of such poets as Poe (whose poems commemorating the death of a beautiful woman are set "out of space, out of time") traces to "springs in family feeling, and a love of legend" (175).

Amy, her young nieces are led to believe, was the perfect southern belle. She was tall, with dark hair, pale skin, lightness of movement, "a good dancer, superb on horseback, with a serene manner, an amiable gaiety tempered with dignity at all hours. Beautiful teeth and hands, of course, and over and above all this, some mysterious crown of enchantment that attracted and held the heart" (176). This model of behavior describes the stereotypical southern lady. The stereotype, in turn, entraps both Amy and the young nieces for whom she represents an ideal. That Amy has felt embalmed by the conventions to which she was forced to conform is clear when she complains, "Mammy, I'm sick of this world. I don't like anything in it. It's so *dull*" (188). Permeating the story with her recollected vitality, she feverishly declares her lover Gabriel a dull sulker, and wishes merely to go to sleep. She finds a way to do so, permanently, as soon as she marries and Mardi Gras is over.

Amy's most audacious rule-breaking is always thwarted, ignored, or forgiven because she is required to embody a family myth. Neither facts nor her inclinations can disrupt that required version of reality: "This loyalty of their father's in the face of evidence contrary to his ideal had its springs in family feeling, and a love of legend that he shared with the others. They loved to tell stories, romantic and poetic, or comic with a romantic humor; they did not gild the outward circumstance, it was the feeling that mattered. Their hearts and imaginations were captivated by their past, a past in which worldly considerations had played a very minor role. Their stories were almost always love stories against a bright blank heavenly blue sky" (175). The so-called facts, and artifacts, of the past leave Miranda feeling "melancholy" but acquiescent. Miranda, too, wants to be loved as Amy once was. Thus she and her sister are "enchanted" by the spell of the past, as her family defines it.

Amy's daring costumes, provocative behavior, and self-destructive escapades never shake her family's insistence that she is a perfect and conventional "lady," one avatar of which is an innocent young girl. Each gesture she makes is therefore reshaped to conform to the family's need for her to play her part. When asked whether she has allowed herself to be kissed at a dance, she replies, "Maybe he did . . . and maybe I wished him to." Her mother retorts, "Amy, you must not say such things. . . . Answer Gabriel's question" (188); that is, provide another and acceptable answer. Finally, Amy apparently hastens her own death by taking an overdose of medicine. Beautiful Amy, we surmise, can endure her life no longer. And Miranda, enjoined to imitate Amy in spite of her inability to do so, is as trapped in the southern-belle stereotype as her aunt once was. But so, of course, are all the young females in her family, all of whom are compared to Amy, to their disadvantage. In belonging "to the world of poetry" (178), Amy resides where flesh-and-blood females can never go. And Miranda's belief that someday she will receive beauty and become a "dead ringer" for Amy is apparently as preposterous as her later ambitions to be a jockey or a tightrope dancer or a pilot.

This southern world of distortion and self-deceit, which Miranda eventually resolves to outgrow and leave behind her, is characterized by a love of theater, music, and "the divinity of man's vision of the unseen" (179). It has no more to do with the women's needs than Gabriel's extravagant presents have to do with Amy's desires. It is a world of form without content. Most of all, it is a world in which girls are never allowed to believe with confidence that they can *know* anything (184). Here young women are prevented from experiencing anything on their own, for their lovers and brothers rush to defend an honor the women would willingly discard. At the end of Part 1, the letters and keepsakes seem "to have no place in the world" (193). Neither, we infer, do the spirited young women.

The family values depicted in Part 1 of "Old Mortality" function to undervalue all girl children by raising before them unattainable standards of feminine perfection. As a result, even when the girls grow into middle-aged matrons like Cousin Molly, they lie about themselves, their ages, and the past they have lived through. And those female offspring like Cousin Eva, the suffragette, are simply discarded or derided for bucking the norm, or for lacking a chin. That the children are corrupted into longing for a romance outside their probable experience is suggested obliquely by their love for the theater, but overtly by Miranda's longing to claim John Wilkes Booth, the flamboyant assassin, as part of the family. The past their imaginations are taught to crave is more dramatic and momentous than any factual records could supply.

By Part 2, the little girls, now grown to ages ten and fourteen, have clearly learned to conform to their family's pattern: thus they invent a Gothic nightmare of a convent to substitute for their thoroughly humdrum parochial school. Their shock is therefore intense upon confronting the real Gabriel, now paunchy, middle-aged, and alcoholic, instead of Amy's dashing lover whom they had always imagined. Gabriel's appearance at the racetrack where their father has taken them reminds the reader of the double signals, and double binds, such a "typically southern" rearing inculcates in its daughters. Gabriel pronounces the girls "pretty as pictures," although he adds, "but rolled into one they don't come up to Amy, do they?" (197). Their father describes them as awkward and a "nest of vipers" (197).

Amy is clearly so alive in memory that even her horse—Miss Lucy—has been perpetuated unto the fourth generation. But even though Miss Lucy IV wins the race, the cost of winning in such southern games horrifies Miranda: "Miss Lucy was bleeding at the nose, two thick red rivulets were stiffening her tender mouth and chin, the round velvet chin that Miranda thought the nicest kind of chin in the world. Her eyes were wild and her knees were trembling, and she snored when she drew breath" (199). The postrace condition of the supposedly beloved winning horse teaches Miranda something about the wider races she has longed to enter: "Miranda stood staring. That was winning, for Miss Lucy. So instantly and completely did her heart reject that victory, she did not know when it happened, but she hated it" (199).

Once the family threesome has encountered Gabriel, they find they cannot shake his unwanted revelations. Insisting on taking them home to show to his wife Miss Honey (whose name causes Miranda at first to mistake her for another horse, and who is clearly treated by Gabriel as callously as livestock), Gabriel reveals as his spouse a grim nemesis. Miss Honey, who has been jerked from rags to riches and back again for all of her married life, "gleamed forth in a pallid, unquenchable hatred and bitterness that seemed enough to bring her long body straight up out of the chair in a fury" (203). Gabriel has obviously been no more concerned for her needs, when they opposed his own, than he was for Amy's. As a result, Honey says distinctly, "I had rather, much rather . . . see my son dead at my feet than hanging around a race track" (204). Having discovered that grown-ups never seem to mean what they say in their descriptions (Gabriel and Miss Honey live, for example, in a disreputable neighborhood "in Elysian Fields"), the little girls discover something further—that being girls, they are not even to be allowed to keep the winnings of the dollars they have been forced to bet on Miss Lucy. The lesson is clear: for females in this world, whether horse or human, winning is losing; the cycle is escapable only through the grave. Whether one reaches the grave through naughty insouciance, as Amy did, or truculent intractability, as Miss Honey will, one cannot break out of the traps imposed by such lovers as Gabriel.

Another ostensible model of female possibilities is provided in Part 3 by Cousin Eva. The strident feminist, Eva at first seems Amy's opposite, only to grow more like her as the tale continues. Both Amy and Eva have pronounced personalities, and both seem to trigger the question, "Why is a strong character so deforming?" (215). Eva is as complacent about the strong hatred she arouses as Amy was once complacent about her loves. Eva's evocation of her own dramatic past is as melodramatic and exaggerated as the family's rendition of the Amy legend. Eva is certainly as bitter about the dullness of her world as the self-destructive Amy once was. And when Eva identifies the family as the root of all wrongs (217), she creates a theatrical extreme in order to glorify it.

Although Eva supplies a version of Amy's life and reputation entirely different from the others', she seems no more accurate than they ever did. In wondering where and when the invention will stop, Miranda begins to infer that, in her family, it has no end. The questions merely escalate: for example, what does *free* mean, if Eva can say of Amy, "She was *too free*" (215); indeed, if Amy was free, what condition would represent *bound*? And who is free of Amy? For Eva and Miranda both remain obsessed with her. And what must Miranda make of Eva's assertion that "it was just sex. . . . she was simply sex-ridden like the rest" (216)? Is it possible to gain any relief from Eva's vision of "festering women stepping gaily towards the charnel house" (216)?

The most disconcerting fact of all, of course, is Miranda's repeated discovery that she and Eva think alike—that family patterns duplicate themselves simultaneously in both their minds. This distressing fact is compounded when Miranda arrives home and finds her family once again falsifying all the facts about Gabriel, even as they plan to cele-

The Louisianas of Katherine Anne Porter's Mind

brate his funeral: "Life for Gabriel . . . was just one perpetual picnic" (219). Thus, having learned that her family falsifies all its facts, and that she herself duplicates the thought patterns of her family, Miranda forces the reader to question whether she has learned any capacity for factual balance at all when she resolves, *"I will be free of them, I shall not even remember them"* (219).

The largest doubts are aroused by Miranda's last declaration: "I don't want any promises, I won't have false hopes, I won't be romantic about myself. I can't live in their world any longer. . . . I don't care. At least I can know the truth about what happens to me, she assured herself silently, making a promise to herself" (221). The narrator, at least, calls all this learning and all this pain and all this resolve into question as she adds to this statement the story's last phrase: "in her hopefulness, her ignorance."

Since Louisiana functions in Katherine Anne Porter's fiction as a place in the writer's *mind*, it is significant that she emphasizes twice the fact that "Holiday" is set in a microcosmic little Brigadoon located "not far from the Louisiana line" (408). The second reference elaborates: the story occurs "a dozen miles away, where Texas and Louisiana melted together in a rotting swamp" (413). The exotic glamor and titillating possibilities Louisiana once suggested have receded just out of reach here, for the tale begins, "At that time I was too young for some of the troubles I was having, and I had not yet learned what to do with them"; as a result, "It seemed to me then there was nothing to do but run away" (407).

The unnamed narrator who recounts "Holiday" in the first person is not Katherine Anne Porter, of course, nor is the story any more factually accurate as autobiography than is "Old Mortality." Nevertheless, it is a coherent fiction manufactured in Porter's mind, and the careful stress on its geographic location is important. It is about where a body goes when a soul feels too oppressed to engage in the adrenalin-charged fantasies of dying quickly after dancing through Mardi Gras or of low-life discoveries to be made on Elysian Fields. Louisiana here is still accessible, but just barely. The story concerns discoveries to be made when there is "nothing to do but run away."

In her time of troubles when the narrator can envision nothing better than isolation and retreat, she arranges a month at an east Texas farm recommended by a friend as a place of idyllic and pastoral perfection. Arriving in the "bitter wind" of March, however, she finds instead only a "desolate mud-colored shapeless scene," and reflects that "there was nothing beautiful in those woods now but the promise of spring, for I detested bleakness" (410). The farmhouse to which she has resigned herself sits "staring and naked, an intruding stranger" (411), and she registers as she enters it, "I was again in a house of perpetual exile" (413). At her request she is shown to the attic room; there she will live, struggling through her puzzles in her upper story much as Godfrey St. Peter does in Cather's *The Professor's House* (to which this detail is probably indebted).

What the narrator finds on her ostensibly self-enclosed and self-sufficient farm is the opposite of everything suggested by Louisiana. First of all, she finds an orderly system: an expandable and inclusive, not exclusive, family, in mode patriarchal, not matriarchal; prosperous, not improvident; Marxist, not Catholic; and disciplined, hardworking, loving, and happy. The Müllers are full of "enormous energy and animal force" (416), and function together as "one human being divided into several separate appearances" (417). The only exception in this serenely homogeneous composite is the crippled and grotesque Ottilie: "The crippled servant girl brought in more food and gathered up plates and went away in her limping run, and she seemed to me the only individual in the house. Even I felt divided into many fragments, having left or lost a part of myself in every place I had travelled, in every life mine had touched, above all, in every death of someone near to me that had carried into the grave some part of my living cells. But the servant, she was whole, and belonged nowhere" (417).

Before the narrator can establish a connection with incessantly shaking Ottilie, and therefore assimilate the truths she must learn before she can return to her own imaginative places, she must first bind up the fragments of herself that she feels she has dropped in every place she has visited and in every death she has experienced. For that task, she retreats instinctively to the bosom of the Müller family.

The Müllers, in providing a perfectly human community, provide also the occasions in which the most intense human emotions center and focus,—birth, marriage, and death; they furnish as well the laughter and tears that naturally attend those events. Beyond that, they supply the necessary community relaxations that occur in weekly dancing parties in the *Turnverein;* the ambiguous political machinations predictable when Father Müller's son-in-law wishes to be both a southern sheriff and a member of an atheist family; the economic ambiguities that inhere in Father Müller's manipulative use of his controlling wealth and his desire to disprove his role as "Kapital"; and a tenuous but dependent relation to the nearest church. As the narrator observes all these human activities, she finds, "I settled easily enough into the marginal life of the household ways and habits" (417). She mends as she pulls herself together; she observes the clear signs of an imminent spring.

The crucial connection she must make before she can finish healing, however, is with Ottilie. Ottilie's "whole body was maimed in some painful, mysterious way, probably congenital, I supposed, though she seemed wiry and tough" (415). A key fact about this figure, particularly from the point of view of such a person as we now know Katherine Anne Porter to have been—always anxious about her appearance and her sexual power—is Ottilie's hideousness, her "mutilated face" and repellent body. A key fact from the point of view of that writer's persona is that Ottilie "can't talk": her face "strained with the anxiety of one peering into a darkness full of danger" (420); her "muteness seemed nearly absolute" (421).

Because in her desperation the narrator has chosen for herself a time of quiet retreat and unprogrammed inactivity, she has the mysterious opportunity, one day, to discover yet another crucial fact about repellent Ottilie. Ottilie owns a photograph she shows to the narrator, and it proves that she was once a normal child of the Müller family:

> The bit of cardboard connected her at once somehow to the world of human beings I knew; for an instant some filament lighter than cobweb spun itself out between that living center in her and in me, a filament from some center that held us all bound to our unescapable common source, so that her life and mine were kin, even a part of each other, and the painfulness and strangeness of her vanished. She knew well that she had been Ottilie, with those steady legs and watching eyes, and she was Ottilie still within herself. For a moment, being alive, she knew she suffered. (426)

The moment over, the two return to their established roles within the household. At lunch, Ottilie reappears dutifully, "and again I had been a stranger to her . . . like all the rest but she was no stranger to me, and could not be again" (426).

The narrator, then, at this point connects with an embodiment of that grotesque part of herself that has been mutilated and shunted aside in childhood. She must next discover what to do with this connection; she takes the Müller household in this crisis as her model: even motherly Annetje "seemed to have forgotten that Ottilie was her sister. So had all the others." In pondering the fact, the narrator realizes that they have forgotten the grotesque part of themselves in pure self-defense, for they know their lives must go on: "Suffering went with life, suffering and labor. While one lived one worked, that was all" (427). The narrator sees no option but to "promise myself that I would forget her, too; and to remember her for the rest of my life" (427). Finally, "I found great virtue and courage in their steadiness and refusal to feel sorry for anybody, least of all for themselves" (428).

Ottilie, of course, cannot be either forgotten or buried, even though the narrator confesses to an intense wish that she would simply and immediately die. But Ottilie has a great deal more left to teach, and the lessons arrive soon. This microcosmic farm cannot escape life's terrors, and thus endures a terrible storm. As thunder crashes, waters rush over the land, drowning chickens and livestock. In meeting the emergency, all work frantically, but the effort overstrains Mother Müller; because they are cut off from medical help, she dies. And Father Müller is left to wail bitterly, "Ach, Gott, Gott. A hundert tousand tollars in the bank . . . and tell me, tell, what goot does it do?" (431).

Waters recede, garish sunshine returns, a funeral takes place, and the family prepares to bury their beloved mother. "On that day," the narrator records, "I realized, for the first time, not death, but the terror of dying" (433). As the hearse leaves the grounds, the narrator lies on her bed in a half-sleep, paralyzed by terror. Through her drowse, she hears the howling of a dog—and wakes to realize that the sound comes from Ottilie. For Ottilie has also come in this moment to the outer rim of her own despair. Both narrator and Ottilie face simultaneously the terror of dying as well as the ultimate bitterness of being left out of human affairs such as burials. Both face in this moment their profound exclusion from human connectedness.

In the moment, the narrator finds within herself the animal energy and force to forge a corrective. She harnesses the shaggy pony to the very cart that first brought her to the farm. She then forces Ottilie into the very seat she once occupied as honored guest, and starts after the funeral cortege. In their frantic, perilous drive toward significant human action and activity, however, the narrator suddenly realizes that Ottilie is enjoying her unconventional escape from the place of endless chores. She is responding to the sunshine and sky. Unmistakably, she is laughing; she is finding joy. In this moment, we as readers understand what Katherine Anne Porter has meant by the moral with which she ended her story's first paragraph: "But this story I am about to tell you happened before this great truth impressed itself upon me—that we do not run from the troubles and dangers that are truly ours, and it is better to learn what they are earlier than later, and if we don't run from the others, we are fools" (407).

The two, then, don't run from the troubles that are truly theirs, for no running can erase their linked experience of permanent mutilation. They don't run, either, from their status as isolatoes. In studying Ottilie's face the narrator understands that "she was beyond my reach as well as any other human reach, and yet, had I not come nearer to her than I had to anyone else in my attempt to deny and bridge the distance between us?" (434). They remain "both equally the fools of life, equally fellow fugitives from death" (435). Yet in running, for once, together, "we would have a little stolen holiday, a breath of spring air and freedom" (435).

The narrator turns the cart away from the rutted main road and toward her favorite escape route and retreating place. In this holiday stolen from inexorable duties, "there would be time enough to drive to the river down the lane of mulberries and to get back to the house before the mourners returned." The running, the holiday, the celebration, the restoration, the rest, will do no harm: "There would be plenty of time for Ottilie to have a fine supper ready for them. They need not even know she had been gone" (435).

In "Holiday" Katherine Anne Porter creates her most upbeat story. Its affirmations are not evasive. Its unity encompasses the worst that human life can offer, to make fools of us all. In teaching us here—with a clearly articulated moral statement—that we are not cowardly to run from troubles that are not ours, she encourages us to find what she has permitted herself: stolen holidays that do no harm and that permit a restored return to the chores of the evening. In assimilating that lesson, we infer, Katherine Anne Porter provided herself a way back to the Louisianas of her mind.

Shirley Ann Grau.
Photo by Carol Lazar, courtesy of Shirley Ann Grau

The Keepers of the House
Scarlett O'Hara and Abigail Howland

*G*ONE WITH THE WIND (1936) is Margaret Mitchell's only surviving work of fiction; *The Keepers of the House* (1964) is Shirley Ann Grau's most ambitious, and in many ways most success-ful. Although the popular appeal of Mitchell's record-breaking classic far surpasses that of *The Keepers,* the books are oddly similar. Both won the Pulitzer Prize; the writers both have been praised for their storytelling skills. Perhaps least apparent, but meriting special atten-tion, is the affinity between the books' dominant themes: gender and racial relations.[1]

In an interview conducted by Kay Bonetti in April, 1989, Shirley Ann Grau expressed her admiration for the "magnificent narrative line" of *Gone with the Wind.* At the same time, she criticized the book's more technical aspects, such as the lack of "subtlety and interesting symbols." Grau considers *Gone with the Wind* as standard an example of mass-market melodrama as one can find. But she also assumes a condescending attitude toward *The Godfather,* the book that, as Paul Schlueter convincingly argues, inspired Grau's own *The Condor Passes.*[2] Despite Grau's similar opinions of these novels—even if those opin-ions can be taken at face value—*Gone with the Wind,* at least, has re-cently attracted critical attention, not only on account of what Eliza-beth Fox-Genovese calls the "immediacy with which it engaged the American imagination," but also by virtue of its special position on the issue of gender.[3] Although, undeniably, *The Keepers of the House* is a more skillfully constructed novel, in terms of technique, then *Gone with the Wind,* the issue of technical superiority is not my concern here.

1. Margaret Mitchell, *Gone with the Wind* (16th rpr.; New York, 1936); Shirley Ann Grau, *The Keepers of the House* (New York, 1964). Hereinafter these novels are cited parenthetically by page number in the text.

2. Kay Bonetti, "Interview with Shirley Ann Grau," American Audio-Prose Library (Columbia, Mo., 1989); Paul Schlueter, *Shirley Ann Grau* (Boston, 1981), 69–71.

3. See Elizabeth Fox-Genovese, "Scarlett O'Hara: The Southern Lady as New Woman," *American Quarterly,* IV (1981), 391–412. For other treatments of this subject, see Anne Goodwyn Jones, *Tomorrow Is Another Day: The Woman Writer in the South, 1859–1936* (Baton Rouge, 1981), 339–50, and Blanche H. Gelfant, *Women Writing in America: Voices in Collage* (Hanover, N.H., 1984), 181–89.

Rather, my focus falls on the kinship between the central heroines of both books: on Abigail Howland's and Scarlett O'Hara's development in the respective narratives; on those characters' embodiment of certain southern stereotypes; and, above all, on the authors' attitudes—best captured by that trite epithet *ambivalent*—toward their created protagonists.

The retrospective sections of both narratives begin at approximately the same time. Abigail, the narrator of *The Keepers of the House*, traces the family history to the first William Howland, who, seduced by the beauty of the land, settled in the book's imaginary territory somewhere between Atlanta and the Mississippi River (reminiscent of Grau's "divided loyalties," for her childhood was split between New Orleans, where she was born, and Montgomery, Alabama). It is 1815, shortly after the battle of New Orleans: "He saw endless stretches of trees, the pines and hickories, big-leafed magnolias and huge live oaks. He saw how plants bloomed in the warmer soil, how they grew double their usual size with no wind to cut them down: dogwood and redbud, flame azalea and laurel" (11). *The Keepers'* geography can be puzzling. Grau has explained that she "went very carefully through the novel and scrambled [its] geography. It's no one place. It's a bit of everything."[4] By saying that *The Keepers* is set in an imaginary territory between New Orleans and Atlanta, I do not mean to imply that it is set somewhere in Mississippi or Alabama. New Orleans and Atlanta, however, are consistent points of reference in the novel: William Marshall Howland sets out from New Orleans when he looks for the site on which to build the house, and his granddaughter, the second Abigail Howland, like Scarlett O'Hara, goes to New Orleans on her honeymoon; but Abigail's grandfather meets his future wife in Atlanta, and when Abigail's mother returns home with her daughter after her short-lived marriage to Gregory Mason, they take an overnight train from Lexington, Virginia, stop for a couple of hours in Atlanta and then take a local train to Madison City. The latter, which is presumably the closest town to the Howlands' estate, does not exist in any of the four states. It could, of course, stand for Madisonville, Louisiana, across Lake Pontchartrain from New Orleans; but William Howland buys his liquor from the Robertsons of Madison City, and their stills are supposedly situated in Honey Island Swamp, which lies far-

---

4. Carlton Creemens, "An Exclusive Tape Recorded Interview with Shirley Ann Grau," *Writer's Yearbook*, XXXVII (1966), 22.

ther east, on the Louisiana-Mississippi border. Other allusions in the novel similarly tend to negate any specific inferences.

Whatever the location, it is on this fertile land that William Marshall Howland starts a plantation, which grows steadily with each succeeding generation. The house Howland builds, at first a primitive structure, develops with the influence of ensuing Howlands, especially women (one of them a rich Catholic heiress from New Orleans, Aimée Legendre), into a home where "even the interior began to have touches of elegance—harmoniums, and inlaid tables and shelves full of china figures" (12).

Gerald O'Hara arrived in America in 1822, but the narrative chronology of *Gone with the Wind* really begins in 1844, when Gerald wins a piece of land in a game of poker, names it Tara, and in less than twenty years turns idle soil into one of the most successful plantations in the county. It takes Scarlett more than sixteen years and the traumatic experience of witnessing the fall of Atlanta to glimpse what her father saw when he first went to estimate the value of the land he had won: "the long avenue of trees leading toward the road . . . twin lines of somber trees . . . the abandoned lawn, waist high in weeds under white-starred young magnolia trees. . . . uncultivated fields, studded with tiny pines and underbrush, that stretched their rolling red-clay surface away into the distance on four sides" (47).

Like William Howland, Gerald O'Hara builds a house that has "no architectural plan whatever," but, Mitchell adds, "with [his wife] Ellen's care and attention, it gained a charm that made up for its lack of design" (57). In both books, then, a house built by a patriarch and serving as the major site of events survives because of the love and courage of its women.

Houses constitute a major metaphor in Grau's fiction. In general, the settings of her novels and short stories are as significant as the characters. In particular, she often uses houses as a metaphor for the female body. In "Ending," from Grau's collection of short stories *Nine Women*, Barbara Eagleton is relieved to see her husband leave for good, and Grau records the corresponding change in the house itself: Barbara "felt the house, empty and quiet now, settle itself at last for the night. She felt a sigh of relief run along beams and floors."[5] Like-

5. Shirley Ann Grau, *Nine Women* (New York, 1986), 122. For more on the significance of houses in Grau's work, see Anthony Bukoski, "The Burden of Home: Shirley Ann Grau's Fiction," *Critique*, IV (Summer, 1987), 181.

wise, in the opening chapter of *The Keepers*, Abigail's feelings of emptiness and loneliness find their echo in the description of the house. The emotional wound becomes physical when evoked in details of torn turf and broken fence. Wishing to hurt others as much as the house has been "hurt," Abigail intends to keep the destruction unrepaired as a reminder.

If Grau's fiction testifies to the physical relationship between a house and the woman inhabiting it, the "keepers" of Grau's houses are typically male. In the story "The Householder," Harry kills a burglar with the gun his father gave him. Remembering his father's conviction that "every householder's got to have a gun," Harry kills not in self-defense, but because the burglar invades *his* house and breaks *his* furniture. Relationships between men and women are likewise in a man's keeping, and more often than not are doomed to failure. The failure is unsurprising given the fact that most of Grau's women are either conveniences (as, for example, in "Patriarch" and "The House-keeper") or nuisances (as in *The Keepers*). The only lasting heterosexual relationship in *The Keepers* is the one between William Howland and his black housekeeper, Margaret Carmichael—the sole woman in the novel for whom William has genuine respect. The only healthy relationship in *Nine Women* is between the lesbian couple portrayed in the story "Home," in which a woman is in charge of both the house and the relationship.

Grau's mature women are "women alone."[6] Their maturation has been all the more painful through being obstructed by the women's attempts to conform to the culture's expectations. Nowhere is this phenomenon more evident than in *The Keepers*, where Abigail's growth is thwarted by her compliance with the role of the southern lady.

Although a good deal of Grau's own family history seeps into the Howland saga (the very name "Howland" belongs to her family, on her mother's side), neither of the maternal figures in the novel resembles Grau's mother. In the interview with Bonetti, Grau's recollections of her mother bring to mind Ellen Robillard: very beautiful, very tall, with black hair, gray eyes, and "dead white" skin. Katherine Onions Grau, in her daughter's words, "subscribed firmly to the dictum that respectable married ladies do not work." Grau hastily adds, however, that "had [her mother] been wealthier or poorer, it would've

---

6. See John Canfield, "Women Alone," *Southern Review*, n.s., XXII (1986), 904–906.

undoubtedly been better for her; wealthier—she wouldn't have cared what people thought; poorer—she wouldn't have had a choice." This is only one of the many instances when Grau's words testify to her ambivalence about gender identity and gender role, the issues that in *The Keepers* reach the proportions of schizophrenia.[7]

The development of Scarlett O'Hara and Abigail Howland interestingly coincides with the process that Jung called "individuation." What merits particular attention in Jung's model is that, unlike other psychoanalytical developmental models, it identifies the beginning of the process of individuation with adult, rather than childhood, experience. Further, it pinpoints the start of this process as the moment the adult becomes conscious of what Jung calls a "persona," a role in society to which that person is expected to conform. Defiance of these expectations marks the next stage in the process of individuation. The following stage is the adult's confrontation with the "shadow," which Jung defines as the "unrecognized dark half of the personality."[8] All these stages can be traced in Scarlett's and Abigail's path to self-awareness.

Individuation, as Jung and other psychoanalysts emphasize, can be initially obstructed by the absence or unreliability of the mother figure. Indeed, both Abigail and Scarlett lose their mothers early in life—Abigail at sixteen, Scarlett at eighteen. Abigail's mother is weak, withering, and unimportant except perhaps as a model of traditional southern feminine behavior. As Abigail confesses, "My mother was a lady and a lady is unfailingly polite and gentle to everyone" (149)—a clear echo of Scarlett's assessment of Ellen—but this role is precisely what Abigail eschews at the novel's conclusion. Scarlett, at least initially, feels obligated to "reproduce" (to borrow a word from Jane Gallop) her mother.[9] Ultimately, however, she comes to believe that everything her mother had told her about life was wrong. Both protagonists derive strength from their relationships with black women who function as surrogate mothers. Mammy is the only female character in Mitchell's novel who profoundly understands Scarlett. Margaret Carmichael, a real stepmother through her secret marriage with William Howland (as Abigail anticipates at one point, "This was my

---

7. Bonetti, "Interview."

8. C. G. Jung, *Two Essays on Analytical Psychology* (Princeton, 1966), 96.

9. Jane Gallop, *The Daughter's Seduction: Feminism and Psychoanalysis* (Ithaca, 1982), 113.

mother, she had raised me, my grandmother too" [221]), sees in Abigail the qualities of character others do not perceive: strength, courage, and moral integrity.

In a further parallel, both protagonists marry men who fail to meet the standards of their society. Scarlett's third marriage, to Rhett Butler, violates the norms of her class because, as several of the novel's personae point out, Captain Butler is "no gentleman." John Tolliver, Abigail's husband, comes from the "northernmost county with the darkest, bloodiest past in the state" (194); Grau has said that in the language of the Old South, he would be called a "wool-hat" or "white trash." Although Rhett, an outcast of a renowned Charleston family, has a far different social background from John's, he too is a self-made man, and similarly is associated with "white trash" through his affiliations with scalawags and carpetbaggers.

Rhett and John share several other traits. They are attractive to women, with the same kind of dark handsomeness. Even though Rhett is plainly a war profiteer and a renegade at heart, there is a brief period in his marriage with Scarlett when for their daughter Bonnie's sake he pursues a political career. He enlists in the Klan; so does John, albeit for a much less noble motive. Yet in both cases we observe the same lack of moral integrity; both men are unscrupulous opportunists, turning everything to their advantage. And the "fierce intensity" that Abigail detects in John also characterizes Rhett.

Whereas critics have tended to treat John Tolliver as a villain, Grau claims to admire his "incredible determination" and says that he was intended not as an evil character, but rather as "a sympathetic picture of a man from a hardscrabble farm, for whom success is absolutely everything." Grau defends Tolliver's reaction to what she calls Abigail's "betrayal." She supports his hypocritically cynical acceptance of what he thinks is William Howland's illegitimate relationship with his black housekeeper, and she finds him absolutely justified in feeling betrayed at the news of their marriage. Grau claims that "if I were to write a sequel, he will have survived very nicely. . . . He will simply adjust himself to suit to whatever society demands."[10]

The problem a critic faces with the characterization of John Tolliver in the novel vis-à-vis Grau's opinion of him is strictly one of intended versus achieved meaning. If Grau intended to model John on Rhett Butler, she failed to give him Rhett's complexity. Rhett has always ap-

10. Bonetti, "Interview."

pealed to the feminine imagination because he combines traditional male qualities (physical strength, assertiveness, boldness, among others) with unconventional traits (recognition of women as sexual beings and sympathy for their desire to "do" something with their lives), together with traits that tradition has associated with women: a desire for verbal and emotional, as well as physical, communication; love for children and family; a strong urge to nurture (he is much more of a mother figure than Scarlett); lack of embarrassment about crying; and a delicacy regarding others' feelings. In him we find a synthesis of strength and tenderness, hence his appeal.

John Tolliver possesses none of these characteristics except the purely "masculine" ones, and yet he is much like Rhett. Mitchell constructed Rhett's character to a broad measure. As appealing to the feminine imagination as he is, Rhett also repels with his grasping opportunism and his cynicism. Grau draws strongly upon these latter traits in her characterization of John Tolliver. John is a cynic not only in his political facade, but also in his private life. At one point he explains to a bewildered Abigail the mechanisms of his hard-won campaign for the state senate: "The Negroes figure I'm not old Judge Lynch himself—and I've tried my damndest to see that they get that message straight. And everybody in the district pretty much knows about your grandpa's bastards. That counts for something, I guess. As for the white people, well, they think I'm for just about whatever they're for. And I've told 'em that myself" (231–32). When Abigail asks John what he "privately" thinks about the Negroes, he cynically responds, "Love 'em dearly. . . . Like your grandfather" (211).

A paradox of both novels is that although the central consciousness in each is that of a woman, only men (Rhett and Ashley, William, and John) are given the ability to think in terms of abstractions. For this reason alone, Anne Goodwyn Jones considers Mitchell's voice in *Gone with the Wind* to be essentially "masculine." The same holds partly true for *The Keepers*. Even though the point of view is exclusively feminine throughout the narrative, for the major part Abigail sees herself through men's eyes: her grandfather's and her husband's. As the narrative unfolds, Abigail resembles the Everywoman of Hélène Cixous' "Sorties": "the nonsocial, nonpolitical, nonhuman half of the living structure . . . tirelessly listening to what goes on inside—inside her belly, inside her 'house.'" Abigail lives from one childbirth to the next, giving birth to four children (and not three, as Schlueter reports), minutely recording the physical changes accompanying each pregnancy.[11] Grau's indisputable achievement, however, lies in conveying precisely the moment when Abigail develops a voice of her own.

The authors' highly ambivalent attitude toward their female protagonists merits particular attention. Much has been written on this aspect of Mitchell's novel, and the arguments need not be rehearsed here. Suffice it to say that inherent in Scarlett's character is an absence of reflection and analysis. Mitchell once admitted to having conceived Melanie Hamilton, not Scarlett, as the real heroine of the book. Scarlett, however, somehow got out of hand and took over the narrative. And this for good reason: Scarlett's crude instincts are counterbalanced by her vivaciousness and effervescence. All are part of the same general trait of energy and vitality, part of the novel's larger theme of life, struggle, and completion versus death, surrender, and depletion—a theme that structures not only characterization, but also the treatment of the novel's historical matter.

That Grau is ambivalent toward her protagonist is perhaps less obvious but becomes apparent once we consider the following details: Abigail's early sources of informal education (her college years seem extraneous to her overall development) are her mother, the neighborhood ladies, and the Bible. She says, for instance, that "listening to the ladies talk," she learned her first skill—that of detecting "signs of Negro blood." That skill enables her to identify the Negro in the Carmichael-Howland children, all of whom are considered white (and not black as Schlueter, among others, assumes). "It's a southern talent, you might say," Abigail adds (143). Another southern talent inherited from her mother is her utter conformity to expectations concerning her gender. Abigail does not find irregular, and certainly is not offended by, systematic male patronizing, whether it be by her grandfather, her husband, or Margaret's son Robert. As she notes, "There are lots of southern men who treat their ladies that way," and, "It's quite pleasant, really" (190). Commentary on the novel seems oddly silent on this aspect of Abigail. Critics instead emphasize the traits Abigail exhibits during and after the dramatic events near the end of the novel. Grau, by contrast, in the interview with Bonetti, bluntly castigated Abigail on all fronts—as not "the brightest" character, and tiresome to boot. To the interviewer's protest that Abigail grows in the

11. Jones, *Tomorrow Is Another Day*, 347; Hélène Cixous, "Sorties," in Hélène Cixous and Catherine Clément, *The Newly Born Woman*, trans. Betsy Wing (Minneapolis, 1986), 66; Schlueter, *Shirley Ann Grau*, 57.

course of the novel, trancends her initial ignorance, and "sees things clearly" at the novel's end, Grau responded with the question "Does she see correctly?" What Grau implies here, Mitchell explicitly states about Scarlett—namely, that "what [Scarlett] understood was written down; what she did not understand—and there were many things beyond her comprehension, they were left to the reader's imagination." Although both writers claim to have little tolerance for the type of woman Mitchell once called "weak-minded," their claims do not withstand even a cursory reading of their novels. Mitchell, as Fox-Genovese has argued, "confused her own identification with Scarlett and had trouble differentiating her function as presentor of Scarlett's vision from her function as commentator on Scarlett."[12] In *The Keepers,* not only does Abigail carry the weight of the entire narrative, but the evolution of almost every character in the novel is also mediated through her consciousness.

The tendency among women to internalize the repressive male constructs that marginalize them informs Grau's text.[13] In fact, all of Margaret and William Howland's three children, including the son, suffer from "a good deal of self-hatred," Grau admits, and Abigail herself is not devoid of self-denigration. She is *expected*—a word firmly rooted in Grau's vocabulary, and indicating that Grau is setting a character within a framework of ready-made "feminine" identity—*expected* to conform to the stereotype of the southern lady, with its notions of inherent scatterbrainedness, nonintellectuality, and dependence, and she squarely realizes this prefabricated "ideal."[14] During her brief courtship with John, she is impressed by his organized and highly authoritarian style and confesses that "since no one had ever told me what to do before, I liked it immensely" (197). When William Howland disappears, and Margaret, John, and Abigail await the news of his death, John tells Abigail that he has offered a monetary reward to the finder. Abigail contends: "I would never have thought of that, but then I never thought of anything" (213). When Margaret delivers her

12. Schlueter, *Shirley Ann Grau,* 55; Richard Harwell, ed., *Margaret Mitchell's "Gone with the Wind" Letters, 1936–1949* (New York, 1976), 102; Fox-Genovese, "Scarlett O'Hara," 410.

13. See, for instance, Joanne Blum, *Transcending Gender: The Male/Female Double in Women's Fiction* (Ann Arbor, 1988), 4.

14. Bonetti, "Interview." See also Jacqueline Boles and Maxine P. Atkinson, "Ladies: South by Northwest," in *Southern Women,* ed. Caroline Matheny Dillman (New York, 1988), 127–40.

first baby for her, Abigail, squatting on the floor, can think of nothing except: "How silly. I can't do anything right. I can't even get to the hospital in time for a baby" (205). Afterward, Margaret pleads with Abigail not to tell anybody that the baby girl was born on the floor: "White ladies don't squat down to drop on the floor" (206). Abigail never mentions the circumstance, and "everybody assumed that the baby had been born on a mattress, proper and decent" (206). This may remind one of Mammy's misgivings about Scarlett's rapid recovery after her first child is born, which Mammy thinks is "downright common—ladies should suffer more" (132). Yet it is the same Abigail who singlehandedly defies the entire city and saves the family home from burning by a gang of hoodlums even though, as she admits, "all my life I had been trained to depend on men."

Firmly inscribed in the category of the lady, and one of its most neurotogenic points, is the expectation that a lady never experiences sexual desire or pleasure, much less admits doing so if she has. Both Jones and Fox-Genovese have written on this point in reference to Scarlett, emphasizing the fact that her sensuality surfaces only with a man who can dominate her. In the only erotic scene of the novel, Scarlett's orgasm is conveyed as the "ecstasy of surrender." In her two passionate encounters with Ashley, one during his furlough in Atlanta, the other in the orchard at Tara, Scarlett promises Ashley that she will slave for him in return for his favors. She says in the former: "I'd cook for you and polish your boots and groom your horse— Ashley, say you love me!" (277), and in the latter: "I'd work for you. . . . I'd do anything for you" (531). Similarly, Abigail recalls the evening, apparently the last in her symbiotic relationship with John, when he tells her, "Woman, . . . let's go to bed." She thinks then that "he was still the most attractive man I'd ever known. I remember that night, even now. I always think of it as the end of the happy times" (232). If both women sound like happy slaves (the point Jones makes in reference to Scarlett), they should. Even the few erotic fantasies Abigail cherishes are linked with her desire for what Jones calls "benevolent paternalism."[15]

The turning points in the narratives, at which both women achieve what might called an inner vision, are remarkably similar. Abigail recollects the car ride from Madison City to the Howland house: "I suppose I've made the trip two hundred times, but now that it is all

15. Fox-Genovese, "Scarlett O'Hara," 414; Jones, *Tomorrow Is Another Day*, 345.

over, I find that I only remember one. Out of all that, only one" (243). Both like and unlike the vision connected with houses in Grau's other works, this is what Grau (in *Evidence of Love*) calls a "myopic vision."[16] The house first looms indistinct in the early morning fog, and Abigail has a short-lived sensation that "it would not be there, would have disappeared like a ghost." As she drives closer, however, she sees the house "vague and indistinct in the fog, but there, just the way it had been for the last five generations. It looked very very large in this light, and empty. Fog covered the fields beneath it, so that it seemed to float without solid ground, just exactly like those fairy castles in a child's story book" (246). Later still, when she goes into *her* house and closes the door "firmly" behind her, she thinks that "there'd been a message of some sort."

The imagery of delusion in this passage, against which Grau projects the clarity of an attained insight, reminds one of an analogous scene in *Gone with the Wind*, where Scarlett's nightmare of running in the fog both becomes reified and takes on a metaphorical meaning near the novel's end, as she finally comprehends that the haven of safety is in Rhett's strong arms. But Rhett doesn't give a damn, and Scarlett, for once, feels defeated; even her old charm ("I'll think of it tomorrow") will not help to direct her thoughts to another channel—until, that is, she thinks of Tara and gathers new strength from her visual recollection of the family estate. In Grau's and Mitchell's descriptions, the image of the house triggers the recognition of familiarity and safety. Abigail sees the blooming azaleas, the yard "familiar and safe . . . full of known things. . . . Empty clothes lines, cords frayed and fluttering" (246). Scarlett remembers "small things": cape jessamine bushes, "the avenue of dark cedars," fluttering curtains. Neither of the two women admits total defeat, even, as Mitchell says, "when it stare[s] them in the face."

It thus appears that the family house is the only place where each woman can find a sustenance independent of the vagaries of human relations. Although I doubt that either Mitchell or Grau wanted to emphasize this point, it nonetheless emerges as an important one at the conclusion of each novel. Both women lose their husbands as they mature and became independent. If Rhett says that he is proud of having a "smart" wife, he at the same time makes it clear that he is in charge of the family. He tells Scarlett during their honeymoon in New

16. Grau, *Evidence of Love* (Boston, 1988).

Orleans that "there's never going to be any doubt in anybody's mind about who wears the pants in the Butler family" (859). By that time, having made the plantation function after the war and having expanded Frank's business in Atlanta into a thriving success, Scarlett has abundantly proved that she can take full charge of the well-being of the family. But Rhett does not need a wife, he needs a child. He tells Scarlett—albeit not entirely convincingly—during their tempestuous conversation at home following Ashley's birthday party that he does not want her body, but her mind. But he also makes it clear that the mind he covets is the mind of a child. He tells Scarlett during their last conversation in the book: "I wanted to take care of you, to pet you, to give you everything you wanted. I wanted to marry you and protect you and give you a free rein in anything that would make you happy— just as I did Bonnie. . . . I wanted you to play, like a child" (1030). Rhett's unguarded love for Scarlett surfaces in the scenes where he acts like a protector of a child (in New Orleans, when Scarlett awakens from her nightmare, and when she tells him that she is pregnant). In both scenes he takes Scarlett on his lap and comforts her the way one comforts a child. The irony of Scarlett's situation is that when she wakes up from her dream of running in the fog and from her romantic dream of Ashley, and emerges as a mature woman, she confronts another dreamer—for Scarlett was as much a part of Rhett's dream as Ashley was of hers.

Moreover, Scarlett is not a child. In fact, Mitchell records the first major change in her heroine at Tara, after the fall of Atlanta; she says that "the girl with her sachet and dancing slippers had slipped away and there was left a woman . . . to whom nothing was left from the wreckage except the indestructible red earth on which she stood" (490). Whenever the well-being of Tara is at stake, Scarlett responds as a mature woman. This is precisely where the two protagonists are most alike: defenders of the family estate, women with spines of steel. Abigail, a subdued woman for the major part of the narrative, declares her independence when she takes full control of events in the climactic scene in *The Keepers*. There is something heroic in this scene, in which Abigail, having dispatched others to a safe hiding place in the woods, remains alone in the house and confronts the entire city with a gun in her hand, much like Scarlett when the Yankee intruder invades the house. Abigail says: "I'm not afraid. . . . I know what to do, I can handle things" (294).

The endings of both books have elicited debate. In *The Keepers*,

Abigail, who has taken arms against a sea of troubles and defended the family house from a gang of racists, is visited by the ghosts of her approving ancestors. She says to them, "I bet you didn't think I could." By this marvelous sleight of hand, Grau makes her point explicit, even as she invites another parallel with *Gone with the Wind*. After the fall of Atlanta, Scarlett returns to Tara to discover that her mother has died and Gerald turned senile, and her mind, spinning with fatigue and the whisky she has drunk on an empty stomach, summons a host of forefathers who "were whispering wordless encouragement to her." She tells them, "Whether you are there or not . . . good night—and thank you" (421). We hear the voices of Scarlett and Gerald O'Hara and of William Howland and his black wife when Abigail thinks the unspoken truth, meant for her courageous first daughter, Abby, to hear, but never uttered aloud: "Child, . . . you don't even know it's possible to love a house and land that much" (274).

Both books' final paragraphs, which draw the past into the present, suggest a number of meanings. Scarlett reminisces about the comfort of Mammy's "broad bosom"; she "wanted Mammy desperately, as she had wanted her when she was a little girl" (1037). And the book concludes with Scarlett's old formula, "Tomorrow is another day." Abigail, like Joan in Grau's *House on Coliseum Street*, huddles "fetus-like against the cold unyielding boards" (309). The regressive longing for home and mother conveyed in these images is characteristic of *écriture féminine* in more than one sense. They suggest what Cixous calls a "pre-oedipal," or "prelinguistic," form of communication wherein, before acculturation, femaleness is conveyed through a mother-infant relationship. Thus is, Janet Todd contends, "the place of *jouissance* crudely defined as the re-experiencing of the physical pleasures of infancy before separation from the mother."[17]

The concluding passages of both books also testify to what Susan Winnett calls "beginning itself," or the "frightening sense of the beginning of a new life," characteristic of female narratology. (Similarly, in the story "Ending," the actual ending is, ironically, only the beginning of the new life for Barbara.) This image of the literal conclusion as a figurative beginning is a recurrent one in Grau's narratives, and brings

17. Janet Todd, *Feminist Literary History* (New York, 1988), 53. Although *écriture féminine* is usually associated with a style that seems alien to both Mitchell and Grau, I would still argue that it pertains to the endings of both texts. Moreover, Grau's identification of the female body with the house throughout her fiction suggests a specifically feminine style of writing.

to mind the regressiveness of final images in the writings of another southern writer associated with Louisiana through her fiction, Kate Chopin.[18] Grau uses the device to conclude *The Keepers, The House on Coliseum Street* (another book with the *house* in its title), and a number of short stories.

There has been much discussion as to what concept ultimately "wins" in *Gone with the Wind.* Fox-Genovese, for instance, maintains that it is Atlanta and urban culture. Conversely, Jones attributes victory in Mitchell's novel to the "old days."[19] My conviction is that if we have to look for a winner at all in either book, it is the woman—or, as Grau puts it, "the keeper of the house." Both writers, each in her own way, argue the inadequacy of the concept of the "lady." Each claims that a woman's aspirations to that role obstruct her growth. And in both books, the woman's survival depends upon her strength—her will and ability to "keep" the house.

18. Susan Winnett, "Coming Unstrung: Women, Men, Narrative, and Principles of Pleasure," *PMLA,* III (1990), 505–18. For this context and also for Chopin's "ambivalences," which likewise resemble Grau's, see Barbara C. Ewell, *Kate Chopin* (New York, 1986), 78–79, 104–105.

19. Fox-Genovese, "Scarlett O'Hara," 397–98.

Berthe Amoss.
Courtesy Berthe Amoss

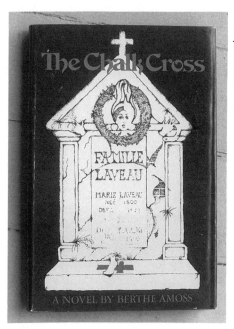

Jacket illustration by
Berthe Amoss for her
novel *The Chalk Cross*.
Courtesy Berthe Amoss

Setting and Local Color
in the Young-Adult Novels of Berthe Amoss

BERTHE AMOSS re-creates Louisiana of the past and the present for young readers through her writing and her illustrations. In Amoss' substantial contribution to the field of children's literature (fourteen books by 1990), she employs the local color of her native New Orleans in presenting vivid and lively scenes and characters. Although she and Mary Alice Fontenot, author of the *Clovis Crawfish* series, are the most prolific Louisiana writers for children today, and although one of Amoss' two teen novels, *The Chalk Cross,* was a runner-up in 1976 for the Edgar (the Mystery Writers of America award) in the best juvenile mystery novel category, she has been virtually overlooked by critics. Two writers, Selma Lanes and John Warren Stewig, praise Amoss in their respective anthologies, but they focus more on her work as an illustrator (and thus her books for young children) than as a writer.[1]

I propose to discuss Amoss as a writer—specifically, as the author of two young-adult books—by examining the various ways in which she employs local color, not only in creating accurate and realistic settings and a suspenseful, mysterious atmosphere, but also in developing contrasting structures (stories alternating between the present and the past), presenting topical themes (such as Catholicism, Voodooism, and racial issues), and portraying strong characters (especially her youthful female protagonists). Amoss has a particular gift for the realistic use of historical backgrounds and southern traditions to which she adds a piquant touch of mystery.

In the two adolescent novels, *The Chalk Cross* (1976) and *Secret Lives* (1979), Amoss focuses on young girls residing in New Orleans during several different historical periods. The protagonists of both books could be described as normal youngsters with typical adolescent interests and a strong sense of curiosity; they are exceptional only in the fact that they are orphaned. They are individualized, not stereotyped;

<hr>

1. Selma Lanes, *Down the Rabbit Hole: Adventures and Misadventures in the Realm of Children's Literature* (New York, 1971), 186; John Warren Stewig, *Children and Literature* (2d ed.; Boston, 1988), 48, 344.

Amoss has said that her characters, although drawn from people she has known, typically assume their own unique qualities and emerge— even for her—"as people." She also often draws on her family history for names as well as to help her visualize her characters, although none is an exact replica of a living person. For example, Addie, the protagonist of *Secret Lives,* has a middle name of "Aspasie," the name of Amoss' great-aunt, and Addie's aunt Eveline is a composite of another aunt, Amoss' grandmother, and other relatives.[2] The surnames in these novels, such as Martin, Laveau, St. Denis, and Dupry, reflect both Amoss' French heritage and that of New Orleans (Amoss loves the city; *The Chalk Cross* is literally dedicated to it).

Both *The Chalk Cross* and *Secret Lives* employ settings in and around New Orleans, with Amoss often mentioning local scenes and historical spots such as Audubon Park, the French Market, the Cabildo, St. Louis Cathedral, the Presbytère bordering Jackson Square, the above-ground tombs in the city's cemeteries, the streetcars, the Holmes department store (now defunct), and the levee. She employs both contemporary time and that of other periods, either in the historical past or in a fictional, imaginary time. Both *The Chalk Cross* and *Secret Lives* possess time schemes that create a two-part structure. In the former book, set in 1976, the central character, Stephanie Martin, mysteriously travels back in time to 1832 and enters another identity, that of Sidonie Laveau ("Donie"), daughter of the Voodoo queen Marie Laveau. The narrative of *Secret Lives* is set in 1937, but several simultaneous imaginary lives are created beyond the present real one for twelve-year-old Addie (short for Adelaide). Addie has a strong sense of place, as is underlined by her spelling out in full and capitalizing the address of her home, Three Twenty Audubon Street—which forces a guest there to think twice when he is invited to coffee at "Three Twenty around five" (45)—but her fruitless attempts to ascertain facts about her dead mother cause her to create an elaborate fictional life for herself in the characters of Jane Whitmore and Edmond Hilary de St. Denis. Jane represents the person Addie has visualized her long-lost mother to be. To cite but one such secret adventure, Jane is rescued against terrible odds by the love of her life, St. Denis, who represents Addie's knight

2. Berthe Amoss, *The Chalk Cross* (New York, 1976); Berthe Amoss, *Secret Lives* (Boston, 1979). Hereinafter both novels are cited parenthetically in the text by page number. The personal information about Amoss, here and throughout, is from my interview with her, November 17, 1987, hereinafter cited as Interview.

in shining armor. Only when Addie determines the truth about her mother can her secret life end, and Jane and St. Denis be laid to rest.

The temporal structure of *The Chalk Cross* contributes to its thematic structure. The story alternates between two periods with increasing frequency after both story lines are introduced, Stephanie's in 1976 and Donie's in 1832; the novel establishes a conflict of authority between Stephanie, who wishes to be an artist, and her guardian, Aunt Louise, who lacks an appreciation for art; meanwhile, her 1832 "mother," Marie Laveau, urges her to continue the family tradition of being a Voodoo queen. The change from one time period to another is skillfully handled, for Amoss is particularly adept at suggesting a variety of sensory causes for Stephanie's slipping back to her "former life" as Donie, and vice versa: the sight of a Creole cottage on St. Ann Street (13) or a portrait of Père Antoine (42), the name of Belle Rose Plantation (57), the thought of a cup of coffee (77), the smell of rosemary (84), the sound of church music (90), a dream about a spider (102), a headache (106), a reading of an account of the yellow fever epidemic of 1832 (124), the chant of the nuns (141), the sound of thunder (142), and others. Amoss excels at depicting the smells, sights, and sounds of New Orleans.

The author uses the city itself to link the two narrative lines through a series of ten black and white drawings revealing Stephanie's former life as Donie 150 years earlier—drawings Stephanie must complete for her art teacher, Mr. Dupry. Stephanie chooses for her topic, "New Orleans: The Place and the People in the 1830s," described as "a fascinating jumble of diverse people, cultures, and religions, predominantly French Catholic with a subculture of black Voodooism" (10–11). Her ten drawings, uniting past with present, depict people: Père Antoine saying his rosary with Donie and her sister Dédé (53), and a quadroon or mulatto woman (85); events: Philomène's wedding in St. Louis Cathedral (102), Donie's initiation as Voodoo queen (133), a slave auction (141), and Donie (or Stephanie) flying over the city, transcending time (149); and places: the Creole cottage on St. Ann Street with Donie's family sitting outside and Donie's mother in the door holding a snake (14), the cottage with Zouzou (who desires Voodoo powers) walking past and Dédé sprinkling salt on the walk in the shape of a cross (38), Belle Rose Plantation (85), and the tomb in St. Louis Cemetery of Marie Laveau, with the red cross on the steps and Donie leaning against the tomb's door (149)—a version of the book's cover, which was illustrated by Amoss. Each drawing represents a significant part of Donie's life and as such becomes important to Stephanie also, both in her existence as Donie in 1832 and as part of her art project in 1976. Donie might well speak for Stephanie when she tells Dédé: "I reckon I was born with pictures tucked in my head, Dédé. Sometimes they form in back of my eyes while I'm looking at something. Then they just spill out on paper" (28). Donie speaks for Amoss as well, for the writer's own artistic gifts echo her ability to paint in words a vivid description of the New Orleans of 1832.[3]

Catholicism, the predominant religion of New Orleans then and now, suffuses *The Chalk Cross* and *Secret Lives*. Virtually all the characters in the two novels are Catholics (as is Amoss herself). The families of Addie and Sandra Lee from *Secret Lives* not only attend mass, but also take comfort in their religion in times of stress. The girls study the Baltimore Catechism with Sister Elizabeth Anne (24), and Addie's Aunt Kate tells her to "say your beads" (77). Aunt Kate had nine First Fridays to her credit when she was only eight; that is, she went to Communion on the first Friday of the month for nine months, "almost guaranteeing" a person's attaining heaven, according to Aunt Eveline (101). Stephanie Martin of *The Chalk Cross* attends l'Académie aux Bois, Collège des Beaux Arts de la Nouvelle Orléans, an exclusive school operated by nuns for 250 years, a fictional place modeled, according to Amoss, on the Ursulines' famous convent academy.[4] When Stephanie finds herself back in 1832, living as Sidonie Laveau, she on several occasions seeks religious advice from the local priest, Père Antoine. Her indecision about whether to accept the Voodoo beliefs of her mother or Catholic doctrine constitutes a major source of conflict for Donie and thus a principal theme of this novel. Donie says, "Could it be that the Power was the same in Voodoo as in the Church and only the ways of tapping it different?" (95). Later, when she notices a statue of the Virgin Mary trampling a snake (representing Satan), Donie thinks of its resemblance to Damballah (135), the snake her mother consults prior to her performing any Voodoo.

Religious beliefs and local customs relating to burial also figure in both novels. For cities like New Orleans, below sea level and surrounded by water, "burials" must of necessity be above ground. The cover of *The Chalk Cross* depicts the probable tomb of Marie Laveau

3. Interview.
4. *Ibid.*

with its red cross, a symbol of Voodoo practice. The tomb Amoss illustrates, located in St. Louis Cemetery No. 1, still has crosses on it.[5] The
cemetery in *Secret Lives* functions not only as a setting, but also as a
motif. The well-known St. Louis Cemeteries contain many prominent
tombs "like little houses" (7), which are reopened for newly deceased
members of the family. Hence Aunt Eveline's concern in *Secret Lives*
that Aunt Kate will die too soon after Uncle Ben. If Uncle Ben has not
yet turned to dust, there will be no room in the tomb for the next
family member. Amoss describes the process, "When the cleaning
men opened the tomb, they burned what was left of the wooden casket
so that it would fall through the grill to the earth below, along with
Uncle Ben's bones" (100).

Aunt Eveline believes tomb burial to be so important that her dying
wish is to have Aunt Kate removed from Metairie Cemetery, in a suburb of New Orleans, where she was buried because Uncle Ben had not
yet decayed enough in the tomb, and placed in the family crypt in St.
Louis Cemetery No. 2.[6] Eveline explains to Addie, "If I could just
solve this nagging problem of Kate! *Stuck* out there! Miles away! In a
hole in the ground! If I could just know Kate was settled in" (174).
Furthermore, Aunt Eveline cautions Addie to die at the right time so
she too can be buried in the family tomb: "Just be careful and *remember:* it's merely a question of timing!" (175).

In both novels the time and place influence the depiction of black
characters. Slavery is an issue in *The Chalk Cross* because, of course, it
was a fact of life in New Orleans of 1832; both slavery and the issue
of color are treated frankly and openly in the novel. Amoss insists,
however, that these topics are of secondary importance as social issues,
and that primary to her is a good story from which a child can draw
meaningful values.[7] The children of Marie Laveau are described as

5. Several theories have been advanced as to the precise burial place of Marie Laveau, one suggesting a wall vault, others suggesting other areas of the cemetery. According to Michael Boudreaux, assistant director of the New Orleans Archdiocesan
Cemeteries, it is generally assumed that Laveau was buried in her family's tomb in St.
Louis No. 1 — the tomb with the red crosses on it. Mr. Boudreaux states that a professor from the University of New Orleans has speculated that Laveau might be buried in
another tomb (with a few more recently added chalk crosses) in St. Louis No. 2, four
blocks away from No. 1; but he stresses that there is no way to know with any certainty.
Telephone interviews with Michael Boudreaux, July 25, 1989, February 25, 1991.

6. Amoss has family buried in St. Louis No. 2 and once had a similar problem.
Interview.

7. *Ibid.*

"coffee-and-cream colored" (13); when they are taunted and called "neither black nor white," they turn to their grandmother for an explanation. She says, "You are an octoroon. . . . Your mother is a quadroon, and I am a mulatto." The response from Denaud, Donie's young brother, is appropriate: "I am a little boy." The grandmother explains further to Donie's younger sister, Dédé: "I am part African, part Indian, and half white. The father of your mother was white, making your mother a quadroon, and your father was also white and that makes you children octoroons." Denaud, "bored with the classifications of color" (24), inquires about his father; and the issue does not recur in that form.

Earlier, Marie Laveau, or "Maman" as her children call her, tells the youngsters not to anger her pet snake, which she regularly consults in her Voodoo practice: "It is he who tells Maman what to do. He understands the long-ago past and sees the future, and he has great Power. What would we do without him? Free, yet black, neither aristocrats nor slaves. It is he who gives us our place in the world. And it is a position of power! Never forget that!" (21). Amoss, steeped in Voodoo traditions of the period, vividly depicts an initiation in which the power is to be passed down from Marie to Donie, mother to daughter. The author distinguishes between those with Voodoo power (Marie), those with limited power (Donie), and those with pretensions to power (Zouzou). The Voodoo chants invoked, along with various gris-gris, amulets, wax dolls, and locks of hair, are authentic. (In assuring the accuracy of these details, Amoss has commented that she consulted Lyle Saxon's compilation of Louisiana folklore, *Gumbo Ya-Ya*, as well as African folklore, contemporary newspaper accounts, and numerous journals by European visitors to New Orleans in the early nineteenth century.)[8] The power of Voodoo for people unable to control many events in their lives by other means is strong, even penetrating the grave, as Donie explains about the red chalk on Maman's tomb: "It is a cry through the wall to the spirit inside and it says, 'Help, help! I have a favor to ask through the tomb and the years, Voodoo Lady. Listen to me! I want, I want . . .'" (15).

The slaves' belief in Voodoo is strong, perhaps inhibiting their ability to do anything more than dream of freedom or civil rights, as Donie learns when she visits Belle Rose. She talks to several blacks

---

8. Lyle Saxon, Edward Dreyer, and Robert Tallant, comps., *Gumbo Ya-Ya: A Collection of Louisiana Folk Tales* (Boston, 1945); Interview.

there who are described as "carefully avoid[ing] the word slave" (68). They believe their master to be good; they live in small, identical houses and have sufficient food so that no one goes hungry. Angèle, however, learns the price of disobedience; she will be sold. She has visions of marrying a slave from another plantation, but that practice is normally forbidden as "not 'set[ting] the right example' for the other slaves" (83). The slave auction where Angèle is to be sold is one of the novel's most vivid scenes. The slaves, nicely dressed for presentation before the buyers, are told: "Look your best when you go into the hall. Stand straight, walk briskly, and *smile*" (110). The better the disposition, the better the job they will be given after purchase, although some are bought primarily for breeding purposes. The excitement and carnival-like atmosphere of the slave auction cap the description, authentic in its setting.

Setting influences theme as well. In *Secret Lives*, a friendship develops between two girls of different races, Holly and Addie. Holly's aunt Nini, the maid, described as "the only sane person" in the house (11), is respected and loved by Addie's family. Holly, visiting her aunt in New Orleans, believes she (Holly) lived another life 150 years ago, and is now a sagoma (a kind of witch doctor) who can see the past and the future (49–50). (Holly's prophetic knowledge echoes that of Marie Laveau's snake in *The Chalk Cross*, and her having lived in a past life likewise recalls Stephanie Martin's former existence.) Holly seems less aware than Addie that the stories from her secret life are fiction. Although both girls use their tales as defense mechanisms to conceal their unhappiness, Holly's may be more persistent because her home life in Chicago is so fraught with tension involving her parents and her three younger siblings; Addie, on the other hand, gradually adjusts to her orphaned condition. But even though Holly's secret life, reflecting her cultural history, differs from Addie's, it nonetheless suggests the universality of youthful daydreams and secret lives.

In all young-adult novels, maturation is fundamental; in this case the setting requires the female protagonists to fulfill their roles as genteel young ladies. Stephanie matures in her roles both as Stephanie and as Donie. Addie develops from a tomboy to a well-adjusted young lady who can dress attractively, dance well, and secure a boyfriend, characteristics widely considered essential for that time and place. Addie also matures enough to befriend her long-time enemy, her pretty cousin Sandra Lee. In fact, so positive is her maturation that the reader does not worry that she is "orphaned" again when the old aunts who cared for her die by the novel's close and she must live with yet another aunt and uncle.

In both novels local-color elements abound; especially notable are the many southern traditions and New Orleans customs in *Secret Lives,* such as never returning a plate empty, drinking a demitasse of coffee, taking flowers to the cemetery on All Saints' Day, or wearing black for a year for certain deceased relatives and lavender for others—a custom observed in Amoss' father's family.[9] Amoss evokes the atmosphere with mention of the places, the names, the flora—such as the magnolias and jasmine—and some of the favorite foods—gumbo, café au lait, calas, and brioches rolled in sugar. Even the beating rain reflects south Louisiana in a way only a native could re-create. The use of local color renders the setting unique and the plots specific, but the characters are universal in their dreams or secret lives, curiosity, resistance to authority, and maturation.

Amoss' informed use of the rich local color of New Orleans—in both her prose and her illustrations—effectively complements the lively blend of fantasy and reality with which she fashions her novels of young adult life. Combining the exotic realities of the city's glamourous past—whether of the 1830s or the 1930s—with the immediate dramas of a young girl's maturation (provocatively flavored with mysteries that never threaten violence), Amoss successfully constructs a fresh and satisfying version of the venerable traditions of southern regional writing.

9. Interview.

Ellen Gilchrist.
Photo by Rhoda K. Faust,
Maple Street Book Shops

Sheila Bosworth.
Photo by Donn Young,
New Orleans

Nancy Lemann.
Photo by Rhoda K. Faust,
Maple Street Book Shops

"New People in the Old Museum of New Orleans"
Ellen Gilchrist, Sheila Bosworth, and Nancy Lemann

> Experiences, reminiscences, episodes, picked up as only women know
> how to pick them up from other women's lives,—or other women's des-
> tinies, as they prefer to call them,—and told as only women know how
> to relate them; . . . that is what interests the women who sit of summer
> nights on balconies. For in those long-moon countries life is open and
> accessible, and romances seem to be furnished real and gratis, in order
> to save, in a languor-breeding climate, the ennui of reading and writing
> books.
>
> —Grace King, *Balcony Stories*

Although an established literary tradition associated with a particular place, region, or city can be of enormous value to a writer, offering inspiration and teaching by example, it can also become an obstacle to success and a threat to the writer's creativity. The danger is especially severe when the materials of the tradition gain such popular approval that publishers, critics, and other readers demand more of the same. Flannery O'Connor spoke to this difficulty when she described the predicament of the southern writer after Faulkner this way: "Nobody wants his mule and wagon stalled on the same track the Dixie Limited is roaring down."[1] The writer who takes New Orleans as a setting faces a similar dilemma, although we might substitute Tennessee Williams' streetcar named Desire for the Dixie Limited as the symbolic vehicle carrying these popular expectations.

George W. Cable, in his collection of stories *Old Creole Days,* pioneered imaginative writing about New Orleans in English. His stories of picturesque Creoles, dark secrets, and old family feuds transformed the exotic surfaces of New Orleans life into the material of fiction. The many writers who followed him gravitated to the same thematic material and descriptive motifs; consequently, by the middle of the twentieth century, the romantic idea of Old New Orleans had ossified into predictable patterns of character, image, and plot.

---

1. Flannery O'Connor, "The Grotesque in Southern Fiction," in *Mystery and Manners,* ed. Sally and Robert Fitzgerald (New York, 1961), 41.

Much of the writing about New Orleans since Cable falls into two traditions, one focusing on the French Quarter, the other on the Garden District. The French Quarter tradition belongs largely to outsiders, who often focus on newcomers haunted by the exoticism of the Quarter. The tradition centered on the Garden District (or, more generally, Uptown New Orleans) offers a more domestic mood, focusing on manners and mores and unfolding in private places. Grace King is one founder of this tradition: she began writing to explain the ways of New Orleans to outsiders and to defend these ways against the perceived attacks of Cable, yet her fiction reveals a cautious testing of social beliefs about the roles of women and blacks. Another is Kate Chopin, who writes critically about Creole societies as an adopted insider; Edna Pontellier in *The Awakening* chafes against the rigid strictures of the established society.[2]

The Garden District tradition has particularly influenced the view of the city held by local writers and by New Orleanians themselves. This literature both grows from and contributes to a perception of upper-class New Orleans society as different and a bit precious. This perception may derive in part, as W. Kenneth Holditch has suggested, from the fact that holding center stage in this society is the glittering artifice of a Carnival ball.[3] Whatever its source, this perception results in a population thought to be set apart from the rest of the world, destined for great things—unrequited love, sexual indiscretion, alcoholism, wasted potential, suicide.

In recent years, this Uptown tradition has come under close scrutiny and revision by Ellen Gilchrist, Sheila Bosworth, and Nancy Lemann; each has written a novel depicting the conflict of a central female character with this tradition; their characters and plots, and even their narrative forms, embody the confrontation with tradition. Among the three, Gilchrist's perspective is unique: the protagonists of her fiction inhabit the margins of this society, and their conflicts with the society take place within fairly traditional narrative forms. Both Bosworth and Lemann, by contrast, offer protagonists who have grown up within this society and whose rejection of it is thus more complex. This complexity shapes unusual narrative forms that unify the rejection of social and literary traditions.

2. J. Randal Woodland, "'In that city foreign and paradoxical': The Idea of New Orleans in the Southern Literary Imagination" (Ph.D. dissertation, University of North Carolina at Chapel Hill, 1987), 134–36.
3. Conversation with W. Kenneth Holditch, August, 1986.

Ellen Gilchrist's rejection of Uptown society and its literary tradition is the simplest and, at the same time, the most complete. The New Orleans residents she includes are often marginal characters themselves; to them and to Gilchrist, the shallowness of upper-class New Orleans society is clear. Her central characters can never be accepted into Uptown society, and generally would spurn such acceptance. In her novel *The Annunciation* (1983), a bride new to the city drives down St. Charles Avenue with her housekeeper sitting beside her; feeling a shared alienation, they imagine themselves "new people in the old museum of New Orleans, Louisiana."[4] This image serves as a useful figure for all of Gilchrist's New Orleans fiction, which places characters new to the city's literary tradition in conflict with the symbols and tokens of the entrenched societal tradition.

Gilchrist's position as an outside observer who sets herself and her main characters in opposition to the Uptown society is most clearly seen in "Looking over Jordan," a story that seems based, at least loosely, on the reception of Gilchrist's work in New Orleans. Its two central characters are Lady Margaret Sarpie, a young woman of a distinguished but declining family who has recently chastised in print Anna Hand, the author of a scandalous book ridiculing the city; and Hand herself, who decides to add a hedonistic dimension to her book tour: "The strange lassitude of New Orleans in summer, the wine at the party, the tiredness in her bones. Why not, she thought. I'll be gone tomorrow. Get drunk, eat sugar, get laid by a native, *be here.*"[5] The native in question is Lady Margaret's brother Armand, and the three are brought together in the Sarpies' old summer home on the north shore of Lake Pontchartrain. Through the interplay of the two women, Gilchrist aligns herself with Anna Hand in opposition to the community's attachment to faded gentility and remembered glamour.

The title story of Gilchrist's first collection, *In the Land of Dreamy Dreams* (1981), traces the threat an outsider poses to the remnant of this gilded age. The action unfolds at a decisive moment: change has come to the New Orleans Tennis Club. Gone are the days when "waiters had brought steaming cups of thick chicory-flavored café au lait out onto the balcony with cream and sugar in silver servers"; now the members must put up with "percolated coffee in Styrofoam cups with

---

4. Ellen Gilchrist, *The Annunciation* (Boston, 1983), 81, hereinafter cited parenthetically by page number in the text.

5. Ellen Gilchrist, *Victory over Japan* (Boston, 1984), 83.

plastic spoons and some kind of powder instead of cream." What's more, in order to pay the mortgage, new members have been allowed in, new members who "didn't belong to the Boston Club or the Southern Yacht Club or Comus or Momus or Proteus."[6]

One of these new members has forced a descendant of the Old Guard to break a once-inviolable code of honor: "There was no denying it. There was no undoing it. At ten o'clock that morning LaGrande McGruder, whose grandfather had been president of the United States Lawn Tennis Association, had cheated a crippled girl out of a tennis match."[7] LaGrande's opponent, Roxanne, is one of the nouveau members; the fact that she and her husband are Jewish makes them even less welcome. The story opens as LaGrande, remembering her Pyrrhic victory over Roxanne, throws her tennis gear into the Mississippi from the Huey P. Long Bridge, marking an ironic populist victory for the Kingfish.

In other stories, Gilchrist creates a variety of characters who, like Roxanne, live on the fringes of Uptown society. An enterprising young pusher sets up shop under an Audubon Park oak tree in "The President of the Louisiana Live Oak Society." Nora Jane Whittington robs an Irish Channel bar to finance a trip west in "The Famous Poll at Jody's Bar." Crystal Weiss, in a series of stories in *Victory over Japan* (1984) and *Drunk with Love* (1986), exemplifies a different kind of marginality: her unwillingness to adopt the roles of happy socialite, devoted wife, and young mother assigned to her by Uptown society drives her into drunken isolation.

Gilchrist offers a more fully developed version of Crystal in the central character of *The Annunciation*. Like Crystal, Amanda McCamey Ashe is an unhappily married woman whose Mississippi Delta origins conflict with the New Orleans Jewish roots of her husband. As a young girl growing up in the Delta, Amanda was fascinated by New Orleans (an experience shared by young women in the fiction of Eudora Welty and Elizabeth Spencer). She encounters the city firsthand at age fourteen when, pregnant by her older cousin, she is sent to a New Orleans home for unwed mothers to give birth. When she moves to New Orleans years later, after her wedding, she recalls her experience as a pregnant and frightened teenager. As her marriage deteriorates, her thoughts turn increasingly to her lost daughter,

6. Ellen Gilchrist, *In the Land of Dreamy Dreams* (Fayetteville, 1981), 65, 62.
7. *Ibid.*, 60–61.

whom she imagines she sees throughout the city. In fact, her daughter is herself unhappily married to a New Orleans lawyer and lives a few blocks from Amanda. Although the women do not meet as mother and daughter in the novel, events at its end suggest that a meeting may be imminent. (A later collection, *Light Can Be Both Wave and Particle,* includes two stories that, according to the book jacket, "provide a new ending to" *The Annuciation.* This additional material clarifies some ambiguities and provides a happier conclusion to the earlier book.)

Amanda rejects New Orleans upper-class society as she gradually awakens to the shallowness of those around her. Gilchrist gives us the substance of Amanda's critique through a flurry of cocktail party chatter that reveals a startling variety of oppressive attitudes, ranging from racism ("She told her brother she was pregnant and he said, good, he'd go on safari and bring her back a little Negro") to the use of children as status symbols ("Did she get into Sacred Heart? Oh, that's a shame"); the chatter, reported with an accurate ear for distinctive New Orleans syntax and intonation, builds to a climax that displays the inevitable results of such oppressions:

> "Shot himself in front of his girlfriend's house while the party was going on. Oh, yes, barely sixteen. They don't know where he got the gun."
> "Hung himself in the closet at Covington."
> "Jumped off a bridge. Just like his daddy before him."
> "Oh, he's disappeared into the Quarter. Won't even take calls. Of course, everyone's known for years. I heard it was a high school boy, an Italian."
> (68–69)

Moving through this world of shallow chatter and deep wounds, Amanda grows ever more conscious that she does not belong in this world of tea parties and suicidal youth. She finds a friend and ally in her housekeeper, Lavertis; their shared alienation from the community contributes to their common sense that they are "new people in the old museum of New Orleans."

These experiences contribute to Amanda's disaffection with her husband and her eventual flight to Fayetteville, Arkansas, where she translates French poetry and takes a young lover. Although Amanda never returns to New Orleans in the course of the novel, she cannot escape the "cargo" of her unknown daughter. Here Gilchrist adopts a motif common in New Orleans fiction. The lost child, the heritage hidden behind locked gates within mysterious courtyards, the dark family secret: these reappear continually in New Orleans writing—in the stories of George W. Cable and Grace King, in *Absalom, Absalom!*, even in Anne Rice's vampire chronicles. The heritage that Amanda passes unwittingly to her daughter is the oppression of Uptown society, an oppression that Amanda overcomes only through understanding herself and taking responsibility for her life; only by leaving New Orleans entirely can she hope to escape the city's snare.

In the novels of Sheila Bosworth and Nancy Lemann, freedom is not so easily won. Although they perceive, with Gilchrist, fatal flaws in the ways Uptown society constitutes itself, each is too deeply rooted in that society to reject it without a struggle. Bosworth's protagonist must reexamine painful childhood memories, and Lemann's protagonist seems so entrenched that she may never escape. To these authors, the structures and manners of New Orleans society are not merely museum exhibits to be examined, analyzed, perhaps laughed at, but active forces that threaten their protagonists, who are both members of the society and observers of it. Their characters are latter-day Quentin Compsons, wanting to be free of the ruins of the old order yet knowing that it is only from those ruins that their freedom can come.

Clay-Lee Calvert, the protagonist of Bosworth's *Almost Innocent* (1984) is, in many ways, a figure familiar to readers of southern literature. Her search is to understand the past (grounded for her in New Orleans) in order to understand herself. In the narrative of Clay-Lee's search, Bosworth conducts her own analytical search, using the literary material of the grand New Orleans novel to subvert the genre itself. Her subversion takes several forms; the details of plot and character that we have come to expect of New Orleans novels are here in abundance, yet Bosworth sets them in a context that questions both their source and their effect. We see these motifs through the central consciousness of Clay-Lee, and through her we understand their impact. The book's narrative circles through recollections and flashbacks, telling the story of Clay-Lee's past as she herself comes to understand it. We learn the story of Clay-Lee's parents and her early life as Clay-Lee herself hears it from her mother's cousin Felicity Léger de la Corde, then Clay-Lee's own memories move the story toward the present.

This nostalgic tone is set in the novel's opening scene. As Clay-Lee and her father have dinner at Galatoire's, Clay-Lee sees their waiter as a link with the past: "Vallon is old now, almost eighty. He used to give my father's father red beans and rice in one of the upstairs rooms, generations ago."[8] Looking at her aging father's youthful smile, Clay-Lee begins examining her past, trying to understand the forces that led to the death of her mother, Constance, and the continuing impact of those forces on her own life.

Many of the traditions Clay-Lee encounters during this self-examination are those of a Catholic upbringing: Lenten regulations, parochial school, catechism, and fasting before First Communion. The memories of these rituals are shaded by a mature understanding of the oppressions of childhood, as when Clay-Lee recalls, with wry humor, the inadvertent breaking of her First Communion fast: "It was the day I made my First Communion, and it was the day I consigned my immortal soul to hell" (92). For the young girl, the damnation of her soul is less important than the embarrassment of not going through a ceremony so meaningful to her mother. Clay-Lee inherits this fixation on the past from Constance, lost in the sorrows of her own childhood. When Clay-Lee's great-uncle (called "Uncle Baby Brother" by all) agrees to pay her tuition to Sacred Heart Academy, the exclusive girls' school that Constance attended, her mother urges upon Clay-Lee the importance of this event: "'Just think,' Constance was telling me, 'Saint Madeleine Sophie Barat founded the Society of the Sacred Heart in France, in 1800, and here you are, almost two hundred years later, way over in Louisiana, about to share in all its history and tradition'" (163).

The rebellious young Clay-Lee fights against the strictures of this history and tradition. When her aunt urges her to read *Lives of the Saints for Little People,* she turns instead to *Louisiana Hayride,* a history of Huey Long's tumultuous career; when her aunt warns her to pray to "the saints instead of making fun of them," she retorts, "Maybe I'll pray to Huey Long instead" (195). We chuckle at this youthful rebellion, but underlying Bosworth's humor is a serious point: the mature Clay-Lee must realize how these traditions imposed themselves on her developing sense of self.

And yet the novel's grounding in New Orleans does not derive solely from its repetition of the old chestnuts of the New Orleans literary tradition; Bosworth balances the sentimental perspective of the past with the more realistic appraisal of the present. Bosworth's clear-

8. Sheila Bosworth, *Almost Innocent* (New York, 1984), 13, hereinafter cited parenthetically by page number in the text.

est use of this dual perspective comes through her use of Mardi Gras, always a prominent motif of the grand New Orleans novel. As the central event of New Orleans social life, Carnival often becomes, as here, a prime setting for serendipitous meetings.

The dramatic manner in which Clay-Lee describes her parents' first meeting suggests how completely her mother's identity was bound to the grand artificiality of New Orleans high society: "She was Constance Blaise Alexander, Queen of Comus, the most magnificent of the Carnival balls, on the night they fell in love" (17). Their masked meeting recalls those that begin George W. Cable's *Grandissimes* and Frances Parkinson Keyes's *Crescent Carnival* and is marked by the equally venerable literary tradition of flaunting custom: "As Constance leaned forward to greet her consort, Rand Calvert, far below, defied tradition by throwing aside his mask to see her face more clearly" (17). The special connection of this family with Mardi Gras goes back even to Constance's birth on Twelfth Night, the traditional beginning of the Carnival season. With the obstetrician still in his satin ball costume, Constance's mother vows to "dress her daughter in only blue or white till she was five years old, as a sign of thanksgiving to the Mother of God for the child's existence" (27).

Yet this romantic view of Carnival is sharply undercut when Constance learns, after her father's sudden death, that he lost most of his money gambling and died penniless because he "borrowed against everything he still owned for the pleasure of seeing you, Mrs. Calvert, as the beautiful debutante and Carnival Queen that you were" (66). We are to see, with Clay-Lee, the absurdity of this gesture, yet Clay-Lee also responds to its grandeur.

As the narrative moves into Clay-Lee's own memories, she recalls a Carnival season that serves as a crucial turning point for the plot. Her recollections of Felicity and her husband Airey's annual Mardi Gras open house are cast as a romantic childhood idyll, yet it sets into motion events that will haunt Clay-Lee well into her adult life. In describing the party, Bosworth captures a certain self-consciously gracious New Orleans social style: "Felicity had not forgotten the light eaters and pregnant ladies, either (and it seemed to me then there were always dozens of the latter, in this city of Catholic wealth and dynasty): waiters circulated with trays of watercress or Virginia ham finger sandwiches, offered iced tea to the mothers-to-be, and poured champagne for their husbands" (125). This fragility cannot prevail against the passage of time: "I don't like the parades any more," recalls Constance; "I used to like them when I lived in the Garden District" (123). Despite the care with which plans have been laid, the party turns out disastrously when Clay-Lee's great-uncle shows up unexpectedly with a surprise guest: "Uncle Baby had brought an octoroon to the de la Cordes' Open House" (131). Damaging as this scene is to the delicate sensibilities of the guests, Uncle Baby Brother's appearance forebodes more lasting damage: his infatuation with Constance will lead to the breakup of the Calverts' marriage and to Constance's death.

The novel's critical view of New Orleans traditions is manifested most clearly in Felicity's narration of the early portion of Constance's story to Clay-Lee. Bosworth draws a sharp contrast between the dying woman and the legendary exploits of her youth: "Tales of her bewitching magnetism, her pitiless heart, ran rife among a certain segment of New Orleans' population. Felicity Léger had trifled with the affections of a brilliant Jewish medical student, wrecked his studies, and robbed him of his future; she had worn underpants fashioned from a Rebel flag to a childhood friend's coming-out party, lifted her skirt, and shown them to the orchestra leader, whose band then burst into the most rousing rendition of 'I Wish I Was in Dixie' ever heard at the Southern Yacht Club" (23). By now Felicity has become the picturesque aging relative, recounting the family history to the adoring Clay-Lee. Bosworth refuses, however, to let Felicity slip fully into a nostalgic haze; into a sensuous account of childhood memories she interjects a jarring reminder of Felicity's present decay:

> All through the rooms were the blending, alternating aromas of sachet-scented bed linens, hand-embroidered by French nuns at a convent in Vermilion Parish; of magnolias and camellias, floating in silver bowls in every room, each spring and summer; of pine logs burning in the wide fireplaces in winter; of freshly baked biscuits and of French-drip coffee in the mornings, gumbos and baked hams and honey-basted plantains at dinnertime. . . .
>
> Felicity paused for a minute, to swallow what looked like a Percodan, then went on. (33–34)

A gashed arm provides the immediate occasion for the Percodan, yet her action suggests that the past itself is a dangerous narcotic, its soothing forces offering both solace and addiction. In her perseverance and her love for Clay-Lee, Felicity recalls other stoic New Orleans ladies, particularly Binx Bolling's aunt, Emily Cutrer, in Walker Percy's *The Moviegoer*. Her desire to pass on something of value to future generations is especially clear in her bequest to Clay-Lee of a collection of books, one a leather-bound edition of Ovid with a letter in it: "'Dear Clay-Lee,' the letter read, 'go on without me, from where we stopped our last Friday night together. If you start at the place where you recall things firsthand—that would be your first years at the house on Camp Street—you will look well and fairly at what you know of your mother's life and your own, and eventually you will see cause and effect. Felicity.'" (73). Added to this was a quote from Ovid: "*Parsque meminisse doloris,* she had written; it is part of grief to remember" (73). Like Binx, Clay-Lee must decide how to interpret these hints from the past and how to integrate them with the knowledge she has gained on her own. Only then can she understand who is responsible for the events of her childhood.

The question of responsibility is posed most clearly by the figure of Rand, Clay-Lee's father, the carefree artist and defier of tradition who, in the opening scene that introduces the book's flashbacks, stumbles drunkenly through dinner at Galatoire's. Rand is the central exhibit before whom Clay-Lee stands, aware that she must understand its meaning for her life before she can move on.

A *Times-Picayune* writer has called Rand "an uptown New Orleans archetype," and reported Bosworth's experience with Rand's avatars: "'I know so many men like that. . . . In fact, three different men have said to me, "Oh, I'm Rand Calvert." And I say "Oh well, yes." . . . I wonder if any other city has them. . . . I'm talking about bright, sophisticated, charming men who have that fatal lethargy. You have a feeling they wouldn't be as charming if they had that drive, that Toledo, Ohio, drive. The charm comes at a price.'"[9]

How to interpret the life of Rand Calvert is a critical question for Bosworth and for her protagonist, just as how to interpret the glamorous fates of men like Rand is a central dilemma in understanding New Orleans and its fiction. To see their doom as a noble expression of the human condition is to risk both sentimentality and the perpetuation of a dangerous myth. To deny any mythic quality is to accept the hard truth of a pathetic and wasted life.

The interpretation of Clay-Lee's story poses another problem, especially for a study of Bosworth in the context of Louisiana women writers, and this problem becomes even more thorny with Lemann's *Lives of the Saints.* Although Bosworth and Lemann trace a woman's search for the meaningful pattern of her life, their protagonists do not, in the end, come to the self-reliant rejection of masculine defini-

9. New Orleans *Times-Picayune,* January 20, 1985, "Dixie" section, 4.

tions that Gilchrist's Amanda achieves, and that a feminist viewpoint might lead us to expect and desire. Clay-Lee and, to an even greater extent, Lemann's Louise are obsessed with the doom that defines the lives of the men they love.

Although we may question, and even condemn, the protagonists' concern with taking care of helpless men, the two women make little progress, if any, in escaping this "codependency" in either novel. The narratives of both books circle back again and again to the cultural expectations that circumscribe the lives of the glamorous, doomed men the women love. Clay-Lee and Louise understand the artificiality of this cultural construct, but they are all but powerless to change it. Their only resource is narrative itself; by pushing the tale to its limits, they can demonstrate its essential fictionality. We as readers must wrestle with the same question: are the glittering young men who populate fictional Uptown society pale southern imitations of Jay Gatsby, or are they, as Nancy Lemann's narrator might put it, The Real Thing?

This question lies at the heart of Lemann's *Lives of the Saints* (1985), a book characterized by manic irony from the title onward. Lemann's rejection of the Uptown tradition is more radical than that of either Gilchrist or Bosworth. Although Lemann's narrator, Louise, like Clay-Lee, is a product of New Orleans society, she is unable to reach the freedom from the past that Clay-Lee finally attains. Louise is driven both to "record the passing parade," as she says, and to turn a withering stare on the pretensions of these Doomed Young Men, thereby freeing them (not the least of her ironic strategies is the capitalization of clichéd concepts that have taken on a life and power of their own). The edges of Louise's picture are beginning to fray, the calm hush of Clay-Lee's reverence replaced by disorder and the refusal to consider such accommodation.

The "saints" of her title are the Collier brothers, Saint Claude Collier (called "Claude") and his younger brother Saint Louis Collier (called "Saint"). Their father, Saint Louis Collier, a former judge and present eccentric, embodies in his dress the fading of a glamorous past: he "always wore seersucker suits that he had had for about fifty years and which were always wrinkled and faded to a kind of yellow color."[10] In describing a summer evening in the Quarter, Lemann

10. Nancy Lemann, *Lives of the Saints* (New York, 1985), 15, hereinafter cited parenthetically by page number in the text.

makes explicit the connection between fashion and nostalgia: "It was Latin American Night in the Quarter, in Jackson Square, starting at eight o'clock. The time is gone when we were 'the gateway to the Americas' and ships left our harbor daily for Havana with all the men wearing white suits. But all the men still wear white suits in New Orleans, on certain summer days" (56). Even the men's white suits here offer a glimpse of nostalgia, recalling as they do days before air conditioning, when crisp white suits bespoke a certain elegance.

Lemann's lack of sympathy for society's pretensions is seen most clearly in her brief portrait of Judge Collier's wife, who—like Joseph Frowenfeld in Cable's *Grandissimes* or Blanche DuBois in *A Streetcar Named Desire*—has had to become acclimated to the city and adapt her exterior view of New Orleans to an understanding of what life there is really like: "She was a Yankee girl Mr. Collier had brought down from Harvard many years ago, and she never got over the shock of New Orleans. As a newlywed, she wanted to wear baggy shirts and work with the professors in her department at Tulane, but somehow this was too unlike her generation, and also, there were always garden parties and witty intrigues and carnival balls. Mrs. Collier had to learn to cope with silver, with crystal, with entertaining, and with other things previously foreign to her" (34). She has made the adjustments that Amanda, in *The Annunciation*, refuses to make, and as a result has become a bitter, pessimistic woman, unable to intervene in her family's inevitable slide toward doom.

Her husband, the Judge, has made his own adjustments. His three passions—gardening, grand opera, and ancient Greek poetry—mark his detachment from the crazed world around him. Although this response is a version of Felicity's admirable stoic detachment, its effects on his sons, who have inherited his sense of doom, are severe. Despite Claude's early promise, he has taken to "hanging around with wino lunatics and racetrack habitués and other weird types of wrecks" (23). His much younger brother, Saint, addicted to Cokes and fatally accident prone, falls to his death from a balcony, a tragedy that leads to his father's nervous breakdown and Claude's further decline.

The classic motifs of New Orleans writing all appear in the novel, but unlike the details in Bosworth's novel, they remain isolated and do not contribute directly to a larger narrative structure. Lemann manifests a curious disinterest in plot; again and again the focus of the narrative shifts from the story to the milieu. One of the narrator's recurring concerns is the weather: "It was a night in the spring, though in New Orleans you can hardly tell the season as it's so often hot. A sweltering night in October can be just the same as a sweltering night in April, for in New Orleans the seasons have only subtle differences, unlike in the North. It was balmy old New Orleans weather in the tropic spring, and everything was green and overgrown" (5).

Again and again Louise tries to define what is distinctive about New Orleans, never finding an answer that satisfies her. Each motif is linked to another in a book-length chain of free association that fails to reveal any larger pattern. The author leads us to the question of what might define New Orleans, yet never settles on an answer that satisfies her. At times an overly close attachment to the past seems to explain the distinctive texture of life in New Orleans: "We got to a bar along the Mississippi coast in one of the small towns. It was a country bar, right on the Gulf, and the entire clientele looked like it had just stepped out of law school, with horn-rimmed glasses predominant. The band was playing old songs from the 1960s era in which New Orleans and environs remain, even though it is twenty years later. They're just always playing old songs where I live" (137).

New Orleans' obsession with the past has been noted ever since the first nineteenth-century travel writers visited the city, but in this novel the usual explanations for such a sense of the past (the city's European heritage or its military defeat) are absent, and the focus instead is on the recent past. For Lemann's characters, living in the past seems largely a means of avoiding the present, ultimately an unsatisfactory means.

Lemann is concerned as well with the potent cultural images of New Orleans—the book at times seems more concerned with these images than with the city itself, becoming a catalog of literary New Orleans. Beth Cooley effectively summarizes the literary landscape of the novel this way: "There is a strange blend of romantic recklessness reminiscent of Mitchell's antebellum Georgia and an almost predetermined destruction reminiscent of Faulkner's antebellum Mississippi. Add to this the nightmarish but voluptuous quality of *A Streetcar Named Desire* and then color it with the ironic humor of Eudora Welty or Walker Percy and you begin to describe the mood of Lemann's New Orleans."[11] Lemann acknowledges the power of these images even as she attempts to rob them of their efficacy. Her detailed descriptions

11. Beth Cooley, "White Summer Suits," *Spectator* (Raleigh, N.C.), September 26, 1985, p. 24.

offer images that are sensuous and seemingly full of meaning, yet rather than linking these images to create a larger thematic pattern, she abruptly shifts our attention to another scene, only to return, a few pages later, to the original image from another perspective. The resulting multifaceted picture speaks to the fragmentation of Louise's own consciousness, and her deeply divided response to the city.

Lemann's fragmentary treatment of Mardi Gras effectively points to differences between Bosworth's approach and hers. In a mood that recalls Faulkner's *Pylon,* New Orleans during the Carnival season becomes a wasteland:

> The ticket takers were lying around on the stairs looking out at the street with the sallow faces of saints, black men wearing gold theater uniforms, sprawled on the stairs looking out to Canal Street as though it were some slow jazz party.
> Carnival, in fact, was pending. (103)

The objective, slightly ominous tone of "pending," more suggestive of a legal judgment than a festival, is a far cry from the vibrancy of earlier literary descriptions of Carnival.

The fragile manners of Felicity's open house in Bosworth's *Almost Innocent* have shattered into the jagged fragments of obsolete fantasies. Consider Louise's artist friend Henry: "In his rooms, Henry hung ominous paintings of Mardi Gras balls, where the queens and debutantes had insanely wide smiles and skeletal frames, holding their scepters rigid in the air. Bland men in tuxedos stood grouped around them, smiling weakly. This was Henry's plea for satire" (65–66). Yet after Lemann holds the old sham-fantasy up to ridicule, she reclaims it in a striking, unexpected image:

> The weather had turned fine. Dark fell. I looked into the glittering night. Suddenly, a parade came out of nowhere and passed through the unsuspecting street, heralded by African drumbeats in the distance vaguely, then the approach of jazz, the smell of sweet olive, ambrosia, the sense of impending spectacle. Then it passed in its fleeting beauty, this glittering dirge, and, as suddenly as it came, I was left, rather stunned, in its wake.
> It is this passing parade which I chronicle. (96)

Only by shattering the old narratives can she regain the experience from the "fragments . . . shored against [her] ruin," in T. S. Eliot's words. And yet, to follow Eliot further, Louise has these experiences of beauty but misses their meaning; she is unable to find the perspective that will make the images cohere.

The manic irony that characterizes Louise's narrative voice is the instrument by which Lemann maintains a distance from the actions she describes. Her aim is to capture the texture of New Orleans life rather than to develop a traditional plot. The novel is divided not into chapters, but into 201 scenes, which range in length from a few lines to a few pages. This formlessness signals a refusal to map out a plot, and hence a doom, for her characters. Given the narrative forms available, Claude's only choices are suicide or alcoholism. Rather than make this choice, Lemann stops the novel. At its end Claude, apparently implicated in a racing scandal, simply leaves: "He stood in his dark suit, blameless. Then he turned down Bourbon directly into that gaudy crowd of humanity, his polite, unobtrusive figure casting among it something of dignity. With his hands in his pockets and his collar turned up against the rain, my beloved Claude receded—and disappeared for years." (144). Lemann leaves us, and Louise, to wrestle with the implications of this mysterious departure.

The hagiography in which the narrator's affections for Claude are masked is heavily ironic; Lemann's is not an orthodox religious imagination. The novel's title is, of course, a pun, a play on traditional religious sensibility. Although its male members are named after saints, the Collier family practices no apparent religion. (Or perhaps they were named after streets—they may as well have been.) When Judge Collier, after Saint's death, begins reading the *Lives of the Saints*, Louise takes it as further evidence of his impending breakdown. Lemann refuses to let her *Lives* become such a martyrology, seemingly the only narrative pattern available. By tracing the surfaces of her characters' lives, rather than describing their ultimate shape, Louise occupies a netherland between the doomed narrative of Clay-Lee Calvert and the flippant irony of Anna Hand; her fragmented narrative signifies a refusal to accept either alternative, as well as a refusal to reject either completely. Her mixture of affection and hate for the city with disgust and love for its inhabitants leads to her narrative of fragmentation and disillusion.

The accumulated tradition of New Orleans literature weighs heavily in the fiction of Gilchrist, Bosworth, and Lemann. Like the humidity of an August afternoon in the French Quarter, remembered people, places, and actions encourage a lassitude and timidity of thought. Why imagine new stories, why invent new destinies, when the old ones are so full of life? Grace King's observation in the passage serving as an epigraph to this essay underlines the point: "Romances seem to be furnished real and gratis, in order to save, in a languor-breeding climate, the ennui of reading and writing books."[12] These furnished romances are not easily ignored.

Gilchrist, Bosworth, and Lemann, each in her own way, have recognized the fatal lethargy of such a course, have understood that the old stories maintain their vitality only by ensnaring new victims and perpetuating their curse. Each writer pits her protagonist against this life-destroying fiction: Amanda and Clay-Lee force the narratives of their lives into new channels; Louise, unable to conceive such a way out, removes herself from the narrative's inexorable move toward doom. For her, the streetcar still rattles through the city streets, giving form to her nightmarish visions. All three authors transform the accumulated popular vision of New Orleans into narrative forms that offer new perspectives on the city's social and literary traditions.

12. Grace King, *Balcony Stories* (1893; rpr. Ridgewood, N.J., 1968), 3.

II
Louisiana Women Writers:
A Bibliography

A Note on the Bibliography

W HO *was* the woman playwright in New Orleans who in 1907 copyrighted a play entitled *The Law and the Lady Down in Dixie,* a melodrama evidencing considerable knowledge of cotton futures, politics, and the Louisiana legal system? Her name, Rose Falls Bres, was on the title page, but I knew nothing more about her in the early 1970s, when I undertook my first foray into researching Louisiana women writers. Very gradually she came into view as I pieced together her professional career as a lawyer in Kentucky, Louisiana, and New York (where she was elected president of the national Women Lawyers Association and was active in the feminist movement). The biographical details of her life outside her profession were more elusive, yet I found finally that I knew more about her than did her close associates years after her death.[1]

A by-product of this search was an intense desire to discover other of Louisiana's women authors and to learn more about ones already familiar to me. Did they, like Bres, write while pursuing other careers? Did they publish while rearing families? What sort of works and with what success? Did they set out to establish their own literary tradition, or did it just evolve?

What was apparent almost from the outset was that no comprehensive bibliography of the state's writers existed. A handful of well-known Louisiana authors were represented quite well in easily accessible biographical dictionaries or bibliographies, but a great many more were isolated or lost entirely to the record. The pioneering works of Alexander N. De Menil (*The Literature of the Louisiana Territory*) and of Thomas P. Thompson (*Louisiana Writers, Native and Resident*), both published in 1904, provided a beginning point for research. A significant contribution was *A Bibliography of Fiction by Louisianians and on Louisiana Subjects,* by Lizzie Carter McVoy and Ruth Bates Campbell (1935), listing fiction written in English. Many entries are annotated, and Louisiana authors when known are indicated, but no biographical information is provided.[2] All of these works

1. See "*The Law and the Lady Down in Dixie: A Drama in Three Acts,* by Rose Falls Bres" (condensed version of the 1907 Bres play with an introduction by Dorothy H. Brown), *New Orleans Review,* VI (1979), 293–300.

2. Alexander N. De Menil, *The Literature of the Louisiana Territory* (1904; rpr. New York, 1971); Thomas P. Thompson, *Louisiana Writers, Native and Resident* (New Orleans,

were valuable in their time but are inadequate today for a comprehensive study of the state's literary history.

The following Bibliography is designed to help establish the canon of Louisiana literature for both scholars and general readers. It is unique in culling from myriad sources a wealth of information attesting to the creativity of women native to or resident in Louisiana and writing in English within the past 150 years. The particular focus on women writers grew in part out of the desire to locate "lost" writers who had been excluded from literary histories. This angle of vision has helped me, as perhaps it will others, to see the writings of these women in a special way.

Setting parameters to determine which women should be considered was not always easy. Women born in Louisiana, whether they continued to live in the state or not, are included. Native Louisianians Grace King, Shirley Ann Grau, and Lee Grue are among those who remained in the state. Other writers born here, such as Lillian Hellman, Minnie Maddern Fiske, Alice Dunbar-Nelson, and Ruth McEnery Stuart, pursued their careers elsewhere. Coming from other states, poets Mary Ashley Townsend and Pinkie Gordon Lane have made Louisiana their home, as have many others who are included in the Bibliography. Townsend became known as the "poet laureate of New Orleans" and Lane in 1989 was officially designated the poet laureate of Louisiana.

Colorful writers such as Mrs. Frances Trollope (1780–1863) and Harriet Martineau (1802–1876) are not included, for although they wrote about New Orleans, they obviously were visitors and did not establish residence in Louisiana. A modern counterpart of these visitors would be Edna Ferber. On the other hand, Katherine Anne Porter, native of Texas, did live in Baton Rouge and wrote an important work while there. Similarly, Zora Neale Hurston's research and writing in the state cause her to be associated with it. Mary Edwards Bryan lived and worked in Natchitoches for a part of her writing career, and other writers, such as Margaret Walker and Ellen Douglas, although identified primarily with other states, did live during formative years in Louisiana or attended school here.

Although women in the state have written in French, Creole, Spanish, and other languages, this study attempts to record only those works written in English. The one exception is Sidonie de la

---

1904); Lizzie Carter McVoy and Ruth Bates Campbell, *A Bibliography of Fiction by Louisianians and on Louisiana Subjects* (Baton Rouge, 1935).

Houssaye, who wrote in French but who is included here to comple-
ment Alice Parker's essay. Her presence is also a reminder of Louisiana's vigorous traditions of non-English writing, as well as an indicator
of the work that remains to be done.[3] Furthermore, despite the excellent and prolific scholarly activity of Louisiana women writers such as
Carol Gelderman and Susan Tucker, the Bibliography had to be confined chiefly to authors of poetry, fiction, and drama (some of whom
may also claim nonfiction works in their canons).[4] A volume of poetry,
a collection of short stories, or a published novel has usually served as
an indicator for inclusion; the publication or the production of several
plays has been the touchstone for drama. Several noteworthy diarists
whose work has been published are also mentioned. And in some rare
instances, writers have been listed who have a verifiable body of stories
or poems published by newspapers, journals, or magazines.

The original intent to be complete has been a challenge, one that
had to be met differently for each major time period. The listing of
the major works of every writer is as inclusive as I could make it, although there are doubtless omissions, particularly of relatively obscure publications. And despite every effort, full publication data
could not always be ascertained. Important reprints and editions are
sometimes noted, but for twentieth-century works, especially, the fascinating stories implicit in this material had to be left untold.

For writers of the nineteenth century and earlier, the biographical
information, when it exists at all, is often quite detailed. Since many
of the early reference works are out of print or not easily obtainable,
it seemed reasonable to include here as much material as space would
permit. With later writers, the biographical data tends to be more
standardized; and the occasional unevenness is a result of selectivity
as well as availability, either from the author herself or from standard
reference works.

Secondary sources represent even more complicated choices. The
intent throughout has been to direct readers and researchers to the
sources of more information, as well as to indicate—especially for
the early years—a writer's acceptance in her own time or afterward
(as signaled by her inclusion in a variety of biographical dictionaries,

3. Mathé Allain of the University of Southwestern Louisiana and J. John Perret of
the University of New Orleans are two French scholars who have contributed to knowledge in this area.

4. See Carol W. Gelderman, *Mary McCarthy: A Life* (New York, 1988) and other
biographies, and Susan Tucker, *Telling Memories Among Southern Women* (Baton Rouge,
1988).

lists of notable women, and checklists of literary works). For major writers such as Lillian Hellman, Margaret Walker, and Kate Chopin, the secondary sources are highly selective, often with a bias toward local or regional resources. For other contemporary writers, secondary material can be scant indeed, and the information about their work was often collected from book jackets, conversations, and/or data forms that the authors filled out.

The method of search for works and authors included the use of earlier bibliographies, literary histories, indexes, directories, church and parish records, newspapers, and many other sources. Where possible, individual works have been examined and read. Literary reputations have been noted from contemporary criticism in publications such as *Harper's, Scribner's, Lippincott's,* the *Century, Appleton's,* and the *Atlantic Monthly* for writers of the nineteenth and early twentieth centuries. For writers of modern times, the many book review sources, scholarly publications, and lists of sales have been useful. Barbara White's *American Women Writers: An Annotated Bibliography of Criticism* (1977) with 415 entries, and the four-volume *American Women Writers* (1978–1982), edited by Lina Mainiero, have helped place new and "recovered" writers within the context of American women writing.[5]

The most formidable single aspect of compiling the Bibliography was establishing biographical data. Misleading inferences of Louisiana affiliation through subject matter, titles, or other facets of works have been checked, resulting in elimination of some entries found in earlier listings. For the names remaining, information varied tremendously, being especially scarce or unreliable for certain nineteenth-century authors. Significantly helpful are such works as May W. Mount's *Some Notables of New Orleans* (1896) with its descriptive and biographical sketches, and Mary T. Tardy's *Living Female Writers of the South* (1872), arranged by states, and Frances Willard's *A Woman of the Century* (1893).[6] These are valuable sources for the researcher, in no small part because of their serious consideration of women as writers. Even these works, however, are in many cases not fully reliable.

5. See Barbara A. White, *American Women Writers: An Annotated Bibliography of Criticism* (New York, 1977), and Lina Mainiero, ed., *American Women Writers: A Critical Reference Guide* (4 vols.; New York, 1979–82).

6. See May W. Mount, *Some Notables of New Orleans: Biographical and Descriptive Sketches of the Artists of New Orleans and Their Work* (New Orleans, 1896); Mary T. Tardy, *The Living Female Writers of the South* (Philadelphia, 1872); and Frances Willard and Mary Livermore, eds., *A Woman of the Century: Leading American Women* (1893; rpr. Detroit, 1967).

Even at the time of the McVoy work, many titles were out of print. In that source and in others, authors are frequently indicated by initials, noms de plume, or maiden names, leading to difficulty in complete identification. Rarely is the chatty information about an author found on a book jacket to entice buyers also placed within the volume itself, where it could be of permanent interest to readers and researchers. Therefore, even if the book is available, the writer may remain a mystery.

The help of writers today and of the general public was solicited through notices in newspapers, magazines, and scholarly journals, with good results.[7] Letters have come from relatives or friends of writers or from readers who do not want a favorite author to be forgotten. Forms were sent to all correspondents for whatever information could be supplied on the lives and works of Louisiana women. Not all suggestions could be included here, but such assistance is much appreciated and resulted in the collection of close to five hundred names now in the file of Louisiana women writers verified as having published poetry, fiction, or drama. Some entries are incomplete, but the majority are supported by biographical and/or publishing data. Some two hundred writers from this group are included in this volume, which, it is hoped, will be of value to future researchers.

Continuing research and writing on authors such as Kate Chopin (by, among others, Tom Bonner and Emily Toth); collections, such as Ann Brewster Dobie's and Mary Dell Fletcher's of Louisiana fiction; studies on movements or eras, such as Carmen M. Lindig's *Path from the Parlor;* reference works such as those edited by Glenn Conrad and by Lucy Core and Lynn Koppel—all combine to help end the mysteries about our writers.[8] This Bibliography is intended as a contribution to that effort to discover and to preserve a significant Louisiana literary legacy.

7. See Paula Devlin, "An Awakening — Discovering Louisiana's Women Writers," *Loyola New Orleans,* II (1983), 18–20, which details the search up to that point and requests submissions of names.

8. See Thomas Bonner, Jr., *The Kate Chopin Companion: With Chopin's Translations from French Fiction* (New York, 1988); Emily Toth, *Kate Chopin* (New York, 1990); Ann Brewster Dobie, ed., *Something in Common: Contemporary Louisiana Short Stories* (Baton Rouge, 1991); Mary Dell Fletcher, *A Century of the Short Story in Louisiana: 1880–1980* (Lafayette, La., 1986); Carmen M. Lindig, *The Path from the Parlor: Louisiana Women, 1879–1920* (Lafayette, La., 1986); Glenn Conrad, ed., *A Dictionary of Louisiana Biography* (Lafayette, La., 1989); and Lucy Core and Lynn Koppel, eds., *Writers Directory 1989* (New Orleans, 1989).

Abbreviations and Short Titles

In order to save space, the following abbreviations and short titles are used for old or specialized resources frequently cited in the Bibliography. Well-known standard references such as *Who's Who* publications are cited by title alone throughout.

American Authors and Books	Burke, W. J., and Will D. Howe. *American Authors and Books, 1640 to the Present Day.* 3d rev. ed; New York: Crown, 1972.
American Women Writers	Lina Mainiero, ed. *American Women Writers: A Critical Reference Guide.* 4 vols. New York: Ungar, 1978–82.
BDSA	Knight, Lucian L., ed. *A Biographical Dictionary of Southern Authors.* 1929; rpr. Detroit: Gale Research, 1978.
BFLLS	McVoy, Lizzie Carter, and Ruth Bates Campbell, eds. *A Bibliography of Fiction by Louisianians and on Louisiana Subjects.* Baton Rouge: Louisiana State University Press, 1935.
CA; CAR; CANR	*Contemporary Authors; Contemporary Authors Revised; Contemporary Authors New Revised.* Detroit: Gale Research, 1962–79.
Contemporary Literary Criticism	*Contemporary Literary Criticism: Excerpts from Criticism of the Works of Today's Novelists, Poets, Playwrights, and Other Creative Writers.* Edited by Sharon Gunton. 56 vols. (1989). Detroit: Gale Research, 1973–.
Dictionary of American Authors	Adams, Oscar Fay. *A Dictionary of American Authors.* 1904; rpr. Detroit: Gale Research, 1969.

Dictionary of Louisiana Biography	*A Dictionary of Louisiana Biography.* Edited by Glenn Conrad. 2 vols. Lafayette: University of Southwestern Louisiana, 1989.
DNAAD	*A Dictionary of North American Authors Deceased Before 1950.* Compiled by W. Stewart Wallace. Toronto: Ryerson Press, 1951.
Living Female Writers of the South	Tardy, Mary T. [Ida Raymon]. *The Living Female Writers of the South.* 1872; rpr. Detroit: Gale Research, 1979.
LSL	Knight, Lucian L., ed. *Library of Southern Literature.* 15 vols. Atlanta: Martin and Hoyt, 1907.
Louisiana: A Guide	Saxon, Lyle, *et al.*, eds. *Louisiana: A Guide to the State.* 1941; rpr. New York: Hastings House, 1959.
Notables of New Orleans	Mount, May W. *Some Notables of New Orleans: Biographical and Descriptive Sketches of the Artists of New Orleans and Their Work.* New Orleans: n.p., 1896.
Something About the Author	Commire, Anne, ed. *Something About the Author: Facts and Pictures About Contemporary Authors and Illustrators of Books for Young People.* 52 vols. (1989). Detroit: Gale Research, 1971–.
Southern Writers	Bain, Robert, John M. Flora, and Louis D. Rubin, Jr., eds. *Southern Writers: A Biographical Dictionary.* Baton Rouge: Louisiana State University Press, 1979.
Twentieth Century Authors	Kunitz, Stanley, and Howard Haycraft. *Twentieth Century Authors: A Biographical Dictionary of Modern Literature.* New York: H. W. Wilson, 1942.
A Woman of the Century	Willard, Frances, and Mary Livermore, eds. *A Woman of the Century: Leading American Women.* 1893; rpr. Detroit: Gale Research, 1967.

Bibliography of Louisiana Women Writers

Nineteenth Century

BAKER, Julie Keim Wetherill (1858–?)

BIOGRAPHY:

Born in Woodville, Mississippi. Daughter of Thomas M. and Sarah Eliza Smith Wetherill. Married Marion A. Baker of the New Orleans *Times-Democrat*. Lived in New Orleans. Novelist; poet; literary critic.

WORKS:

Wings: A Novel. Philadelphia: Lippincott, 1878.
The Wandering Joy. New York: Broadway, 1910.

SECONDARY SOURCES:
BDSA.
Who's Who.

BONNET, Marie Marguerite (1865–?)

BIOGRAPHY:

Born in New Orleans. Daughter of Jean François Bonnet. Moved to Pennsylvania in the 1920s.

WORKS:

Sweet William. Chicago: A. C. McClurg, 1890.
Little Marjorie's Love Story. Chicago: A. C. McClurg, 1891.
Prince Tip-Top. Chicago: A. C. McClurg, 1892.
My Lady. Chicago: A. C. McClurg, 1894.
A Child of Tuscany. Chicago: A. C. McClurg, 1895.
Pierette. Chicago: A. C. McClurg, 1896.
A Little House in Pimlico. Chicago: A. C. McClurg, 1898.
Tales of an Old Château. Chicago: A. C. McClurg, 1900.
Bernardo and Laurette. Chicago: A. C. McClurg, 1902.
Clotilde: A Story of Old New Orleans. Chicago: A. C. McClurg, 1903.

SECONDARY SOURCES:

BDSA.
Dictionary of Louisiana Biography.

BURCKETT, Florence ("Edith Lee") (?–?)

BIOGRAPHY:

Born in Vicksburg, Mississippi. Daughter of "a merchant of New Orleans." Moved to New Orleans in childhood. Made debut in the New Orleans *Times* around 1868. Prose writer.

WORK:

Wildmoor: A Novel. Philadelphia: Lippincott, 1875.

SECONDARY SOURCE:

Living Female Writers of the South.

CADY, Helena Maxwell (1849–?)

BIOGRAPHY:

Born in New Orleans. Daughter of Patrick W. Maxwell, civil engineer engaged in erecting sugar engines and building bridges and railroads. Grandfather was Dr. John Maxwell of Dundee, Scotland, surgeon in the British army. Spent her youth in Cuba. Married Mr. (?) Cady in 1870; seven children. Lived in Arkansas after the Civil War. Became interested in medicine, graduated from the Homeopathic School of Physicians and Surgeons as an M.D. Practiced medicine in Little Rock for several years, then moved to Louisville, Kentucky. Active in philanthropic and civic affairs. Worker in the Woman's Christian Temperance Union, Woman Suffrage Association, and other groups. Writer of prose and poetry.

WORKS:

None available.

SECONDARY SOURCE:

A Woman of the Century.

CANFIELD, Gertrude Augusta (1836–?)

BIOGRAPHY:

Born in Vicksburg, Mississippi. Married Major Canfield (killed in battle of Mansfield, Louisiana, 1864; lawyer by profession). Lived in Rapides Parish, Louisiana. Novelist; poet.

WORKS:

My Cousin Anne: A Novel.
Works appeared in *Louisiana Democrat* and New Orleans *Crescent.*

SECONDARY SOURCE:

Living Female Writers of the South.

CARROLL, Mother Teresa Austin ("Mother Austin"; "A Member of the Order of Mercy") (1835–1909)

BIOGRAPHY:

Born in Clonmel, County Tipperary, Ireland, as Margaret Anne Carroll. Became a Sister of Mercy. Came to New Orleans in 1869; lived thirty years in New Orleans. Died in Mobile, Alabama.

WORKS:

Glimpses of Pleasant Homes: A Few Tales for Youth. New York: Catholic Publication Society, 1861.

Life of Catherine McAuley, Foundress and First Superior of the Institute of Religious Sisters of Mercy. New York: Sadlier, 1865.

Happy Hours of Childhood: A Series of Tales for the Little Ones. New York: O'Shea, 1867.

Sunbeams. New York: O'Shea, 1867.

Angel Dreams: A Series of Tales for Children. New York: Catholic Publication Society, 1871.

By the Seaside. New York: O'Shea, 1872.

Life of the Venerable Clement Mary Hofbauer, Priest of the Congregation of the Most Holy Redeemer. New York: Catholic Publication Society, 1877.

Life of St. Alphonsus Liguori, Bishop and Doctor of the Church—Founder of the Congregation of the Most Holy Redeemer. New York: O'Shea, 1879.

Marie Antoinette: An Historical Drama. New York: Catholic Publication Society, 1880.

Mary Beatrice and Her Step-Daughters: An Historical Drama for Girls. New York: Catholic Publication Society, 1880.

Meditations for a Novena to Our Lady of Mercy and Reflections for the Renovation Retreat. New Orleans: T. Fitzwilliam, 1881.

Four Days in the Life of Mary Queen of Scots: A Drama for Young Ladies. New Orleans: T. Fitzwilliam, 1882.

The Tudor Sisters: An Historical Drama. New Orleans: T. Fitzwilliam, 1883.

Scenes from the Life of Catherine of Aragon: An Historical Drama. New Orleans: T. Fitzwilliam, 1885.

Ursulines in Louisiana, 1727–1824. New Orleans: Hyman Smith, 1886.

Leaves from the Annals of the Sisters of Mercy. 4 vols.

Vol. I. New York: O'Shea, 1881.

Vol. II. New York: Catholic Publication Society, 1883.

Vol. III. New York: Catholic Publication Society, 1889.

Vol. IV. New York: O'Shea, 1895.

Essays—Educational and Historic; or, X Rays on Some Important Episodes. New York: O'Shea, 1899.

In Many Lands. New York: O'Shea, 1904.

The Father and the Son: St. Alphonsus and St. Gerard. St. Louis, Mo.: Herder, 1905.

A Catholic History of Alabama and the Floridas. New York: Kenedy, 1908.

Edited and translated numerous works. Also contributed articles to *American Catholic Quarterly Review, Irish Monthly, Catholic World,* and *Magnificat.*

SECONDARY SOURCES:

Catholic Builders of the Nation. Boston: Continental, 1923.

Manly, Louise. *Southern Literature.* Richmond, Va.: Johnson, 1895.

Thompson, Thomas P. *Louisiana Writers, Native and Resident.* New Orleans: American Printing, 1904.

CHOPIN, Kate O'Flaherty (1850–1904)

BIOGRAPHY:

Born in St. Louis. Daughter of Thomas and Eliza Faris O'Flaherty. Educated at the Convent of the Sacred Heart, St. Louis. Married Oscar Chopin of Louisiana, 1870; six children. Lived in New Orleans and in Cloutierville, Natchitoches Parish, Louisiana. Novelist; short-story writer.

WORKS:

At Fault: A Novel. St. Louis: Nixon-Jones Printing Co., 1890.

Bayou Folk (short stories). Boston: Houghton Mifflin, 1894.

A Night in Acadie (short stories). Chicago: Way and Williams, 1897.

The Awakening: A Novel. Chicago: H. S. Stone, 1899.

The Complete Works of Kate Chopin. Edited by Per Seyersted. Baton Rouge: Louisiana State University Press, 1969.

A Kate Chopin Miscellany. Edited by Per Seyersted and Emily Toth. Natchitoches: Northwestern State University of Louisiana, 1979.

A Vocation and a Voice. Edited by Emily Toth. New York: Viking Penguin, 1991.

The Chopin Papers are held by the Missouri Historical Society, St. Louis.

SECONDARY SOURCES:

Bonner, Thomas, Jr. *The Kate Chopin Companion: With Chopin's Translations from French Fiction.* New York: Greenwood Press, 1988.

Elfenbein, Anna Shannon. *Women on the Color Line: Evolving Stereotypes and the Writings of George Washington Cable, Grace King, Kate Chopin.* Charlottesville: University Press of Virginia, 1989.

Ewell, Barbara C. *Kate Chopin.* New York: Ungar, 1986.

Seyersted, Per. *Kate Chopin: A Critical Biography.* Baton Rouge: Louisiana State University Press, 1969.

Skaggs, Peggy. *Kate Chopin.* Boston: Twayne, 1985.

Taylor, Helen. *Gender, Race, and Region in the Writings of Grace King, Ruth McEnery Stuart, and Kate Chopin.* Baton Rouge: Louisiana State University Press, 1989.

Toth, Emily. *Kate Chopin.* New York: William Morrow, 1990.

CLACK, Marie Louise (1830–1901)

BIOGRAPHY:

Married Colonel Clack, lawyer of Norfolk, Virginia (died in battle of Mansfield, Louisiana, 1864). Married M. Richardson of New Orleans in 1870. Poet; fiction writer.

WORKS:

Our Refugee Household. New York: Blelock, 1866.

General Lee and Santa Claus: Christmas Gift to Her Little Southern Friends (children's book). New York: Blelock, 1867.

"My Experiences of the Civil War of 1861–1865" (experiences in New Orleans as a refugee during the Civil War; personal narratives).

"During Civil Wars: Four Stories." Dedicated to Madame Edmond Deslonde of New Orleans.

SECONDARY SOURCE:

Living Female Writers of the South.

COLLINS, Mrs. E. Burke (See SHARKEY, Emma Augusta)

COWEN, Samuella ("Le Clerc") (1842–?)

BIOGRAPHY:

Daughter of Samuel Wright Mardis (United States congressman from the state of Alabama; died before Cowen was born). Family moved to New Orleans. Grew up, was educated, and was married in New Orleans. Husband served in Richmond in the Army of Virginia.

WORKS:

Creola (novelette). N.p., n.d.

Contributed to the *Mirror, Southern Literary News,* and *Illustrated News.*

SECONDARY SOURCE:

Living Female Writers of the South.

CRESWELL, Julia Pleasants (1821–1886)

BIOGRAPHY:

Born in Huntsville, Alabama. Daughter of Colonel J. J. Pleasants of Virginia (later Alabama secretary of state). Married Judge David Creswell (planter near Shreveport, lawyer by profession) in 1854; four children. Died in Jackson, Louisiana. Poet; novelist.

WORKS:

Aphelia and Other Poems, by Two Cousins of the South. With Thomas Bibb
Bradley. New York: Scribner, 1854.

Callamura (allegorical novel). Philadelphia: Claxton, Remsen, and Haffelfinger, 1868.

SECONDARY SOURCE:

Living Female Writers of the South.

DALSHEIMER, Alice Solomon ("Sylvia Dale") (1845–1880)

BIOGRAPHY:

Born in New Orleans. Married Mr. (?) Dalsheimer, lawyer. Never published in book form. Died in New Orleans. Poet; short-story writer.

WORKS:

"Motherhood" and "Twilight Shadows" (poems) appeared in New Orleans daily papers.

SECONDARY SOURCE:

Living Female Writers of the South.

DAVIS, Mollie Evelyn Moore (1852–1909)

BIOGRAPHY:

Born Mary Evelina Moore in Talladega, Alabama. Daughter of John
and Marian Lucy Crutchfield Moore. Married Thomas Edward Davis,
later editor in chief of the New Orleans *Picayune*, 1874. Lived in the
French Quarter. Wrote under "Mrs. M. E. M. Davis," "Mollie Moore
Davis," and "Mollie E. Moore." Died in New Orleans. Poet; novelist;
dramatist.

WORKS:

Minding the Gap and Other Poems. Houston: Cushing and Cave, 1867.

Poems by Mollie E. Moore. Houston: E. H. Cushing, 1869.

Poems by Mollie E. Moore. Houston: E. H. Cushing, 1872.

In War Times at La Rose Blanche (semiautobiography). Boston: D. Lothrop, 1888.

The Mistress of Odd Corner. Boston: Two Tales, 1892.

Under the Man-Fig Tree. Boston: Houghton Mifflin, 1895.

A Christmas Masque of St. Roch; Père Dagobert; and *Throwing the Wanga*
(drama). Chicago: A. C. McClurg, 1896.

An Elephant's Track and Other Stories. New York: Harper, 1897.

Under Six Flags: The Story of Texas. Boston: Ginn, 1897.

The Wire Cutters: A Novel. Boston: Houghton Mifflin, 1899.

The Queen's Garden. Boston: Houghton Mifflin, 1900.

Jaconetta: Her Loves. Boston: Houghton Mifflin, 1901.

Tulane Songs. New Orleans: Tulane University, 1901.

A Bunch of Roses and Other Parlor Plays. Boston: Small, Maynard, 1903.
The Little Chevalier. Boston: Houghton Mifflin, 1903.
Christmas Boxes (a comedy). Zionsville, Ind.: S. Warner, 1907.
A Dress Rehearsal. Zionsville, Ind.: S. Warner, 1907.
His Lordship. Zionsville, Ind.: S. Warner, 1907.
The New System (a comedy). Zionsville, Ind.: S. Warner, 1907.
The Price of Silence. Boston: Houghton Mifflin, 1907.
Queen Anne Cottages (romantic comedy). Zionsville, Ind.: S. Warner, 1907.
The Flagship Goes Down: A Broadside Poem. Houston: n.p., 1908.
The Moons of Balbanca. Boston: Houghton Mifflin, 1908.
Ode to Texas: Written for the Occasion of the Ladies' Bazaar for the Benefit of San Jacinto Battle Ground. Houston: n.p., 1908.
Selected Poems of Mollie Moore Davis. New Orleans: Green Shutter Book Shop, 1927.

SECONDARY SOURCES:
American Women Writers, I.
LSL, III, 1909.
New Orleans *Picayune,* January 2, 1909.
Wilkinson, Clyde W. "The Broadening Stream: The Life and Literary Career of Mary Evelyn Moore Davis." Ph.D. dissertation, University of Illinois, 1947.

DAVIS, Varina Anne Jefferson (1864–1898)

BIOGRAPHY:
Born in Richmond, Virginia. Daughter of Jefferson Davis (president of the southern Confederacy) and Varina Howell Davis. Referred to as "Daughter of the Confederacy." Studied in France and Germany. Spent much time in New Orleans. Novelist.

WORKS:
An Irish Knight of the Nineteenth Century (sketch of the life of Robert E. Emmet). New York: John W. Lovell, 1888.
The Veiled Doctor: A Novel. New York: Harper, 1895.
A Romance of Summer Seas: A Novel. New York: Harper, 1898.

SECONDARY SOURCES:
Davis, Varina Howell. *Jefferson Davis, Ex-President of the Confederate States of America: A Memoir by His Wife.* New York: Belford, 1890.
Ferrell, C. C. "The Daughter of the Confederacy: Her Life, Character, and Writings," *Mississippi Historical Society Publications,* II (1899), 64–84.
New Orleans *Picayune,* September 19, 1898.
Rowland, Eron. *Varina Howell: Wife of Jefferson Davis.* 2 vols. New York: Macmillan, 1927–31.

DAWSON, Sarah Ida Fowler Morgan (1842–1909)

BIOGRAPHY:

Born in New Orleans. Daughter of Thomas Gibbes (district court judge) and Sarah Waller Fowler Morgan. Married Captain Francis Warrington Dawson, newspaper editor, 1874; two children. Wrote for husband's paper, the Charleston *News and Courier*, under the pen names "Mr. Fowler" and "Feu Follet." Lived in Baton Rouge, Port Hudson (Louisiana), and Charleston. Moved to Paris, France, after husband's death. Wrote children's stories, French translations of the Br'er Rabbit tales. Her well-written diary, which recorded her experiences during the Civil War, was published by her son after her death. Died in Paris, May 5, 1909.

WORKS:

Les Aventures de Jeannot Lapin. 1903.

A Confederate Girl's Diary. Edited by Warrington Dawson. Boston: Houghton Mifflin, 1913.

A Confederate Girl's Diary. Civil War Centennial Edition. Edited by James I. Robertson, Jr. Bloomington: Indiana University Press, 1960.

The Civil War Diary of Sarah Morgan. Edited by Charles East. Athens: University of Georgia Press, 1991.

Contributions appeared in the Charleston *News and Courier, Mon Journal* of Paris, *Cosmopolitan*, etc.

SECONDARY SOURCES:

Coulter, E. M. *Travels in the Confederate States.* Norman: University of Oklahoma, 1948.

Dictionary of Louisiana Biography, I.

Dunaway, Philip, and Mel Evans. *A Treasury of the World's Great Diaries.* Garden City, N.Y.: Doubleday, 1957.

East, Charles. "Sarah Morgan's Civil War: A Firsthand Experience of War in Louisiana." *Cultural Vistas*, II (Spring, 1991), 11–14, 30–32.

Freeman, D. S. *The South to Posterity.* New York: Scribner's, 1939.

King, Grace. *Memories of a Southern Woman of Letters.* New York: Macmillan, 1932.

National Cyclopedia of American Biography, XXIII.

Wilson, Edmund. *Patriotic Gore: Studies in the Literature of the American Civil War.* New York: Oxford University Press, 1962.

The Sarah M. Dawson and Family Papers are in the archives of LSU. Additional Dawson and Morgan Papers are at Duke University.

DE LA HOUSSAYE, Sidonie ("Louise Raymond") (1820–1894)

BIOGRAPHY:

Born August 17, 1820, in St. John the Baptist Parish, Louisiana. Name on baptismal certificate is Hélène Perret. Daughter of Ursin and Françoise Paine Perret. Family moved to St. Mary Parish in 1828, where father became successful sugar planter and owner of Belle Vue Plantation above the town of Franklin. Little institutional education except for three months at age twelve at Sacred Heart Convent in St. James Parish. Married Alexander LePelletier De La Houssaye, steamboat captain, 1833 (?) (died 1863); six children (four sons, one daughter survived). Lived in St. Martinville, then in Franklin, where she ran a school until the Civil War. Postmistress in Franklin for a brief time. Resumed teaching in 1874 and intermittently through the next ten years. Reared eight grandchildren after the death of her daughter in 1875. Wrote for New Orleans periodicals such as *L'Abeille, Le Meschacébé,* and *Le Franco-Louisianais,* which published her stories and novels in serial form. In 1890 received the gold medal of *lauréate* of the Athénée Louisianais, New Orleans literary society founded to preserve the French language in Louisiana. Died February 18, 1894; interred in Franklin. Translator; novelist.

WORKS:

Pouponne et Balthazar. New Orleans: Librairie de l'Opinion, 1888.

Charles et Ella. Bonnet Carré [Reserve], La.: Imprimerie du Meschacébé, 1892.

Amis et fortune. Bonnet Carré, La.: Imprimerie du Meschacébé, 1893.

Les Quarteronnes de la Nouvelle-Orléans. Première Partie: Octavia la Quarteronne. Bonnet Carré, La.: Imprimerie du Meschacébé, 1894.

Les Quarteronnes de la Nouvelle-Orléans. Deuxième Partie: Violette la Quarteronne. Bonnet Carré, La.: Imprimerie du Meschacébé, 1895.

Pouponne and Balthazar. Translated and with an introduction by J. John Perret. Lafayette: Center for Louisiana Studies, University of Southwestern Louisiana, 1983.

Unpublished manuscripts in Louisiana State University Libraries, Baton Rouge.

SECONDARY SOURCES:

Cable, George W. *Strange True Stories of Louisiana.* New York: Scribner's, 1907.

Caulifield, Ruby Van Allen. *The French Literature of Louisiana.* New York: Columbia University Press, 1929.

Perret, J. John. "A Critical Study of the Life and Writings of Sidonie de la Houssaye." Ph.D. dissertation, Louisiana State University, 1966.

———. " '*Strange True Stories of Louisiana':* History or Hoax?" *Southern Studies,* XVI (1977), 41–53.

DINNIES, Anna Peyre Shackelford (1805–1886)

BIOGRAPHY:

Born in Georgetown, South Carolina. Daughter of W. F. Shackelford, judge. Educated at the Female Seminary of the Miss Ramsays in Charleston. Married John C. Dinnies, bookseller and publisher, 1830.

Also wrote under "Moina," "Rachel," "Anna Peyre Shackelford," "Mrs. Anna Peyre." Moved to New Orleans, 1849. Died in New Orleans. Poet; journalist.

WORKS:

The Floral Year (one hundred compositions in twelve groups, embellished with bouquets of flowers drawn and colored from nature, each flower illustrated with a poem). Boston: B. B. Mussey, 1847.

SECONDARY SOURCES:

American Women Writers, I.

Hale, S. J. *Flora's Interpreter and Fortuna Flora; or, The American Book of Flowers and Sentiments.* Boston: Sanborn, Carter, Bazin, 1848.

Living Female Writers of the South.

DORSEY, Sarah Anne Ellis ("Filia") (1829–1879)

BIOGRAPHY:

Born in Natchez, Mississippi. Daughter of Thomas George Percy and Mary Routh Ellis. Married Samuel Worthington Dorsey, planter in Tensas Parish, Louisiana, 1853. Died in New Orleans.

WORKS:

Recollections of Henry Watkins Allen, Ex-Governor of Louisiana. New York: M. Doolady; New Orleans: J. A. Gresham, 1866.

Lucia Dare. New York: M. Doolady, 1867.

Agnes Graham: A Novel. Philadelphia: Claxton, Remsen, and Haffelfinger; New Orleans: J. A. Gresham, 1869.

Athalie; or, A Southern Villeggiatura: "A Winter's Tale." New Orleans: J. A. Gresham, 1872.

Panola: A Tale of Louisiana. Philadelphia: T. B. Peterson, 1877.

Contributions appeared in periodicals, including the *Churchman* and the *Southern Literary Messenger.*

SECONDARY SOURCES:

Evans, W. A. "Sarah Anne Ellis Dorsey," *Journal of Mississippi History,* 1944.

Living Female Writers of the South.

New Orleans *Times,* July 5, 1879.

DUPUY, Eliza Ann (1814–1881)

BIOGRAPHY:

Born in Petersburg, Virginia. Daughter of Jesse (shipowner) and Mary Anne Thompson Sturdivant Dupuy. Was a governess in Natchez, Mississippi. Wrote about forty stories, mostly for the New York *Ledger.* Spent latter part of life in Louisiana and Mississippi. Also wrote under "Annie Young." Died in New Orleans. Novelist; short-story writer.

WORKS:

Merton: A Tale of the Revolution. N.p., *ca.* 1828.

Celeste, the Pirate's Daughter: A Tale of the South and West. Cincinnati: Stratton and Barnard, 1845.

The Conspirator. New York: Appleton, 1850.

The Separation, the Divorce, and the Coquette's Punishment. Cincinnati: J. A. and U. P. James, 1851.

Adventures of a Gentleman in Search of Miss Smith. Cincinnati: Edwards and Goshorn, 1852.

Florence; or, The Fatal Vow. Cincinnati: L. Stratton, 1852.

Emma Walton; or, Trials and Triumphs. Cincinnati: J. A. and U. P. James, 1854.

Annie Selden; or, The Concealed Treasure. Cincinnati: E. Mendenhall, 1854.

Ashleigh: A Tale of the Olden Time. Cincinnati: H. B. Pearson, 1854.

The Country Neighborhood. New York: Harper, 1855.

The Huguenot Exiles; or, The Times of Louis XIV (historical novel). New York: Harper, 1856.

The Planter's Daughter: A Tale of Louisiana. Philadelphia: T. B. Peterson, 1857.

The Mysterious Marriage: A True Romance of New York Life. Philadelphia: T. B. Peterson, 1858.

Why Did He Marry Her? New York: F. M. Lupton, 1870.

Michael Rudolph: "The Bravest of the Brave." New York: F. M. Lupton, 1870.

The Cancelled Will. Philadelphia: T. B. Peterson, 1872.

Who Shall Be Victor? Philadelphia: T. B. Peterson, 1872.

All for One; or, The Outlaw's Bride. Philadelphia: T. B. Peterson, 1873.

The Dethroned Heiress. Philadelphia: T. B. Peterson, 1873.

The Gypsy's Warning. Philadelphia: T. B. Peterson, 1873.

The Mysterious Guest. Philadelphia: T. B. Peterson, 1873.

Was He Guilty? Philadelphia: T. B. Peterson, 1873.

The Hidden Sin. Philadelphia: T. B. Peterson, 1874.

The Clandestine Marriage. Philadelphia: T. B. Peterson, 1875.

The Discarded Wife; or, Will She Succeed? Philadelphia: T. B. Peterson, 1875.

A New Way to Win a Fortune. Philadelphia: T. B. Peterson, 1875.

The Shadow in the House: A Husband for a Lover. N.p., 1881.

SECONDARY SOURCES:

American Women Writers, I.

Dupuy, B. H. *The Huguenot Bartholomew Dupuy and His Descendants.* N.p., 1908.

Fleming, Walter J. *The South in the Building of the Nation.* Vol. XI. Southern Historical Publ. Society, 1909.

Freeman, Julia Dean [Mary Forrest]. *Women of the South Distinguished in Literature*. New York: Richardson, 1866.
Living Female Writers of the South, I.

FIELD, Martha Reinhard Smallwood ("Catharine Cole") (1855–1898)

From *Notables of New Orleans*

BIOGRAPHY:
Born in Lexington, Missouri. Daughter of Colonel W. M. Smallwood, who became editor of the New Orleans *Picayune*. Educated at Mace Lefranc Institute, New Orleans. Married Charles W. Field, stockbroker in San Francisco; one child. Widowed after three years. Wrote for the San Francisco *Post*. Returned to New Orleans. Writer and editor of the New Orleans *Times-Democrat* and the New Orleans *Picayune*. Travel writer, essayist, and poet for these and other periodicals. Said to have founded the first circulating library in New Orleans. Her daughter, Flo, also a writer, worked on the *Double Dealer,* a literary magazine, and was a playwright. Died December 20, 1898, in Chicago. Interred in New Orleans.

WORKS:
"Queen Anne Fronts and Mary Jane Backs." In *The Louisiana Book,* edited by Thomas McCaleb. New York: R. F. Straughan, 1894.
Catharine Cole's Book. Chicago: Way and Williams, 1897.
The Way to Paradise. N.p., n.d.

SECONDARY SOURCES:
Dabney, Thomas E. *One Hundred Great Years: The Story of the "Times-Picayune" from Its Founding to 1940*. Westport, Conn.: Greenwood Press, 1972.
Jackson, Joy J. *New Orleans in the Gilded Age: Politics and Urban Progress, 1880–1896*. Baton Rouge: Louisiana State University Press, 1968.
A Woman of the Century.

GROENEVELT, Sara Bartlett ("Stanley M. Bartlett" and others) (?–?)

BIOGRAPHY:
Born near Natchitoches, Louisiana. Daughter of Dr. Sylvanus Bartlett of Maine and Julia Finch Gresham of Kentucky. Educated at girls'

high school in New Orleans; studied music in Europe. Married Eduard Groenevelt. Lived in New Orleans and Chicago. Poet; writer of fiction and nonfiction.

WORKS:

Wrote poems and prose for the New Orleans *Times-Democrat,* the Chicago *Current,* and other publications.

SECONDARY SOURCE:
A Woman of the Century.

HARPER, Eliza Elliott ("Sindera") (1834–?)

BIOGRAPHY:

Born in Jones County, Georgia. Daughter of Colonel John L. Lewis of Claiborne Parish. Family moved to Minden, Louisiana, in 1846. Married Dr. James D. Harper.

WORKS:

Publications appeared in the Louisville *Journal* and other periodicals.

SECONDARY SOURCE:
Living Female Writers of the South.

HEWITT, Emma Churchman (1850–?)

BIOGRAPHY:

Born in New Orleans. Was associate editor of *Ladies Home Journal, Home,* and *Washington Leisure Hours.* Poet; nonfiction writer.

WORKS:

Ease in Conversation; or, Hints to the Ungrammatical. Philadelphia: Curtis, 1887.
Hints to Ballad Singers. Philadelphia: Curtis, 1889.
Queen of Home: A Book For the Household. Philadelphia: Miller-Megee, 1889.
The Three Little Denvers. Philadelphia: G. W. Jacobs, 1902.
How to Train Children. Philadelphia: G. W. Jacobs, 1908.
How to Live on a Small Income. Philadelphia: G. W. Jacobs, 1909.

SECONDARY SOURCES:
BDSA.
A Woman of the Century.

HOLMES, Sarah Katherine Stone (1841–1907)

BIOGRAPHY:

Born at Mississippi Springs, Mississippi. Daughter of William Patrick (cotton planter) and Amanda Susan Ragan Stone. Educated by tutors and at Elliott's Academy, Nashville, Tennessee. Married Henry Bry Holmes in 1869 at Walton Bend Plantation in Mississippi; four children. Lived at Stonington Plantation near Delta, Louisiana, as a child. Family lived at Brokenburn, a large cotton plantation in northeast Louisiana northwest of Vicksburg, Mississippi, when the Civil War began. Fled to Texas with widowed mother and other family members, stopping at Delhi and Monroe, Louisiana, for two months. Arrived in Lamar County, Texas, in 1863; later moved to Tyler where other refugees had settled. Returned to Brokenburn in 1865. Lived many years in Tallulah, Louisiana; leader in social, cultural, civic, and religious life of the town. Died December 28, 1907, in Tallulah.

WORK:
> *Brokenburn: The Journal of Kate Stone, 1861–1868.* Edited by John Q. Anderson. Baton Rouge: Louisiana State University Press, 1955.

SECONDARY SOURCE:
> Wilson, Edmund. *Patriotic Gore: Studies in the Literature of the American Civil War.* New York: Oxford University Press, 1962.

HOMES, Mary Sophie Shaw Rogers ("Millie Mayfield") (1850–?)

BIOGRAPHY:
> Born in Frederick City, Maryland. Daughter of Thomas Shaw. Married Norman Rogers (died). Married Luther Homes in 1864. Family moved to Louisiana after father's death. Resided in Louisiana. Poet; novelist.

WORKS:
> *Carrie Harrington; or, Scenes in New Orleans* (novel). New York: A. Atchison, 1857.
> *Progression; or, The South Defended* (poems). Cincinnati: Applegate, 1860.
> *A Wreath of Rhymes.* Philadelphia: Lippincott, 1869.
> Contributed articles, essays, sketches, and poems to the New Orleans *Daily Crescent* and *True Delta.*

SECONDARY SOURCES:
> *BDSA.*
> *Living Female Writers of the South.*

HOSKINS, Josephine R. ("Jacqueline"; "Hildegarde") (?–?)

BIOGRAPHY:
> Born in New York. Daughter of a French immigrant (father). Moved to New Orleans around 1859.

WORKS:
> "Love's Stratagem" (novelette). *Southern Monthly,* December, 1861, January, 1862.

"Life and Writings of Mrs. Jameson" (essay). *Southern Monthly,* n.d. Contributed to *Catholic World.*

SECONDARY SOURCE:
Living Female Writers of the South.

HUMPHREYS, Sara Gibson (1830–?)

BIOGRAPHY:

Born on a plantation in southwestern Louisiana. Daughter of the Hon. Tobias Gibson and Louisiana Breckenridge Hart of Kentucky. Educated in Virginia and Philadelphia. Married Joseph A. Humphreys of Kentucky.

WORKS:

"Negro Libertines of the South," *Bedford's Magazine,* n.d.
"Man and Woman in the Bible and in Nature" Publishing data unknown.

SECONDARY SOURCE:
A Woman of the Century.

JAMISON, Cecilia Viets Dakin (1837–1909)

BIOGRAPHY:

Born in Yarmouth, Nova Scotia. Daughter of Viets and Elizabeth Bruce Dakin. Educated in Canada, New York, Boston. Married George Hamilton, 1860 (?); married Samuel Jamison, lawyer, 1878. Lived and worked in New Orleans after marriage to second husband. Published in *Scribner's, Harper's, Appleton's Journal, St. Nicholas,* and *Journal of American Folklore.* Died April 11, 1909, Roxbury, Massachusetts. Novelist; short-story writer.

WORKS:

Woven of Many Threads. Boston: J. R. Osgood, 1871.
A Crown from the Spear. Boston: J. R. Osgood, 1873.
Ropes of Sand (short stories). Boston: J. R. Osgood, 1873.
My Bonnie Lass. Boston: Estes and Lauriat, 1877.
The Story of an Enthusiast, as Told by Himself. Boston: Ticknor, 1889.
Lady Jane. New York: Century, 1891.
Toinette's Philip. New York: Century, 1894.
Seraph, the Little Violiniste. Boston: W. A. Wilde, 1896.
Thistledown. New York: Century, 1903.
Penhallow Family: A Story. Boston: W. A. Wilde, 1905.

SECONDARY SOURCE:
American Women Writers, II.

JANVIER, Margaret Thompson ("Margaret Vandergrift") (1844–1913)

BIOGRAPHY:

Born in New Orleans. Daughter of Francis de Haes and Emma Newbold Janvier. Educated in New Orleans public schools. Lived much of her life in New Jersey. Died February 13, 1913, Moorestown, New Jersey. Poet; fiction writer.

WORKS:

Clover Beach. Philadelphia: Henry T. Coates, 1880.
The Absent-Minded Fairy. Philadelphia: Ketterlinns Printing House, 1884.
Doris and Theodora. Philadelphia: Porter and Coates, 1884.
Rose Raymond's Wards. Philadelphia: Porter and Coates, 1885.
Ways and Means. Philadelphia: Henry T. Coates, 1886.
The Dead Doll and Other Verses. Boston: Ticknor, 1889.
Little Helpers. Philadelphia: Henry T. Coates, 1889.
Holidays at Home: For Boys And Girls. Chicago: W. B. Conkey, 1900.
Under the Dog Star. Chicago: W. B. Conkey, 1900.
Umbrellas to Mend. Boston: R. G. Badger, 1905.
Little Belle and Other Stories. Philadelphia: Henry T. Coates, n.d.
The Queen's Body-Guard. Philadelphia: Porter and Coates, 1883.

SECONDARY SOURCES:
American Authors and Books.
American Women Writers, II.
BDSA.

JEFFREY, Rosa Griffith Vertner Johnson (1828–1894)

BIOGRAPHY:

Born in Natchez, Mississippi. Married Claude M. Johnson of Louisiana. Married Alexander Jeffrey of New York. Died October 6, 1894. Poet; novelist.

WORKS:

Poems. Boston: Ticknor and Fields, 1857.
Woodburn. New York: Sheldon, 1864.
Daisy Dare and Baby Power (poems). Philadelphia: Claxton, Remsen, and Haffelfinger, 1871.
The Crimson Hand and Other Poems. Philadelphia: Lippincott, 1881.
Marah (novel). Philadelphia: Lippincott, 1884.

SECONDARY SOURCES:
American Authors and Books.
BDSA.
Living Female Writers of the South.

JOHNSTON, Maria Isabella Barnett (1835–?)

BIOGRAPHY:

Born in Fredericksburg, Virginia. Daughter of Judge Richard Barnett. Married C. L. Buck (died in war); three children. Married Dr. W. R. Johnston (died). Lived in New Orleans, 1881–1887. Also lived in Madison Parish, Louisiana. Novelist; short-story writer; journalist.

WORKS:

The Siege of Vicksburg (novel). Boston: Pratt Bros., 1869.
The Freedwoman. N.p., 1886.
Jane: A Novel. N.p., 1892.
Contributed stories and articles to New Orleans *Picayune,* New Orleans *Times-Democrat,* Boston *Woman's Journal, Planters' Journal.* Also edited St. Louis *Spectator.*

SECONDARY SOURCES:
BDSA.
A Woman of the Century.

JONES, Alice Ilgenfritz (?–1906)

BIOGRAPHY:
Unknown.

WORKS:

Unveiling a Parallel: A Romance. Boston: Arena, 1893.
Beatrice of Bayou Teche. Chicago: A. C. McClurg, 1895.
The Chevalier de St. Denis. Chicago: A. C. McClurg, 1900.

SECONDARY SOURCE:
BDSA.

KEPLINGER, E. M. ("Queen of Hearts") (?–?)

BIOGRAPHY:

Born in Baltimore. Married Samuel Keplinger in Mobile, Alabama. Taught in the public schools of New Orleans for many years. Published poems in the *Southern Ladies' Book, Sunday Times,* and elsewhere.

WORKS:

Berenice: A Novel. New Orleans: Miss S. M. Haight, 1878.
Contributed to the New Orleans *Sunday Times.*

SECONDARY SOURCES:
BDSA.
Living Female Writers of the South.

LESLIE, Miriam Follin (Mrs. Frank Leslie) (1836–1914)

From Madeleine B. Stern, *Purple Passage: The Life of Mrs. Frank Leslie* (1953; rpr. Norman: University of Oklahoma Press, 1971); with the author's permission

BIOGRAPHY:

Born in New Orleans. Daughter of Charles Follin and Susan Danforth Follin. Educated in Cincinnati schools. As a girl, toured briefly with actress Lola Montez. Married David Charles Peacock, 1854; married Ephraim George Squier, 1856; married Frank Leslie, 1873; married William C. Kingsbury Wilde, 1891. Wrote under: "Frank Leslie," "Miriam Florence Follin Leslie," "Miriam F. Squier." Called the "Queen of Publishers' Row" and the "Amazon of Publishing." Had a varied career as actress, translator, writer of prose, editor, and publisher. Greatest achievements were in editing and publishing; edited *Frank Leslie's Lady's Magazine* in the 1860s, *Frank Leslie's Lady's Journal* in the 1870s, and many other publications. Attended Abraham Lincoln's inauguration in 1861 and reported Queen Victoria's Jubilee. Lived in New York City and Saratoga, New York. Traveled extensively in Europe. Left a bequest of nearly two million dollars to Mrs. Carrie Chapman Catt for suffrage work. Died September 18, 1914.

WORKS:

Translator. *Travels in Central America,* by A. Morelet. New York: Leypoldt, Holt and Williams, 1871.

California: A Pleasure Trip from Gotham to the Golden Gate. New York: G. W. Carleton, 1877.

Rents in Our Robes. Chicago: Belford, Clarke, 1888. Art Press, 1890.

Are Men Gay Deceivers? New York: F. T. Neely, 1893.

Are We All Deceivers? New York: F. T. Neely, 1896.

A Social Marriage. New York: F. T. Neely, 1899.

The Froth of Society (drama; translated from Dumas). 1893.

SECONDARY SOURCES:

American Women Writers, II.

Ross, Ishbel. *Charmers and Cranks.* New York: Harper and Row, 1965.

Stern, Madeleine B. *Purple Passage: The Life of Mrs. Frank Leslie.* Norman: University of Oklahoma, 1953.

———. *Queen of Publishers Row.* New York: Julian Messner, 1965.

A Woman of the Century.

MALONEY, Teresa De Lacy (1839–?)

BIOGRAPHY:
Born in Manchester, England. Parents moved to New Orleans when Maloney was an infant. Had four children. Poet.

WORKS:
The Legend of Nonnenwerth and Other Poems. San Jose, Calif.: J. J. Owen, 1876.
Contributed to New Orleans *Times.*

SECONDARY SOURCE:
Living Female Writers of the South.

MANSFIELD, Blanche McManus (1869–?)

BIOGRAPHY:
Born in Louisiana. Educated in New Orleans and Paris. Married Milburg Francisco Mansfield in 1898. Juvenile fiction; illustrator.

WORKS:
The True Mother Goose. Boston: Lamson Wolfe, 1895.
How the Dutch Came to Manhattan. New York: E. R. Herrick, 1897.
Childhood Songs of Long Ago. New York: E. R. Herrick, 1897.
The Voyage of the Mayflower. New York: E. R. Herrick, 1897.
Bachelor Ballads. New York: New Amsterdam Book Co., 1898.
The Quaker Colony. New York: E. R. Herrick, 1899.
The Sov'rane Herb and the Smoker's Year . . . Boston: L. C. Page, 1904.
Romantic Ireland. With husband. 2 vols. Boston: L. C. Page, 1904.
Our Little Cousin series. 8 vols. Boston: L. C. Page, 1905–11.
The American Woman Abroad. New York: Dodd, Mead, 1911.
Colonial Monographs. N.p., n.d.
Told in the Twilight. N.p., n.d.

SECONDARY SOURCES:
American Authors and Books.
BDSA.

MASSENA, Agnase M. C. ("Creole") (1845–?)

BIOGRAPHY:
Born in New Orleans. Resided in Plaquemines Parish, Louisiana. Edited a paper in Louisiana.

WORK:
Marie's Mistake: A Woman's History. Boston: Pratt Bros., 1869.

SECONDARY SOURCE:
Living Female Writers of the South.

MENKEN, Adah Isaacs (1835–1868)

BIOGRAPHY:

Born in Milneburg, a New Orleans suburb. Daughter of Auguste and Marie Théodore. Married Alexander Menken, 1856; divorced. Married John C. Heenan, 1859; divorced. Married Robert H. Newell, 1862; divorced. Married James Barkley, 1866. Talented actress; achieved international reputation on stage in wide variety of roles in the United States, England, and the Continent; chiefly known for daring performances in Byron's *Mazeppa* and other equestrian shows. Acquainted with many literary notables, such as Bret Harte, Joaquin Miller, Algernon Swinburne, George Sand, and Alexander Dumas the elder. Died August 10, 1868, Paris. Essayist; playwright; poet.

WORKS:

Infelicia (poems). Philadelphia: Lippincott, 1868.

Writings included poems and essays in newspapers such as the New York *Clipper,* the *Sunday Mercury,* and the Cincinnati *Israelite.*

The Adah Isaacs Menken Diary is in the Harvard University Theater Collection.

SECONDARY SOURCES:

American Women Writers, III.

BDSA.

Falk, Bernard. *The Naked Lady; or, The Storm Over Adah.* London: Hutchinson, 1934.

Lesser, Allen. *Weave a Wreath of Laurel: The Lives of Four Jewish Contributors to American Civilization.* New York: Coven Press, 1938.

Mankowitz, Wolf. *Mazeppa: The Lives, Loves, and Legends of Adah Isaacs Menken.* London: Blond and Briggs, 1982.

MERRICK, Caroline Elizabeth Thomas (1825–1908)

BIOGRAPHY:

Born in Cottage Hall Plantation, East Feliciana Parish, Louisiana. Daughter of Captain David and Elizabeth Patillo Thomas. Married Edwin Thomas Merrick (elected chief justice of the Louisiana Supreme Court in 1855); five children. Louisiana suffrage and temperance leader. Lived in Clinton, Louisiana, and New Orleans. Died in New Orleans; buried in Metairie Cemetery. Short-story writer.

WORKS:

Old Times in Dixie Land: A Southern Matron's Memories (autobiography). New York: Grafton, 1901.

Published a series of stories and sketches of the Negro people in Louisiana.

SECONDARY SOURCES:

BDSA.

Dictionary of American Authors.

A Woman of the Century.

MILLER, Dora Richards (18?–?)

BIOGRAPHY:

Married Anderson Miller, lawyer from Mississippi, 1862; two children. Lived in Arkansas for a time. Educated in New Orleans. Writer; teacher.

WORKS:

A Woman's Diary of the Siege of Vicksburg: Under Fire from the Gunboats. New York: n.p., 1885. Later published in *Strange True Stories of Louisiana.* New Orleans: G. W. Cable, 1889.

Contributions appeared in the *Century* and newspapers. Wrote a column with George Washington Cable.

SECONDARY SOURCE:

A Woman of the Century.

MILLER, Martha Carolyn Keller (?–?)

BIOGRAPHY:

Unknown.

WORKS:

The Fair Enchantress; or, How She Won Men's Hearts. Philadelphia: T. B. Peterson, 1883.

Love and Rebellion: A Story of the Civil War and Reconstruction. New York: T. S. Ogilvie, n.d.

Aletheia; or, At Last it Biteth Like a Serpent, and Stingeth Like an Adder. New Orleans: Press of New Orleans Christian Advocate, n.d.

Severed at Gettysburg. New York: T. S. Ogilvie, n.d.

SECONDARY SOURCES:

BDSA.

BFLLS.

NICHOLSON, Eliza Jane Poitevent Holbrook ("Pearl Rivers") (1849–1896)

Courtesy the Historic New Orleans Collection, Museum/ Research Center, Acc. No. 1981.369.44

BIOGRAPHY:

Born in Pearlington, Hancock County, Mississippi. Daughter of William J. and Mary A. Russ Poitevent. Educated at the Amite (Louisiana) Female Seminary. Married Colonel A. M. Holbrook, 1872 (died in 1876). Married George Nicholson, newspaperman, 1878; two children. Became first woman in the world to own and manage a major newspaper, the New Orleans *Daily Picayune.* Rescued the paper from bankruptcy and added new sections on medicine and household hints and for young people. Gave Dorothy Dix her start. Promoted civic causes in education and animal protection. Elected president of the Women's National Press Association in 1884. Died in New Orleans. Poet; newspaperwoman.

WORKS:

Lyrics by Pearl Rivers. Philadelphia: Lippincott, 1878.

Two Poems (by "Pearl Rivers"). N.p., 1900.

Contributions appeared in numerous newspapers, including the New Orleans *Times,* New Orleans *Picayune,* New York *Home Journal,* and New York *Ledger.*

SECONDARY SOURCES:

American Women Writers, III.

Harrison, James H. *Pearl Rivers: Publisher of the Picayune.* New Orleans: Tulane University, 1932.

Holditch, W. Kenneth. "Eliza Jane Poitevent, Pearl Rivers, and the Old Lady of Camp Street." *Louisiana Literature,* IV (1987), 27–56.

New Orleans *Picayune,* February 16, 1896.

New Orleans *Times-Democrat,* February 16, 1896.

Ross, Ishbel. *Ladies of the Press.* New York: Harper, 1936.

NIXON, Jennie Caldwell (1839–?)

BIOGRAPHY:

Born in Shelbyville, Tennessee. Taught at Sophie Newcomb College (New Orleans); chair in English literature. Wrote essays, fiction, poetry.

SECONDARY SOURCE:
A Woman of the Century.

NOBLES, Catherine (?–?)

BIOGRAPHY:
Born in New Orleans. Clubwoman and writer.

WORKS:
Wrote for various newspapers and journals.

SECONDARY SOURCE:
A Woman of the Century.

PORTER, Annie (?–?)

BIOGRAPHY:
Unknown.

WORKS:
"Doctor Alphege" (melodrama). *Lippincott's Magazine,* XXII (1878), 526*ff.*
My Village in the South (serialized novel). *Lippincott's Magazine,* XXIII–XXIV (1879).
"At Last" (melodrama set in New Orleans and the Atchafalaya swamp). *Lippincott's Magazine,* XXXIII (1884), 383 ff., 488 ff., 575 ff.
"Miss Martin." *Atlantic Monthly,* XLIII (1889), 797 ff.
"Ninon" (New Orleans slave story). *Scribner's Monthly,* XVII (1895), 372 ff.

SECONDARY SOURCE:
Kirk, John Foster. Supplement to *Allibone Critical Dictionary of English Literature and British and American Authors.* 1891; rpr. Detroit: Gale Research, 1965.

PUGH, Eliza Lofton Phillips (1841–1889)

BIOGRAPHY:
Born in Bayou Lafourche, Assumption Parish, Louisiana. Daughter of Colonel George and Sarah McRhea Phillips. Educated at Miss Hull's Seminary in New Orleans. Married William W. Pugh, planter of Assumption Parish. Novelist; writer of short stories and sketches.

WORKS:
Not a Hero: A Novel. New York: Blelock, 1867. Published in England as: *Judith Grant; or, The Tempted Wife.*
In a Crucible: A Novel. Philadelphia: Claxton, Remsen, & Haffelfinger; New Orleans: J. A. Gresham. 1872.

SECONDARY SOURCES:
American Women Writers, III.
BDSA.
Living Female Writers of the South.

RIPLEY, Eliza Moore Chinn McHatton (1832–1912)

BIOGRAPHY:
Born February 1, 1832, in Lexington, Kentucky. Daughter of Judge Richard Henry and Betsey Holmes Chinn. Family moved to New Orleans in 1835. Married James Alexander McHatton in Lexington, 1852 (died 1865). Married Dwight Ripley in 1873. Lived ten years at Arlington Plantation, Mississippi. Traveled to Mexico, then to Cuba, during the Civil War. With second husband, lived in the northern United States. Died July 13, 1912.

WORKS:
From Flag to Flag: A Woman's Adventures and Experiences in the South During the War in Mexico and in Cuba. New York: Appleton, 1889.
Social Life in Old New Orleans: Being Recollections of My Girlhood. New York: Appleton, 1912. Printed earlier in New Orleans *Times-Democrat.*

SECONDARY SOURCES:
American Women Writers, III.
DNAAD.
Louisiana: A Guide.
Tallant, Robert. *The Romantic New Orleanians.* New York: Dutton, 1950.

SAXON, Elizabeth Lyle (1832–1915)

BIOGRAPHY:
Born in Greenville, Tennessee. Daughter of Andrew Jackson and Clarissa N. Crutchfield Lyle. Educated by Caroline Lee Hentz at Tuskegee, Alabama. Married Lydell A. Saxon of South Carolina, 1849; three children. In 1879, led band of New Orleans women in securing petition for equal suffrage. Helped organize state Women's Christian Temperance Union in 1883. Spoke and wrote on work reforms for women and children. Wrote on labor for New Orleans *Item* in 1890s. Active in civic and social life of New Orleans. Died in Memphis, March 14, 1915. Poet; fiction writer; suffragist.

WORKS:
Wrote stories and poems from an early age; published in newspapers 1853–1857.
A Synopsis of All Religious Beliefs. New York: New York Public Library, 1880.

A Southern Woman's War Time Reminiscences. Memphis: Press of the Pilcher, 1905.

Poems of Elizabeth Lyle Saxon. Compiled by grandson, Lyle Saxon. Dallas: C. C. Cockrell, 1932.

SECONDARY SOURCES:
Dictionary of Louisiana Biography.
National Cyclopedia of American Biography, XVI.
New Orleans *Times,* June 11, 1879.
A Woman of the Century.

SHARKEY, Emma Augusta Brown ("Mrs. E. Burke Collins") (1858–19?)

BIOGRAPHY:
Born in Rochester, New York. Daughter of W. S. Brown. Married E. Burke Collins, lawyer (died). Married Robert R. Sharkey, Mississippi cotton planter. Moved to Louisiana with husband for health reasons; spent summers near Tangipahoa, Louisiana, and winters in New Orleans. Novelist; journalist.

WORKS:
Bonny Jean, and a Severe Threat. New York: Street and Smith, 1887.
Sold for Gold. Cleveland: Arthur Westbrook, 1889.
A Debt of Vengeance. New York: Street and Smith, 1890.
The Cost of a Promise; or, Her Sorry Mistake. New York: Street and Smith, 1891.
Her Dark Inheritance. Cleveland: Arthur Westbrook, 1892.
A Gilded God: A Novel. Springfield, Mass.: Springfield Pub. Co., 1893.
Long Since Forgiven: or, Her Cherished Ring. New York: Street and Smith, 1901.
Her Life's Desire; or, Won by Patience. New York: Street and Smith, 1905.
The Wife He Chose; or, A Jest of Fate. New York: Street and Smith, 1908.

SECONDARY SOURCE:
A Woman of the Century.

SLAUGHTER, Marianna Marbury (1838–?)

BIOGRAPHY:
Born near St. Francisville, Louisiana, January 31, 1838. Lived in Monroe, Ruston, Mt. Lebanon, and Shreveport (all in Louisiana). Writer of short stories, sketches, novels.

WORKS:
A Texas Courtship. N.p., 1875.
Music by Telegraph. N.p., 1875.
Pleasant Riderhood on the War Path. N.p., 1876.

Pleasant Riderhood Grows Confidential. N.p., 1876.
Sunny Thoughts from Louisiana. N.p., 1878.
Rue's Christmas Carol. N.p., 1878.
Driftwood. N.p., 1879.
The Man with a Hobby. N.p., 1879.
Little Secesh. N.p., 1892.

SECONDARY SOURCE:

Alexander, Albert George. "Louisiana Writers, 1875–1900." M.A. thesis. Nashville: George Peabody College, 1931.

STUART, Ruth McEnery (1852–1917)

Courtesy the Historic New Orleans Collection, Museum/Research Center, Acc. No. 69-67-LP

BIOGRAPHY:

Born in Marksville, Avoyelles Parish, Louisiana. Daughter of James and Mary Routh Stirling McEnery. Educated in New Orleans private and public schools. Married Alfred Oden Stuart, cotton planter of Hempstead County, Arkansas, 1879; one child. Sometime editor of *Harper's Bazaar.* Seventy or more short stories and novels published in top periodicals of her time. From 1894 to 1986, stories included in twenty or more anthologies, at least sixteen after her death. More than a dozen of her books still in print as of 1991. Died in New York City, May 6, 1917. Novelist; poet.

WORKS:

Carlotta's Intended: A Novel. Philadelphia: Lippincott, 1891; rpr. Freeport, N.Y.: Books for Libraries, 1969.
A Golden Wedding and Other Tales. New York: Harper, 1893; rpr. New York: Garrett Press, 1969.
The Story of Babette, a Little Creole Girl. New York: Harper, 1894.
Gobolinks; or, Shadow Pictures for Young and Old. With Albert Bigelow Paine. New York: Century, 1896.
Sonny . . . [A Story]. New York: Century, 1896.
Solomon Crow's Christmas Pockets and Other Tales. New York: Harper, 1897; rpr. Freeport, N.Y.: Books for Libraries, 1969.
The Snow-Cap Sisters: A Farce. New York: Harper, 1897.
In Simpkinsville: Character Tales. New York: Harper, 1897; rpr. Freeport, N.Y.: Books for Libraries, 1969.

Moriah's Mourning, and Other Half-Hour Sketches. New York: Harper, 1898; rpr. Freeport, N.Y.: Books for Libraries, 1969.

Holly and Pizen, and Other Stories. New York: Century, 1899.

The Woman's Exchange of Simpkinsville. New York: Harper, 1899.

Napoleon Jackson: The Gentleman of the Plush Rocker. New York: Century, 1902; rpr. Freeport, N.Y.: Books for Libraries, 1972.

George Washington Jones: A Christmas Gift that Went A-Begging. Philadelphia: H. Altemus, 1903.

The River's Children: An Idyll of the Mississippi. New York: Century, 1904.

Sonny, A Christmas Guest. New York: Century, 1904.

The Second Wooing of Salina Sue and Other Stories. New York: Harper, 1905; rpr. New York: Garrett Press, 1969.

Aunt Amity's Silver Wedding and Other Stories. New York: Century, 1909.

The Unlived Life of Little Mary Ellen. Indianapolis: Bobbs-Merrill, 1910.

Sonny's Father. New York: Century, 1910.

The Haunted Photograph. New York: Century, 1911; rpr. Freeport, N.Y.: Books for Libraries, 1974.

Daddy Do-Funny's Wisdom Jingles. New York: Century, 1913.

The Cocoon: A Rest-Cure Comedy. New York: Hearst's International Library, 1915.

Plantation Songs and Other Verses. New York: Appleton, 1916.

Simpkinsville and Vicinity: Arkansas Stories of Ruth McEnery Stuart. Edited by Ethel C. Simpson. Fayetteville: University of Arkansas Press, 1983.

SECONDARY SOURCES:

BDSA.

Dictionary of Louisiana Biography, II.

Frisby, James R., Jr. "New Orleans Writers and the Negro: George Washington Cable, Grace King, Ruth McEnery Stuart, Kate Chopin, and Lafcadio Hearn, 1870–1900." Ph.D. dissertation, Emory University, 1972.

Hall, W. *The Smiling Phoenix: Southern Humor from 1865 to 1914.* Gainesville: University of Florida Press, 1965.

Simpson, Ethel C. "Ruth McEnery Stuart: The Innocent Grotesque." *Louisiana Literature,* IV (1987), 57–74.

Taylor, Helen. *Gender, Race, and Region in the Writings of Grace King, Ruth McEnery Stuart, and Kate Chopin.* Baton Rouge: Louisiana State University Press, 1989.

THOMPSON, Mary Agnes ("Nesta LaNovice") (?–?)

BIOGRAPHY:

Born in New Orleans. Daughter of Isaac Thompson of Glasgow, Scotland, and Celia Brady Thompson of Sligo, Ireland. Lived in New Orleans.

WORKS:
"Dat Christmas Eve." *Current Topics*, II, No. 6 (New Orleans after the war), 3*ff.*
Metairie and Other Old Aunt Tilda of New Orleans Sketches. 1892. Originally appeared in the New Orleans *Picayune* and *Times-Democrat.*

SECONDARY SOURCE:
BDSA.

TOWNSEND, Mary Ashley Van Voorhis ("Xariffa") (1832–1901)

BIOGRAPHY:
Born in Lyons, New York. Daughter of James G. and Catherine Van Winkle Van Voorhis. Educated at District School and the Academy. Married Gideon Townsend, banker of New Orleans, 1852; three children. Moved with family to New Orleans in 1860. Wrote for the New Orleans *Delta, Crescent,* and *Picayune.* Also wrote under the pseudonyms "Michael O'Quillo," "Crab Crossbones," and "Henry Rip." Died in Galveston, Texas. Poet; novelist.

WORKS:
The Brother Clerks: A Tale of New Orleans. New York: Derby, 1857.
Xariffa's Poems. Philadelphia: Lippincott, 1870.
The Captain's Story: A Poem. Philadelphia: Lippincott, 1874.
Down the Bayou and Other Poems. Boston: J. R. Osgood, 1882.
The World's Cotton Centennial Exposition: A Poem. New Orleans: L. Graham and Son, 1885.
"A Poem Written for the Dedication of the Howard Memorial Library." New Orleans *Times-Democrat,* March 5, 1889.
Easter Sunrise. New Orleans: Seebold, 1889.
Distaff and Spindle: Sonnets. Philadelphia: Lippincott, 1895.

SECONDARY SOURCES:
American Women Writers, IV.
LSL, XII.
Meyer, Audrey May. *Mary Ashley Townsend: Xariffa, 1832–1901.* New Orleans: n.p., 1938.
New Orleans *Picayune,* June 9, 1901.
New Orleans *Times-Democrat,* June 8, 1901.

WAITZ, Julia LeGrand ("Julia Ellen LeGrand") (1829–1881)

BIOGRAPHY:
Born in Ann Arundel County, Maryland. Daughter of Claudius F. and Anna Maria Croxall LeGrand. Moved to Louisiana at an early age. Married Adolf Waitz, May, 1867, in Galveston, Texas. Had a school

for girls in New Orleans with her sister, Virginia. Left manuscripts of journal and two novels and poems. Lived in New Orleans. Died in 1881, Galveston. Poet; teacher.

WORK:

The Journal of Julia LeGrand, New Orleans, 1862–1863. Edited by Kate Mason Rowland and Mrs. Morris L. Croxall. Richmond, Va.: Everett Waddey, 1911.

SECONDARY SOURCES:

Dictionary of Louisiana Biography.

Parker, Alice. "The Civil War Journal of Julia LeGrand Waitz (1861–1863)." *New Orleans Review* (Spring, 1988), 69–72.

WALWORTH, Jeannette Ritchie Hadermann (1837–1918)

BIOGRAPHY:

Born in Philadelphia. Daughter of Charles Julius Hadermann (German baron and president of Jefferson College, Mississippi) and Matilda Norman von Winsingen. Married Major Douglas Walworth of Natchez, Mississippi, 1873. Died in New Orleans. Novelist.

WORKS:

Forgiven at Last. Philadelphia: Lippincott, 1870.

Dead Men's Shoes. Philadelphia: Lippincott, 1872.

Against the World. Boston: Shepard and Gill, 1873.

Heavy Yokes. Boston: W. F. Gill, 1876.

Nobody's Business. New York: Authors' Publishing Co., 1878.

Matsy and I (poems). Memphis: Rogers, 1883.

The Bar Sinister: A Social Study. New York: Cassell, 1885.

The New Man at Rossmere. New York: Cassell, 1886.

Old Fulkerson's Clerk. New York: Cassell, 1886.

Without Blemish: Today's Problem. New York: Cassell, 1886.

Scruples: A Novel. New York: Cassell, 1886.

Southern Silhouettes. New York: H. Holt, 1887.

At Bay. N.p., 1887.

The Silent Witness. New York: Cassell, 1888.

That Girl from Texas. Chicago: Belford, Clarke, 1888.

A Strange Pilgrimage. New York: A. L. Burt, 1888.

True to Herself. New York: A. L. Burt, 1888.

The Martlet Seal. Philadelphia: Lippincott, 1889.

Baldy's Point. New York: Cassell, 1889.

A Splendid Egotist. Chicago: Belford, Clarke, 1889.

On the Winning Side. New York: P. F. Collier, 1893.

An Old Fogy. New York: Merriam, 1895.

Ground Swells. Philadelphia: Lippincott, 1896.

Uncle Scipio: A Story of Uncertain Days in the South. New York: R. F. Fenno, 1896.
Where Kitty Found Her Soul. New York: F. H. Ravell, 1896.
Three Brave Girls. New York: Whittaker, 1897.
Fortune's Tangled Skein. New York: Baker and Taylor, 1898.
Green Withes. Philadelphia: Lippincott, 1899.
A Little Radical. New York: Street and Smith, 1900.
History of New York in Words of One Syllable. Chicago: Belford, Clarke, 1889.
His Celestial Marriage. New York: Mershon, n.d.

SECONDARY SOURCES:
American Women Writers, IV.
BDSA.
Living Female Writers of the South.

WEBB, Laura S. ("Stannie Lee") (?–?)

BIOGRAPHY:
Born in Alabama.

WORKS:
Heart Leaves (verse). Mobile, Ala.: n.p., 1868.
Custer's Immortality (poem). New York: New York Evening Post Steam Press, 1876.
A Requiem for Lee. New Orleans: Pelican, n.d.

SECONDARY SOURCE:
BDSA.

WHITAKER, Lily C. (1850–?)

BIOGRAPHY:
Born in Charleston, South Carolina. Daughter of Nathaniel (clergyman) and Mary Scrimzeour (author) Whitaker. Educated in New Orleans. Contributed to *Southern Quarterly Review,* of which her father was editor. Poet; dramatist.

WORKS:
Donata and Other Poems. Baltimore: J. B. Piet, 1881.
Young American Progressive Hobby Club: A Farce in One Scene for Fourteen Males and One Female. New York: E. S. Werner, 1896.
Fourteen or more school plays were produced.

SECONDARY SOURCES:
Allibone Supplement.

BDSA.
DNAAD.

WHITAKER, Mary Scrimzeour Furman Miller (1820–1906)

BIOGRAPHY:
Born in Beaufort District, South Carolina. Daughter of Reverend Samuel Furman. Married John Miller. Married Nathaniel Whitaker, clergyman. Educated in Edinburgh. Died in New Orleans. Poet; novelist.

WORKS:
Poems. Charleston, S.C.: J. B. Nixon, 1850.
Albert Hastings: A Novel. New York: Blelock, 1868.

SECONDARY SOURCES:
BDSA.
Dictionary of American Authors.
Living Female Writers of the South.

WILLARD, Florence J. O'Connor (?–?)

BIOGRAPHY:
Born in Louisiana. Lived in New Orleans. Novelist; poet.

WORKS:
The Heroism of the Confederacy; or, Truth and Justice. London: n.p., 1862; New Orleans: A. Eyrich, 1869.
Contributed to New Orleans *Mirror,* New Orleans *Sunday Times.*

SECONDARY SOURCES:
BDSA.
Living Female Writers of the South.

WILLIAMS, Marie Bushnell (?–?)

BIOGRAPHY:
Born in Baton Rouge. Daughter of Judge Charles Bushnell. Married Josiah P. Williams, planter of Rapides Parish, 1843. Lived near Alexandria and later in Opelousas. Wrote for the New Orleans *Sunday Times.* Poet; prose writer.

WORK:
Tales and Legends of Louisiana (lyrical poem). N.p., n.d.

SECONDARY SOURCES:
BDSA.
Living Female Writers of the South.

WINDLE, Catharine F. (?–1870)

BIOGRAPHY:

Born in Lancaster, Pennsylvania. Daughter of Reverend William and Mrs. Forrester Ashmead. Married George W. Windle of Wilmington, Delaware, 1849. Moved to New Orleans with husband immediately after marriage. Poet.

WORKS:

Poems, N.p., 1848.

Contributions appeared in *Graham's* and *Sartain's* magazines, New Orleans *Delta,* and *True Delta.*

SECONDARY SOURCE:

Living Female Writers of the South.

YEISER, Sarah C. Smith ("Aunt Charity"; "Azelee") (?–?)

BIOGRAPHY:

Born in Vermont. Married Dr. Philip Yeiser of Alexandria, Louisiana. Taught for many years in New Orleans.

WORKS:

Contributions appeared in the New Orleans *Crescent.*

SECONDARY SOURCE:

Living Female Writers of the South.

Twentieth Century (Deceased)

AARON, Grace Tarleton (1893–?)

BIOGRAPHY:

Born in Patterson, St. Mary Parish, Louisiana. Daughter of Dr. Thomas W. Tarleton (a physician) and Louise Wilson Tarleton. Educated at Patterson High School and at Mrs. Blake's Private School, New Orleans. Married Morris Aaron of Natchitoches Parish in April, 1918. First poems published in 1930. Contributed to newspapers and poetry journals. Member of Shreveport Poetry Society. Third winner of short-story contest of Louisiana Federated Women's Clubs, 1935. Member of the D.A.R. Poet; short-story writer.

WORKS:

Cane River and Other Poems. Natchitoches, La.: Lesche Club, 1967. Posthumously published.

SECONDARY SOURCE:

Dictionary of Louisiana Biography, I.

AUSTIN, Martha Waddell (18?–?)

BIOGRAPHY:
Born in New Orleans. Daughter of Major John E. and Shauline Yerger (Creath) Austin. Educated at Newcomb College and Radcliffe College. Poet; journalist; novelist.

WORKS:
Veronica. New York: Doubleday, Page, 1903.
Tristram and Isoult. Boston: Richard G. Badger, 1905.
Contributions in New Orleans *Picayune.*

SECONDARY SOURCE:
BDSA.

BELL, Sallie Lee Riley (1885–?)

BIOGRAPHY:
Born in New Orleans. Daughter of Robert Lee (physician) and Sallie O'Pry Riley. Educated at Newcomb College. Married Thaddeus Park Bell, physician, 1909. Novelist; dramatist; author of stories for children.

WORKS:
Until the Daybreak. Grand Rapids: Zondervan, 1950.
The Street Singer. Grand Rapids: Zondervan, 1951.
Through Golden Meadows. Grand Rapids: Zondervan, 1951.
The Queen's Zest: A Romance of Louis XVI. Grand Rapids: Zondervan, 1952.
By Strange Paths: A Novel of Old Louisiana. Grand Rapids: Zondervan, 1952.
River Fetters: A Romance of the Early Christian Era. Grand Rapids: Zondervan, 1953.
Unto the Uttermost. Grand Rapids: Zondervan, 1954.
The Substitute. Grand Rapids: Zondervan, 1955.
The Thunderbolt: A Novel of Ancient Israel. Grand Rapids: Zondervan, 1956.
The Torchbearer. Grand Rapids: Zondervan, 1956.
The Wayward Heart. Grand Rapids: Zondervan, 1957.
The Bond Slave. Grand Rapids: Zondervan, 1957.
The Silver Cord. Grand Rapids: Zondervan, 1958.
Ginger. Grand Rapids: Zondervan, 1958.
The Long Search. Grand Rapids: Zondervan, 1959.
The Snare. Grand Rapids: Zondervan, 1959.
The Last Surrender: A Romance of the War Between the States. Grand Rapids: Zondervan, 1959.
The Hidden Treasure. Grand Rapids: Zondervan, 1960.

Beyond the Shadows. Grand Rapids: Zondervan, 1960.
The Shattered Wall. Grand Rapids: Zondervan, 1961.
Her Bridge to Happiness. Grand Rapids: Zondervan, 1961.
The Singing Angel. Grand Rapids: Zondervan, 1961.
The Love That Lingered. Grand Rapids: Zondervan, 1962.
The Secret Conflict. Grand Rapids: Zondervan, 1963.
Love at the Cross Roads. Grand Rapids: Zondervan, 1963.
The Interrupted Melody. Grand Rapids: Zondervan, 1964.
Romance Along the Bayou. Grand Rapids: Zondervan, 1964.
Light from the Hill. Grand Rapids: Zondervan, 1965.
The Trail. Grand Rapids: Zondervan, 1966.
The Promise. Grand Rapids: Zondervan, 1966.
Last Cry. Grand Rapids: Zondervan, 1967.
The Hidden Dream. Grand Rapids: Zondervan, 1967.
Down a Dark Road. Grand Rapids: Zondervan, 1968.
Tangled Threads. Grand Rapids: Zondervan, 1968.
Overshadowed. Grand Rapids: Zondervan, 1969.

SECONDARY SOURCES:
CA.
CANR.
Who's Who of American Women.

BRES, Rose Falls (Rosetta C. Falls) (1869–1927)

BIOGRAPHY:

Born in New Orleans, one of five children. Daughter of Isaac W. and Rosetta Falls. Married William A. Bres, cotton broker, 1902(?). Early newspaper work, then legal career, being admitted to the Bar in Kentucky, Louisiana, and New York. President of National Women Lawyers Association, 1925–1927, after serving as editor of its publication, the *Women Lawyers' Journal*, 1921–1924. Counsel for the Lucy Stone League. Also edited *Oyez!*, a magazine published by women lawyers. Wrote articles for many publications. Died in Jacksonville, Florida, November 14, 1927.

WORKS:

Chênière Caminada; or, The Wind of Death. New Orleans: Hopkins Printing Office, 1893.
The Story of the Yellow Fever. New Orleans: n.p., 1905.
Turn of the Wheel: A Humorous One Act Sketch. Copyright July 12, 1907.
A Fairy Tale: A One Act Sketch. Copyright August 9, 1907.
"*The Law and the Lady Down in Dixie: A Drama in Three Acts,* by Rose Falls Bres" (condensed version of the 1907 Bres play with an introduction by Dorothy H. Brown). *New Orleans Review,* VI (1979), 293–300.
Law and the Woman. Brooklyn, N.Y.: American Printing Office, 1917.

Maids, Wives, and Widows: The Law of the Land and of the Various States as It Affects Women. New York: Dutton, 1918.
Articles in *Delineator, American Magazine,* and others.

SECONDARY SOURCES:
American Women Writers, I.
"Rose Falls Bres: An Appreciation." *Women Lawyers' Journal,* XVI (January, 1928), 3.

BRISTOW, Gwen (1903–1980)

Courtesy the Historic New Orleans Collection, Museum/Research Center, Acc. No. 1983.215.99

BIOGRAPHY:
Born in Marion, South Carolina. Daughter of Louis Judson Bristow (minister) and Caroline Cornelia Winckler Bristow. Educated at Judson College; Columbia University School of Journalism; Anderson College. Married Bruce Manning, 1929. Reporter for the New Orleans *Times-Picayune,* 1925–1934. Died in New Orleans. Novelist; poet; journalist.

WORKS
The Alien and Other Poems. N.p., 1926.
The Invisible Host. With Bruce Manning. New York: Mystery League, 1930. Drama adaptation by Owen Davis, *The Ninth Ghost.* New York: French, 1932.
The Gutenberg Murders. With Manning. New York: Mystery League, 1931.
The Mardi Gras Murders. With Manning. New York: Mystery League, 1932.
Two and Two Make Twenty-two. With Manning. New York: Mystery League, 1932.
Deep Summer. New York: Crowell, 1937.
The Handsome Road. New York: Crowell, 1938.
This Side of Glory. New York: Crowell, 1940.
Gwen Bristow: Self Portrait (publicity pamphlet). New York: Crowell, 1940.
Tomorrow Is Forever. New York: Crowell, 1943. Film, 1946.
Jubilee Trail. New York: Crowell, 1950. Film, 1953.
Celia Garth. New York: Crowell, 1959.
The Plantation Trilogy. New York: Crowell, 1962. Published with additional historical material in the preface of each book.
Calico Palace. New York: Crowell, 1970.
Golden Dreams. New York: Crowell, 1980.

SECONDARY SOURCES:
American Women Writers, I.
CANR.
Chicago Tribune, August 19, 1980. Obituary.
New Orleans Review, (Spring, 1988), 15–20.

BRYAN, Mary Edwards (1838–1913)

BIOGRAPHY:

Born in Lloyd, Jefferson County, Florida. Daughter of Major John D. Edwards (planter and state senator) and Louisa Crutchfield Houghton Edwards. Educated at Fletcher Institute in Georgia. Married Iredell E. Bryan, planter, of Louisiana; five children. Lived and worked in Natchitoches, Louisiana. Became editor of Natchitoches *Tri-Weekly* in 1866; associate editor of *Sunny South*, a weekly, 1874–1884. Moved to New York, 1885, Georgia, 1895. Died in Clarkston, Georgia. Poet; novelist; journalist.

WORKS:

Mrs. Manch. New York: Appleton, 1880.

Wild Work: Story of the Red River Tragedy. New York: Appleton, 1881.

The Bayou Bride. New York: G. Munro, 1886.

Kildee; or, The Sphinx of the Red House. New York: G. Munro, 1886.

Munro's Star Recitations for Parlor, School, and Exhibition. Edited by Iredell Bryan. New York: G. Munro, 1887.

A Stormy Wedding. New York: Street and Smith, 1887.

My Own Sin: A Story of Life in New York. New York: G. Munro, 1888.

Uncle Ned's White Child. New York: G. Munro, 1889.

The Ghost of the Hurricane Hills; or, A Florida Girl. New York: G. Munro, 1891.

Ruth the Outcast. New York: G. Munro, 1891.

His Legal Wife. Cleveland: Westbrook, 1894.

The Girl He Bought; or, Bonny and Blue. New York: G. Munro's Sons, 1895.

Nan Haggard, the Heiress of Dead Hopes Mine. New York: G. Munro's Sons, 1895.

Poems and Stories in Verse. Atlanta: C. P. Byrd, 1895.

Her Husband's Ghost. Cleveland: Westbrook, 1896.

Maple Leaf Amateur Reciter: A Book of Choice Dialogues for Parlor, School, and Exhibition. Edited by Bryan. N.p., 1908.

His Wife's Friend. New York: Street and Smith, 1908.

Three Girls. Cleveland: Westbrook, 1912.

Bayou Tree. N.p., n.d.

A Fair Judas. N.p., n.d.

Fugitive Bride. New York: Street and Smith, n.d.

His Greatest Sacrifice. New York: Street and Smith, n.d.
Sinned Against. New York: Street and Smith, n.d.

SECONDARY SOURCES:
American Women Writers, I.
Julia Dean Freeman [Mary Forrest]. *Women of the South Distinguished in Literature.* New York: Richardson, 1866.
Patty, James S. "A Woman Journalist in Reconstruction Louisiana." *Louisiana Studies,* III (1964), 77–104.

CARVER, Ada Jack (1890–1972)

BIOGRAPHY:
Born in Natchitoches, Louisiana. Daughter of Marshall Hampton and Ada Whitfield Jack Carver. Educated at Judson School, Marion, Alabama, and Louisiana state Normal School (graduated 1911). Married John B. Snell, 1918. Died in Minden, Louisiana. Dramatist; short-story writer. Received O. Henry and *Harper's* short-story prizes in 1925 for "Redbone"; O. Henry prizes in 1926 for "Treeshy" and 1927 for "The Singing Woman"; O'Brien prize in 1926 for "Maudie"; and the Bellasco Cup in 1926 for her play *The Cajun.*

WORKS:
The Cajun: A Drama in One Act. New York: S. French, 1926.
Bagatelle. N.p., 1927.
The Clock Strikes Tomorrow (children's play). Produced 1935.
Short stories appeared in the *Century, Harper's,* and other magazines.

SECONDARY SOURCES:
American Women Writers, I.
Ford, Oliver Jackson III. "Ada Jack Carver: A Critical Biography." Ph.D. dissertation, University of Connecticut, 1975.
New Orleans Review, XV (Spring, 1988), 84–88.

CLAUDEL, Alice Moser (1918–1982)

BIOGRAPHY:
Born in New Orleans. Daughter of Herbert Mayberry and Jeannette McLeod Hayes Moser. Educated at Sophie Wright High School, New Orleans; University of South Carolina; Tulane University (B.A. 1964, M.A. 1968). Married Enrique A. Rivera Baz, 1935; divorced, 1941; one son. Married Calvin Andre Claudel, 1943. Cofounding editor, with Calvin Andre Claudel, of *New Laurel Review.* Lived in Chalmette, Louisiana. Poet; short-story writer.

WORKS:
Southern Season. Pikeville, Ky.: Pikeville College Press of the Appalachian Studies Center, 1972.

Represented in: Allan Swallow, ed. *Three Lyric Poets*. Albuquerque: University of New Mexico Press, 1944. Work also appeared in *Chariton Review, New America, Descant,* and others.

SECONDARY SOURCE:
CANR.

COLLINS, Mary Barrow (See LINFIELD, Mary Barrow Collins)

CONVERSE, Florence (1871–?)

BIOGRAPHY:
Born in New Orleans. Daughter of George T. and Caroline Edwards Converse. Educated at Wellesley College. Novelist; editor; poet. Worked on the *Churchman*, 1900–1908; the *Atlantic Monthly*, 1908–1930. Short stories appeared in the *Atlantic Monthly, Century, Collier's,* and others, and included "Belated Conscience," "Cooperative Ghosts," "Maggie's Minstrels," "Moorland Magic," "Quality of Mercy," and "Three Gifts." Died in Wellesley, Massachusetts.

WORKS:
Diana Victrix: A Novel. Boston: Houghton Mifflin, 1897.
The Burden of Christopher. Boston: Houghton Mifflin, 1900.
Long Will: A Romance of the Days of Piers Plowman. New York: Dutton (Everyman's Library), 1903.
Long Will: A Story of England in the Time of Chaucer. New York: Dutton, 1905.
The House of Prayer. New York: Dutton, 1908.
A Masque of Sibyls. London: J. M. Dent, 1910.
The Children of Light. Boston: Houghton Mifflin, 1912.
The Story of Wellesley (nonfiction). Boston: Little, Brown, 1915.
The Blessed Birthday: A Christmas Miracle Play. New York: Dutton, 1919.
Translator (from the French). *Birds of a Feather,* by Marcel Nodand. Garden City, N.Y.: Doubleday, Page, 1919.
Garments of Praise: A Miracle Cycle. New York: Dutton, 1921.
Into the Void: A Bookshop Mystery. Boston: Little, Brown, 1926.
The Holy Night: A Masque. Boston: Atlantic Press, 1929.
Sphinx. New York: Dutton, 1931.
Efficiency Expert (poetry). New York: John Day, 1934.
Collected Poems. New York: Dutton, 1937.

SECONDARY SOURCES:
American Authors and Books.
BDSA.
Who Was Who Among North American Authors, 1921–1939.

CROSS, Ruth Palmer (1887–1981)

BIOGRAPHY:

Born near Paris, Texas. Daughter of Walter Derohan and Willie Alta Cole Cross. Educated at Paris High School, University of Texas, University of Chicago, University of California, and Columbia University. Lived in Winsted, Connecticut, 1925–1945. Married G. W. Palmer, 1926. Moved to Winnfield, Louisiana, 1957. Papers are in Northwestern Louisiana State University Library. Died in Louisiana, September 30, 1981. Wrote short stories, novels, plays, nonfiction.

WORKS:

A Question of Honor. New York: F. M. Lupton, 1917. Later made into a film.

The Golden Cocoon. New York: Harper, 1924.

The Unknown Goddess. New York: Harper, 1926.

Enchantment. London: Longmans, Green, 1930.

The Big Road. London: Longmans, Green, 1931.

Soldier of Good Fortune. Dallas: B. Upshaw, 1936.

Back Door to Happiness. New York: J. H. Hopkins, 1937.

Eden on a Country Hill (nonfiction). New York: H. C. Kinsey, 1938.

Wake Up and Garden! (nonfiction). Englewood Cliffs, N.J.: Prentice-Hall, 1942.

The Beautiful and the Doomed. Natchitoches, La.: Northwestern Louisiana State University, 1976.

Published in *Holland's Magazine, Best American Short Stories, Saturday Evening Post,* and others.

SECONDARY SOURCES:
Dictionary of Louisiana Biography, I.
Who Was Who Among North American Authors, 1921–1939.

DAY, Dorothy (1897–1980)

BIOGRAPHY:

Born in Brooklyn, New York. Daughter of John J. and Grace Satterlee Day. Educated at the University of Illinois, 1914–1916. Married Forster Batterham, 1925; marriage dissolved; one child. Worked for the New Orleans *Item* in the 1920s. Died November 29, 1980, New York City. Editor; journalist; social reformer; writer. Influential Catholic writer and feminist.

SECONDARY SOURCE:
CA.

DIX, Dorothy (See GILMER, Elizabeth Meriwether)

DUNBAR-NELSON, Alice Ruth Moore (1875–1935)

BIOGRAPHY:

Born in New Orleans. Daughter of Joseph (seaman) and Patricia Wright (seamstress) Moore. Educated at Straight College; became teacher and social worker. Married Paul Laurence Dunbar, poet, 1898; separated, 1902 (Dunbar died in 1906). Married Henry A. Callis, 1910; divorced, date unknown. Married Robert John Nelson, 1916. Died in Philadelphia. Poet; dramatist; fiction writer; journalist.

WORKS:

Violets and Other Tales (twelve poems and seventeen tales and sketches). Boston: Monthly Review Press, 1895.

The Goodness of St. Rocque and Other Stories (collection of local-color tales). New York: Dodd, Mead, 1899.

Masterpieces of Negro Eloquence. Edited by Robert Nelson. New York: Bookery Publishing Co., 1914.

Paul Laurence Dunbar, Poet Laureate of the Negro Race. Philadelphia: R. C. Ransom, 1914.

Mine Eyes Have Seen (drama). *Crisis,* XV (1918), 271–75.

The Dunbar Speaker and Entertainer. Edited by Robert Nelson. Naperville, Ill.: J. L. Nichols, 1920.

The Negro in Louisiana: People and Music. N.p., n.d.

An Alice Dunbar-Nelson Reader. Edited by R. Ora Williams. Washington, D.C.: University Press of America, 1978.

Give Us Each Day: The Diary of Alice Dunbar-Nelson. Edited by Gloria T. Hull. New York: W. W. Norton, 1984.

The Works of Alice Dunbar-Nelson. Edited by Gloria T. Hull. 3 vols. New York: Oxford University Press, 1988.

SECONDARY SOURCES:

American Women Writers, III.

Hull, Gloria T. *Rewriting the Renaissance: Three Women Poets of the Harlem Twenties.* Bloomington: Indiana University Press, 1987.

Kerlin, Robert. *Negro Poets and Their Poems.* N.p., 1935.

Metcalf, E. W., ed. *The Letters of Paul and Alice Dunbar: A Private History.* Berkeley: University of California Press, 1973.

Whiteman, Maxwell. "A Century of Fiction by American Negroes, 1853–1952: A Descriptive Bibliography." *Journal of Negro History* (January, 1936).

ELDER, Susan Blanchard (1835–1923)

BIOGRAPHY:

Born in Fort Jessup, Sabine Parish, Louisiana. Daughter of General Albert Gallatin Blanchard (U.S. Army general and Confederate brigadier general) and Susan Thompson Blanchard. Educated at Girls'

High School in New Orleans and St. Michael's Convent of the Sacred Heart, St. James Parish. Married Charles D. Elder, 1855. Lived in Selma, Alabama, during Civil War. Returned to New Orleans. Taught science and math at Picard Institute and New Orleans High School. Wrote for New Orleans *Morning Star* and other Catholic journals. After husband's death in 1890, lived with daughter in Cincinnati. Died in Cincinnati. Poet; novelist; dramatist.

WORKS:

James the Second. N.p., 1874.

Savanarola. N.p., 1875.

Ellen Fitzgerald: A Southern Tale. N.p., 1876.

The Leos of the Papacy. N.p., 1879.

Character Glimpses of the Most Reverend William Henry Elder, D.D. N.p., 1911.

Elder Flowers: A Collection From the Poems of Mrs. Susan B. Elder. New Orleans: L. Graham, 1912.

The Life of Abbé Adrian Rouquette. New Orleans: L. Graham, 1913.

A Mosaic in Blue and Gray. N.p., 1914.

Ellen Loswell; or, Life in New Orleans Under Two Flags: A Play. N.p., n.d.

SECONDARY SOURCES:

American Authors and Books.

American Women Writers, I.

Cincinnati *Enquirer,* November 4, 1923.

Living Female Writers of the South.

FISKE, Minnie Maddern Davey (1865–1932)

Courtesy Louisiana Collection, Howard-Tilton Memorial Library, Tulane University

BIOGRAPHY:

Born in New Orleans; christened Marie Augusta Davey. Only child of Thomas W. (theatrical touring company manager from Wales) and Elizabeth Maddern Davey. Child actress in plays by Shakespeare and others. Adopted "Minnie Maddern" as stage name after father left (1869) and she and her mother went to New York City. Both parents dead by 1879, and she made her home with her mother's sister, Emma Stevens. Educated in convent schools in Cincinnati and St. Louis between acting engagements. Debuted as adult actress May 15, 1882, New Park Theater, New York City. Married

LeGrand White, musician, 1883; divorced, 1888. Married Harrison Grey Fiske, editor of the New York *Dramatic Mirror,* 1890; he wrote plays for her and became her manager. As "Mrs. Fiske," became one of America's great actresses. Championed works of Henrik Ibsen and starred in his plays, beginning in 1894. Appeared in films from 1913 to 1915 to help stave off bankruptcy, which came anyway. Continued her stage career until she became ill in 1932. Received many honors, including honorary degrees from Smith College (1926) and University of Wisconsin (1927). Died at home in Hollis, New York, February 15, 1932. Actress; playwright; director; producer.

WORKS:

Between 1890 and 1894, wrote at least four one-act plays: *The Rose, The Eyes of the Heart, Common Clay* and *Not Guilty* (information on performances not available). Known to have adapted and revised many plays by others.

A Light from St. Agnes (lyric tragedy in one act). New York: R. L. Huntzinger, 1925. Made into opera by Frank Harling.

Fontenelle (full-length play). With Paul Kester. No other information available.

Mrs. Fiske, Her Views on Actors, Acting, and the Problems of Production. Edited by Alexander Woollcott. 1917; rpr. New York: Blom, 1968.

Correspondence with Mrs. Dashiell of New Orleans in Howard-Tilton Memorial Library, Tulane University.

SECONDARY SOURCES:

BDSA.

Binns, Archie (with Olive Kooken). *Mrs. Fiske and the American Theatre.* New York: Crown, 1955.

Burns, Morris U. "Minnie Maddern Fiske." In *Notable Women in the American Theatre,* edited by Alice M. Robinson, Vera M. Roberts, and Milly S. Barranger. Westport, Conn.: Greenwood Press, 1989.

Oxford Companion to American Literature.

Strang, Lewis C. *Famous Actresses of the Day in America.* 2d Series. Boston: L. C. Page, 1902.

Woollcott, Alexander, New York *Times,* January 19, 1916, p. 12.

GARCIA, Celine Fremaux (1850–1935)

BIOGRAPHY:

Born in Donaldsonville, Louisiana. Daughter of Leon Joseph (engineer and state land officer) and Flore Caroline deMontilly Fremaux, both of old French families who came to New Orleans. One sister, four brothers. Family lived in Donaldsonville, New Orleans, Baton Rouge, Jackson, and Port Hudson in Louisiana, and in Mobile, Alabama. Educated by mother and in the Miller School (associated with Centenary College, Shreveport), and at the Judson Institute (Alabama). Finished high school in New Orleans. Taught in New Orleans public schools. Married Joseph Garcia, businessman, 1871; four children. Lived in New Orleans.

WORKS:

Celine Remembering Louisiana, 1850–1871 (memoir). Edited by Patrick J. Geary. Athens: University of Georgia Press, 1987. Personal account of nonplantation, middle-class family written by a woman of French Catholic immigrant background.

SECONDARY SOURCES:

Antler, Joyce. New York *Times,* July 31, 1988, p. 19.

Brasseaux, Carl A. *Journal of American History,* LXXV (March, 1989), 1327.

Jackson, Joy. *Choice,* XXVI (Summer, 1988), 204.

GILMER, Elizabeth Meriwether ("Dorothy Dix") (1861–1951)

Courtesy the Historic New Orleans Collection, Museum/Research Center, Acc. No. 1974.25.27.147

BIOGRAPHY:

Born in 1861 (some say 1870) in Woodstock, Montgomery County, Tennessee. Daughter of William Douglas and Maria Winston Meriwether. Educated at Female Academy of Clarksville and at Hollins Institute, Botecourt Springs, Virginia. Married George O. Gilmer, 1882. Literary editor of the New Orleans *Daily Picayune;* started "Lagniappe" section. Died in New Orleans; buried in Metairie Cemetery. Fiction writer; journalist.

WORKS:

Fables of the Elite. New York: R. F. Fenno, 1902.

What's Sauce for the Gander Is Sauce for the Goose. N.p., 1912.

Woman's Lack of Pride. New York: Political Equality Association, 1912.

Dorothy Dix on Woman's Ballot. New York: National American Woman Suffrage Association, 1914.

Mirandy. New York: Hearst's International Library, 1914.

Hearts à la Mode. New York: Hearst's International Library, 1915.

Mirandy Exhorts: A Black Mammy Story. Philadelphia: Penn, 1922.

My Trip Around the World. Philadelphia: Penn, 1924.

Dorothy Dix: Her Book—Everyday Help for Everyday People. New York: Funk and Wagnalls, 1926.

Mexico. Gulfport, Miss.: C. Rand, 1934.

How to Win and Hold a Husband. 1939; rpr. New York: Arno Press, 1974.

SECONDARY SOURCES:

American Women Writers, II.

Deutsch, Hermann B. "Dorothy Dix Talks." In *Saturday Evening Post Biographies of Famous Journalists,* edited by John E. Drewry. Athens: University of Georgia Press, 1942.

Dolson, Hildegarde. "Dear Miss Dix—This Is My Problem," *Reader's Digest,* February, 1945, pp. 39–42.

Kane, Harnett T., and Ella Bentley Athur. *Dear Dorothy Dix: The Story of a Compassionate Woman.* Garden City, N.Y.: Doubleday, 1952.

New York *Times,* December 16, 1951 (obituary).

Ross, Ishbel. *Ladies of the Press.* New York: Harper, 1936.

GODCHAUX, Elma (1896–1941)

BIOGRAPHY:

Born in Napoleonville, Louisiana. Daughter of Edward (planter) and Ophelia Gumbel Godchaux. Educated at Radcliffe College. Married Walter Kahn; divorced; one daughter. Died in New Orleans, April 3, 1941. Novelist; short-story writer.

WORKS:

Stubborn Roots: A Novel. New York: Macmillan, 1936.

Short stories appeared in the *Southern Review, Frontier and Midland,* and other journals. Three stories have been anthologized as follows:

"Wild Nigger." In *The Best Short Stories of 1935,* edited by Edward J. O'Brien. Boston: Houghton Mifflin, 1935.

"Chains." In *O. Henry Memorial Award Prize Stories of 1936,* edited by Harry Hansen. New York: Doubleday, Doran, 1937. In *The Best Short Stories of 1937,* edited by Edward J. O'Brien. Boston: Houghton Mifflin, 1937. In *Louisiana in the Short Story,* edited by Lizzie Carter McVoy. Baton Rouge: Louisiana State University Press, 1940.

"The Horn That Called Bambine." In *A Southern Harvest,* edited by Robert Penn Warren. Boston: Houghton Mifflin, 1937. In *An Anthology of Stories from the Southern Review,* edited by Cleanth Brooks and Robert Penn Warren. Baton Rouge: Louisiana State University Press, 1953. In *A Century of the Short Story in Louisiana, 1880–1980,* edited by Mary Dell Fletcher. Lafayette: Center for Louisiana Studies, University of Southwestern Louisiana, 1986.

SECONDARY SOURCES:

American Women Writers, II.

BFLLS.

Goldstein, A. "The Creative Spirit." In *The Past As Prelude: New Orleans, 1718–1968,* edited by Hodding Carter. New Orleans: Pelican, 1968.

GOREAU, Laurraine Roberta (1919–1985)

BIOGRAPHY:

Born in New Orleans. Daughter of Nelson Goram (inventor and manufacturer) and Anna Wilson Goreau; one of five children. Managing editor of the Lafayette (La.) *Daily Advertiser* in the 1940s; the Superior (Wisc.) *Daily Telegraph* in the 1950s; editor of Women's Section of the *Item* and then the *States-Item* in New Orleans. Retired for health reasons; moved to Carrollton, Georgia. Newspaperwoman; biographer; songwriter.

WORKS:

Just Mahalia, Baby: The Mahalia Jackson Story. Waco, Tex.: Word, 1975; rpr. New Orleans: Pelican, 1984.

The Ballad of Catfood Grimes (folk opera based on a poem by Hodding Carter). Performed February 20, 1983, New Orleans.

Wrote songs recorded by Mahalia Jackson, Pete Fountain, and Ronnie Kole, among others.

SECONDARY SOURCES:

New Orleans *Times-Picayune,* February 20, 1983, Sec. 2, p. 3.

Who's Who Among American Women in Communications.

Who's Who in the South and Southwest.

HARDIN, Charlotte Prentiss (1882–?)

BIOGRAPHY:

Born in New Orleans. Married William Johnston Hardin, 1909.

WORKS:

"Windscents." *Atlantic Monthly,* 1907.

"Chanson Louis XIII." *Atlantic Monthly,* 1908.

"Musings of a Pre-Raphaelite Painter." *Atlantic Monthly,* 1909.

SECONDARY SOURCE:

BDSA.

HARRISON, Edith Ogden (Mrs. Carter Henry Harrison, Jr.) (?–1955)

BIOGRAPHY:

Born in New Orleans. Daughter of Judge Robert Nash and Sarah Beatty Ogden. Educated at Convent of the Sisters of Mercy and Peabody High School, New Orleans. Married Carter Henry Harrison, Jr. (mayor of Chicago), 1887; two children. Novelist; dramatist; juvenile-fiction author.

WORKS:

Prince Silver Wings and Other Fairy Tales. Chicago: A. C. McClurg, 1902.

The Star Fairies and Other Fairy Tales. Chicago: A. C. McClurg, 1903.

Legends of the Earth and Sky. Chicago: A. C. McClurg, 1904.
Moon Princes. Chicago: A. C. McClurg, 1905.
The Moon Princess: A Fairy Tale. Chicago: A. C. McClurg, 1907.
The Flaming Sword and Other Legends of the Earth and Sky. Chicago: A. C. McClurg, 1908.
Ladder of Moonlight. Chicago: A. C. McClurg, 1909.
Mockingbird Lane. Chicago: A. C. McClurg, 1909.
The Mockingbird; Sunrise and Sunset. Chicago: A. C. McClurg, 1909.
Polar Star, Aurora Borealis. Chicago: A. C. McClurg, 1909.
Princess Sayrane: A Romance of the Days of Prester John. Chicago: A. C. McClurg, 1910.
Glittering Festival. Chicago: A. C. McClurg, 1911.
The Lady of the Snows (novel). Chicago: A. C. McClurg, 1912.
Enchanted House and Other Fairy Stories. Chicago: A. C. McClurg, 1913.
Clemencia's Crisis (novel). Chicago: A. C. McClurg, 1915.
Below the Equator: The Story of a Tour Through the Countries of South America. Chicago: A. C. McClurg, 1918.
All the Way 'Round: The Story of a Fourteen-Month Trip Around the World. Chicago: A. C. McClurg, 1922.
Lands of the Sun: Impressions of a Visit to Tropical Lands. Chicago: A. C. McClurg, 1925.
Gray Moss. Chicago: R. F. Seymour, 1929.
The Scarlet Riders. Chicago: R. F. Seymour, 1930.
Strange to Say: Recollections of Persons and Events in New Orleans and Chicago. Chicago: A. Kroch, 1949.

SECONDARY SOURCES:
BDSA.
Who's Who.
Who's Who of American Women.

HELLMAN, Lillian Florence (1905–1984)

Photo by Robert Tobey
© Vineyard Gazette, Inc.

BIOGRAPHY:
Born in New Orleans. Daughter of Max Bernard Hellman (businessman) and Julia Newhouse Hellman. Educated at New York University; Columbia University. Married Arthur Kober, writer, 1925; divorced, 1932. Dramatist; wrote many screenplays and adaptations; nonfiction writer.

WORKS:

The Children's Hour. New York: Knopf, 1934. Film, 1962.

Days to Come. New York: Knopf, 1936.

These Three. Film, 1936.

The Little Foxes. New York: Random House, 1939. Film, 1941.

Watch on the Rhine. New York: Random House, 1941. Film, 1943.

The Searching Wind. New York: Viking, 1944. Film, 1946.

Another Part of the Forest. New York: Viking, 1947. Film, 1948.

Regina (opera). 1949.

Monteserrat (adapted from Robles). New York: Dramatists Play Service, 1950.

The Autumn Garden. Boston: Little, Brown, 1951.

The Lark (adapted from Anouilh). New York: Random House, 1956.

Candide: A Comic Operetta Based on Voltaire's Satire. New York: Random House, 1957.

Toys in the Attic. New York: Random House, 1960. Film, 1963.

My Mother, My Father, and Me (adapted from Blechman). New York: Random House, 1963.

An Unfinished Woman: A Memoir. Boston: Little, Brown, 1970.

Pentimento: A Book of Portraits. Boston: Little, Brown, 1973. Film, *Julia*, 1977.

Scoundrel Time. Boston: Little, Brown, 1976.

Maybe: A Story. Boston: Little, Brown, 1980.

SECONDARY SOURCES:

Adler, Jacob. "The Rose and the Fox: Notes on the Southern Drama." In *South: Modern Southern Literature in its Cultural Setting*, edited by Louis D. Rubin, Jr., and Robert Jacobs. Garden City, N.Y.: Dolphin Books, 1961.

Bryer, Jackson R., ed. *Conversations with Lillian Hellman*. Jackson: University Press of Mississippi, 1986.

Feibleman, Peter. *Lilly: Reminiscences of Lillian Hellman*. New York: William Morrow, 1988.

Goodman, Charlotte. "The Fox's Cubs: Lillian Hellman, Arthur Miller, and Tennessee Williams." In *Modern American Drama: The Female Canon*, edited by June Schlueter. Teaneck, N.J.: Fairleigh Dickinson University Press, 1990.

Lederer, Katherine. *Lillian Hellman*. Boston: Twayne, 1979.

Rollyson, Carl. *Lillian Hellman: Her Legend and Her Legacy*. New York: St. Martin's, 1988.

Southern Writers.

Wright, William. *Lillian Hellman: The Image, the Woman*. New York: Simon and Schuster, 1988.

HURSTON, Zora Neale (1903–1960)

BIOGRAPHY:

Born in Eatonville, Florida. Daughter of John (preacher and carpenter) and Lucy Ann Potts (seamstress) Hurston. Educated at Howard University; Barnard College; Columbia University. Died in Fort Pierce, Florida. Novelist; dramatist; folklorist.

WORKS:

Jonah's Gourd Vine. Philadelphia: Lippincott, 1934.
Mules and Men. Philadelphia: Lippincott, 1935.
Their Eyes Were Watching God. Philadelphia: Lippincott, 1937.
Tell My Horse (nonfiction). Philadelphia: Lippincott, 1938.
Moses, Man of the Mountain. Philadelphia: Lippincott, 1939.
Dust Tracks on a Road (autobiography). 1939; rpr. Urbana: University of Illinois, 1984.
Seraph on the Suwanee. New York: Scribner, 1948.

SECONDARY SOURCES:

American Women Writers, II.
Borders, Florence Edwards. "Zora Neale Hurston: Hidden Woman." *Callaloo*, II (1979), 89–92.
Gayle, Addison, Jr. "The Outsider." In *The Way of the New World: The Black Novel in America*. New York: Anchor/Doubleday, 1976.
Hemenway, Robert. *Zora Neale Hurston: A Literary Biography*. Urbana: University of Illinois Press, 1977.
Howard, Lillie P. *Zora Neale Hurston*. New York: Twayne Pub., 1980.
Turner, Darwin T. "Zora Neale Hurston: The Wandering Minstrel." In *In a Minor Chord: Three Afro-American Writers and Their Search for Identity*. Carbondale: Southern Illinois University Press, 1971.

KEYES, Frances Parkinson (1885–1970)

Courtesy the Historic New Orleans Collection, Museum/ Research Center, Acc. No. 1974.25.27.496

BIOGRAPHY:

Born in Charlottesville, Virginia. Daughter of John Henry (professor of Greek) and Louise Johnson Wheeler. Married Henry Wilder Keyes (governor of New Hampshire, 1917–1919, United States senator, 1919–1937); three children. Lived in Beauregard House, 1113 Chartres St., New Orleans. Died in New Orleans. Poet; fiction writer.

WORKS:

The Old Gray Homestead. Boston: Houghton Mifflin, 1919.

The Career of David Noble. New York: F. A. Stokes, 1921.

Letters from a Senator's Wife. New York: Appleton, 1924.

Queen Anne's Lace. New York: Liveright, 1931.

Lady Blanche Farm: A Romance of the Commonplace. New York: Liveright, 1931.

Silver Seas and Golden Cities: A Joyous Journey Through Latin Lands. New York: Liveright, 1931.

Senator Marlowe's Daughter. New York: Messner, 1933.

The Safe Bridge. New York: Messner, 1934.

The Happy Wanderer (poems). New York: Messner, 1935.

Honor Bright. New York: Messner, 1936.

Capital Kaleidoscope: The Story of a Washington Hostess. New York: Harper, 1937.

Written in Heaven: The Story on Earth of the Little Flower of Lisieux. New York: Messner, 1937.

Parts Unknown. New York: Messner, 1938.

The Great Tradition. New York: Messner, 1939.

Along a Little Way. New York: Kenedy, 1940.

Fielding's Folly. New York: Messner, 1940.

The Sublime Shepherdess. New York: Messner, 1940.

All That Glitters. New York: Book League of America, 1941.

The Grace of Guadalupe. New York: Messner, 1941.

Crescent Carnival. New York: Messner, 1942.

Also the Hills. New York: Messner, 1943.

The River Road. New York: Messner, 1945.

Came a Cavalier. New York: Messner, 1947.

Once on Esplanade: A Cycle Between Two Creole Weddings. New York: Dodd, 1947.

Dinner at Antoine's. New York: Messner, 1948.

All This Is Louisiana. New York: Harper, 1950.

The Cost of a Bestseller. New York: Messner, 1950.

Joy Street. New York: Messner, 1950.

Thérèse: Saint of a Little Way (rev. ed. of *Written in Heaven*). New York: Messner, 1950.

The Old Gray Homestead and *The Career of David Noble* (two novels in one volume). New York: Liveright, 1951.

Steamboat Gothic. New York: Messner, 1952.

Bernadette of Lourdes. New York: Messner, 1953.

The Royal Box. New York: Messner, 1954.

Frances Parkinson Keyes' Cookbook. Garden City, N.Y.: Doubleday, 1955.

St. Anne: Grandmother of Our Savior. New York: Hawthorn, 1955.

Blue Camellia. New York: Messner, 1957.

Land of Stones and Saints. Garden City, N.Y.: Doubleday, 1957.
Victorine. New York: Messner, 1958.
Frances Parkinson Keyes' Christmas Gift. New York: Hawthorn, 1959.
Mother Cabrini: Missionary to the World. New York: Farrar, Straus, 1959.
Station Wagon in Spain. New York: Farrar, Straus, 1959.
The Chess Players. New York: Farrar, Straus, 1960.
Roses in December (autobiography). Garden City, N.Y.: Doubleday, 1960.
The Rose and the Lily: The Lives and Times of Two South American Saints.
  New York: Hawthorn, 1961.
Madame Castel's Lodger. New York: Farrar, Straus, 1962.
The Restless Lady and Other Stories. New York: Liveright, 1963.
Three Ways of Love. New York: Hawthorn, 1963.
A Treasury of Favorite Poems. New York: Hawthorn, 1963.
The Explorer. New York: McGraw-Hill, 1964.
I, the King. New York: McGraw-Hill, 1966.
Tongues of Fire. New York: Coward-McCann, 1966.
The Heritage. New York: McGraw-Hill, 1968.
All Flags Flying (Memoirs). New York: McGraw-Hill, 1972.

SECONDARY SOURCES:
American Women Writers, II.
Breit, Harvey. *The Writer Observed.* New York: World, 1956.
Ehlers, Leigh A. "'An Environment Remembered': Setting in the Nov-
  els of Frances Parkinson Keyes." *Southern Quarterly,* XX (Spring,
  1982), 54–65.
Fitzgibbon, Robert and Ernest V. Heyn. *My Most Inspiring Moment: En-
  counters with Destiny Relived by Thirty-eight Best-Selling Authors.* Garden
  City, N.Y.: Doubleday, 1965.
Hogan, Pendleton. *Lunch with Mrs. Keyes: A Short Biography of Frances
  Parkinson Keyes.* New Orleans: Keyes Foundation, 1989.

KING, Grace Elizabeth (1852–1932)

BIOGRAPHY:
Born in New Orleans. Daughter of William Woodson (lawyer) and
Sarah Ann Miller King. Educated at Institut St. Louis; Institut Cénas.
Published widely in periodicals of the day. Lectured on Sidney Lanier
at Cambridge University in 1891 during one of several extensive trips
to Europe. Awarded honorary doctorate at Tulane University in
1915. Received the Palmes d'Officier de l'Instruction Publique of the
French government in 1918. Honored by the Louisiana Historical Society in 1923. Historian; fiction writer.

WORKS:
"Earthlings." *Lippincott's Monthly Magazine,* II (1888), 599–679.
Monsieur Motte. New York: A. C. Armstrong and Son, 1888.

Jean-Baptiste Le Moine, Sieur de Bienville. New York: Dodd, Mead, 1892.
Tales of a Time and Place. 1892; rpr. New York: Garrett Press, 1969.
Balcony Stories. 1893; rpr. New York: Gregg Press, 1968.
A History of Louisiana. With J. R. Ficklen. Baton Rouge: University Publishers, 1894.
New Orleans: The Place and the People. New York: Macmillan, 1895.
De Soto and His Men in the Land of Florida. New York: Macmillan, 1898.
Stories from Louisiana History. With J. R. Ficklen. New Orleans: L. Graham and Son, 1905.
The Pleasant Ways of St. Medard. New York: Henry Holt, 1916.
Creole Families of New Orleans. New York: Macmillan, 1921.
Madame Girard, an Old French Teacher of New Orleans. New Haven, 1922; rpr. from the *Yale Review.*
La Dame de Sainte Hermine. New York: Macmillan, 1924.
A Splendid Offer: A Comedy for Women (one-act play). N.p., 1926.
Mt. Vernon on the Potomac: History of the Mt. Vernon Ladies' Association of the Union. New York: Macmillan, 1929.
Memories of a Southern Woman of Letters. New York: Macmillan, 1932.
Grace King of New Orleans: A Selection of Her Writings. Edited by Robert Bush. Baton Rouge: Louisiana State University Press, 1973.

SECONDARY SOURCES:
American Women Writers, II.
Bush, Robert. *Grace King: A Southern Destiny.* Baton Rouge: Louisiana State University Press, 1983.
Elfenbein, Anna Shannon. *Women on the Color Line: Evolving Stereotypes and the Writings of George Washington Cable, Grace King, Kate Chopin.* Charlottesville: University Press of Virginia, 1989.
Kirby, David. *Grace King.* Boston: Twayne, 1980.
Slayton, G. C. "Grace Elizabeth King: Her Life and Works." Ph.D. dissertation, University of Pennsylvania, 1974.
Taylor, Helen. *Gender, Race, and Region in the Writings of Grace King, Ruth McEnery Stuart, and Kate Chopin.* Baton Rouge: Louisiana State University Press, 1989.
Vaughan, Bess. "A Bio-Bibliography of Grace Elizabeth King." *Louisiana Historical Quarterly,* XVII (October, 1934), 752–70.

LEA, Fannie Heaslip (1884–1955)

BIOGRAPHY:
Born in New Orleans. Daughter of James John (newspaperman) and Margaret Heaslip Lea. Educated at Newcomb College and Tulane University. Married Hamilton Pope Agee, 1911; divorced, 1926; one child. Died in New York City. Novelist; poet; dramatist; short-story writer; journalist.

WORKS:

Quicksands. New York: Sturgis and Walton, 1911.

Jaconetta Stories. New York: Sturgis and Walton, 1912.

Sicily Ann: A Romance. New York: Harper and Bros., 1914.

Chloe Malone. Boston: Little, Brown, 1916.

The Dream-Maker Man. New York: Dodd, Mead, 1925.

With This Ring. New York: Dodd, Mead, 1925.

With or Without. New York: Dodd, Mead, 1926.

Wild Goose Chase. New York: Dodd, Mead, 1929.

Lollie: A Play. 1929. Presented on Broadway, 1930.

Happy Landings. New York: Dodd, Mead, 1930.

Goodbye, Summer. New York: Dodd, Mead, 1931.

Take Back the Heart (poems). New York: Dodd, Mead, 1931.

Half-Angel. New York: Dodd, Mead, 1932.

Summer People. New York: Dodd, Mead, 1933.

Dorée. New York: Dodd, Mead, 1934.

Men and Angel. New York: Nicholson, 1935.

Anchor Man. New York: Dodd, Mead, 1935.

Crede Byron (play). New York: Dodd, Mead, 1936.

The Four Marys. New York: Dodd, Mead, 1937.

Once to Every Man. New York: Dodd, Mead, 1938.

Not for Just an Hour. New York: Dodd, Mead, 1939.

Nobody's Girl. New York: Dodd, Mead, 1940.

There Are Brothers. New York: Dodd, Mead, 1940.

Sailor's Star. New York: Dodd, Mead, 1944.

The Devil Within. New York: Dodd, Mead, 1948.

Verses for Lovers (and Some Others). New York: Dodd, Mead, 1955.

SECONDARY SOURCES:

American Women Writers, II.

Twentieth Century Authors.

LINFIELD, Mary Barrow Collins (1891–?)

BIOGRAPHY:

Born at Poplar Stand Plantation, West Feliciana Parish, Louisiana. Daughter of William Lawrence Barrow and Bessie Hampton Barrow. Educated at Millsaps College; Tulane University; University of Chicago.

WORKS:

Punishment. Under pen name "Lawrence Highland." Boston: Four Seas, 1926.

Young Woman In Love. New York: Macaulay, 1929.

Instruct My Heart. New York: Parnassus, 1934.

Japonica Grove. Garden City, N.Y.: Doubleday, Doran, 1935.

Day of Victory. Garden City, N.Y.: Doubleday, Doran, 1936.

SECONDARY SOURCE:
Who Was Who Among North American Authors, 1921–1939.

NESOM, Anne Reiley (1885–1951)

BIOGRAPHY:
Born in St. Francisville, Louisiana.

WORKS:
Blue Haze: Cabin in the Pines. Tigard, Ore.: n.p., 1935.
Sweet Bay: Louisiana Verse. Cleveland: The Press of Flozari, 1940.
Turns on the Trail That Lead by Treasures of Darkness Toward Peaceful Goals (poems). St. Francisville, La.: E. Robinson, 1947.

SECONDARY SOURCES:
Agnew, Janet M., comp. *A Southern Bibliography: Poetry, 1929–1938.* Library School Bibliography Series, No. 3. Edited by Margaret M. Hardman. *University Bulletin*, n.s., Vol. XXXII, No. 11. Baton Rouge: Louisiana State University, 1940.
Bridges, Katherine. *The Poets of Louisiana: A Handlist.* Natchitoches: Northwestern Louisiana University, 1966.

NEUGASS, Miriam Dorothy Newman ("Isidora Newman") (1878–?)

BIOGRAPHY:
Born in New Orleans. Daughter of Isidore (banker) and Rebecca Kiefer Newman. Educated at Columbia University. Married Edwin A. Neugass of New Orleans in 1901; three children. Invented "Dixie" dolls. Fiction writer.

WORKS:
Fairy Flowers: Nature Legends of Facts and Fantasy. New York: Henry Holt, 1926.
Shades of Blue. New York: Henry Harrison, 1927.
Flowers: Facts and Fables. New York: Snellgrove, 1937.

SECONDARY SOURCE:
None.

NEWMAN, Isidora (See NEUGASS, Miriam Dorothy Newman)

NEWTON, Alma (Mrs. Alma Newton Anderson) (1886–?)

BIOGRAPHY:
Born in Jefferson County, Mississippi. Daughter of Algernon Emmet and Mattie Hunt Newton. Educated at Newcomb College; Cincinnati Conservatory of Music. Married to James M. Anderson of Mississippi, 1907–1914; one child. Novelist.

WORKS:

The Love Letters of a Mystic. New York: John Lane, 1916.
Memories. New York: Duffield, 1917.
The Blue String and Other Sketches. New York: Duffield, 1918.
A Jewel in the Sand. New York: Duffield, 1919.
Dreaming True. New York: John Lane, 1921.
Shadows. New York: John Lane, 1921.
An Old-Fashioned Romance. New York: Minton, Balch, 1924.

SECONDARY SOURCE:
Who Was Who in America.

PERRY, Stella George Stern (1877–1953?)

BIOGRAPHY:

Born in New Orleans. Daughter of George and Carolyn Silverstein Stern. Educated at Southern Academic Institute, New Orleans; Newcomb College; Barnard College, Columbia University. Married George Hough Perry of New York, September 19, 1906 (died 1945); one son. Author and humanitarian. Advertising and editorial writer in New York, 1899–1906. Active in many civic organizations and humanitarian groups. Lived in Brooklyn.

WORKS:

Go to Sleep. New York: Stokes, 1911.
Melindy. New York: Moffat, Yard, 1912.
The Kind Adventure. With four illustrations in color by Maria L. Kirk and Carlton Glidden. New York: Stokes, 1914.
When Mother Lets Us Act (children's plays). New York: Moffat, Yard, 1914.
All the Children (pageant on child labor for the 1915 Panama Exposition).
The Sculpture and Murals of the Panama-Pacific International Exposition (official handbook). San Francisco: Wahlgreen, 1915.
The Sculpture of the Exposition. With A. Sterling Calder. San Francisco: Elder, 1915.
Little Bronze Playfellows. San Francisco: Elder, 1915.
Clever Mouse (six booklets). San Francisco: n.p., 1916.
Angel of Christmas. New York: Stokes, 1917.
The Girls' Nest. New York: Stokes, 1918.
Palmetto. New York: Stokes, 1920.
Come Home. New York: Stokes, 1923.
Down the Avenue of Ninety Years. N.p., 1924.
Barbara of Telegraph Hill. New York: Stokes, 1925.
The Defenders. New York: Stokes, 2 printings in 1927.
Extra Girl. New York: Stokes, 1929.

"Richardson: General Server." *North American Review*, CCXXVIII (October, 1929), 392–98.

SECONDARY SOURCES:
American Authors and Books.
Dictionary of Louisiana Biography, II.
Who Was Who in America.

PITKIN, Helen (See SCHERTZ, Helen Christine [Pitkin])

PORTER, Katherine Anne (1890–1980)

BIOGRAPHY:
Born in Indian Creek, Texas, as Callie Russell Porter. Daughter of Harrison Boone and Mary Jones Porter. Educated at home and in southern girls' schools. Married John Henry Koontz, railway clerk, 1906. Married Eugene Pressly, 1933; divorced, 1938. Married Albert Eskine, 1938; divorced, 1942. Died in Silver Springs, Maryland. Novelist; short-story writer. Awarded Pulitzer Prize for Fiction in 1966.

WORKS:
My Chinese Marriage. New York: Duffield, 1921.
What Price Marriage. New York: J. H. Sears, 1927.
Flowering Judas. New York: Harcourt, Brace, 1930.
Hacienda: A Story of Mexico. New York: Harrison, 1934.
Noon Wine. New York: Schuman's, 1937.
Pale Horse, Pale Rider. New York: Harcourt, Brace, 1939.
The Leaning Tower and Other Stories. New York: Harcourt, Brace, 1944.
Days Before. Salem, N.H.: Ayer, 1952.
The Days Before: Collected Essays and Occasional Writings. New York: Harcourt, Brace, 1952.
The Old Order: Stories of the South. New York: Harcourt, Brace, 1955.
Fiction and Criticism of Katherine Anne Porter. Pittsburgh: University of Pittsburgh Press, 1957.
Ship of Fools. Boston: Little, Brown, 1962. Film, 1965.
The Collected Stories of Katherine Anne Porter. New York: Harcourt, Brace and World, 1965.
A Christmas Story. New York: Dial, 1967.
The Collected Essays and Occasional Writings of Katherine Anne Porter. New York: Delacorte, 1970.
The Never-Ending Wrong. Boston: Little, Brown, 1977.

SECONDARY SOURCES:
American Women Writers, III.
CA.
Curley, Daniel. "Katherine Anne Porter: The Larger Plan." *Kenyon Review*, XXV (Autumn, 1963), 671–95.

Givner, Joan. *Katherine Anne Porter: A Life.* New York: Simon and Schuster, 1982.

Hardy, John Edward. *Katherine Anne Porter.* New York: Ungar, 1973.

Hartley, Lodwick, and George Core, eds. *Katherine Anne Porter: A Critical Symposium.* Athens: University of Georgia Press, 1969.

Liberman, M. M. *Katherine Anne Porter's Fiction.* Detroit: Wayne State University Press, 1971.

SCHERTZ, Helen Christine Pitkin (1877–?)

BIOGRAPHY:

Born in New Orleans. Daughter of John Robert Graham Pitkin (U.S. ambassador) and Helen Fearing Fuller Pitkin. Educated at Newcomb College. Married (1909) Christian d'Augsburg Schertz, native of Germany, chemist and owner of drugstores in New Orleans. Staff writer for the New Orleans *Times-Democrat.* Founder of the New Orleans Spring Fiesta, charter member of Le Petit Théatre

From *Notables of New Orleans*

du Vieux Carré, and active in Louisiana Historical Society, the Stuart Clan, American Pen Women, and many other civic and philanthropic groups. Poet; journalist.

WORKS:

Over the Hills (poem). Evanston, Ill.: W. S. Lord, 1903.

An Angel by Brevet: A Story of Modern New Orleans. Philadelphia: Lippincott, 1904.

The Betrayal (poem). New Orleans: n.p., 1913.

A Walk Through French Town in Old New Orleans. New Orleans: New Orleans Journal, 1918.

Legends of Louisiana. New Orleans: New Orleans Journal, 1922.

SECONDARY SOURCES:

Dictionary of Louisiana Biography, II.

Notables of New Orleans.

Who's Who of American Women.

SCOTT, Evelyn ("Ernest Souza") (1893–1963)

BIOGRAPHY:

Born in Clarkesville, Tennessee, as Elsie Dunn. Daughter of Seeley and Maude Thomas Dunn of New Orleans. Moved to New Orleans at age eighteen. Attended Newcomb College. Common law marriage, Frederick Creighton Wellman (Cyril Kay Scott), 1913; one son. Lived in Brazil seven years, then returned to U.S. Married John Metcalfe, English novelist, 1928. Wrote her first fiction at age nine, published her first story at thirteen, and began her professional career at sixteen. Wrote under "Evelyn Scott" and "E. Souza." Poet; novelist; dramatist.

WORKS

Precipitations. New York: N. L. Brown, 1920.

Love: A Drama in Three Acts. N.p., 1921.

The Narrow House. New York: Boni and Liveright, 1921.

Narcissus. New York: Harcourt, 1922.

Bewilderment. London: Duckworth, 1922.

Escapade. New York: Cape and Smith, 1923.

The Golden Door. New York: F. Seltzer, 1925.

In the Endless Sands: A Christmas Book for Boys and Girls. With Cyril Kay Scott. New York: Henry Holt, 1925.

Ideals: A Book of Farce and Comedy. New York: A. and C. Boni, 1927.

Migrations: An Arabesque in Histories. New York: A. and C. Boni, 1927. London: Duckworth, 1927.

The Wave. New York: Cape and Smith, 1929.

Witch Perkins: A Story of the Kentucky Hills. New York: Henry Holt, 1929.

On William Faulkner's "The Sound and the Fury." New York: Cape and Smith, 1929.

Blue Rum. New York: Cape and Smith, 1930.

The Winter Alone. New York: Cape and Smith, 1930.

A Calendar of Sin: American Melodramas. New York: Cape and Smith, 1931.

Eva Gay: A Romantic Novel. New York: Smith and Haas, 1933.

Breathe upon These Slain. New York: Smith and Haas, 1934.

Billy the Maverick. New York: Henry Holt, 1934.

Background in Tennessee. New York: R. M. McBride, 1937.

Bread and a Sword. New York: Scribner's, 1937.

The Shadow of the Hawk. New York: Scribner's, 1941.

Unpublished works: "Before Cock Crow: A Novel" (1930–62); "Escape Into Living: A Novel" (1951–62); "The Gravestones Wept" (poetry; 1950–60); "The Youngest Smiles" (poetry; 1955–60).

SECONDARY SOURCES:

American Women Writers, IV.

Callard, D. A. *Pretty Good for a Woman: The Enigmas of Evelyn Scott.* New York: W. W. Norton, 1985.

Southern Writers.

Twentieth Century Authors.

SMYTH, Nathalie Bouligny (1856–1912)

BIOGRAPHY:

Born in New Orleans. Daughter of Gustave Bouligny and Octavia Fortier Bouligny. Family from Milan, Italy, and then Spain. Married Dr. Andrew Woods Smyth, chief surgeon of Charity Hospital, May 21, 1881. One daughter, Arthemise (married Rev. David Hay, Presbyterian minister). Died June 22, 1912; buried in Londonderry, Ireland.

WORK:

Poems of Nathalie Bouligny Smyth. Belfast: McCaw, Stevenson and Orr, 1923.

SECONDARY SOURCE:

Biographical note by John Rutherford. Copy in Historic New Orleans Collection.

WETMORE, Elizabeth Bisland ("B. L. R. Dane") (1861–1929)

BIOGRAPHY:

Born at Camp Bisland, Fairfax Plantation, St. Mary Parish, Louisiana. Daughter of Dr. Thomas S. and Margaret (Brownson) Bisland. Married Charles W. Wetmore in 1891. Contributed to the New Orleans *Times-Democrat.* Became an editor of *Cosmopolitan* magazine. Novelist; journalist.

WORKS:

A Widower Indeed. With Rhoda Broughton. New York: Appleton, 1891.

A Flying Trip Around the World. New York: Harper, 1891.

Old Greenwich. New York: Knickerbocker, 1897.

Courtesy the Huntington Library, San Marino, California

A Candle of Understanding: A Novel. New York: Harper, 1903.

The Secret Life; Being the Book of a Heretic. New York: J. Lane, 1906.

The Life and Letters of Lafcadio Hearn. 2 vols. London: Archibald Constable, 1906.

Seekers in Sicily; Being a Quest for Persephone by Jane and Peripatetica. With Anne Hoyt. New York: J. Lane, 1909.

At the Sign of the Hobby Horse. Boston: Houghton Mifflin, 1910.

The Japanese Letters of Lafcadio Hearn. Boston: Houghton Mifflin, 1910.

The Case of John Smith: His Heaven and His Hell. New York: Putnam, 1916.

The Truth About Men and Other Matters. New York: Avondale, 1927.

Three Wise Men of the East. Chapel Hill: University of North Carolina Press, 1930.

SECONDARY SOURCES:

BDSA.

Dictionary of Louisiana Biography, II.

Ross, Ishbel. *Ladies of the Press.* New York: Harper, 1936.

Tinker, Edward L. *Lafcadio Hearn's American Days.* New York: Dodd, Mead, 1924.

Verdery, Katherine. "Elizabeth Bisland Wetmore" (biographical and critical essay plus excerpts from three works). In Vol. XIII of *LSL.*

Williams, Susan Miller. "L'enfant terrible: Elizabeth Bisland and the South." *Southern Review,* n.s., XXII (Autumn, 1986), 680–96.

A Woman of the Century.

Contemporary Writers

AMOSS, Berthe (1925–)

BIOGRAPHY:

Born in New Orleans. Daughter of Sumter Davis Marks (lawyer) and Berthe Lathrop Marks. Educated at Tulane University; University of Hawaii; and in Germany and Belgium. Married Walter James Amoss, Jr., president of Lykes Bros. Steamship Co.; six sons. Children's books writer and illustrator. Original watercolor illustrations are in the following collections: Kerlan Collection, University of Minnesota Library; University of Southern Mississippi, de Grummond Collection; Louisiana State Library; Howard Tilton Memorial Library, Tulane University. Teaches at Tulane University. Wrote column on children's books for New Orleans *Times-Picayune,* 1980–1991. Lives in New Orleans.

WORKS:

It's Not Your Birthday. New York: Harper and Row, 1966.

Tom in the Middle. New York: Harper and Row, 1968.

By the Sea. New York: Parents Magazine Press, 1969.

The Marvellous Catch of Old Hannibal. New York: Parents Magazine Press, 1970.

Old Hasdrubal and the Pirates. New York: Parents Magazine Press, 1971.

The Very Worst Thing. New York: Parents Magazine Press, 1972.

The Big Cry. Indianapolis: Bobbs-Merrill, 1972.

The Great Sea Monster; or, A Book by You. New York: Parents Magazine Press, 1976.

The Chalk Cross. New York: Seabury, 1976.

The Witch Cat. New Orleans: Preservation Resource Center of New Orleans, 1977.

The Loup Garou. Gretna, La.: Pelican, 1979.

Secret Lives. Boston: Little, Brown, 1979.

What Did You Lose, Santa? New York: Harper and Row, 1987.

The Mockingbird Song. New York, Harper and Row, 1988.

Old Hannibal and the Hurricane (picture book). New York: Hyperion/ Disney, 1991.

Columbus Discovers America: Window Storybook. New Orleans: More Than a Card, 1991.

Forthcoming (1992): "Burn the Witch" (novel for older children).

SECONDARY SOURCES:

Brown, Dorothy H., and Barbara C. Ewell. "Fiction and Louisiana Women Writers." *Louisiana Literature,* V (Fall, 1988), 24–43.

CA.

CANR.

Something About the Author.

ARCENEAUX, Thelma Hoffman Tyler

BIOGRAPHY:

Born in Thibodaux, Louisiana. Married Arthur Tyler; two children. Married Junius Arceneaux, 1963; three children; five adopted children. Poet; fiction writer (short stories and novel); article writer.

WORKS:

Reaching for the Unreachable (poems). Tyler, Tex.: Merchants Press, 1970.

They Emerged from the Shade: A Novel. Detroit: Harlo, 1974.

SECONDARY SOURCE:

Nykoruk, Barbara, ed. *Authors in the News.* Biography News Library. Vol. I of 2 vols. Detroit: Gale Research, 1976–77.

BALLARD, Cordelle Kemper (1897–)

BIOGRAPHY:

Born in New Orleans. Daughter of sugar planter and engineer, St. Mary Parish, Louisiana. Educated at Newcomb College; Tulane University; University of Michigan. Married Lyman Jay Ballard, naval architect; divorced. Career in the American Red Cross. Charter member of the American Association of Social Work. Decorated in 1946 by French and Italian Red Cross Societies. Lived in Louisiana, Michigan, New York, New Jersey, Pennsylvania, Illinois, France, Italy. Resides in Bridgeport, Connecticut. Fiction and nonfiction writer.

WORKS:

Writer of nine short stories published in *Womankind* (1981), the *Attakapas Gazette* (1981 and 1984), and *Expanding Horizons* (1979, 1980, and

1981). In manuscript, two novels, an autobiography, and "The Future of Aging."

SECONDARY SOURCES:
None.

BANKS, Sara Jeanne Gordon Harrell (1937–)

BIOGRAPHY:
Born in Tuscaloosa, Alabama. Daughter of Preston Brooks (purchasing agent) and Anee Frierson Cooper Harrell. Lived in Savannah, Georgia, as a child. Educated at Georgia Southern College; University of North Carolina at Chapel Hill; University of Georgia; Emory University. Married Caleb Burch Banks, steamship association employee, 1964; one child.

WORKS:
Semo: A Dolphin's Search for Christ. St. Louis, Mo.: Concordia, 1977.
Tomo-chi-chi. Minneapolis: Dillon, 1977.
Cottage By the Sea. St. Louis, Mo.: Concordia, 1977.
John Ross. Minneapolis: Dillon, 1979.
Willowcat and the Chimney Sweep. Atlanta: Peachtree, 1980.
Grove of Night. New York: Avon, 1981.
Mallory's Island. St. Louis, Mo.: Concordia, 1986.
In progress: "Annie Rising Fawn" (novel); "Mulberry Silk" (historical novel).
Contributor to *DeKalb Literary Journal, Environmental Quality, Georgia Conservancy, Chandler Review,* and *Marian.*

SECONDARY SOURCE:
CA.

BARRON, Ann Forman ("Annabel Erwin")

BIOGRAPHY:
Born in Oakdale, Louisiana. Daughter of Royal Clinton (professor) and Anne Erwin (pianist) Forman. Educated by private tutors. Married Del D. Barron; two children. Lives in Fort Worth, Texas. Published in *Redbook, Reader's Digest,* and other periodicals.

WORKS:
Murder Is a Gentle Kiss. New York: Bouregy, 1960.
Spin a Dark Web. New York: Bouregy, 1961.
Strange Legacy. New York: Fawcett, 1969.
Dark Vengeance. New York: Fawcett, 1972.
Serpent in the Shadows. New York: Berkeley, 1973.
Bride of Menace. New York: Fawcett, 1973.

Banner Bold and Beautiful. New York: Fawcett, 1975.
Liliane (as Annabel Erwin). New York: Warner Books, 1976.
Firebrand. New York: Fawcett, 1977.

SECONDARY SOURCE:
CA.

BLACKWELL, Muriel Fontenot (1929–)

BIOGRAPHY:

Born in Pine Prairie, Louisiana. Daughter of Philip L. (oil worker) and Alma Johnson Fontenot. Educated at Louisiana College; Louisiana State University; University of Tennessee. Married William Lloyd Blackwell, minister, 1950; two children. Lives in Brentwood, Tennessee. Poet; novelist; short-story writer.

WORKS:

Prairie Potpourri (poems). Baton Rouge: Claitors Book Store, 1967.
Potter and Clay (poems). Nashville: Broadman, 1975.
The Secret Dream. Nashville: Broadman, 1981.
It Was for Me (one-act musical play for children). Nashville: Broadman, 1982.
The Dream Lives On (juvenile novel; sequel to *The Secret Dream*). Nashville: Broadman, 1984.
The Keeping Shelf. Nashville: Broadman, 1985.
Work has been represented in anthologies, including the *National Anthology of Poetry;* numerous stories in journals; many guidance and help books for teachers and parents.

SECONDARY SOURCE:
CA.

BLAKE, Jennifer (See MAXWELL, Patricia)

BORENSTEIN, Audrey Farrell (1930–)

BIOGRAPHY:

Born in Chicago. Daughter of Robert C. Farrell and Rose Schageman Farrell. Educated at University of Illinois; Louisiana State University. Married Walter Borenstein, 1953; two children. Taught at Louisiana State University, 1958–1960, Cornell College, 1965–1969, State University of New York at Buffalo, 1970. Novelist; short-story writer.

WORKS:

Redeeming the Sin: Essays on Social Science and Literature. New York: Columbia University Press, 1978.
First prize in fiction from *Zeitgeist,* 1966, for "Rachel"; creative writing

fellowship from National Endowment for the Arts, 1976–77; contributor of articles, stories, poems, and reviews to literary journals including *Antioch Review, Kansas Quarterly,* and *Croton Review.*

SECONDARY SOURCE:
   CA.

BOSWORTH, Sheila (1948–)

BIOGRAPHY:
   Born in New Orleans. Educated at Sacred Heart Academy; Newcomb College. Married Hilton Bell, attorney; two children. Lives in Covington, Louisiana. Novelist.

WORKS:
   Almost Innocent. New York: Simon and Schuster, 1984.
   Slow Poison. New York: Knopf, 1992.

SECONDARY SOURCES:
   Brown, Dorothy H., and Barbara C. Ewell. "Fiction and Louisiana Women Writers." *Louisiana Literature,* V (Fall, 1988), 24–43.
   New Orleans *Times-Picayune,* November 26, 1984, January 20, 1985, September 20, 1986, February 25, 1990.

BROSMAN, Catharine Savage (1934–)

BIOGRAPHY:
   Born in Denver, Colorado. Daughter of Paul Victor (teacher) and Della L. Stanforth Hill. Educated at Rice University; University of Grenoble, France. Married to Patrick Savage, 1955–1964. Married Paul W. Brosman, Jr., 1970; one child. Lives in New Orleans; Andrew W. Mellon Professor of Humanities, Tulane University. Recipient of many awards and honors. Poet; scholar.

WORKS:
   Watering. Athens: University of Georgia Press, 1972.
   Abiding Winter. Florence, Ky.: Robert L. Barth, 1983.
   Journeying from Canyon de Chelly. Baton Rouge: Louisiana State University Press, 1991.
   In progress: "Woman in Red" (poems).
   Contributions have appeared in numerous periodicals and anthologies, including *Southern Poetry Review, Southwest Review, Texas Quarterly, Southern Humanities Review, Shenandoah, Sewanee Review, New Southern Poets* (Chapel Hill: University of North Carolina Press, 1974), *Best Poems of 1973* (Palo Alto, Cal.: Pacific Books, 1974), and *Anthology of Magazine Verse* (Beverly Hills: Monitor Books, 1981, 1984). Manuscripts kept in Howard-Tilton Memorial Library, Tulane University.

SECONDARY SOURCES:

CA.

Fischer, John Irwin. "Community and the Individual Life: Catharine Savage Brosman's 'Watering.'" *Southern Review,* n.s., IX (Summer, 1973), 710–12.

Healey, James. *Prairie Schooner,* XLVIII (Summer, 1974), 183.

Richardson, D. E. In *Southern Review,* n.s., XII (October, 1976), 881–82.

Virginia Quarterly Review, XLIX (Winter, 1973), xiii.

Who's Who in America.

BROWN-GUILLORY, Elizabeth (1954–)

Courtesy Dillard University

BIOGRAPHY:

Born in Lake Charles, Louisiana. Daughter of Leo and Marjorie Savoy Brown. Grew up in Church Point, Louisiana. Educated at University of Southwestern Louisiana; Florida State University. Married Lucius M. Guillory; one daughter. Taught at Dillard University. Currently teaches English and African-American literature at University of Houston. Twelve of her plays have been produced, in New Orleans, New York, and elsewhere. Lives in Houston. Playwright; scholar.

WORKS:

Bayou Relics. Colorado Springs: Contemporary Drama Service/Meriwether, 1983.

M'am Phyllis. New Orleans: n.p., n.d.

Marry Me, Again. New Orleans: n.p., n.d.

Snapshots of Broken Dolls. Colorado Springs: Contemporary Drama Service/Meriwether, 1987.

Their Place on Stage: Black Women Playwrights in America. Westport, Conn.: Greenwood Press, 1988.

Wines in the Wilderness: Plays by African-American Women from the Harlem Renaissance to the Present. Editor. Anthology with introduction and biographical notes. New York: Praeger, 1990.

SECONDARY SOURCES:

Bryan, Violet Harrington. "Evocation of Place and Culture in the Works of Four Contemporary Black Louisiana Writers: Brenda Osbey, Sybil Kein, Elizabeth Brown-Guillory, and Pinkie Gordon Lane." *Louisiana Literature,* IV (1987), 49–65.

Ewell, Barbara C., and Dorothy H. Brown. "Drama, Poetry, and Louisiana Women Writers." *Louisiana Literature,* VI (Spring, 1989), 37–56.

CAMPBELL, Edna Freeman (1906–)

BIOGRAPHY:

Born in Independence, Louisiana. Daughter of James Irving and Lena Robertson Freeman. Married James Howard Campbell; two children. Women's editor of the Hammond *Daily Star,* 1961–1980. Feature writer for the Baton Rouge *Morning Advocate,* 1969–1986. Member of Louisiana Press Women; named "Woman of the Year" in 1970 in state competition. Poet.

WORKS:

Poems and articles have appeared in *Louisiana Lyrics, Louisiana Leaders* (1969), *Vignettes of Louisiana History* (1968), and other publications. Many articles on Louisiana history.

SECONDARY SOURCES:

International Who's Who in Poetry.
Personalities of the South. Raleigh, N.C.: American Biographical Institute, 1969.
Who's Who in the South and Southwest.
Who's Who of American Women.

CANFIELD, Sandra Kay Patterson ("Karen Keast"; "Sandi Shane"; "Sandra Canfield") (1944–)

BIOGRAPHY:

Born in Longview, Texas. Daughter of Ira and Ruby Patterson. Married Charles Keast Canfield, Jr. Resides in Shreveport, Louisiana. Novelist.

WORKS:

Suddenly the Magic. New York: Berkley/Jove, 1984.
Notorious. New York: Berkley/Jove, 1985.
Forbidden Dream. New York: Berkley/Jove, 1985.
Dark Lightning. New York: Berkley/Jove, 1986.
Tender Treason. New York: Berkley/Jove, 1986.
Conquer the Night. New York: Berkley/Jove, 1986.
(All of the foregoing were written as "Karen Keast.")
No Perfect Season (as "Sandi Shane" with Penny Richards). New York: Harlequin, 1985.
Sweet Burning (as "Sandi Shane" with Penny Richards). New York: Harlequin, 1985.
Cherish This Moment. Toronto: Harlequin, 1986.

SECONDARY SOURCE:
New Orleans *Times-Picayune,* July 21, 1991.

CARMER, Elizabeth Black (1904–)

BIOGRAPHY:

Born in New Orleans. Educated at Newcomb College, degree in design. Married to Carl Carmer, writer. Contributor to *Theatre Arts Monthly* and *Harper's Bazaar.* Lives in Irvington-on-Hudson, New York. Writer and illustrator. Works are in the Kerlan Collection at the University of Minnesota.

WORKS:

Wildcat Furs to China: Cruise of the Sloop "Experiment." New York: Knopf, 1945.

Illustrator. *Eagle in the Wind.* By Carl Carmer. New York: Aladdin Books, 1948.

Francis Marion: Swamp Fox of the Carolinas. New York: Garrard, 1962.

The Susquehanna from New York to the Chesapeake. New York: Garrard, 1964.

Captain Abner and Henry O. With Carl Carmer. New York: Garrard, 1965.

Mike Fink and the Big Turkey Shoot. New York: Garrard, 1965.

Tony Beaver, Griddle Skater. New York: Garrard, 1965.

The Hurricane's Children. New York: D. McKay, 1967.

Pecos Bill and the Long Lasso. New York: Garrard, 1968.

SECONDARY SOURCE:
Something About the Author.

CARR, Pat Moore ("Pat M. Esslinger") (1932–)

BIOGRAPHY:

Born in Grass Creek, Wyoming. Daughter of Stanley Moore and Bea Parker Moore. Educated at Rice University; Tulane University. Married Jack H. Esslinger, 1955; divorced, 1970. Married Duane Carr, 1971; four children. Professor of English and writer. On faculty of Dillard University; University of New Orleans; University of Texas, El Paso; currently at Western Kentucky University, Bowling Green. Awards include South and West Fiction Award (1969); Best American Short Stories Honor Roll (1974); Green Mountains Short Story Award (1986); First Stage Drama Award (1991).

WORKS:

From Beneath the Hill of the Three Crosses Procesion de Navidad (as Esslinger; short stories). Fort Smith, Ark.: South and West Press, 1970.

The Grass Creek Chronicle (novel). El Paso: Endeavors in Humanity, 1976.
Bernard Shaw. New York: Ungar, 1976.
The Women in the Mirror. Iowa City: Iowa University Press, 1977. Winner Iowa Fiction Award.
Night of the Luminaries (short stories). Austin: Slough Press, 1986.
Sonahchi (short stories). El Paso: Cinco Puntos Press, 1988.
In progress: "The Village of Women" (novel).

SECONDARY SOURCES:
CA.
CANR.

CASSIN, Maxine (1927–)

BIOGRAPHY:
Born in New Orleans. Daughter of Alvin (accountant) and Dora Hurwitz Kaplan (Russian immigrants). Educated at Newcomb College; Tulane University. Married Joseph Cassin in 1954; one child. Editor and publisher of New Orleans Poetry Journal Press Books. Lives in New Orleans. Poet.

WORKS:
Nine by Three. With Robert Lawrence and Felix Stefanile. Eureka, Calif.: Hearse Press, 1962.
A Touch of Recognition. Denver: A. Swallow, 1962.
The Maple Leaf Rag: An Anthology of New Orleans Creole Poetry. Coeditor and contributor. New Orleans: Poetry Journal Press, 1980.
Turnip's Blood: Poems. Baton Rouge: Sisters Grim Press, 1985.
Poems have appeared in numerous periodicals and anthologies, including *Chicago Review;* New York *Herald Tribune;* New York *Times; New Republic; New Orleans Review; The Chicago Review Anthology,* edited by David Ray (Chicago: University of Chicago Press, 1959); *Three Dimensions of Poetry,* edited by Vincent Stewart (New York: Scribner's, 1969); and others.

SECONDARY SOURCES:
Minneapolis *Star Tribune,* March 9, 1986, p. 11G.
New Orleans *Times-Picayune,* June 11, 1989.
Strother, Garland. Review of *Turnip's Blood.* Louisiana Library Association *Bulletin* (Spring, 1986), 155–56.

CHERRY, Kelly

BIOGRAPHY:
Born in Baton Rouge. Daughter of J. Milton (violinist and professor of music theory) and Mary Spooner (violinist and writer) Cherry. Edu-

cated at Mary Washington College; University of Virginia; University of North Carolina–Greensboro. Married Jonathan Silver, 1966; divorced, 1969. Teacher and writer in residence, University of Wisconsin, Madison.

WORKS:

Sick and Full of Burning (novel). New York: Viking Press, 1974.

Lovers and Agnostics (poems). Charlotte, N.C.: Red Clay Press, 1975.

Relativity: A Point of View. Baton Rouge: Louisiana State University Press, 1977.

Augusta Played. Boston: Houghton Mifflin, 1979.

Conversion (stories). New Paltz, N.Y.: Treacle Press, 1979.

Songs for a Soviet Composer (poems). St. Louis, Mo.: Singing Wind Press, 1980.

Loneliness: Words for a Secular Canticle. Winston-Salem, N.C.: Palaemon Press, 1980.

In the Wink of an Eye. New York: Harcourt Brace Jovanovich, 1983.

Lost Traveller's Dream. New York: Harcourt Brace Jovanovich, 1984.

Natural Theology (poems). Baton Rouge: Louisiana State University Press, 1988.

My Life and Dr. Joyce Brothers: A Novel in Stories. Chapel Hill: Algonquin, 1990.

The Exiled Heart: A Meditative Autobiography. Baton Rouge: Louisiana State University Press, 1991.

Works have appeared in *Best Short Stories* (Boston: Houghton Mifflin, 1972), *Pushcart Prize II* (New York: Avon Press, 1977), *Southern Review, Georgia Review, Fiction, Southern Poetry Review,* and others.

SECONDARY SOURCES:

CA.

CANR.

CLAYTON, Jo (1939–)

BIOGRAPHY:

Born in Modesto, California. Daughter of Howard Garland (farmer) and Bessie Jones Clayton. Educated at University of California, Berkeley; Modesto Junior College; University of Southern California; University of New Orleans. High-school English teacher with Orleans Parish School Board since 1971. Novelist; short-story writer.

WORKS:

Diadem for the Stars. New York: DAW Books, 1977.

La Marchos. New York: DAW Books, 1978.

Irsud. New York: DAW Books, 1978.

Maeve. New York: DAW Books, 1979.

SECONDARY SOURCES:
CA.
New Orleans *Times-Picayune,* February 10, 1985.

COKER, Carolyn ("Allison Cole")

BIOGRAPHY:
> Born in Tulsa, Oklahoma. Daughter of Samuel Bennet (businessman) and Bernice Woods Cole (teacher). Educated at University of Oklahoma; Southern Methodist University; Tulane University. Married Franklin C. Coker, tax consultant; divorced; one child. Lives in Sierra Madre, California. Novelist.

WORKS:
> *The Other David.* New York: Dodd, Mead, 1984.
> *Back Toward Lisbon.* New York: Dodd, Mead, 1985.
> *The Vines of Ferrara.* New York: Dodd, Mead, 1986.
> *The Head of the Lion.* New York: Dodd, Mead, 1987.

SECONDARY SOURCE:
CA.

COLLINS, Meghan (1926–)

BIOGRAPHY:
> Born in New Orleans. Daughter of Willard and Maude Gamble Roberts. Educated at Barnard College; California State College at Hayward. Married Sterrett A. Burges, 1945; divorced, 1974; three children. Married John S. Collins, 1974. Novelist.

WORKS:
> *Maiden Crown.* Boston: Houghton Mifflin, 1979.
> *The Willow Maiden.* New York: Dial, 1986.
> Contributor to magazines including *Ms., Saturday Review, Friends' Journal, California Living.*

SECONDARY SOURCE:
CA.

CONNOLLY, Vivian ("Andrea Harris"; "Susanna Rosse") (1925–)

BIOGRAPHY:
> Born in Pittsburgh, Pennsylvania. Daughter of James N. (management consultant) and Esther Reedy Hauser. Educated at Ohio State University; Manhattan (N.Y.) State School of Nursing; University of California. Married Harry H. Eckstein, September, 1946; divorced. Married John R. Connolly, clockmaker, 1969. Teacher at Louisiana State University School of Nursing, New Orleans, 1975–77. Psychiatric nursing specialist; free-lance writer.

WORKS:

South Coast of Danger. New York: Tower, 1973.
Fires of Ballymorris. New York: Dell, 1975.
The Velvet Prison. New York: Dell, 1977.
An Irish Affair (as Andrea Harris). New York: Playboy Press, 1978.
A Scream Away (as Andrea Harris). New York: Playboy Press, 1978.
Windfall (as Andrea Harris). New York: Playboy Press, 1979.
Byzantine Encounter (as Andrea Harris). New York: Playboy Press, 1979.
To Love as Eagles. New York: Playboy Press, 1979.
Dance on a Tightrope (as Susanna Rosse). New York: Playboy Press, 1980.
The Counterfeit Bride. New York: Fawcett, 1980.
Five Ports to Danger. New York: Tower, 1980.
Cecilia. New York: Fawcett, 1981.
Love in Exile. New York: Harlequin, 1983.
Published in *American Mercury, Irish Times, American Journal of Nursing, Irish Independence,* and others.

SECONDARY SOURCES:
CA.
CANR.
New Orleans *Times-Picayune,* May 7, 1983, November 1, 1987.

CORRINGTON, Joyce Elaine Hooper (1936–)

Courtesy Joyce Corrington

BIOGRAPHY:
Born in Houston. Daughter of Charles Foster and Ruby Sparks Hooper. Educated at Rice University; Louisiana State University; Tulane University. Married John William Corrington, writer and teacher, 1960 (died 1989); four children. Chemistry professor and former chair of department at Xavier University. Places of residence: Houston, Baton Rouge, New Orleans; now lives in Malibu, California. Coauthor with husband of screenplays, television series, and mystery novels.

WORKS:

Screenplays:
"Von Richthofen and Brown," United Artists (released as *The Red Baron,* 1971).
"I Am Legend," Warner Bros., 1971 (released as *The Omega Man,* 1971).
Box Car Bertha, American International Production, 1972.

Battle for the Planet of the Apes, Twentieth Century Fox, 1973.
The Arena, New World Pictures, 1973.
Killer Bees, World Vision Enterprises, 1974.
Television series:
Head writer with John W. Corrington for Columbia Broadcasting Systems, Inc.: "Search for Tomorrow" (1978–80); "Texas" (1980–81); "General Hospital" (1981–82); "Capitol" (1982).
Books:
So Small a Carnival. New York: Viking/Penguin, 1986.
A Project Named Desire. New York: Viking/Penguin, 1987.
A Civil Death. New York: Viking/Penguin, 1987.
The White Zone. With John William Corrington. New York: Viking/Penguin, 1990.
Editor. *The Collected Stories of John William Corrington.* Columbia: University of Missouri Press, 1990.

SECONDARY SOURCES:
CANR.
New Orleans *Times-Picayune,* July 20, 1986.
Who's Who in Entertainment.

COULTER, Hope Norman (1961–)

BIOGRAPHY:
Born in New Orleans. Daughter of Tom David (pathologist) and Hope Johns (journalist) Norman. Grew up in Alexandria, Louisiana. Educated at Harvard University. Studied African literature at University of Zambia as Rotary fellow. Married Nate Coulter, attorney, 1983; one child. Lives in Little Rock, Arkansas. Received Porter Fund Award in 1989. Writer; editor.

WORKS:
The Errand of the Eye. Little Rock: August House, 1988.
Dry Bones. Little Rock: August House, 1990.

SECONDARY SOURCES:
CA.
New Orleans *Times-Picayune,* January 6, 1991.

CRONE, Moira (1952–)

BIOGRAPHY:
Born in Goldsboro, North Carolina. Daughter of James Clarence (accountant) and Ethel Donnelly Crone. Educated at Smith College; Johns Hopkins University. Married Rodger L. Kamenetz, poet and writer, October 14, 1974; two children. Teaches creative writing at

Louisiana State University, Baton Rouge. Member of board of Bethesda Writers' Century, 1981, and Fiction Collective, New York.

WORKS:

The Winnebago Mysteries and Other Stories. New York: Fiction Collective, 1982.

The Life of Lucy Fern. New York: Cambridge Book Co., 1983.

A Period of Confinement: A Novel. New York: Putnam, 1986.

In progress: "Remember Who Loves You" (novel).

Published in *The New Yorker, Mademoiselle, Ohio Review, Southern Review, Western Humanities Review,* and others. Also in anthologies: *American Made* (New York: Fiction Collective, 1986); *New Stories by Southern Women* (Columbia: University of South Carolina Press, 1989).

SECONDARY SOURCE:

CA.

CRUZ, Joan Carroll (1931–)

BIOGRAPHY:

Born in New Orleans. Daughter of Daniel Joseph (radio operator) and Josephine Eiffert Carroll. Educated at Tulane University; Notre Dame College (now St. Louis University). Married Louis Edgar Cruz, June 12, 1954; five children. Lives in New Orleans.

WORKS:

Desires of Thy Heart. New York: Tandem Press, 1977.

The Incorruptibles (nonfiction). New York: Tan Books, 1978.

Relics (nonfiction). Huntington, Ind.: Our Sunday Visitor, 1984.

SECONDARY SOURCE:

CA.

DANIELS, Kate (1953–)

BIOGRAPHY:

Born in Richmond, Virginia. Educated at University of Virginia; Columbia University School of the Arts. Married to Geoff Macdonald; two sons. Taught at University of Virginia; University of Massachusetts at Amherst; Louisiana State University. Winner of several fellowships and many awards for poetry. Lives in Durham, North Carolina. Poet; teacher; critic.

WORKS:

The White Wave: Poems. Pittsburgh: University of Pittsburgh Press, 1984. Manuscript winner of Agnes Lynel Starrett Award, 1983.

Of Solitude and Silence: Writings on Robert Bly. Coeditor with Richard Jones. Boston: Beacon, 1982.

The Niobe Poems. Pittsburgh: University of Pittsburgh Press, 1988.

Forthcoming: *The Achievement of Muriel Rukeyser.* Coeditor. Ann Arbor: University of Michigan Press.

In progress: "Muriel Rukeyser: A Life in Poetry" (biography). New York: Random House.

Also represented in:

Godine Anthology of Contemporary Poetry. Boston: Godine, 1991.

The Best of Crazyhorse. Fayetteville: University of Arkansas Press, 1990.

1984 Anthology of Magazine Verse. Beverly Hills: Monitor, 1984.

Poetry and Politics: An Anthology of Essays. New York: William Morrow, 1985.

The Pushcart Anthology: Best of the Small Presses VII. New York: Pushcart Press, 1982.

Working Classics: Poems on Industrialization. Champaign-Urbana: University of Illinois Press, 1990.

Many journals.

SECONDARY SOURCE:
CA.

DAVIDSON, Jean (1937–)

BIOGRAPHY:
Born in Spanish Fort, Mississippi. Daughter of Walter Leon and Eva Pettus Jeffries. Educated at Louisiana College; Louisiana State University. Married John A. Davidson, 1965; one child. Fiction writer.

WORK:
The Devil's Horseman. New York: Doubleday, 1976. Won first prize in gothic novel contest by Lancer Books and *Writer's Digest,* 1972.

SECONDARY SOURCES:
None.

DAVIS, Diane Wicker ("Delaney Devers") (1946–)

BIOGRAPHY:
Born in Baton Rouge. Daughter of Benjamin Franklin Wicker, Jr., of Zachary, Louisiana, and Katrina Walters Wicker of Baskin, Louisiana. Educated at Louisiana State University; Northwestern State College; Wright State University, Ohio. Married Frank James Davis (major in USAF) of Covington, Louisiana, 1967. Resides in Shreveport. Romance writer.

WORKS:
The Heart Victorious (as Devers). New York: Jove, 1984.

Call Back the Dawn (as Diane Wicker Davis). New York: Avon, 1985. Set in antebellum Mansfield, Louisiana.

Lucky's Woman (as Devers). New York: Jove, 1985.

Smiles of a Summer Night (as Devers). New York: Jove, 1986. Contemporary romance set near Thibodaux, Louisiana.

Places in the Heart (as Devers). New York: Berkley, 1987.

SECONDARY SOURCES:
None.

DAVIS, Suzannah Nelson (1950–)

BIOGRAPHY:

Born in Shreveport. Daughter of Gordon and Lynn Nelson, past publishers and editors of the Coushatta (La.) *Citizen*. Educated at Louisiana State University. Married J. Q. Davis, 1971; three children. Member of North Louisiana Romance Writers and Romance Writers of America. Resides in Coushatta, Louisiana. Romance writer.

WORKS:

No Bed of Roses. New York: Walker, 1984.

Not for Any Price. New York: Dell Candlelight Ecstasy, 1986.

Prisoner of Passion. New York: Dell Candlelight Ecstasy, 1986.

SECONDARY SOURCES:
None.

DAVIS, Thadious Marie (1944–)

BIOGRAPHY:

Born in New Orleans. Educated at Southern University, Baton Rouge; Atlanta University; Boston University. Currently professor of English at Brown University. Poet; activist; scholar.

WORKS:

Poems published in many periodicals, including *New Orleans Review, Black Scholar, Obsidian, South and West, Callaloo,* and others.

Many scholarly publications, including *Faulkner's "Negro": Art and the Southern Context* (Baton Rouge: Louisiana State University Press, 1982).

Editor. *Afro-American Writers from the Harlem Renaissance to 1940.* Detroit: Gale Research, 1987.

SECONDARY SOURCES:

Directory of American Scholars.

Ewell, Barbara C., and Dorothy H. Brown. "Drama, Poetry, and Louisiana Women Writers." *Louisiana Literature,* VI (Spring, 1989), 37–56.

DOHAN, Mary Helen (1914–)

BIOGRAPHY:

Born in Cincinnati. Daughter of Joseph Francis (manufacturer's representative) and Anastasia Enneking Dohan. Educated at Newcomb College; Tulane University. Married Robert D. Samsot, attorney, 1938; two children. Professor at Newcomb College and Dominican College. Fiction writer; poet; essayist.

WORKS:

Our Own Words (nonfiction). New York: Knopf, 1974.

Represented in *Best American Short Stories,* ed. Martha Foley and David Burnett. Boston: Houghton Mifflin, 1966.

Contributor of stories, poems, and articles to periodicals, including *Atlantic, Redbook,* and *Smithsonian.*

SECONDARY SOURCE:

CA.

DOUGLAS, Ellen (See HAXTON, Josephine Ayres)

DUBUS, Elizabeth Nell ("Beth Michel") (1933–)

BIOGRAPHY:

Born in Lake Charles, Louisiana. Daughter of Andre Jules (civil engineer) and Katherine Burke Dubus. Educated at University of Southwestern Louisiana; Louisiana State University. Divorced; five children. Textbook writer and editor. Sister of Andre Dubus, novelist and short-story writer. Volunteer Activist of the Year, Baton Rouge, 1978. Resides in Baton Rouge. Romance novelist; writer of short stories and nonfiction.

WORKS:

Marguerite Tanner. New York: Tower Books, 1982.

Cajun. New York: Seaview/Putnam, 1983.

Acadian. New York: Putnam, 1984.

Where Love Rules. New York: Putnam, 1985.

Mixed Doubles (two-act play). With Henry Avery. 1984.

To Love and To Dream. New York: Putnam, 1986.

Twilight of the Dawn. New York: St. Martin's, 1989.

Fiction and nonfiction published in many newspapers and periodicals, including *Redbook, Good Housekeeping,* the *North American Review, Woman's Day,* and *Woman's World.*

SECONDARY SOURCES:

Boyd, Pam. "With Cajun Author Beth Dubus, Writing Comes Last." Lafayette *Raging Cajun* (Fall, 1985), 10–11.

Millett, Fred B. *Contemporary American Authors: A Critical Survey and 219 Biographies.* 1940; rpr. New York: AMS Press, 1970.
New Orleans *Times-Picayune,* July 9, 1989.

DUREAU, Lorena (See NEWSHAM, Lorraine)

DUGAS, Clarisse Elizabeth Boutte

BIOGRAPHY:

Born in Broussard, Louisiana. Educated at University of Southwestern Louisiana; Florida State University. Poet; teacher.

WORKS:

Work published in the *Southwestern Review, Orphic Lute, Acadie Tropicale, Blue Unicorn, Salome, Revue de Louisiane, The Lyric,* and *International University Poetry Quarterly.*
Also in *Voices of the Majestic Sage: An Anthology,* edited by Sal Butacci and Susan Gerstle. Saddle Brook, N.J.: New Worlds Unlimited, 1984.

SECONDARY SOURCES:
None.

FENNELLY, Tony (1945–)

BIOGRAPHY:

Born in Orange, New Jersey. Daughter of Thomas Richard and Mary V. Lynch (librarian) Fennelly. Educated at University of New Orleans. Married Richard Catoire, 1972. Lives in New Orleans. Mystery writer.

WORKS:

The Theology of Time Travel. New York: Ellipsis, 1976.
The Glory Hole Murders. New York: Carroll and Graf, 1985.
The Closet Hanging. New York: Carroll and Graf, 1987.

SECONDARY SOURCES:
CA.
Impact, November 15, 1985.
New Orleans *Times-Picayune,* April 20, 1986, March 13, 1989.

FONTENOT, Mary Alice ("Mary Alice Riehl") (1910–)

BIOGRAPHY:

Born in Eunice, Louisiana. Daughter of Elias Valrie and Kate King Barras. Married to Sidney J. Fontenot, 1925–1963 (died); three children. Married Vincent L. Riehl, Sr., 1966. Lives in Lafayette, Louisiana. Author of juvenile fiction; nonfiction writer; journalist.

WORKS:
Clovis Crawfish and His Friends. Baton Rouge: Claitors, 1962.
Clovis Crawfish and the Big Betail. Baton Rouge: Claitors, 1963.
Clovis Crawfish and the Singing Cigales. Baton Rouge: Claitors, 1965.
The Ghost of Bayou Tigre. Baton Rouge: Claitors, 1965.
Clovis Crawfish and Petit Papillon. Baton Rouge: Claitors, 1966.
Clovis Crawfish and the Spinning Spider. Baton Rouge: Claitors, 1968.
The Cat and St. Landry: A Biography of Sheriff D. J. "Cat" Doucet of St. Landry Parish. With Vincent L. Riehl, Sr. Baton Rouge: Claitors, 1972.
Clovis Crawfish and the Curious Crapaud. Baton Rouge: Claitors, 1970.
Clovis Crawfish and Michelle Mantis. Baton Rouge: Claitors, 1976.
Acadia Parish, Louisiana: A History to 1920. 2 vols. Baton Rouge: Claitors, 1976, 1979.
Clovis Crawfish and the Orphan Zo-Zo. Gretna, La.: Pelican, 1983.
The Louisiana Experience (as Riehl). With Julie Landry. Baton Rouge: Claitors, 1983.
Clovis Crawfish and Etienne Escargot. Gretna, La.: Pelican, 1985.
Clovis Crawfish and His Friends. Gretna, La.: Pelican, 1985.
The Star Seed: A Story of the First Christmas. Baton Rouge: Claitors, 1985.
In progress: "Early Families of Acadia Parish."
Represented in *Contes et Comptines du Bayou* (elementary-school French reader). Edited by Kenneth Douet. Lafayette, La.: n.p., 1980.

SECONDARY SOURCES:
CA.
Veach, Damon. *Louisiana Literary Legacy.* Baton Rouge: Louisiana Writers Guild, 1984.

FRIEDMANN, Patty (1946–)

BIOGRAPHY:
Born in New Orleans. Daughter of Werner and Marjorie Cahn Friedmann. Educated at Newman School; Smith College. Married Robert Skinner, novelist and university librarian, 1979; two children. Lives in New Orleans.

WORKS:
Too Smart to Be Rich: A Satiric Look at Being a "Yuffie." New Orleans: Celestial Press, 1987.
The Exact Image of Mother. New York: Viking, 1991.

Photo by David Spelman, courtesy Patty Friedmann

SECONDARY SOURCES:
New Orleans *Times-Picayune,* March 24, 1991.
Persellin, Ketura. *Boston Phoenix Literary Section,* May, 1991, p. 16.
Publishers Weekly, February 1, 1991, pp. 67–68.

GEHMAN, Mary (1943–)

BIOGRAPHY:

Born in Bucks County, Pennsylvania. Daughter of Leroy Straus (farmer and factory worker) and Frances Lerch Gehman. Educated at Millersville State College (Pennsylvania); Loyola University of New Orleans; University of New Orleans. Married Mauricio Ney Rodriguez, 1972; divorced; two sons. Has taught English in high school and at Loyola University and Delgado Community College. Licensed tour guide since 1984, conducting walking tours about the contributions of women to New Orleans history. Has lived in New Orleans since 1970. Writer; editor; historian.

WORKS:

Published poems and articles in *New Orleans Magazine,* New Orleans *Times-Picayune, Figaro,* and others; regular contributor to *Fodor's New Orleans.*

Editor, *Distaff,* New Orleans monthly women's newspaper, 1973–1982.

Women and New Orleans: A History. New Orleans: Margaret Media, 1985.

In progress: a history of Creoles of color in New Orleans.

SECONDARY SOURCES:
Directory of Women's Media, 1980–.
Human Resource File of the Research Clearinghouse Center for Research on Women, Memphis State University, 1985–.

GEREIGHTY, Andrea Saunders (1938–)

BIOGRAPHY:

Born in New Orleans. Daughter of Andrew Jackson (businessman) and Jeanne Theresa Martin Saunders. Educated at University of New Orleans; Exeter College, England. Married Dennis A. Gereighty, Jr., 1959; three children. Lives in Metairie, Louisiana. Poet; short-story writer.

WORKS:

Illusions and Other Realities (poems). New Orleans: Medusa, 1974.

In progress: "Restless for Cool Weather" (poems).

Works have appeared in the following periodicals and anthologies: *Seven Stars Poetry Review, San Francisco Quarterly, Ellipsis,* New Orleans *Distaff, College Poetry Review, Poetry People, New Laurel Review, Pontchartrain Review,* and *Beggar's Bowl.*

SECONDARY SOURCES:
None.

GEX-BREAUX, Quo Vadis (1950–)

BIOGRAPHY:
Born in New Orleans. Daughter of Wilbert (laborer) and Marion Porter Gex. Educated at Boston University; Tulane University. Married Raymond R. Breaux; two children. Development officer at New Orleans school. Lives in New Orleans. Poet; journalist.

WORKS:
Dark Waters (poems). New Orleans: N'Kombo Press, 1969.
In progress: "Jazz Rain." New Orleans: Congo Square.
Poems have appeared in *N'kombo Magazine, Xavier Review, Hoodoo Literary Magazine, Black River Journal,* and others; also in *Word Up: Black Poetry of the Eighties from the Deep South,* edited by Kalamu ya Salaam. Atlanta: Beans and Brown Rice, 1990.

SECONDARY SOURCES:
Jet, January 25, 1973.
New Orleans *States-Item,* October 13, 1972.
New Orleans *Times-Picayune,* October 7, 1990.

GILCHRIST, Ellen (1935–)

BIOGRAPHY:
Born in Vicksburg, Mississippi. Daughter of William Garth Gilchrist (engineer) and Aurora Alford Gilchrist. Has three sons. Educated at Millsaps College; University of Arkansas. Lives in Fayetteville, Arkansas. Poet; novelist; short-story writer. Winner of American Book Award for Fiction, 1984.

WORKS:
The Land Surveyor's Daughter (poems). San Francisco: Lost Roads, 1979.
In the Land of Dreamy Dreams (short stories). Fayetteville: University of Arkansas Press, 1981.
The Annunciation. Boston: Little, Brown, 1983.
Victory over Japan (short stories). Boston: Little, Brown, 1984.
Drunk with Love (short stories). Boston: Little, Brown, 1986.
Falling Through Space: The Journals of Ellen Gilchrist. Boston: Little, Brown, 1987.
Riding Out the Tropical Depression: Selected Poems, 1975–1985. New Orleans: Faust, 1987.
The Anna Papers. Boston: Little, Brown, 1988.
Light Can Be Both Wave and Particle (short stories). Boston: Little, Brown, 1989.

Blue-Eyed Buddhist and Other Stories. London: Faber, 1990.
I Cannot Get You Close Enough: Three Novellas. Boston: Little, Brown, 1990.
Net of Jewels. Boston: Little, Brown, 1992.

SECONDARY SOURCES:
CA.
Lowry, Beverly. "Redheaded Hellions in the Crape Myrtle," *New York Times Book Review,* September 23, 1984, p. 18.
New Orleans *Times-Picayune,* September 20, 1986, February 25, 1990.
Yardley, Jonathan. "Knockout 'Victory': The Best Stories Yet from Ellen Gilchrist," Washington *Post,* September 12, 1984, pp. B1, 10.

GOERTZ, Arthemise (1905–)

BIOGRAPHY:
Born in New Orleans. Daughter of John and Mary Helena Miller Goertz. Educated at Newcomb College; International Students Institute (Tokyo). Married Hector A. Alfonso (died in World War II). Married Charles O. Roome, 1950. Tutored the daughters of Japanese consul in New Orleans. Lives in Mandeville, Louisiana. Novelist.

WORKS:
South of the Border. New York: Macmillan, 1939.
Give Us Our Dream. New York: McGraw-Hill, 1947.
The Moon Is Mine. New York: McGraw-Hill, 1949.
New Heaven, New Earth. New York: McGraw-Hill, 1951.
A Dream of Fuji. New York: McGraw-Hill, 1953.

SECONDARY SOURCES:
American Novelists.
Current Biography, 1953.

GRAHAM, Alice Walworth (1905–)

BIOGRAPHY:
Born in Natchez, Mississippi. Daughter of John Perriander and Alice Leslie Gordon Walworth. Educated at Mississippi State College for Women; Louisiana State University. Married Richard Norwood Graham, civil engineer. Resided in New Orleans. Novelist.

WORKS:
Lost River. New York: Dodd, Mead, 1938.
The Natchez Woman. Garden City, N.Y.: Doubleday, 1950.
Romantic Lady. Garden City, N.Y.: Doubleday, 1952.
Indigo Bend. Garden City, N.Y.: Doubleday, 1953.

The Vows of the Peacock. Garden City, N.Y.: Doubleday, 1955.
Shield of Honor. Garden City, N.Y.: Doubleday, 1957.
Cibola. Garden City, N.Y.: Doubleday, 1962.
The Summer Queen. Garden City, N.Y.: Doubleday, 1973.

SECONDARY SOURCES:
CAR.
CANR.

GRAU, Shirley Ann (1929–)

BIOGRAPHY:
Born in New Orleans. Daughter of Adolph Eugene and Katherine Onions Grau. Educated at Newcomb College. Married James Kern Feibleman, professor at Tulane, 1955 (died 1987); four children. Lives in New Orleans. Novelist; short-story writer. Winner of Pulitzer Prize, 1965.

WORKS:
The Black Prince and Other Stories. New York: Knopf, 1955.
The Hard Blue Sky. New York: Knopf, 1958.
The House on Coliseum Street. New York: Knopf, 1961.
The Keepers of the House. New York: Knopf, 1964. Pulitzer Prize, 1965.
The Condor Passes. New York: Knopf, 1971.
The Wind Shifting West (stories). New York: Knopf, 1973.
Evidence of Love. New York: Random House, 1977.
Nine Women. New York: Knopf, 1985.
Writers and Writing. Edited by A. W. Fields. Lafayette: University of Southwestern Louisiana, 1988.

SECONDARY SOURCES:
American Women Writers, II.
CA.
Gosset, Louise Y. *Violence in Recent Southern Fiction.* Durham: Duke University Press, 1965.
Grau, Joseph A., and Paul Schlueter. *Shirley Ann Grau: An Annotated Bibliography.* New York: Garland, 1981.
New Orleans *Times-Picayune,* February 25, 1990.
Rohrberger, Mary. "Shirley Ann Grau and the Short Story." In *Women Writers of the Contemporary South,* edited by Peggy Whitman Prenshaw. Jackson: University Press of Mississippi, 1984.
Schlueter, Paul. *Shirley Ann Grau.* Boston: Twayne, 1981.
Wagner-Martin, Linda. "Shirley Ann Grau's Wise Fiction." In *Southern Women Writers: The New Generation,* edited by Tonette Bond Inge. Tuscaloosa: University of Alabama Press, 1990.

GRIFFIN, Emilie Russell Dietrich (1936–)

Courtesy Emilie Griffin

BIOGRAPHY:
Born in New Orleans. Daughter of Norman Edward and Helen Russell Dietrich. Educated at Tulane University; National University of Mexico; Notre Dame Seminary (New Orleans). Married Henry William Griffin, editor and writer, 1963; three children. Worked as advertising writer/producer. Received awards for television commercials and at Venice Film Festival. Playscript award, Louisiana Council for Music and Performing Arts. Journalist; novelist; inspirational writer; playwright.

WORKS:

The Only Begotten Son: A Play (1971).

Turning: Reflections on the Experience of Conversion. Garden City, N.Y.: Doubleday, 1980.

Clinging: The Experience of Prayer. New York: Harper and Row, 1984.

His Holiness Pope John Paul II Visits the City of New Orleans. New Orleans: Archdiocese of New Orleans, 1987.

Carnage at Christhaven (serial mystery novel by members of the Chrysostom Society). San Francisco: Harper and Row, 1989.

Chasing the Kingdom: A Parable of Faith. New York: Harper and Row, 1990.

Contributor to journals and periodicals including *America, New Catholic World, Modern Liturgy,* and *Journal of Advertising.*

SECONDARY SOURCES:

CA.

CANR.

New Orleans *Times-Picayune,* July 13, 1980, May 27, 1990.

New York Times Book Review, July 13, 1980.

GRUE, Lee Meitzen (1934–)

Photo by Bryce Lankard, courtesy Lee Meitzen Grue

BIOGRAPHY:

Born in Plaquemine, Louisiana. Daughter of Leroy Robert Meitzen (geophysicist) and Catherine McCullar Meitzen. Educated at Tulane University; University of New Orleans; Warren Wilson College. Married Ronald David Grue, Mississippi River pilot; three children. Editor of *World Port* (commercial magazine on the Mississippi River) and of *New Laurel Review* (literary magazine). Director of New Orleans Poetry Forum. Poet.

WORKS:

Trains and Other Intrusions: A Chapbook of Poetry. New Orleans: New Orleans Poetry Forum, 1974.

French Quarter Poems. New Orleans: Long Measure, 1979.

In the Sweet Balance of the Flesh (poems). Austin: Plain View Press, 1991.

In progress: "Goodbye, Silver, Silver Cloud" (short stories).

Poems and short stories have appeared in numerous literary magazines, newspapers, and anthologies. Has edited several books of poems by children in New Orleans public schools, including *Going Downtown New Orleans, Get My Mama Some Good Red Beans,* 1975.

SECONDARY SOURCES:

Directory of Poets and Writers.

Ewell, Barbara C., and Dorothy H. Brown. "Drama, Poetry, and Louisiana Women Writers." *Louisiana Literature,* VI (Spring, 1989), 37–56.

New Orleans *Times Picayune,* September 20, 1986.

Who's Who of American Women.

HALDEMANN, Linda Wilson (1935–)

BIOGRAPHY:

Born in Washington, D.C. Daughter of John Barnett (attorney) and Mildred Beckwith Wilson. Educated at Loyola University, New Orleans; Pennsylvania State University. Married Harry Haldemann, professor of English, 1959; four children. Lives in Indiana, Pennsylvania. Novelist; opera article writer.

WORKS:

Star of the Sea. Garden City, N.Y.: Doubleday, 1978.

The Last Born of Elvinwood. Garden City, N.Y.: Doubleday, 1978.

Articles in *Opera News* and *Opera Journal.*

SECONDARY SOURCE:
CA.

HALL, Martha Lacy (1923–)

BIOGRAPHY:

Born in Magnolia, Mississippi. Daughter of William Monroe and Elizabeth Goza Lacy. Educated at Whitworth College for Women, Brookhaven, Mississippi. Married Robert Sherrill Hall, Jr., electrical and mechanical engineer, 1941 (died 1991); three children. Worked for the Memphis *Press-Scimitar.* Editor at the Louisiana State University Press, 1968–1979; managing editor, 1979–1984; currently fiction editor. Lives in Baton Rouge. Short-story writer.

WORKS:

Call It Living: Three Stories. Athens, Ga.: Press of the Nightowl, 1981.

Music Lesson: Stories. Urbana: University of Illinois Press, 1984.

The Apple Green Triumph and Other Stories. Baton Rouge: Louisiana State University Press, 1990.

Stories published in the *Southern Review, New Orleans Review, Sewanee Review, Virginia Quarterly, Shenandoah,* and other literary journals. Works frequently cited in *Best American Short Stories;* story "Joanna" is in *Selected Stories from the Southern Review, 1965–1985,* edited by Lewis P. Simpson *et al.* Baton Rouge: Louisiana State University Press, 1988. "The Apple-Green Triumph" was selected for inclusion in the 1991 edition of *Prize Stories: The O. Henry Awards* (New York: Doubleday, 1991).

SECONDARY SOURCES:
None.

HAMILTON, Anne Butler (1944–)

BIOGRAPHY:

Educated at University High School, Baton Rouge; Sweet Briar College; University of Wisconsin; Louisiana State University; Humboldt State University. Married Charles Stewart Hamilton; two children. Short-story and nonfiction writer.

WORKS:

Little Chase and Big Fat Aunt May (stories). Baton Rouge: VAAPR, 1981.

Son of Immigrants: James M. Imahara. Privately published, 1981.

Little Chase and Big Fat Aunt May Recipe Book. Baton Rouge: VAAPR, 1983.

Little Chase and Big Fat Aunt May Ride Again. Baton Rouge: VAAPR, 1983.

The Herman and Little Leon Stories. Baton Rouge: Damon, 1984.

A Tourist's Guide to West Feliciana Parish. New Orleans: Habersham Corp., 1984.

Works have appeared in *1982 Louisiana Anthology,* compiled by Damon Veach (Baton Rouge: VAAPR, 1982); *Louisiana Life; New Orleans Magazine; Baton Rouge Magazine; Country Roads Magazine; Pacifica; Country People; Mississippi Magazine;* and others.

SECONDARY SOURCE:
Veach, Damon. *Louisiana Literary Legacy.* Baton Rouge: Louisiana Writers Guild, 1984.

HAXTON, Josephine Ayres ("Ellen Douglas") (1921–)

BIOGRAPHY:
Born in Natchez, Mississippi. Daughter of Richardson (engineer) and Laura Davis Ayres. Educated at University of Mississippi. Married Kenneth Haxton, 1945; divorced; three sons. Lived in Arkansas and in Alexandria, Louisiana, as a child; worked briefly at the Gotham Book Mart in New York. Writer-in-residence, Northeast Louisiana University, Monroe (1976–1979), at the University of Mississippi (1979–) and at the University of Virginia (1983); Welty Professor at Millsaps College, Jackson, Mississippi; Zale Writer-in-Residence at Tulane (1991). Her awards include the Houghton Mifflin Fellowship Award, finalist for the National Book Award (1962), and Mississippi Institute of Arts and Letters Award (twice); two National Endowment for the Arts Fellowships; and the Fellowship of Southern Writers Fiction Award (1989). Lives in Jackson, Mississippi. Novelist; short-story writer.

WORKS:
Moon of Violence (romance mystery). New York: Bouregy/Avalon, 1960.
A Family's Affairs. Boston: Houghton Mifflin, 1962.
Black Cloud, White Cloud: Two Novellas and Two Stories. Boston: Houghton Mifflin, 1963.
Walker Percy's "The Last Gentleman." New York: Seabury, 1969.
Apostles of Light. Boston: Houghton Mifflin, 1973.
The Rock Cried Out. New York: Harcourt Brace Jovanovich, 1979.
A Lifetime Burning. New York: Random House, 1982.
A Long Night. Jackson, Mississippi: Nouveau Press, 1986.
The Magic Carpet and Other Tales. Jackson: University Press of Mississippi, 1987.
Can't Quit You, Baby. New York: Atheneum, 1988.
In progress: a novel.

SECONDARY SOURCES:
Broughton, Panthea Reed, and Susan Millar Williams. "Ellen Douglas." In *Southern Women Writers: The New Generation,* edited by Tonette Bond Inge. Tuscaloosa: University of Alabama Press, 1990.

New Orleans *Times-Picayune,* August 7, 1988.
New Yorker, March 3, 1973.
New York Times Book Review, February 18, 1973, October 31, 1982.
Speir, Jerry. "Of Novels and the Novelist: An Interview with Ellen Douglas." *University of Mississippi Studies in English,* n.s., V (1984–1987), pp. 231–48.
Stockwell, Joe. *Ellen Douglas.* Jackson: Mississippi Library Commission, 1977.

HEAD, Gwen (1940–)

BIOGRAPHY:
Born in New Orleans. Daughter of Harry (journalist) and Elsie Scott Head. Educated at Southern Methodist University; Trinity University; St. Mary's University. Married Allan Charles Schwartzman, investor, May 23, 1963. Taught at Aspen Writers' Conference, 1978. Received Helen Buttis Prize for *Poetry, Northwest,* 1968, and named Anne Sexton Fellow at Bread Loaf Writers' Conference, 1975. Fiction prize at Aspen Writers' Conference for "Substantial Risk." Lives in Seattle. Poet; fiction writer.

WORKS:
Special Effects. Pittsburgh: University of Pittsburgh Press, 1975.
The Ten Thousandth Night. Pittsburgh: University of Pittsburgh Press, 1979.

SECONDARY SOURCE:
CA.

HEBERT, Julie (1954–)

Courtesy Julie Hebert

BIOGRAPHY:
Born in Morgan City, Louisiana. Daughter of Earl (accountant and comptroller) and Nelwyn Shepherd Hebert (landlady). Educated at Nicholls State University, Thibodaux, Louisiana. One daughter. Has received an Emmy award, two National Endowment for the Arts Directing Fellowships, and a Marin Arts Council Playwrighting Fellowship. Currently Theater Artistic Producing Director for the Contemporary Arts Center in New Orleans. Her plays have been produced in Los Angeles, San Francisco, San Di-

ego, and elsewhere. Lives in New Orleans. Playwright; director; author of performance texts.

WORKS:

Almost Asleep (1985). In *Best of the West*. Los Angeles: Padua Hill Press, 1991.

Other plays include *Purgatory* (1983); *True Beauties* (1984; Best Play, 1987, Bay Area Critics Circle; Drama-Logue Awards); *Strongbox* (1986); *In the Privacy of Strangers* (1987); *Ruby's Bucket of Blood* (1990); *The Knee Desires the Dirt* (1991). Performance texts: *Died Suddenly* (1988), *Beneath the Thin Skin* (1989).

SECONDARY SOURCES:

New Orleans *Times-Picayune*, October 25, 1991.
Who's Who in American Theater.

HOLLAND, Isabelle (1920–)

BIOGRAPHY:

Born in Basel, Switzerland. Daughter of Philip (U.S. Foreign Service officer) and Corabelle Anderson Holland. Educated at University of Liverpool; Tulane University. Lives in New York. Novelist; short-story writer.

WORKS:

Cecily. Philadelphia: Lippincott, 1967.
Amanda's Choice. Philadelphia: Lippincott, 1970.
The Man Without a Face. Philadelphia: Lippincott, 1972.
Heads You Win, Tails You Lose. Philadelphia: Lippincott, 1973.
Kilgaren. New York: Weybright, 1974.
Trelawny. New York: Weybright, 1974.
Journey for Three. Boston: Houghton Mifflin, 1975.
Of Love and Death and Other Journeys. Philadelphia: Lippincott, 1975.
Moncrieff: The Long Search (gothic novel). New York: Weybright, 1976.
Bump in the Night. New York: Doubleday, 1988.
A Fatal Advent. New York: Doubleday, 1989.

SECONDARY SOURCES:

CAR.
Contemporary Literary Criticism.
New York Times Book Review, May 3, 1970.

HUGHES, M. E.

BIOGRAPHY:

Born in New Orleans, grew up in New Iberia, Louisiana. Educated at Baylor University; American Academy of Dramatic Arts; M.A. from Bennington College. Teaches writing at Hunter College at Adelphi

University, New York City. Newspaper reporter; editor; costume designer; teacher; novelist.

WORK:

Precious in His Sight: A Novel. New York: Viking/Penguin, 1988.

SECONDARY SOURCE:

New Orleans *Times-Picayune,* January 15, 1989.

JEFFERSON, Sonia Wilmetta Johnson (1925–)

BIOGRAPHY:

Born in Mississippi. Daughter of Geylon Johnson and Minnie Toney Johnson. Educated at Alcorn College; University of Illinois. Married Nephus Jefferson, Jr.; one child. Resides in Baton Rouge. Artist; writer; educator of the deaf.

WORKS:

Thirteenth Child. Baton Rouge: Franklin Press, 1973.

Poems for People. Baton Rouge: Franklin Press, 1975.

Cat Girl. Baton Rouge: Franklin Press, 1978.

Short Stories. Baton Rouge: Franklin Press, 1978.

Work has also been published in newspapers and magazines, including *Church and Home.*

SECONDARY SOURCES:

None.

KANE, Julie Ellen (1952–)

Photo by Peggy Stewart, courtesy Julie Kane

BIOGRAPHY:

Born in Boston. Daughter of Edwin (radio/ TV newscaster) and Nanette Spillane Kane (grade school teacher). Educated at Cornell University; Boston University; Louisiana State University. Came to Baton Rouge to work in a federal antipoverty program; technical writer and editor in New Orleans, where she was a director of the Maple Street Bar Literary Reading Series. First woman to hold the George Bennett Fellowship in Writing at Phillips Exeter Academy (Exeter, New Hampshire, 1975–1976); other awards include the Poetry Atlanta Prize (1990), the *Mademoiselle* Magazine College Poetry Competition (1973), and the National Council of Teachers of English Creative Writing Award (1970). Lives in New Orleans.

WORKS:

Two Into One. With Ruth Adatia. London: Only Poetry, 1982.
Body and Soul. New Orleans: Pirogue Press, 1987.
The Bartender Poems. London: Greville Press, 1991.
Poems have appeared in *From a Bend in the River* (New Orleans: Contemporary Arts Center, 1991); *Prairie Smoke* (Pueblo, Colo.: Pueblo Poetry Project, 1990); *Anthology of Magazine Verse and Yearbook of American Poetry,* 1981; *Touching This Earth: Poems by Women* (New Wilmington, Pa.: Dawn Valley Press, 1977); *I, That Am Ever Stranger: Poems on Women's Experience* (New Wilmington, Pa.: Dawn Valley Press, 1974); *The First Anthology* (Ithaca, N.Y.: Society for the Humanities, 1974); as well as in numerous journals.

SECONDARY SOURCES:
New Orleans *Times-Picayune,* August 16, 1987, June 11, 1989.

KEIN, Sybil (1939–)

BIOGRAPHY:

Born in New Orleans; named Consuela Moore. Daughter of Francis (bricklayer) and Augustine Boudreaux Moore. Educated at Xavier University; University of New Orleans; University of Michigan. Married Felix Provost, 1959; divorced; three children. Teaches at the University of Michigan, Flint. Lives in Flint, Michigan, and New Orleans. Poet; playwright; author of children's books.

WORKS:

Visions from the Rainbow. Flint, Mich.: N. D. Hosking, 1979.
Gombo People: Poésie Créole de la Nouvelle Orléans/New Orleans Creole Poetry. New Orleans: Leo J. Hall, 1981.
Delta Dancer: New and Selected Poems. Detroit: Lotus, 1984.
Get Together (play; 1970). In *Wines in the Wilderness,* edited by Elizabeth Brown-Guillory. New York: Praeger, 1990.
Writer of twenty-eight plays, ten of which have been produced: *Saints and Flowers,* 1965; *Projection One,* 1966; *The Black Box,* 1967; *The Christmas Holly,* 1967; *Deep River Rises,* 1970; *The Reverend,* 1970; *Get Together,* 1970; *When I Grow Up,* 1974; *Rogues Along the River Flint,* 1977; and *River Rogues,* 1979. Also has written several juvenile books.
Poems and plays have appeared in numerous periodicals and anthologies, including *Callaloo, Obsidian, Beloit Poetry Journal, Black American Literature Forum, English Journal, American Dream* (Lexington, Mass.: Ginn, 1977), and *Introduction to Theatrical Arts* (Dubuque: Kendall Hunt, 1971).
In progress: "Des Gardenia et Roses: Les Chansons Créoles" (Creole songs in five languages).

SECONDARY SOURCES:

Bryan, Violet Harrington. "Evocations of Place and Culture in the Works of Four Contemporary Black Louisiana Writers: Brenda Osbey, Sybil Kein, Elizabeth Brown-Guillory, and Pinkie Gordon Lane." *Louisiana Literature,* IV (1987), 49–65.

Miami *News,* September 28, 1985.

New Orleans Magazine, April, 1972.

KELLY, Regina Zimmerman (1898–)

BIOGRAPHY:

Born in New Orleans. Daughter of Joseph A. and Theresa Antoni Zimmerman. Educated at University of Chicago (Ph.D., 1920). Married Norman H. Kelly, 1920. Children's-story writer; biographer.

WORKS:

King Richard's Squire: A Tale of Chaucer's England. New York: Crowell, 1937.

Young Geoffrey Chaucer. New York: Lothrop, Lee and Shepard, 1952.

And the Deaf Shall Hear. Newark, N.J.: Family Circle, 1952.

Lincoln and Douglas: The Years of Decision. New York: Random House, 1954.

Beaver Trail. New York: Lothrop, Lee and Shepard, 1955.

Henry Clay: Statesman and Patriot. Boston: Houghton Mifflin, 1960.

Abigail Adams: The President's Lady. Boston: Houghton Mifflin, 1962.

Chicago: Big-Shouldered City. Chicago: Reilly and Lee, 1962.

New Orleans: Queen of the River. Chicago: Reilly and Lee, 1963.

Paul Revere: Colonial Craftsman. Boston: Houghton Mifflin, 1963.

Picture Story and Biography of Marquette and Joliet. Chicago: Follett, 1965.

Picture Story and Biography of John Adams. Chicago: Follett, 1965.

James Madison: Statesman and President. Boston: Houghton Mifflin, 1966.

Franklin Delano Roosevelt. Chicago: Follett, 1966.

One Flag, One Land. Chicago: Reilly and Lee, 1967.

John F. Kennedy. Chicago: Follett, 1969.

Miss Jefferson in Paris. New York: Coward, McCann and Geoghegan, 1971.

SECONDARY SOURCE:

CAR.

LANE, Pinkie Gordon (1923–)

Courtesy Pinkie Gordon Lane

BIOGRAPHY:
Born in Philadelphia, Pennsylvania. Daughter of William Alexander and Inez Addie West Gordon. Educated at Spelman College; Atlanta University; Louisiana State University (where she was the first black woman to receive a Ph.D.) Married Ulysses Simpson Lane (deceased); one son. Teacher in Florida and Georgia public schools (1949–1955); professor at Southern University in Baton Rouge since 1959; professor of English emerita since 1986. Has lectured, read, and given workshops throughout the United States and in Ghana, Cameroon, and Zambia. Awards include Baton Rouge Women of Achievement (1984); Women in the Mainstream, New Orleans World Exposition (1984); College English Association National Award in Poetry (1988); and Image Award, National Association for the Advancement of Colored People (1990). Poet laureate of Louisiana (since 1989). Active in many civic and cultural organizations. Resident of Baton Rouge since 1956. Poet; teacher.

WORKS:
Wind Thoughts (poems). Fort Smith, Ark.: South and West, 1972.
Discourses on Poetry. Editor and contributor. Fort Smith, Ark.: South and West, 1972.
Poems by Blacks. Editor and contributor. Fort Smith, Ark.: South and West, 1973.
Mystic Female (poems). Fort Smith, Ark.: South and West, 1978.
I Never Scream: New and Selected Poems. Detroit: Lotus, 1985.
Girl at the Window (poems). Baton Rouge: Louisiana State University Press, 1991.
Works have appeared in *Journal of Black Poetry, Personalist, Hoodoo, Louisiana Review, Ms., New Orleans Review,* and others. Also represented in *Word Up: Black Poetry of the Eighties from the Deep South,* edited by Kalamu ya Salaam (Atlanta: Beans and Brown Rice, 1990).

SECONDARY SOURCES:
Bryan, Violet Harrington. "Evocations of Place and Culture in the Works of Four Contemporary Black Louisiana Writers: Brenda Osbey, Sybil Kein, Elizabeth Brown-Guillory, and Pinkie Gordon Lane." *Louisiana Literature,* IV (1987), 49–65.
CAR.

Harris, Trudier, and Thadious Davis, eds. *Afro-American Poets Since 1955*. Detroit: Gale Research, 1985.

Hero, Danella P. "A Conversation with Louisiana's Poet Laureate: Pinkie Gordon Lane." *Louisiana Literature,* VII (1990), 14–27.

Newman, Dorothy W. "Lane's Mystic Female." *Callaloo,* V (1979), 153–55.

New Orleans *Times-Picayune,* November 3, 1991.

LARSON, Susan ("Suzanne Michelle") (1951–)

BIOGRAPHY:

Born in Salina, Kansas. Daughter of Donald E. (oil refinery worker) and Hilda Luetje Larson. Grew up near Houston. Educated at Rice University; University of Houston. Married Julian Wasserman, professor, 1975; two children. Bookseller for many years and book reviewer for the Houston *Post*. Reviews and essays have appeared in *Matrix, Ultra,* and *Centerline*. Currently book editor for the New Orleans *Times-Picayune*. Lives in New Orleans. Romance novelist (with coauthor Barbara Michels); journalist.

WORKS:

Enchanted Desert. New York: Silhouette Desire Romances, 1982.
Silver Promises. New York: Silhouette Desire Romances, 1983.
No Place for a Woman. New York: Silhouette Desire Romances, 1983.
Political Passions. New York: Silhouette Desire Romances, 1983.
Forbidden Melody. New York: Silhouette Desire Romances, 1983.
Stormy Serenade. New York: Silhouette Desire Romances, 1984.
Recipe for Love. New York: Silhouette Desire Romances, 1984.
Fancy Free. New York: Silhouette Desire Romances, 1984.
Sweetheart of a Deal. New York: Silhouette Desire Romances, 1984.
Starstruck Lovers. New York: Silhouette Desire Romances, 1985.

SECONDARY SOURCES:
None.

LEAKE, Joanna Brent ("Joanna Brent")

BIOGRAPHY:

Born in Baton Rouge. Daughter of Alan (advertising executive) and Adalie Margules Brent (interior designer). Educated at Vassar College; State University of New York at Buffalo. Married David M. Leake (architect); one daughter. Taught at University of New Orleans, 1977–. Short-story writer; juvenile-fiction writer.

WORKS:

A Child Likes (poems for children). Baton Rouge: Louisiana Arts and Science Center, 1971.

A Few Days in Weasel Creek. New York: Seaview Books, 1979. Film, CBS TV, 1982.

SECONDARY SOURCES:
None.

LEMANN, Nancy (1956–)

BIOGRAPHY:
Born in New Orleans. Educated at Brown University; Columbia University. Resides in New York City.

WORKS:
Lives of the Saints: A Novel. New York: Knopf, 1985.
The Ritz on the Bayou (novel form used for report on a Louisiana trial). New York: Knopf, 1987.
Sportsman's Paradise. New York: Knopf, 1992.

SECONDARY SOURCES:
CA.
Contemporary Literary Criticism.
New York *Times,* May 15, 1985.

L'ENFANT, Julia Claire Chandler (1944–)

BIOGRAPHY:
Born in Hodge, Louisiana. Daughter of Weldon K. Chandler and Era Byrd Pullen Chandler. Educated at Louisiana State University and University of New Orleans. Married Howard W. L'Enfant, Louisiana State University professor of law, 1966; one child. Lives in Baton Rouge. Teacher; fiction writer.

WORKS:
Short stories in the *Southern Review* and other journals.
The Dancers of Sycamore Street: A Novel. New York: St. Martin's, 1983.

SECONDARY SOURCE:
CA.

LEVY, Maya (1939–)

BIOGRAPHY:
Born in Hammond, Louisiana. Educated at Southeastern Louisiana University, Hammond. Married Lee K. Levy; three children. Resides in Hammond.

WORK:
Daughters: A Play. Boston: Baker's Plays, 1986.

SECONDARY SOURCES:
None.

LYSTAD, Mary Hanemann (1928–)

BIOGRAPHY:

Born in New Orleans. Daughter of James and Mary Douglas Hanemann. Educated at Newcomb College; Columbia University; Tulane University. Married Robert Lystad, 1953; five children. Lives in Washington, D.C. Social psychologist; writer. Awards won for children's books with psychological themes.

WORKS:

Millicent the Monster. New York: Harlin Quist, 1968.
Jennifer Takes Over P.S. 94. New York: Putnam, 1972.
James the Jaguar. New York: Putnam, 1972. *Weekly Reader* Book Club selection.
That New Boy. New York: Crown, 1973.
The Halloween Parade. New York: Putnam, 1973.

SECONDARY SOURCE:
CANR.

McFERREN, Martha Dean (1947–)

BIOGRAPHY:

Born in Henderson, Texas. Daughter of Manley Edward and Emma Louise Turner McFerren. Educated at North Texas State University (B.S., M.L.S.); Warren Wilson College (M.F.A.). Married Dennis Scott Wall, 1977. Awards: Artist Fellowship in Literature, Louisiana State Arts Council, 1983; Yaddo Fellowship, 1985; National Endowment for the Arts Grant, 1991. Lives in New Orleans. Poet.

WORKS:

Delusions of a Popular Mind. New Orleans: Poetry Journal Press, 1983.
Get Me Out of Here! Green Harbor, Mass.: Wampeter Press, 1984.
Contours for Ritual. Baton Rouge: Louisiana State University Press, 1987.
Published in *Georgia Review, College English, Louisiana Literature, Shenandoah, Southern Review, Open Places, Helicon Nine, New Laurel Review, Stone Country, Literary Review,* and others.

SECONDARY SOURCE:

Struebling-Beasley, Kristen, and Danella Primeaux Hero. "Salvaged Memories: New Orleans Artists, Southern Writers, and Common Sensibility." *Helicon Nine,* Nos. 17/18 (Spring, 1987), 60–92.

MARTIN, Valerie (1948–)

Photo by Thomas Victor, courtesy
Valerie Martin

BIOGRAPHY:
Born in Sedalia, Missouri. Daughter of John Roger (sea captain) and Valerie Fleischer Metcalf. Educated at University of New Orleans; University of Massachusetts. Married Robert M. Martin, artist; divorced; one child. Taught at University of New Orleans, New Mexico State University, University of Alabama, Mt. Holyoke College; currently at University of Massachusetts, Amherst. Novelist; short-story writer.

WORKS:
Love (short stories). Amherst, Mass.: Lynx House, 1976.
Set in Motion. New York: Farrar, Straus and Giroux, 1978.
Alexandra. New York: Farrar, Straus and Giroux, 1979.
A Recent Martyr. Boston: Houghton Mifflin, 1987.
The Consolation of Nature and Other Stories. Boston: Houghton Mifflin, 1988.
Mary Reilly. New York: Doubleday, 1990.
Stories and articles have appeared in *Ricochet, Black Warrior Review, New York Times Book Review, New Orleans Review, Southern Review,* and elsewhere.

SECONDARY SOURCES:
Brown, Dorothy H., and Barbara C. Ewell. "Fiction and Louisiana Women Writers." *Louisiana Literature,* V (1988), 24–43.
CA.
New Orleans *Times-Picayune,* September 20, 1986, May 24, 1987, February 4, 1990.
USA Today, January 26, 1990.

MATHIS, Cleopatra (1947–)

BIOGRAPHY:
Born in Ruston, Louisiana. Daughter of James C. (police officer) and Maxine Theodos Walton. Educated at Louisiana Polytechnic University; Tulane University; Southwest Texas State University; Columbia University. Married William J. Mathis, 1973; one child. Poet; teacher.

WORKS:
Aerial View of Louisiana (poems). New York: Sheep Meadow, 1980.
The Bottom Land (poems). New York: Sheep Meadow, 1982.

Numerous poems have also appeared in anthologies and magazines, including *New Yorker, Nation, American Poetry Review, Southern Review,* and *Poetry Now.*

SECONDARY SOURCE:
CA.

MAXWELL, Patricia ("Jennifer Blake"; "Maxine Patrick"; "Patricia Ponder"; "Elizabeth Treahearne" [joint pseudonym]) (1942–)

BIOGRAPHY:
Born in Winn Parish, Louisiana. Daughter of John H. (electrician) and Daisy Durbin Ponder. Married Jerry R. Maxwell, automobile dealer, 1957; four children. Lives in Quitman, Louisiana. Novelist; poet; short-story writer.

WORKS:
The Secret of Mirror House. New York: Fawcett, 1970.
Stranger at Plantation Inn. New York: Fawcett, 1971.
Storm at Midnight. Coauthor with Carol Albritton (as "Elizabeth Treahearne"). New York: Ace Books, 1973.
The Bewitching Grace. New York: Popular Library, 1974.
Bride of a Stranger. New York: Fawcett, 1974.
The Court of the Thorn Tree. New York: Popular Library, 1974.
Dark Masquerade. New York: Fawcett, 1974.
Love's Wild Desire. New York: Popular Library, 1977.
The Notorious Angel. New York: Ballantine, 1977.
The Storm and the Splendor. New York: Fawcett, 1979.
Tender Betrayal. New York: Popular Library, 1979.
Captive Kisses. New York: Signet, 1980.
Golden Fancy. New York: Fawcett Gold Medal Books, 1980.
Love at Sea. New York: Signet, 1980.
April of Enchantment. New York: Signet, 1981.
Embrace and Conquer. New York: Ballantine, 1981.
Royal Seduction. New York: Ballantine, 1983.
Midnight Waltz. New York: Fawcett Columbine, 1984.
Surrender in Moonlight. New York: Fawcett Columbine, 1984.
Fierce Eden. New York: Ballantine, 1985.
Royal Passion. New York: Ballantine, 1986.
Spanish Serenade. New York: Fawcett Columbine, 1990.
Contributor of poetry, short stories, and articles to periodicals.

SECONDARY SOURCES:
CA.
CANR.
Falk, Kathryn, ed. *Love's Leading Ladies.* New York: Pinnacle, 1982.
New Orleans *Times-Picayune,* July 21, 1991.

Stahls, Paul F., Jr. "The Many Romances of Patricia Maxwell." *Louisiana Life*, II (September–October, 1982), pp. 138–41.

MEYERER, Margaret Renfroe (1924–)

BIOGRAPHY:

Born in Birmingham, Alabama. Daughter of Morton C. and Maud Powers Renfroe. Educated at Louisiana State University. Married Albert Meyerer, Jr.; three children. Married Thomas J. Standfill. Has lived in Jasper, Alabama; Grand Isle, Louisiana. Resides in Baton Rouge. Teacher; poet.

WORKS:

Poems in periodicals and anthologies, including *American Poetry Anthology* (Santa Cruz, Calif.: American Poetry Association, 1985, 1986). *Heartbreak: Poems.* New York: Vantage, 1985.

SECONDARY SOURCE:

Who's Who in U.S. Writers, Editors, and Poets, 1986–87.

MILLICAN, Arthenia Jackson Bates (1920–)

BIOGRAPHY:

Born in Sumter, South Carolina. Daughter of Shepard (educator) and Susan Emma David (craftswoman) Jackson. Educated at Morris College; Atlanta University; Louisiana State University. Taught English at Southern University, Baton Rouge. Lives in Baker, Louisiana. Poet.

WORKS:

Seeds Beneath the Snow: Vignettes from the South. New York: Greenwich Press, 1969.
The Deity Nodded. Detroit: Harlo, 1973.
Such Things from the Valley (poems). Norfolk, Va.: Millican, 1977.
"The Bottoms of Hills: Tales of Virginia Life" (unpublished collection of short stories).

Contributions have also appeared in *Black World, Obsidian, Callaloo,* and others.

SECONDARY SOURCES:

Brown, Dorothy H., and Barbara C. Ewell. "Fiction and Louisiana Women Writers." *Louisiana Literature*, V (Fall, 1988), 24–65.
CA.

"Legitimate Resources of the Soul: An Interview With Arthenia Bates Millican," *Obsidian* (Spring, 1977), 14–34.

New Orleans *Times-Picayune,* September 20, 1986.

"Reflections: Arthenia Bates Millican." In *Sturdy Black Bridges: Visions of Black Women in Literature,* edited by Roseann P. Bell, Bettye J. Parker, and Beverly Guy-Sheftall. Garden City, N.Y.: Anchor/Doubleday, 1979.

Who's Who Among Black Americans, 1990–91.

World Who's Who of Women.

MITCHELL, Judith Paige

BIOGRAPHY:

Born in New Orleans. Daughter of George J. (engineer) and Ester Finerowsky Segal. Attended Tulane University. Married Alvin M. Binder, Mississippi lawyer, 1951; divorced; three children. Married Abram S. Ginnes, 1969; divorced. Lives in Beverly Hills, California. Name legally changed to Mitchell. Writes as "Paige Mitchell." Novelist; television scriptwriter.

WORKS:

A Wilderness of Monkeys. New York: Dutton, 1965.

Love Is Not a Safe Country. New York: Dutton, 1967.

The Mayfly. New York: Bantam, 1971.

The Covenant. New York: Atheneum, 1973.

Act of Love: The Killing of George Zygmanik (nonfiction). New York: Knopf, 1976.

Wild Seed. Garden City, N.Y.: Doubleday, 1982.

"Geisha" (television drama). CBS TV, 1986.

"Roses Are for the Rich" (television series). CBS TV, 1987. Based on novel by Jonell Lawson.

SECONDARY SOURCES:

Best Sellers, June, 1976.

CANR.

New York Times Book Review, May 27, 1973, April 4, 1976.

MORGAN, Berry (1919–)

BIOGRAPHY:

Born in Port Gibson, Mississippi. Daughter of John Marshall and Bess Berry Taylor Brumfield. Educated at Loyola University, New Orleans; Tulane University. Has four children. Instructor at Northeast Louisiana University, Monroe. Novelist; short-story writer.

WORKS:
Pursuit. Boston: Houghton Mifflin, 1966.
The Mystic Adventures of Roxie Stoner (short stories). Boston: Houghton Mifflin, 1974.
In progress: "Fornica Creek" (novel).
Stories have appeared in the *New Yorker.*

SECONDARY SOURCES:
CA.
New Orleans *Courier,* December 12, 1973.

NEWSHAM, Lorraine ("Lorena Dureau")

BIOGRAPHY:
Born in New Orleans. Spent fifteen years as editor and opera singer in Mexico. Fiction writer; teacher.

WORKS:
The Last Casquette Girl. New York: Pinnacle, 1981.
Iron Lace (romance). New York: Pocket Books, 1983.
Lynette. New York: Pinnacle, 1983.
Beloved Outcast. Toronto: Paperjacks, 1987.

SECONDARY SOURCES:
New Orleans *Times-Picayune,* December 25, 1985, May 31, 1987.
Veach, Damon. *Louisiana Literary Legacy.* Baton Rouge: Louisiana Writers Guild, 1984.

O'BRIEN, Sharon (1942–)

Courtesy Sharon O'Brien

BIOGRAPHY:
Born in New Orleans. Daughter of John D. and Anna May Smith O'Brien. Educated at the University of Miami; University of New Orleans; Tulane School of Public Health and Tropical Medicine; University of Birmingham (England). Has worked as editor, public-relations director; co-owner of management consulting firm. Has won numerous writing and editing awards from International Business Communicators, the Press Club of New Orleans, and the Louisiana Hospital Association. Lives in Gretna, Louisiana. Playwright.

WORKS:

The Emperor's New Clothes (1970); *Rapunzel* (1970); *Robin Hood* (1973); *Rumpelstiltskin* (1973); *Lafitte* (1975); *Puss 'n' Boots* (1977); *Mother Goose* (1977); *Sheets* (1979); *Spilt Milk* (1980); *Lake Vista* (1981); *Bloomsday 1941* (1991).

SECONDARY SOURCES:

Gretna (La.) *West Bank Guide*, October 18, 1978.
Who's Who in the South and Southwest.

OSBEY, Brenda Marie (1957–)

Photo by Chandra McCormick,
courtesy Brenda Marie Osbey

BIOGRAPHY:

Born in New Orleans. Daughter of Lawrence Osbey (boxer) and Lois Emelda Hamilton. Educated at Dillard University; Université Paul Valéry, France; University of Kentucky at Lexington. Taught at UCLA, Dillard University. Now at Loyola University, New Orleans. Honors include the Academy of American Poets Loring-Williams Prize, an Associated Writing Programs Poetry Award (1984), a National Endowment for the Arts Fellowship (1990), and fellowships at the Macdowell Colony, the Fine Arts Work Center, and the Bunting Institute of Radcliffe College at Harvard University. Lives in New Orleans. Poet.

WORKS:

Ceremony for Minneconjoux. Lexington, Ky.: Callaloo Poetry Series, 1983.
In These Houses. Middletown, Conn.: Wesleyan Press, 1988.
Desperate Circumstance, Dangerous Woman. Brownsville, Ore.: Story Line Press, 1991.
Poems have appeared in numerous periodicals, including *Obsidian, Essence, Callaloo, TENDRIL, Southern Exposure, Southern Review, American Poetry Review,* and *American Voice.*
Represented in *The Made Thing: An Anthology of Contemporary Southern Poetry* (Fayetteville: University of Arkansas Press, 1987); *Early Ripening: American Women's Writing Now* (London: Pandora, 1986).

SECONDARY SOURCES:

Bryan, Violet Harrington. "Evocations of Place and Culture in the Works of Four Contemporary Black Louisiana Writers: Brenda Osbey, Sybil Kein, Elizabeth Brown-Guillory, and Pinkie Gordon Lane." *Louisiana Literature,* IV (1987), 49–65.

Esolen, Gary. "New Orleans Poet." *Gambit,* March 10, 1984, p. 1.

New Orleans *Times-Picayune,* April 22, 1984, November 3, 1991.

Oppengart, Bea. "Poetry: 'Ceremony for Minneconjoux,' the Callaloo Poetry Series." Louisville *Courier-Journal,* May 13, 1984, p. 19.

OWEN, Lyla Hay ("Lyla Lagarde") (1943–)

Courtesy Lyla Hay Owen

BIOGRAPHY:

Born in New Orleans. Daughter of Obed Nellson and Lucretia Ruth Breechen Lagarde. Educated at Rochester Institute of Technology; Columbia University. Married Herbert Arthur Shapiro; divorced; one son. Married Vidal Lee Hay; divorced. Married Paul Owen; divorced; two daughters. Awarded an Artist Fellowship in Theater, Louisiana Division of the Arts (1986–1987); served as poet-in-schools, St. Charles Parish. Playwright; poet; writer of fiction and nonfiction; lyricist.

WORKS:

Creoles of New Orleans: Gens de Couleur/People of Color. With photographs by Owen Murphy. New Orleans: First Quarter Press, 1987.

Numerous plays, produced in New Orleans and elsewhere, as well as children's musicals between 1970 and 1989. Her poetry, fiction, articles, and interviews have appeared in the *New Laurel Review, New Leaves Review,* New Orleans *Times-Picayune, Vieux Carré Courier, Figaro, Gambit,* and others.

SECONDARY SOURCE:

New Orleans *Times-Picayune,* May 25, 1987.

OWEN, Sue (1942–)

Courtesy Sue Owen

BIOGRAPHY:

Born in Clarinda, Iowa. Daughter of Theodore R. (small businessman) and Elizabeth Jeanne Roderick Matthews. Educated at University of Wisconsin; Goddard College. Married Thomas Owen, professor, in 1964. Awards include 1988 Ohio State University Press/The Journal Award in Poetry; fellowships at Port Townsend Writers' Conference, Wesleyan Writers' Conference, and the Aspen Writers' Conference. Environmental activist. Lives in Baton Rouge. Poet.

WORKS:

Nursery Rhymes for the Dead. New York: Ithaca House, 1980.

The Book of Winter. Columbia: Ohio State University Press, 1988.

Contributions have also appeared in numerous periodicals including *Harvard Magazine, Iowa Review,* the *Nation, Ploughshares, Poetry, Southern Review,* and *Virginia Quarterly Review.*

Represented in the following anthologies: *The Anthology of Magazine Verse, Intro 10* (Norfolk, Va.: Hendel and Reinke, 1979) and *The Best of Intro* (Norfolk, Va.: Associated Writing Programs, 1985); and *USA Poetry* (Göteborg, Sweden: n.p., 1984).

SECONDARY SOURCES:

Ewell, Barbara C., and Dorothy H. Brown. "Drama, Poetry, and Louisiana Women Writers," *Louisiana Literature,* VI (Spring, 1989), 37–56.

Library Journal, December, 1980.

New Orleans *Times-Picayune,* September 20, 1986, June 11, 1989.

Southern Review, n.s., XIX (Winter, 1983), 229–32.

Who's Who of American Women.

RICE, Anne ("Anne Rampling"; "A. N. Roquelaure") (1941–)

BIOGRAPHY:

Born in New Orleans. Daughter of Howard (sculptor) and Katherine Allen O'Brien. Educated at Texas Woman's University; San Francisco State University; University of California, Berkeley. Married Stan Rice, poet and painter; two children (one deceased). Novelist.

WORKS:

"The Idol of the Flies" (novelette). In *Alfred Hitchcock's Stories My Mother Never Told Me.* New York: Random House, 1963.

Interview with the Vampire. New York: Knopf, 1976.

The Feast of All Saints. New York: Simon and Schuster, 1979.

Photo by Stan Rice, courtesy Anne Rice

Cry to Heaven. New York: Knopf, 1982.

The Claiming of Sleeping Beauty (as A. N. Roquelaure). New York: Dutton, 1983.

Beauty's Punishment (as A. N. Roquelaure). New York: Dutton, 1984.

The Vampire Lestat. New York: Knopf, 1985.

Exit to Eden (as Anne Rampling). New York: Arbor House, 1985.

Beauty's Release (as A. N. Roquelaure). New York: Dutton, 1985.

Belinda (as Anne Rampling). New York: Arbor House, 1986.

Queen of the Damned. New York: Knopf, 1988.

The Mummy: or, Ramses the Damned. New York: Ballantine, 1989.

The Witching Hour. New York: Knopf, 1990.

SECONDARY SOURCES:

Allison, Dorothy. "Sex, Sin, and the Pursuit of Literary Excellence in Anne Rice's Triple Threat." *Village Voice Literary Supplement,* December, 1986, p. 1.

CA.

CANR.

Holditch, W. Kenneth. "Interview with Anne Rice." *Lear's Magazine,* II (October, 1989), 86–89.

Ramsland, Katherine. *Prism of the Night: A Biography of Anne Rice.* New York: Dutton, 1991.

Roberts, Bette B. "Anne Rice's Interview with the Vampire." *New Mexico Humanities Review,* II (Spring 1979), 49–55.

SALOY, Mona Lisa (1950–)

Photo by James Terry III, courtesy Mona Lisa Saloy

BIOGRAPHY:
Born in New Orleans. Daughter of Louis Joseph Saloy (laborer, supervisor), Sr., and Olga Saloy Fitch (seamstress). Educated at the University of Washington; San Francisco State University; Louisiana State University. Taught at Laney College (Oakland, Calif.); San Francisco State University; University of California (Berkeley); Louisiana State University; Dillard University. Awards include National Endowment for the Arts Poet-in-Residence at the San Francisco African American Historical and Cultural Society and coordinator of the Arts-in-Education Program in Baton Rouge. Has worked extensively with poetry in the schools programs and received the Delta Sigma Theta Arts Excellence Award in Literature in 1989. Lives in New Orleans. Poet; essayist; fiction writer; playwright.

WORKS:
Poems have appeared in *Jazz Society, Cricket, Five Fingers Poetry, Haight-Ashbury Literary Journal, Poems for Peace Quarterly, Black Scholar, Washington Review, Testimony,* and others.

Anthologies include *From a Bend in the River* (New Orleans: Contemporary Arts Center, 1991); *Louisiana Laurels* (Baton Rouge: Arts Council of Greater Baton Rouge, 1991); *Word Up: Black Poetry of the Eighties from the Deep South* (Atlanta: Beans and Brown Rice, 1990); *Clay Drum: Anthology of San Francisco Writing* (San Francisco: Retribution Press, 1981); and *Dark Waters, North West Anthology of Black Writers and Poets* (Seattle: United Black Artists Guild, 1977).

In progress: "Between Laughter and Tears: Black Mona Lisa Poems"; "Still Color Struck" (collection of short fiction); a novel; and a book-length poem.

SECONDARY SOURCE:
Jenkins, Joyce. "Some Information." *Poetry Flash,* No. 143 (February, 1985).

SHAIK, Fatima (1952–)

BIOGRAPHY:
Born in New Orleans. Daughter of Mohamed and Lily LaSalle Shaik. Educated at Xavier University; Boston University; New York Univer-

sity. Married James Little, painter, 1984; one child. Worked as a reporter for New Orleans *Times-Picayune* and Miami *News* in the 1970s. Editor and free-lance writer for McGraw-Hill. Awarded National Endowment for the Humanities Fellowship. Lives in New York City. Novelist; short-story writer.

WORKS:

✓ *The Mayor of New Orleans: Just Talking Jazz* (collection of novellas). Berkeley, Calif.: Creative Arts Book Co., 1987.
Work appears in *Parachute Shop Blues* anthology (New Orleans: Xavier University Press, 1972), *Southern Review,* and elsewhere.

SECONDARY SOURCES:
New Orleans *Times-Picayune*, January 24, 1988, June 18, 1989.

SHANKMAN, Sarah ("Alice Storey")

BIOGRAPHY:
Born in West Monroe, Louisiana. Has lived in New York and New Orleans; now resides in San Francisco. Wrote for *Atlanta Magazine.* Writer and editor of *New Orleans Magazine* in the 1960s.

WORKS:
Keeping Secrets. New York: Simon and Schuster, 1988.
First Kill All the Lawyers (as "Alice Storey"). New York: Pocket Books, 1988.
Then Hang All the Liars (as "Alice Storey"). New York: Pocket Books, 1989.
Now Let's Talk of Graves. New York: Pocket Books, 1990.
She Walks in Beauty. New York: Pocket Books, 1991.

SECONDARY SOURCE:
DeMers, John. "Secrets Worth Sharing." New Orleans *Times-Picayune,* August 21, 1988.

SMITH, Julie (1944–)

BIOGRAPHY:
Born in Annapolis, Maryland. Daughter of Malberry (lawyer) and Claire Tanner (school counselor) Smith. Educated at University of Mississippi. Newspaper writer for New Orleans *Times-Picayune,* 1965–1966; San Francisco *Chronicle,* 1968–1979. Partner in editorial consulting firm, Invisible Ink, San Francisco, 1979–. Lives in Santa Barbara, California.

WORKS:
Death Turns a Trick. New York: Walker, 1982.
The Sourdough Wars. New York: Walker, 1984.
True-Life Adventure. New York: Mysterious Press, 1985.

Tourist Trap. New York: Mysterious Press, 1986.
Huckleberry Fiend. New York: Mysterious Press, 1987.
New Orleans Mourning. New York: St. Martin's, 1990.
The Axeman's Jazz. New York: St. Martin's, 1991.
Stories in *Miniature Mysteries: 100 Malicious Little Mystery Stories* (New York: Taplinger, 1981); *The Arbor House Treasury of Mystery and Suspense* (New York: Arbor House, 1981); *Alfred Hitchcock's Mystery Magazine; Ellery Queen's Mystery Magazine;* and *Mike Shane Mystery Magazine.*

SECONDARY SOURCES:
CA.
New Orleans *Times-Picayune,* September 28, 1991.

SONIAT, Katherine "Bonnie" (1942–)

BIOGRAPHY:
Born in Washington, D.C. Educated at Newcomb College and Tulane University. Married Eric Treathaway, poet and professor, 1984; two sons. Taught at Hollins College (Virginia); now at Virginia Polytechnic Institute and State University. Awards include Camden Poetry Prize; Virginia Prizes in Poetry (1989); Ann Stanford Poetry Prize; and fellowships from the Academy of American Poets and the Bread Loaf Writers' Conference. Lives in Catawba, Virginia. Poet.

WORKS:
Notes of Departure. Camden, N.J.: Walt Whitman Center, 1985.
The Giant Side of Seasons. Milton, Mass.: Chowder Press, 1985.
Winter Toys. Maryville, Mo.: Green Tower Press, 1989.
Cracking Eggs: Poems. Orlando: University of Central Florida Press, 1990.
Poetry published in *Southern Review, Poetry, American Scholar, Poetry Northwest, Louisiana Literature, Fiddlehead, Georgia Review,* and others. In progress: "A Shared Life" (poems); "Coming into the River Parishes" (poems); and "The Flower Girl" (young adult novel).

SECONDARY SOURCES:
New Orleans *Times-Picayune,* March 17, 1985, June 11, 1989.

TANEY, Retta M. (1942–)

BIOGRAPHY:
Born in New Orleans. Daughter of Walter and Mercedes Barfield Taney. Educated at Dominican College; St. John's University (New York); Tulane University. Teaches at Xavier University. Awards include two winning plays in the BBC (radio) Africa Series Competition. Plays have been produced in New Orleans, Edinburgh, London, and Cambridge (England). Playwright; scholar.

WORKS:

Io, Catherine. In *Xavier Review,* special issue, VI (1986).

Restoration Revivals on the British Stage, 1944–1979: A Critical Survey. Lanham, Md.: University Press of America, 1985.

Plays: *Brigand's Visit* (1966); *Visitation* (1968); *Io, Catherine* (1986); *Baraza Notes* (1987) (radio play with Johanna Kitasimbwa); *Bridge* (1990) (radio play with Johanna Kitasimbwa).

SECONDARY SOURCE:

Farrell, Joseph. "Around the Festival Fringe: *Io, Catherine.*" *Scotsman* (Edinburgh, Scotland), August 22, 1985.

TOTH, Emily Jane (1944–)

BIOGRAPHY:

Born in New York City. Daughter of John J. and Dorothy Ginsberg Fitzgibbons. Educated at Swarthmore College; Johns Hopkins University. Married Bruce Toth of Cleveland, 1967. Scholar and writer. Has taught at Morgan State University, University of New Orleans, University of North Dakota, University of Richmond, and Pennsylvania State University. Resides in Baton Rouge. Professor of English, Louisiana State University. Biographer; editor.

WORKS:

The Curse: A Cultural History of Menstruation. With Janice Delaney and Mary Jane Lupton. New York: Dutton, 1976.

A Kate Chopin Miscellany. With Per Seyersted. Natchitoches, La.: Northwestern State University, 1979.

Inside Peyton Place: The Life of Grace Metalious. Garden City, N.Y.: Doubleday, 1981.

Daughters of New Orleans (historical novel). New York: Bantam, 1983.

Regionalism and the Female Imagination. New York: Human Sciences Press, 1985.

Kate Chopin (biography). New York: William Morrow, 1990.

Editor. *A Vocation and a Voice,* by Kate Chopin. New York: Viking Penguin, 1991.

Forthcoming: "Kate Chopin's Notebooks."

SECONDARY SOURCES:

CA.

Who's Who of American Women.

TRUST, Estelle Louise (1915–)

BIOGRAPHY:

No information available.

WORKS:

Louisiana Night. Shreveport, La.: n.p., 1942.
Anne Bronte. Dallas: Story Book Press, 1954.
The Hazelwood Wand (poems). Shreveport, La.: Literary Calendar Press, 1958.

SECONDARY SOURCES:

Who's Who of American Women.
International Who's Who of Poetry.

VILLARRUBIA, Jan (1948–)

BIOGRAPHY:

Born in New Orleans. Daughter of Forrest (manager) and Audrey Levy Villarrubia. Educated at Louisiana State University. Married Charles Merrell, 1978. Lives in New Orleans. Poet; dramatist; journalist.

WORKS:

Plays: *Night Blooming Cereus* (1984); *Odd Fellows Rest* (1986); *Yellow Roses That Big* (1989).

Poems and articles have appeared in numerous periodicals, including *Literary Review, Louisiana Renaissance, Mississippi Valley Review, Negative Capability, New Laurel Review, Pontchartrain Review, Wind Literary Journal,* and *Gambit*.

SECONDARY SOURCE:

Arts Spectrum, June–September, 1986, p. 14.

WALKER, Margaret Abigail (1915–)

BIOGRAPHY:

Born in Birmingham, Alabama. Daughter of Sigismund (Methodist minister) and Marion Dozier Walker. Attended New Orleans schools; Gilbert Academy. Higher education at Northwestern University; University of Iowa. Married Firnist James Alexander, 1943; four children. Was professor of English, Jackson State College, Jackson, Mississippi, and director of Institute for the Study of the History, Life, and Culture of Black Peoples, also in Jackson. Resides in Jackson. Poet; novelist.

WORKS:

For My People (poems). New Haven: Yale University Press, 1942.
Jubilee (novel). Boston: Houghton Mifflin, 1965.
Ballad of the Free (poems). Detroit: Broadside Press, 1966.
Prophets for a New Day (poems). Detroit: Broadside Press, 1970.
How I Wrote Jubilee. Chicago: Third World Press, 1972.
October Journey (poems). Detroit: Broadside Press, 1973.

A Poetic Equation: Conversations Between Margaret Walker and Nikki Giovanni. Washington, D.C.: Howard University Press, 1974.

D(a)emonic Genius of Richard Wright. Washington, D.C.: Howard University Press, 1982.

Richard Wright: Daemonic Genius. New York: Warner Books, 1988.

This Is My Century: New and Collected Poems. Athens: University of Georgia Press, 1989.

"How I Wrote Jubilee" and Other Essays on Life and Literature. Edited by Maryemma Graham. New York: Feminist Press, 1990.

God Touched My Life: The Inspiring Autobiography of the Nun Who Brought Song, Celebration, and Soul to the World (Sister Thea Bowman). San Francisco: Harper and Row, 1992.

SECONDARY SOURCES:

Black World, XXI (December, 1971).

CA.

Contemporary Literary Criticism, I (1973), VI (1976).

Evans, Mari. *Black Women Writers, 1950–1980: A Critical Evaluation.* Garden City, N.Y.: Doubleday, 1982.

Negro Digest, February, 1967, January, 1968.

New York Times Book Review, August 2, 1942, September 25, 1966.

New York Times Literary Supplement, November 4, 1942.

Powell, B. J. "Black Experience in Margaret Walker's 'Jubilee' and Lorraine Hansberry's 'The Drinking Gourd.'" *CLA Journal* (December, 1977), 304–11.

Rowell, Charles. "Poetry, History, and Humanism: An Interview with Margaret Walker." *Black World,* XXV (1975), 4–17.

Tate, Claudia, ed. *Black Women Writers at Work.* New York: Continuum, 1983.

WATSON, Pauline Bennett (1925–)

BIOGRAPHY:

Born in New Iberia, Louisiana. Daughter of Luke and Rosalie Catalano Bennett. Educated at Palmer Institute of Authorship. Married Jimmy T. Watson, 1947; five children. Lives in Turnball, Texas. Writer of juvenile stories, adult fiction, articles.

WORKS:

A Surprise for Mother. Englewood Cliffs, N.J.: Prentice-Hall, 1976.

Cricket's Cookery. New York: Open Court, 1986.

A Day with Daddy. Englewood Cliffs, N.J.: Prentice-Hall, 1986.

Curley Cat Babysits. New York: Harcourt Brace Jovanovich, 1987.

Published in *Cricket's Choice,* edited by Clifton Fadiman and Marianne Carns (New York: Open Court, 1975). Also in *My Weekly Reader,*

Cricket, Woman's Day, Southern Living, Reader's Digest, Parents' Magazine, and others.

SECONDARY SOURCES:
CA.
CAR.
Something About the Author.

WEBB, Bernice Larson (19?–)

Courtesy Bernice Webb

BIOGRAPHY:
Born in Ludell, Kansas. Daughter of Carl Godfred and Ida Genevieve Tongish Larson. Educated at University of Kansas; University of Aberdeen, Scotland. Married Robert MacHardy Webb, 1961; two children. Professor of English at University of Southwestern Louisiana. Lives in Lafayette, Louisiana. Poet; dramatist; short-story writer; literary critic.

WORKS:
The Basketball Man: James Naismith (biography). Lawrence: University of Kansas Press, 1973.
Poetry on the Stage: William Poel, Producer of Verse Drama. Salzburg, Austria: Universitat Salzburg, 1979.
Beware of Ostriches (poems). Baton Rouge: Legacy, 1978.
Picking at "the Goophered Grapevine." Bowling Green, Ky.: Kentucky Folklore Society, 1979.
Lady Doctor on a Homestead: Mary Amelia Hay. Colby, Kansas: Western Plains Heritage, 1986.
Two Peach Baskets. Lafayette, La.: Spider Press, 1991.
Poems have been published in many journals, including *New Laurel Review, Kansas Quarterly, Ball State Forum, Stone Country,* and *Epos.* Short stories have appeared in *DePaul Literary Magazine, Kansas Magazine, Kansas Quarterly,* and others.

SECONDARY SOURCES:
CAR.
International Authors and Writers Who's Who.
Who's Who of American Women.

WEINBERGER, Betty Kiralfy (1932–)

BIOGRAPHY:
Born in Columbus, Georgia. Daughter of Victor J. and Raye C. Kiralfy. Educated at Tulane University; Columbia University; the University of Chicago. Married Stanley R. Weinberger, attorney, 1960; two children. Resides in Glencoe, Illinois. Counselor, social worker. Writer of children's stories, nonfiction.

WORKS:
I Saw a Purple Cow. With Ann Cole, Carolyn Haas, and Elizabeth Haller. Boston: Little, Brown, 1972.
A Pumpkin in a Pear Tree. With Ann Cole, Carolyn Haas, and Elizabeth Haller. Boston: Little, Brown, 1976.
Children Are Children Are Children. With Ann Cole. Boston: Little, Brown, 1978.
Also published in periodicals.

SECONDARY SOURCE:
CA.

WHITE, Gail (1945–)

BIOGRAPHY:
Born in Pensacola, Florida. Daughter of Robert (car dealer) and Jeanne Nelson Brockett. Educated at Stetson University. Married Arthur White, 1967. Currently works at Tulane Medical School. Poetry editor of *Piedmont Literary Review.* Lives in New Orleans. Poet; short-story writer.

WORKS:
Pandora's Box. San Jose, Calif.: Samisdat Press, 1977.
Irreverent Parables. Benson, Ariz.: Border-Mountain Press, 1978.
Fishing for Leviathan. Belford, Maine: Wings, 1982.
The Way We Come Home. West Lafayette, Ind.: Sparrow Press, 1985.
All Night in the Churchyard. New Orleans: Proof Rock, 1986.
Sibyl and Sphinx. With Barbara Loots. Kansas City, Mo.: Rockhill Press, 1988.
Contributions have appeared in numerous magazines, including *American Scholar, Southern Poetry Review, Christian Century, Lyric,* and *DeKalb Literary Arts Journal;* also in *Anthology of Magazine Verse and Yearbook of American Poetry.*

SECONDARY SOURCE:
Who's Who of American Women.

WIDMER, Mary Lou (1926–)

Courtesy Mary Lou Widmer

BIOGRAPHY:

Born in New Orleans. Daughter of Earl S. and Alma Pigeon Schultis. Educated at Loyola University, New Orleans. Married Albert F. Widmer, attorney; two children. Resides in New Orleans. Novelist; nonfiction writer.

WORKS:

Night Jasmine (romance). New York: Dell, 1980.

Beautiful Crescent: A History of New Orleans. With Joan B. Garvey. New Orleans: Garner Press, 1982.

Lace Curtain: A Novel. New York: Charter Books, 1985.

New Orleans in the Thirties. New Orleans: Pelican, 1989.

New Orleans in the Forties. New Orleans: Pelican, 1990.

New Orleans in the Fifties. New Orleans: Pelican, 1991.

In progress: "Quadroon" (novel).

SECONDARY SOURCE:

New Orleans *Times-Picayune,* December 8, 1985, July 21, October 13, 1991.

WIER, Dara Dixon (1949–)

BIOGRAPHY:

Born in New Orleans. Daughter of Arthur Joseph (director of vocational school) and Grace Barrois Dixon. Educated at Louisiana State University; Longwood College; Bowling Green State University. Married Allen Wier, writer and teacher, 1969; divorced 1983. Married Michael Pettit, poet, 1983. Resides in Amherst, Massachusetts. Teacher; writer; poet.

WORKS:

Published in *New Republic, North American Review, Quartet, Hollins Critic, Southern Review,* and anthologies such as *Intro Six* (Garden City, N.Y.: Doubleday, 1974).

Blood, Hook and Eye: Poems. Austin: University of Texas Press, 1977.

All You Have in Common: Poems. Pittsburgh: Carnegie-Mellon University Press, 1984.

The 8-Step Grapevine: Poems. Pittsburgh: Carnegie-Mellon University Press, 1988.

The Book of Knowledge (poems). Pittsburgh: Carnegie-Mellon University Press, 1988.

SECONDARY SOURCES:
CA.
CANR.

WILLIAMS, Patti McGavran (1936–)

BIOGRAPHY:
Born in Fort Pierce, Florida. Daughter of Jack (mechanic) and Lucille VanWinkler McGavran. Educated at Stetson University; Columbus College. Married Harold Page Williams, 1955; two children. Taught elementary school in New Orleans, 1962–1972. Resides in Florida.

WORKS:
Husbands: A Novel. New York: Plainfield, N.J.: Logos International, 1976.
Hurting and Healing: How to Cope with Hurt Feelings. Smithtown, N.Y.: Exposition Press, 1980.

SECONDARY SOURCE:
CA.

WILTZ, Chris (1948–)

Photo by David Richmond, courtesy Chris Wiltz

BIOGRAPHY:
Born in New Orleans. Daughter of Adolphe Michael (accountant) and Merle Hiers (underwriter) Wiltz. Educated at the University of Southwestern Louisiana; Loyola University, New Orleans; University of New Orleans; San Francisco State University. Married to Kenneth McElroy, 1970; divorced. Married to Joseph Pecot, communications company president; one child. Resides in New Orleans. Novelist.

WORKS:
The Killing Circle. New York: Macmillan, 1981.
A Diamond Before You Die. New York: Warner Books, 1988.
The Emerald Lizard. New York: Dutton, 1991.

Completed manuscript: "The Glass House" (novel). In progress: "Three Sisters" (novel).

SECONDARY SOURCES:
CA.
New Orleans *Gambit,* September 12, 1981.
New Orleans *Times-Picayune,* March 13, 1989, January 20, September 28, 1991.

Contributors

PATRICIA BRADY is director of publications at the Historic New Orleans Collection. She earned her Ph.D. in history at Tulane University and then was assistant professor of History at Dillard University. She is editor of *The Encyclopedia of New Orleans Artists, 1718–1918* (1987); *Nelly Custis Lewis's Housekeeping Book* (1982); and *George Washington's Beautiful Nelly: The Letters of Eleanor Parke Custis Lewis to Elizabeth Bordley Gibson, 1794–1851* (1991). A specialist in cultural and social history, she frequently writes on the arts and domestic life.

DOROTHY H. BROWN is professor of English in City College of Loyola University of New Orleans. Teaching, especially dramatic literature from Shakespeare to modern women writers, is her special love, but her research has ranged from contemporary British theater to women writers of Louisiana, her adopted home of more than thirty years. She is currently at work on a book for Chadwyck-Healey, Ltd., on American women playwrights.

VIOLET HARRINGTON BRYAN is associate professor of English at Dillard University. She has published articles on African-American writers and on black urban culture in New Orleans. Her book *Dialogues of Race and Gender: The Myth of New Orleans in Literature* is forthcoming from the University of Tennessee Press.

LINDA S. COLEMAN is associate professor of English and director of the Writing Center and Writing Across the Curriculum at Eastern Illinois University. Her interest in Louisiana women writers began during her years in Grace King's native New Orleans. Currently, she is at work on a study of the life-writing of first- and second-generation British female Quakers.

BARBARA C. EWELL is professor of English in City College of Loyola University of New Orleans. She has published essays on feminist criticism and pedagogy and on authors as various as Michael Drayton and Margaret Atwood, and is author of *Kate Chopin* (1986). Her current research focuses on the short stories of southern women writers.

SYLVIA PATTERSON ISKANDER, professor of English at the University of Southwestern Louisiana, specializes in both eighteenth-century British literature and children's literature. She is author of

Rousseau's "Emile" and Early Children's Literature (1971), and her work appears in such journals as the *Children's Literature Quarterly* and the international *Children's Literature Journal.*

CLARA JUNCKER is associate professor of American Literature and Culture at the Copenhagen Business School, Denmark. She has taught in the Department of English/Writing Programs at the University of California, Los Angeles, and at Tulane University. She has published widely on nineteenth- and twentieth-century American literature, literary theory, and composition theory, and has edited a collection of African-American women's writing, *Black Roses* (1985). She is president of the Danish Association for American Studies.

ELIZABETH MEESE is professor of English and adjunct professor of Women's Studies at the University of Alabama. She has written three books, *Crossing the Double-Cross: The Practice of Feminist Literary Criticism* (1986), *(Ex)Tensions: Re-Figuring Feminist Criticism* (1990), and *(Sem)erotics: Theorizing Lesbian Writing* (1992), and coedited (with Alice Parker) two volumes of feminist critical scholarship.

ELZBIETA H. OLEKSY is associate professor of English at the University of Lodz, Poland, and visiting professor at Southern Seminary College. She is the author of *Battle and Quest in the American Fable of the Nineteen-Sixties* (1983) and *Plight in Common: Hawthorne and Percy* (1991), as well as a number of articles on American fiction. She is currently working on a comparative study of women's fiction of the American South and recent Polish women's writing, and she is editing a collection of papers on gender in Walker Percy's fiction.

ALICE PARKER is associate professor of French and Humanities at the University of Alabama, where she is also director of the Women's Studies Program. Her research focuses on eighteenth-century women writers in France and contemporary feminist writers in France and Quebec. She has edited (with Elizabeth Meese) two volumes of critical essays and is presently writing a book on the avant-garde texts of Nicole Brossard.

ELLEN PEEL teaches in the Department of World and Comparative Literature and the Department of English at San Francisco State University. Her major areas of research are feminist criticism and theory, the novel, and literary theory. She is currently working on a book entitled *Beyond Utopia: Persuasion, Narrative, and Skeptical Feminism.*

MERRILL SKAGGS is dean of the Graduate School and professor of English at Drew University. She has published widely on nineteenth- and twentieth-century literature of the South. Her books include *The Folk of Southern Fiction* (1972), *The Mother Person* (with Virginia Barber, 1975), and most recently, *After the World Broke in Two: The Later Novels of Willa Cather* (1990).

J. RANDAL WOODLAND teaches in the Writing Programs of the University of California at Los Angeles. A Louisiana native, he recently earned his Ph.D. in English at the University of North Carolina at Chapel Hill. He is currently completing a book on the "idea of New Orleans" in the southern literary imagination.

Index